Practical Workflow for SAP

SAP PRESS

Edited by Bernhard Hochlehnert, SAP AG

SAP PRESS is a joint initiative of SAP and Galileo Press. The know-how offered by SAP specialists combined with the expertise of the publishing house Galileo Press offers the reader expert publications in the field. SAP PRESS features first hand information, expert advice and provides useful skills for professional decision making.

SAP PRESS offers a variety of books on technical and business related topics for the SAP-user. For further information, please also visit our website: *www.sap-press.com*

Rüdiger Buck-Emden
mySAP CRM
Solution for Success
2002, 312 pp.
ISBN 1-59229-003-5

Thomas Schneider
SAP Performance Optimization Guide
The Official SAP Guide
2002, 504 pp.
ISBN 1-59229-007-8

Paul Read
SAP Database Administration with Microsoft SQL Server 2000
2002, 328 pp.
ISBN 1-59229-005-1

Alan Rickayzen, Jocelyn Dart,
Carsten Brennecke, Markus Schneider

Practical Workflow for SAP

Effective Business Processes using
SAP's WebFlow Engine

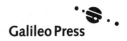

Galileo Press

ISBN 1-59229-006-X

Editing: Wiebke Hübner
Proofreading: Bruce Mayo, Konstanz, Germany
Cover design: department, Cologne, Germany
Production: Iris Warkus
Typesetting: reemers publishing services gmbh, Krefeld, Germany
Printed and bound by Bercker Graphischer Betrieb, Kevelaer, Germany

Contents

Preface from the Industry

Workflow... How can one word evoke so many similar yet different definitions? It is a generic word used to describe all of the steps required to accomplish a given task (i.e. workflow is the "*flow of work*"). These tasks can be carried out in a work environment, a social setting, or in personal situations. Each day our life is comprised of a series of both unique and connected workflows. These workflows can be manual or automated.

A workflow has several components. The first component is the triggering event. Note that the trigger relates to something that has already happened. Following the triggering event one or more steps in the workflow process occur. A simple example of a manual workflow is parents waking their children to begin the process of getting ready for school. In reality, this is a series of workflows. The first event might be waking the children, followed by the steps of dressing; the workflow finishes when the children notify their parents they are dressed and ready for breakfast. Being ready for breakfast is the triggering event to notify the parents to begin the process of cooking and serving the food. Putting the dirty dishes on the counter might be the triggering event to begin the dish washing process.

As these examples show, we continually trigger and complete workflows daily. Even in our daily routines, we attempt to automate the workflows for efficiency and timesavings. Most studies of business processes find that a significant amount of the process time is spent waiting for the next step to occur. These wait times can consume as much as 90% of the entire process. In the examples above, automation might be applied to the first triggering event by the use of an alarm clock. Rather than the parents having to know the exact time to go to the children's room, they can set the clock. This also eliminates the time spent walking to their room. Another way to automate the workflow might be to have a timer turn on the cooking equipment at a specified time.

The above examples are provided to emphasize the point that *workflows never go away, rather they tend to be done inefficiently,* resulting in lengthy processing. Workflow is about communication, providing the next person in the process with a notification of when to take action.

Extending these ideas to the business environment, it is evident that a great deal of value can be captured by process automation. This value capture is significantly enhanced if a business has implemented SAP, as we have done at Eastman Chemical Company. Business processes utilizing SAP typically are comprised of several transactions. Each transaction completes a step in the process. In some instances completion of the transaction passes data to another process. As an example, consider processing a sales order. During the creation of the sales order the user enters pertinent sales information. Another step in the process involves the creation of an invoice, which in turn automatically creates the necessary financial posting. At Eastman Chemical Company, we utilize SAP's WebFlow Engine to enhance numerous business processes, including but not limited to the sale order process, EDI/IDOC error handling, material master creation, and purchasing. The sales order workflows allow us to review orders for problems related to credit or material availability and resolve them within minutes. In addition, WebFlow provides a clear and detailed itemization of process steps, down to the second, telling what was done, when and by whom. WebFlow eliminates the need for less efficient means of notification. Land mail gets lost, phone calls are not answered or returned and normal e-mail is lost in the mass of regular e-mail. When a required action does not occur within a specific period of time, after a notification WebFlow lets us automatically escalate the notification. In terms of the daily wake-up routine described above, escalation gives us something like a bigger alarm clock ring on the other side of the room that rings when the children turn off the first alarm and go back to bed.

As with most business processes, timely communication between the persons executing the steps of the process is critical. SAP provides WebFlow to model the workflow process in a manner that allows for accurate and timely movement of the data from one person to the next. Notifications normally are automatic and sent by varied technology. *Simply stated, SAP WebFlow is about getting the right data to the right person, at the right place, at the right time.* By doing this, companies can more fully capture the value of the integrated SAP modules by linking the appropriate people to the required task. A good example is the credit check that is often necessary when a sales order is taken. If the customer exceeds their credit limit when the sales order is entered, WebFlow will see this event and will send an immediate notification to the appropriate credit representative (not just any credit representative, but the proper one) to take action. This notification will include the order in question and an automated link to the transaction in SAP where the credit can be released or blocked.

Given that WebFlow will improve the process flow, irrespective of whether the process involves human interaction or is completely automatic, how does this translate to the corporate bottom line? Increasingly corporations are challenged to provide an economic return for the investment required to implement IT projects such as creation of workflow. WebFlow compresses the cycle time of a process, resulting in more time available for those in the process to work with other value-adding projects. It also increases the accuracy by enforcing required data input, data validation, and by eliminating the potential for keying errors.

I hope that this book will help reap the enormous benefits for your business that can be realized with SAP's WebFlow Engine.

Tom Walker

Systems Associate
Eastman Chemical Company

Preface from SAP

Almost 20 years ago, when I worked at an insurance company, a department manager got me thinking about our urgent need for better support for business case processing. A recurring problem at this time was how to deal with unpaid premiums for specific kinds of insurance policies over various stages of escalation—the business process was a challenging mixture of automated periodic batch processing, single case dialog transactions and legal processes, all based on rules and policies that could change from time to time. The department leader wanted an easy way to keep processes consistent and well documented, one which would also be easy to learn and understand for new employees. For me, this was the starting point to really think about business process and workflow management.

When I joined SAP in 1993, I was struck with the major difference between SAP's goals for a broad standard solution and the very specific requirements of an insurance company: SAP had to provide a single generic tool to support the tremendous variety of business processes that SAP's customers were driving.

The goals we identified were:

1. The system needs to support distributed processing—distributed in time, distributed in the organization. The system has to be modular and interoperable—other workflow and process management systems should be able to trigger processes within SAP and vice versa, and different user groups need to access their task through different groupware products.

2. The system needs to support a flexible and changing organization. Flexibility is needed regarding people involved as well as sequence of steps. It must be very straightforward to change organizational structure, roles, responsibilities, and business rules without changing the underlying application building blocks.

3. The system needs to be embedded in the technology layer of an SAP solution— no extra installation effort, easy to configure, easy to administer and monitor and able to leverage on other technologies in this layer, such as document management, messaging and security.

4. SAP must not only deliver a tool, but predefined workflow solutions that can be simply switched on or customized for the specific needs of a company within hours, not weeks.

To pick just one of these goals as an example, *Interoperability* is a key factor for SAP customers. Large companies with complex IT landscapes (resulting from mergers and dynamic business practices), dependent on collaboration with partners need to keep their business processes synchronized and under control. SAP is a founding and permanent active member of such open organizations as the Workflow Management Coalition (WFMC), and BPMI.org, supporting not only the definition of standards, but also their implementation and test in real life interoperability exercises.

These goals have passed the test of time and technological evolution. SAP has embedded the WebFlow Engine in its Web Application Server, making it available to all application components and solutions of the mySAP.com e-business platform.

For the last seven years, SAP customers have been quietly automating and improving their business processes with the help of SAP's workflow management tool. The latest release, the WebFlow Engine, has come a long way from the initial R/3 3.0 offering—with support for SOAP, XML messaging, Web services, and the new and varied user interfaces that are emerging. This is why the authors felt the time was right for a book that would describe the new features, together with a distillation of the knowledge gained from these last seven years of SAP workflow in practice.

So what you see today, and what is described in this book, is a mature and proven workflow and process management system. It works in thousands of installations and it helps to bring higher reliability and quality, more flexibility, and better transparency to many day-to-day business processes in hundreds of companies. And WebFlow is a change agent: it supports a smooth transition from more manually driven to more automated business process operation. Automation can be done step by step, in a non-disruptive way.

I very much want to thank the authors, Carsten Brennecke, Jocelyn Dart, Alan Rickayzen and Markus Schneider, for sharing their unique blend of in-depth development knowledge together with consulting experience to make this book so valuable. The authors provide a broad overview of SAP's WebFlow Engine, as well as real life examples and tips and tricks (thanks also to the generous feedback from customers) to get the best value out of the system. I also want to thank the WebFlow development team for their tremendous achievements and their spirit of innovation and cooperation.

Franz J.Fritz

Vice President Technology Architecture and Product Management
SAP AG

Who Should Read This Book?

This book presents a practical approach to using SAP's WebFlow Engine. It is not a tutorial (there are excellent tutorials in the SAP Library help documentation available on the Web or in the system) nor is it simply a high level description of workflow in the SAP environment. Rather, it is a distillation of the experience that we and our colleagues have gathered in this field, experience that we believe can be useful to companies, project leaders, consultants and developers.

The book is divided into four parts, to make it easier for you decide where and how far to read.

High-level overview including benefits	Chapter 1
Project work and what happens after going live	Chapters 2—6
Workflow development, if you intend to extend SAP-provided workflows or develop your own	Chapters 7—14
Examples of the use of workflow in mySAP.com	Chapter 15—18

The choice of examples for chapters 15 to 18 was a particularly difficult one because there are so many worthy candidates, such as Product Life Cycle Management (PLM), Utilities and Employee Self Services (ESS) to name but a few areas where workflow is used successfully and intensively. In the end, we chose examples that are easily understandable for readers outside their respective fields of application, which at the same time illustrate a wide variety of concepts covered in earlier chapters.

Although this is not a tutorial, and not a complete guide either, we could not resist including many tips and tricks, which we believe would be useful to even the most experienced of readers in this field. If you are new to workflow, we hope you will not be distracted by these excursions.

This book is based on Release 6.10 of the SAP Web Application Server, which is part of the platform on which the different mySAP.com solutions are built (e.g. mySAP CRM or mySAP SRM). The basic workflow engine was first available in the 3.0 Basis Release (the basis of R/3 3.0), and was called "SAP Business Workflow". When a Release is mentioned in the book, it implicitly refers to the SAP Web Application Server (for Release 6.10 or later) or the SAP Basis system (for releases earlier than 6.10).

Acknowledgements

Writing any book is a major undertaking, requiring much hope, optimism, dedication and persistence on the part of the authors, and copious amounts of encouragement from friends and colleagues. We would like to thank the following people without whose help and support this book would never have been written:

Stefan Bäuerle, Rüdiger Buck-Emden, Thomas Frisch, Ralf Götzinger, Carla Gioertz, Jay Hill, Ulrich Keil, Sky Kimbal, Nathalie Kratz, Markus Kinateder, Alastair McRobb, Erwin Pinter, Mark Pyc, Gerald Rickayzen, David Rouse, Gerhard Scherer, Monika Schleicher, Patrick Schmidt, Phil Soady, David Stead, Jörg Stuhrmann, Rainer Weber and Christian Wernet for their time and patience in reviewing chapters and their many excellent suggestions for improving the content. Very special thanks to Thomas Kosog for some excellent tips included in this book.

Dr. Ulrich Mende (author of "SAP Business Workflow") for the example of deadlines based on factory calendars, and for his generous encouragement.

Terry Bramblet, Patrick Green, Dale Davis, Myra Gill and Bernd Freitag for their tremendous support from our user community and especially, Susan Keohan who moderates the SAP-WUG newsgroup. The many, many members of the SAP-WUG from around the world who delight us with their creativity and interest in SAP's WebFlow Engine.

Wiebke Hübner, Tomas Wehren, Bruce Mayo, Günter Lemoine, Joachim Hartmann and Bernhard Hochlehnert for the production support for this book.

Last but certainly not least, our families and friends, who have patiently supported us through it all.

Part 1
Using SAP Supplied Workflows

1 Introduction to SAP's WebFlow Engine

A brief overview of what can be achieved using SAP's WebFlow Engine, how it affects your organization and what it is included in the deliverables. You need no previous knowledge of SAP or workflow management in order to read this chapter.

1.1 What is SAP's WebFlow Engine?

SAP's WebFlow Engine is the SAP tool for managing business processes over the Internet as well as internally within and between mySAP components.

SAP's WebFlow Engine guides the business process through the complex world of a company's infrastructure, ensuring that the automatic parts of the process flow through with a minimum of fuss. At the same time the WebFlow Engine helps the people involved in the process to do their part, too. To facilitate this it has to be able to provide the user with everything he or she needs to take part in the process, as well as monitoring deadlines and triggering escalation procedures when a process starts to drag.

> **Tip** Initially SAP wanted to differentiate between the new capabilities of the WebFlow Engine from its forerunner, SAP Business Workflow. But this distinction turned out to be purely academic. Internal processes often expand to cover steps taking place over the Internet, and pure e-processes inevitably extend themselves to automate internal departmental processing as well. Separate tools would have meant integration hurdles. Fortunately, however, the same engine was driving both the traditional steps in the process as well as the Internet steps, meaning that this book does not need to distinguish between WebFlow and SAP Business Workflow.[1]

Once you have mastered the workflow functionality, you will see that extending it to the Web is easy. This is a reflection on the success of SAP's in integrating its software infrastructure with the Internet on different fronts, for example in the mySAP Enterprise Portal and the SAP Web Application Server.

Traditionally, business processes were often about approvals—approval of purchase requisitions, approval of leave of absence and so on. Nowadays business

---

1 New features are clearly marked with the Release that they became available to make things simpler for those of you working on older Releases. The basic workflow functionality has been available since R/3 Release 3.0.

processes are more often than not concerned with pooling know-how from different teams of experts to reach a result. Examples of this are:

▶ Producing a marketing brochure

▶ Answering a customer enquiry

▶ Correlating an engineering change in a product that has already reached the production line.

Such processes will typically take between a day and several weeks to complete. There are workflows that run through in an average of under ten minutes, and there's no doubt that in the future, as the trend to Web Portals increases, this sort of time will be the rule rather than the exception.

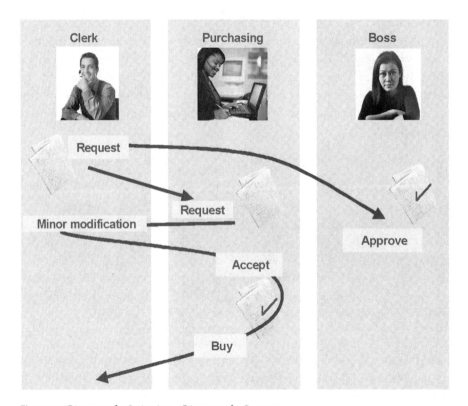

Figure 1.1 Diagram of a Swim-Lane Diagram of a Process

Notice how in figure 1.1 we've gone to the trouble of showing the different participants in this example of a business process. You'll see later that the human factor is one of the most important (and interesting) aspects of SAP's WebFlow Engine.

How the users access the process depends on your local installation. Some will access it through their native SAP GUIs for Windows or JAVA. Others access it through a Web Interface in their Extranet or Intranet Inbox while others interact through their groupware. Some even take part through their native workflow system, linked directly to SAP's WebFlow Engine as part of a collaborative process.

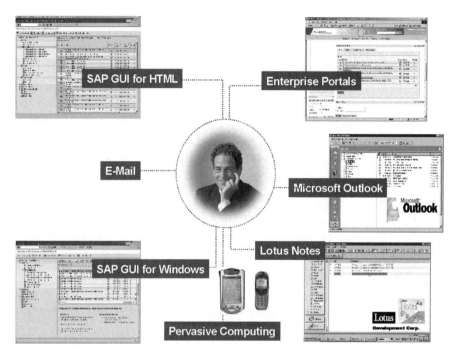

Figure 1.2 Diagram of Different User Communities Linked in One Process

It helps to think of SAP's WebFlow Engine in two parts.

1. The definition tools, which allow you to model the business process.

2. The runtime environment.

You can think of the definition in terms of clicking together model railway tracks to specify how a process should proceed. The *definition tools*, which are of most interest to the consultant or developer modeling the process, will be described in detail in this book.

The *runtime environment* makes sure that the process rides smoothly down the tracks and provides all sorts of utilities to make sure that the participants in the process can enhance the quality of the process as it runs. Because most processes, no matter how well defined, will require ad hoc detours or short cuts, the runtime environment allows for suitable flexibility in the predefined process definition.

The runtime environment is of most interest to the administrators and owners of a process. This is the part of SAP's WebFlow Engine system that can be leveraged to improve the performance of the process even further. It is unfortunate that although a lot of effort goes into process design and the structuring of the work-flow definition, the runtime environment contains many powerful features that are often overlooked. That is why this book goes beyond the description of the process modeling to cover the runtime environment, too.

Workflow, the engine of e-process management, is highly proactive, not just in terms of dispatching the tasks to the participants when action is required, but also in terms of giving participants all the information and tools that they need to make the process a success. This is a message that we are going to repeat over and over again in this book because the quintessence of a good workflow process is its proactive nature. Instead of hoping that the participants know what to do and do it as diligently as possible, you monitor the process and make it as comfortable for the participants as possible.

If you like, think of SAP's WebFlow Engine as a sort of Master Of Ceremonies at a big occasion: making sure that the ceremony is carried out smoothly in the cor-rect order, discretely ironing out problems as they arise, and guiding trainees through their individual duties so that everyone, guests and staff alike, leaves the occasion with glowing smiles.

1.2 Workflow or WebFlow?

SAP's WebFlow Engine is the tool. But what are the things that actually run? Are they automated processes, e-Processes, WebFlows, process instances or workflows?

Here are three current definitions of workflow management and e-Process man-agement.

> *"Workflow management consists of the automation of business procedures during which documents, information or tasks are passed from one participant to another in a way that is governed by rules or procedures." [Workflow Management Coali-tion (WfMC)]*[2]

> *Workflow is: "Software that integrates business rules and people, independent of the triggering event, to enable and control access to knowledge and information while coordinating all the roles in a business process, including internal workers, customers, suppliers, software agents and applications." [GIGA]*[3]

---

2 Quote reproduced here with kind permission from Layna Fischer of the Workflow Manage-ment Coalition.

3 This quote is taken from "Workflow Defined", February 2000, from the GIGA Information Group. The paper was a collaboration between Connie Moore of GIGA and Derek Miers of Enix Consulting.

"Ovum defines e-process as workflow technology that addresses the needs of e-business" [Ovum][4]

Because the WebFlow Engine can be involved in all of these, we will simply refer to them all as workflows. This is not saying that the Internet processes don't have a special role to play. Quite the opposite—which is why so much time and effort has been invested in, and continues to be invested in, the development of SAP's WebFlow Engine's Internet capabilities. However, most business processes still run behind company firewalls, as close to the business applications as possible. Neglecting more traditional aspect of process automation would not bring the benefits that makes one company significantly more competitive than the next.

1.3   Can I Do Without SAP's WebFlow Engine?

There are two alternatives to using SAP's WebFlow Engine. You can do without workflow altogether. In other words you can rely on written instructions, word of mouth and prayers to make sure that your business processes run efficiently and reliably. In a small company, where everybody knows everyone else's name, this is probably acceptable.

However, once a company exceeds this size such methods are not likely to work well. The business processes will run, but there will be little transparency; there will be no engine to drive the processes at the business level and there will be no engine to drive the work or bring the information needed to perform the work to the employees. Without this, the business processes will run, but they will be slow, yield many failures and be very difficult to change.

> **Tip** 'Workflow' is sometimes seen as costly and time-consuming to implement, but this impression often comes ironically from lack of transparency and chaos in companies that do not yet use workflow. Once you have automated your processes with SAP's WebFlow Engine (which fulfils the three objectives of providing transparency, driving business processes, and driving tasks to the people), it is very easy to implement changes and to measure their success.

There are very few companies around today that can afford the luxury of inefficient, slow and error-prone processes. The Internet, with its speed and its choice of partners and services, does not eliminate the need for workflow. Quite the opposite: because the Internet is only a point-to-point medium, with no memory of what has happened previously and no knowledge about what should happen

---

4 "E-process: Workflow for the E-business" from Ovum January 2001

next, it merely exacerbates the chaos. It makes an engine that monitors and drives the process all the more important.

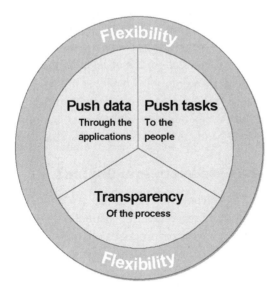

Figure 1. 3 The Primary Goals of Workflow

The second alternative is to use a workflow engine in your SAP environment from a different vendor. In many cases this would amount to looking a gift horse in the mouth, because SAP supplies hundreds of best-business-practice workflow templates for SAP's WebFlow Engine, along with tight business application integration with the tool. Both the engine and the best-business-practice workflow templates are automatically included and installed in every SAP component.

On the other hand, if your company has already invested a lot of money in a different vendor's tool, then the continued use of this tool could be an intelligent proposition. If this applies in your case, we genuinely hope that you will be able to put to use some of the more general tips in this book. It will also be worth your while looking at chapter 11, *E-Process Interfaces*. This describes the opportunity to integrate processes driven by SAP's WebFlow Engine easily and robustly with your own non-SAP tool. This solution would at least save you from the upgrade problems and reliability problems associated with trying to get an external tool to drive the processes in the mySAP.com installation.

1.4   In Which Situations Should I use SAP's WebFlow Engine?

Later in this book you'll be given more exact guidelines for deciding when to automate a process using SAP's WebFlow Engine. In this section we'll highlight the primary features so that you can decide on the spot (such as during a conversation over lunch) whether or not SAP's WebFlow Engine is likely to be appropriate for the task in hand. Saying "yes, definitely" on the spot does not, however, free you from the more detailed evaluation that will need to follow later.

Contrary to what you might expect, you do *not* have to take into account whether or not the process is executed over the Internet in order to make your decision. This is because the complete development and run-time environment has been optimized to allow you to take traditional workflows and port them to the Internet with a minimum of fuss. This is absolutely essential, because you often need to extend the boundaries of a traditional internal business process outwards so that it no longer simply involves members of one department, but merges partner companies or occasional users with no SAP GUI and no SAP skills into the process.

When this happens, you need to extend the workflow definition quickly and cheaply. It would be counterproductive if you had to create the whole process anew. So adding a Web user interface or inserting steps in the workflow to collaborate with business processes in a partner's system is a very simple matter. The question now boils down to "Is workflow technology going to help in my situation?"

1.4.1   Primary Factors

The primary factors influencing the decision to use workflow are:

1. Human involvement
2. Repetition
3. Fruits of success
4. Cost of failure

The following sections will describe these points in more detail but it is worth stressing at this point that many mySAP.com components rely on WebFlow to automate their processes. So a significant factor is "Does SAP provide a workflow which already covers your needs in this area?" Even if the SAP-provided workflow does not exactly match your requirements you will find that it is a very good starting point, because the component is already 'workflow-aware'.

Factor 1: Human Involvement

One of the key features of all workflow systems is the ability to manage the people involved in a process. The workflow should coax the best out of the participants and compensate for their shortcomings too. This is the fascination of creating a good business process: workflow is very people-oriented. Not just in the user interface, but also in the way the participants work together in a team. Workflow supports this teamwork.

When the process is extended to the Web this becomes even more important. Contrary to some early perceptions, the Internet does not solve all problems on its own. It simply allows a faster and tighter integration between the people involved in the business process.

In fact, the Internet leads to an increase in the number of participants involved in a business process, and it also extends the geographic availability of the participants. Whereas five years ago you might have had a small group of participants in the same building, now you can have hundreds of participants scattered around the globe. And many of the new participants will be anonymous to the rest. It is easy to see why the first attempts to use the Internet failed: because there was no workflow in place to harness the potential anarchy.

The people involved in a process are the deciding factor. Although the WebFlow Engine is equally good at handling processes that involve no human interaction because of its high volume capabilities, scalability, and open interfaces, it is the human aspect that is the most difficult to tame. Because automated processes without human interaction, often classed as Business Process Automation (BPA) scenarios, inevitably mutate to include human interaction as the scope of the process definition expands, a company committing itself to a purely BPA tool would quickly run into a dead-end. Even in BPA scenarios, the human factor eventually becomes the most critical factor governing the success of the implementation. An example of a process that does not involve humans would be a fully automatic production process in the chemical industry. An example of a process that does involve humans is shown in figure 1.4, where customer creates an appointment for a car to be repaired via the courtesy services of the insurance company's claims department.

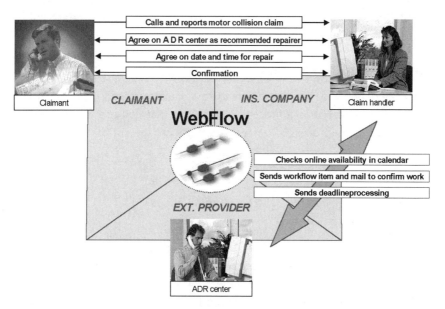

Figure 1.4 Example—Insurance Claim Appointment Scenario: The Insurance Company and the External Service Provider Cooperate in a Networked Team to Produce and Provide the Service for the Claimant

Factor 2: Repetition

The more often a process repeats itself, the better the return on the investment made in modeling the process. It is as simple as that.

This does not mean that there is no point in using WebFlow if the process does not repeat itself many times a day. If you activate one of the standard workflow templates delivered as part of your SAP component and use it as-is, the cost of automating the process is trivial, so it does not need to run often to give a return on investment. However, if you have a process that runs in a thousand variations, you might think carefully about modeling only the core of the process rather than creating one thousand workflow definitions.

Another exception to the repetition rule is a process that should rarely if ever occur, such as a catastrophe plan. This is related to the fourth factor, cost of failure, but is worth mentioning here. Emergency and exception procedures are good examples of processes worth automating, because they have to follow a predefined path and they have to follow this path as fast as possible, compensating for human nature along the way.

So don't be dogmatic about the repetition factor. It is certainly important but by no means an absolute criterion.

Factor 3: The Fruits of Success

This may seem obvious, but you do need to calculate roughly how much you stand to gain by automating a process. The criteria that you use to measure the success will vary from process to process but these are the critical factors.

1. Cost savings that can be realized
2. How much the speed of the process can be improved
3. How much the quality of the outcome can be improved.

While you do not want to waste time and money or unnecessary research, it is essential that you get some sort of estimate of the expected savings before an implementation gets a go-ahead. Every project is an opportunity to document the usefulness of workflow, but the opportunity is wasted if you don't make a before and after snapshot. Unfortunately, projects often lose sight of this in the rush to go live. The snapshot will be of great value later, when other departments approach you about automating other processes. A quantified measure of success is invaluable to senior management too. They will be keen to spread the use of a successful technology, once they can be shown in easy-to-understand terms that it is a success.

This book will go into more detail later about how to calculate these costs, but we'll describe some of the factors involved here.

Cost savings are influenced by the reduction in time that a participant actively spends in the process. Questions to ask when evaluating the cost savings are:

▶ Is the information that participants need provided together with the task when it arrives on their screen, or do they have to do further research?

▶ Can you redistribute parts of a task to unskilled colleagues rather than expecting the skilled (and highly paid) employee to do it all?

▶ Can you automate some of the steps so that the system performs part of the task rather than expecting an employee to do it all?

Replacing complex navigation inside transactions by simple forms-based steps will often create substantial savings on their own.

The *speed of the process* is almost certain to increase dramatically when the workflow goes live. Reducing process time from two weeks to one to two days is typical of most of the workflow projects done using SAP's WebFlow Engine. As well as estimating and comparing the timesaving, you should also prepare a list of intangible benefits. For example: Is a customer served more quickly? Does a new product take less time to reach the market? Is production downtime reduced?

The *quality of the results* of the process is the most difficult to estimate, but is becoming increasingly important. Traditionally workflow is often used for approvals procedures, approvals being deemed a necessary evil in corporate life. Workflow can, of course, degenerate to an approval process within a hierarchy of rubber-stamping managers, with all applications being approved at some level without question. There is little point in implementing rubber-stamping approvals.

However, if the approvers are chosen correctly, and the information brought to them with the task is helpful, the quality of the decisions being made will improve. This is important because good decisions are the single most important factor for a company's success. SAP's WebFlow Engine has been used to improve decision-making to reduce waste of materials (e.g. as part of an engineering change), reduce wasting money (e.g. helping to process incoming invoices) and reduce waste of human resources (e.g. during service management). So you can see that to measure the fruits of success you will have to ask many questions about the process and conduct research in many different directions. But be warned! Don't make the mistake made by the big business process reengineering projects of recent years and get carried away trying to invent the perfect process design.

Simply automating the core of the process can often make the biggest savings.

Factor 4: The Cost of Failure

Strictly speaking, the cost of failure should appear as a by-product when you estimate the "fruits of success". However, because the cost of a process failing is often the most significant cost, and because this factor is often neglected during requirements gathering, it deserves separate attention. How much does it cost to recall a car because an engineering change request has delivered the wrong result? How much damage does it do to a printer company's image if an out-of-date version of the printer driver is delivered to the customers? The cost of a process failing can be enormous. If it fails to finish in time or delivers the wrong result, you will see lost customers, production standstills or heavy maintenance bills. You can be sure that it is the failures rather than the successes that make the headlines, so make sure the cost of failure is taken into account when you decide whether or not to automate a process.

In practice, even the best business process stalls or goes wrong occasionally, irrespective of whether or not workflow is being used. However, workflow writes audit logs, making it easier to chase down the sources of errors and correct them as quickly as possible. Workflows can also trigger escalation procedures, for example, when too much time elapses before a participant moves on to the next step. Often this is simply a matter of identifying a user who is sitting on a task too long (maybe they are on vacation) and forwarding it elsewhere. Using workflow, it is a matter of a few mouse clicks to identify the holdup. With paper or e-mail based scenarios this can consume a few hours of actual work, spread over several days.

1.5 High-Level Overview of What Can be Achieved With SAP's WebFlow Engine

Irrespective of the process being automated, you will certainly achieve the following general benefits:

- ▶ The duration of the process is reduced dramatically.
- ▶ The process definition becomes transparent. Everyone knows what they are doing and why, even when there is high staff turnover.
- ▶ Each process instance (i.e. each separate run of the process) is transparent. During the process run and afterwards you can track who did what, when.
- ▶ The process is under control. You can change the definition on the fly to improve it or to react to sudden changes in the environment.

Of course, in addition to these gains there are benefits, such as cost savings or fewer failures that are specific to the process you are automating. These will often be the most significant benefits and the reason for automating the process in the first place.

However, the four general points mentioned above are relevant to all processes, and they are supported by features embedded in the tool. In other words, these benefits can be realized with a minimum of effort in the process analysis and a minimum of effort in the implementation. These are the benefits you get for free, when you use SAP's WebFlow Engine to automate your process.

Because SAP's WebFlow Engine is integrated directly into the SAP Web Application Server and because the SAP components mesh with it directly, the administration involved in making sure that the process runs day-in day-out is almost negligible (this is based on actual feedback from SAP user groups). We will describe this in more detail in a later chapter but it is worth knowing this right at the beginning, to get an idea of the balance in favor of the benefits.

The next section describes some of these features and will give you an idea of how they help you achieve this result.

1.6 Brief Overview of Features

To meet the large variation in scenario requirements and customer environments, SAP's WebFlow Engine offers a wealth of features and integration possibilities. Providing these in one single tool gives you a consistent approach and allows for future expansion of the process. Hundreds of workflow templates are delivered to kick-start the SAP implementation.

1.6.1 Robust Integration into the mySAP.com Components

The direct integration into the mySAP.com transactions, Internet Application Component (IAC) Web transactions, and portals has to be one of the single biggest advantages of using SAP's WebFlow Engine. For example, as you can see from figure 1.5, when a user inspects a record she can jump straight to graphical logs of the processes that used this record, seeing when it was processed and who was involved in processing it.

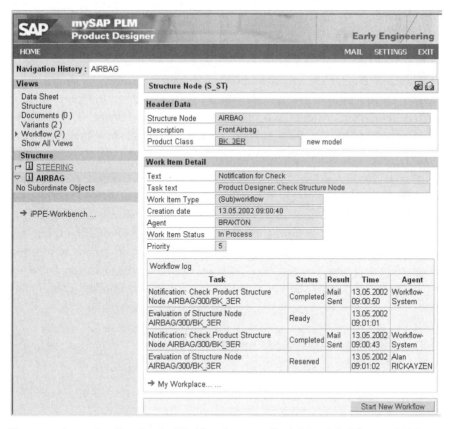

Figure 1.5 Screenshot Showing the Workflow Summary (Log) Being Called from an SAP Transaction

Alternatively, an operator can start an ad hoc workflow process related to the record without having to worry about who is involved in the process or how the process runs. The workflow deals with this automatically. This is useful to avoid the situation where an operator recognizes that something is wrong but does not know how to correct it or who to contact. Without workflow the user will probably turn a blind eye to the situation and hope that someone else deals with it. However, if a workflow has been defined, they simply trigger the workflow and let the workflow follow a preset routine, correctly notifying the other participants along the way.

In addition, many parts of SAP's WebFlow Engine use existing mySAP services to perform fundamental duties rather than duplicating these. Examples of this are: organizational management; communication services and security infrastructures.

These are the advantages, but you should also be aware that many applications trigger workflows directly, relying on SAP's WebFlow Engine to drive the processes through the component (see example in figure 1.5). In other words, SAP's WebFlow Engine provides an intrinsic part of the SAP component's functionality.

1.6.2 Graphical Workflow Builder

The Workflow Builder allows you to build or enhance a process by simply dragging and dropping the individual tasks (based on transactions, function modules etc.) into the process definition. A full suite of modeling elements is available to pick and drop into the workflow definition. Different types of branches, loops and escalation paths can be added with conditions automatically determining which path to follow.

Various types of forms (SAP, Lotus Notes, Microsoft Outlook, HTML) can be generated and maintained from the Workflow Builder so that a given step in the workflow can be accessed from a variety of environments without requiring the process definition to be remodeled. Indeed, the forms can be generated for multiple platforms simultaneously so that one user can access the task using an HTML form in the Web whereas another executes the task directly from her Lotus Notes inbox.

1.6.3 Graphical Status Visualization

There are a variety of different process logs that can be displayed:

▶ Graphical (based on the graphic workflow definition)
▶ Summary (used by the operational user to determine what has been done so far by whom)

- Chronological (for auditing purposes)
- Technical (for debugging a process)

You can navigate directly to these logs from the application transactions involved in the business process (e.g. while viewing an engineering change request). This is available automatically (providing that the application has enabled this) without the need for customizing, and it has the bonus of providing a useful link between seemingly unrelated business objects within a cross-application business process.

1.6.4 Routing Mechanisms

Routing algorithms can be selected for determining the users performing the tasks. This automatic dispatching is very important when you want to avoid wasting time waiting for a supervisor to manually dispatch a task to someone in her department. The most complex algorithms can be resolved by calling function modules, but most needs are satisfied by simply assigning users or organizational units according to simple criteria without the need for programming.

Organizational Management, which is part of the SAP Web Application Server, can be used to simplify the user administration. This is an option that many SAP customers take. Other mechanisms such as office distribution lists, subscription mechanisms or (if the situation warrants it) on-the-fly supervisor user assignments can be used instead.

1.6.5 Deadline/Escalation Management

Deadlines are an important part of process management. They are used to remind users (or supervisors) about tasks that are waiting to be performed. They can also be used to control the process directly. For example, deadline management can specify that if a fourth level approval is not performed within two days, then the request can automatically be sent through to the final stage of processing, with notifications being sent to the appropriate people. Escalation works in the same way, with corrective action being called automatically when a deadline is missed.

1.6.6 Synchronization Management

Sophisticated event handling allows your process to trigger automatically, based on changes (status, HR, change documents, etc.) taking place within the SAP component. These events can also be used to synchronize processes with each other. For example if a supplier is blocked, the engineering change request relying on this supplier can be sent back to the business approval stage before the change goes live.

1.6.7 Integration with Groupware Products and mySAP.com

Allowing users to access the task list through their standard e-mail client or user portal (Microsoft Outlook, Lotus Notes, IAC Web Inbox and the mySAP Enterprise Portal) is a major step in getting them to accept the business process. Direct integration is especially important for sporadic but critical processes. SAP's WebFlow Engine provides this integration, seamlessly, without the need to take special steps when creating the workflow.

1.6.8 Ad Hoc Process Enhancers (Queries, Attachments, Forwarding)

Once the workflow is up and running, the users increase its efficiency by using attachments (to justify a decision, for example) or queries (to get additional information). Other users can view these long after the process has finished. This is clearly an advantage over e-mails, because the e-mails will be deleted or remain hidden in recipients' inboxes. Attachments and queries (with their answers) can be read directly from the workflow log by anyone with the correct authorization.

In addition steps or step-sequences (subworkflows) can be added to a workflow while it is running and these are immediately visible in the graphic workflow log. Reviewers can be added on the fly and predetermined agents downstream in the process can be replaced (authorization and configuration permitting).

1.6.9 Integration with Other Systems Across the Internet

Even a traditional process is going to need support for the Internet sooner or later. SAP's WebFlow Engine supports Wf-XML, the open interface defined by the Workflow Management Coalition to enable workflow systems provided by different vendors to co-operate with each other. In addition, you can send your own SOAP messages or call Web services directly from the workflow.

1.6.10 Desktop Integration (Microsoft Word, Lotus SmartSuite, etc.)

Sometimes it is useful to have workflows that produce PC based documents. For example, a workflow that creates a contract based on a standard Microsoft Word Template can be defined, filling in the details with the data accumulated during the workflow execution. This is particularly useful for creating complicated documents where the formatting as well as the content is important. In this example, the legal department, which is involved later in the process, still has the chance to add their own changes before the final contract is agreed on. And if you rely on outsourced experts such as translators, lawyers or writers, think how much time can be saved and how much control can be gained if you integrate them into the process via the Internet.

1.6.11 Information System

Although this is not usually the primary concern when kicking off a project with SAP's WebFlow Engine project, the information system often becomes significant later on. Once your workflow is up and running the system collects statistics.

SAP's WebFlow Engine provides some standard reports as well as a powerful information gathering technology, the Workflow Information System (WIS). The standard reports are of the form "how often does the process run?", "how long does it take?" or "what is the workload of my department?" You can use WIS to customize sophisticated reports, which give you a clear idea of how to improve the process. For example, you can look at "how much processing time is involved in failed engineering change requests?" or "how often does the northern sales division fail to deliver an offer on time?" or "how often are purchase requisitions under $20 refused and how much time is spent processing them?" Often the result of the analysis will simply be to increase or decrease the number of users available for one of the tasks (perhaps on a seasonal basis). Or you might find that some critical information is missing on the FAQ about the workflow procedure on your company's intranet.

You do not have to use the reporting, but you are losing a golden opportunity if you do not.

1.6.12 Robust Extensible Architecture

Although the underlying object-oriented methodology used in creating workflow definitions was greeted suspiciously in the first Release (R/3 3.0), this has proved to be one of the biggest assets of the system. Process definitions are quicker to adapt to changes in the business process and changes in the business applications than traditional forms-based workflow management systems. A company's business process must be able to change at very short notice and existing custom workflows have to adapt automatically to the new features in a new SAP Release so this has flexibility, and ability to adapt is one of the most prized assets of the WebFlow Engine. In the meantime, the object-oriented approach, which includes features used extensively in WebFlow such as event-handling and the use of methods and attributes, is a cornerstone of all modern software development.

Similarly the WebFlow Engine itself has stood the test of time, and is equally at home dealing with traditional approval processes (forms-based too) as at dealing with modern XML-message based techniques.

1.7   Summary

We have avoided formal terminology in this chapter to make it easier for anyone without workflow experience to read. However, at this stage it is worth defining a few terms that will crop up through the subsequent chapters, so that you can dip in to them in whatever order you choose, but still know what is being discussed.

- The *workflow definition* is the set of rules that determine the path that the process takes.
- A *workflow instance*, which is often simply referred to as the *workflow*, is a single workflow run.
- The *tasks* are the steps in the process, which have to be performed either by people or automatically by the software.
- A *work item* is the task instance that is performed as a single workflow step.
- *Agents* are the people who process the tasks (via the work items).
- *Participants* are everybody involved in the process, including those who simply receive a notification that something has or hasn't been done.
- The *container* is the place where all data used in the workflow is collected.
- The *binding* is the set of rules that define which data is passed to which part of the process.

To help visualize this, look at table 1.1, which illustrates the terminology with a simple purchase requisition procedure. More exact definitions will be given in the relevant chapters, but this is enough to keep you going for the moment.

Terminology	Example
Workflow definition	How a purchase requisition is processed, from the initial request to the creation of a purchase order.
Workflow	The processing of a single purchase requisition for an office printer.
Agent	Requisitioner, manager, member of the IT dept and a member of the purchasing department.
Participant	Office colleagues of the requisitioner, who will later receive news of the new printer.

Table 1.1 Examples to Illustrate Workflow Terminology

Terminology	Example
Task	Check that the office does not already have this equipment.
Work item	Check that there is currently no printer in room I1.29.
Container content	Office (I1.29), Equipment (printer)
Binding	The room number of the office and the equipment type is required to perform this task, but NOT the requisitioner's cost center.

Table 1.1 Examples to Illustrate Workflow Terminology (cont.)

SAP's WebFlow Engine has taken SAP Business Workflow to the Internet.

The traditional gains of workflow are:

▶ Process control

▶ Faster throughput

▶ Higher quality of the results

▶ Coping with staff turnover, frustration thresholds and reduced available time for training

▶ Cutting down costs

▶ Flexibility to change the process on the fly

These gains can be won in the SAP environment, irrespective of the component being used and irrespective of the type of user involved (employee, partner, external resource, etc.). A good indicator of whether to use workflow is if the process involves several different people. If the process repeats itself often or if it simply cannot afford to fail, then you have an even higher incentive to use workflow.

SAP's WebFlow Engine is an industry-proven e-Process management tool with no compromises regarding the functionality delivered, regarding the functionality, stability and performance delivered.

2 Requirements Gathering Strategy

What you need to ask and know in order to assess whether or not to automate the process and what degree of automation can be achieved. At the end of this section you will have a good idea about how to proceed with the project.

2.1 Introduction

Gathering requirements for a workflow, as you would perhaps expect, is very similar to gathering requirements for a business process. Much the same information would need to be gathered if you were about to write up the business process in a procedures manual. Even if you simply intend to activate one of the workflows delivered in your SAP component, it is worth digesting this chapter to see how even the most mundane things, such as the description that accompanies a work item, can be optimized to increase the success of your project.

The key questions behind any business process or workflow can be summarized as:

▶ **Who Should?**

- Who is involved in the process?
- Who actually does/will do the work, i.e. who are the agents?
- Who is indirectly involved? This could be people who need to be notified but don't actually participate directly, or people who will do related tasks outside of the workflow that the workflow needs to know about.

▶ **Do What?**

- What tasks/activities need to be performed?
- Will the tasks be performed in the same system as the workflow, in another system, or are they manual?
- Does someone need to be directly involved in performing the task, or can the task be automated?

▶ **To What?**

- What entities (objects) and data are involved?
- If I want someone to perform a task, what data do they need to see and/or use to complete it?
- If the task is to be automated, what data does the system need to complete it?

▶ **When?**

  ▷ What starts the process?

  ▷ How do we know when a task/activity is complete?

  ▷ How do we know when the process as a whole is finished?

▶ **In What Order?**

  ▷ What is the sequence of tasks?

  ▷ Are tasks dependent on each other?

  ▷ Can they be done in parallel?

  ▷ Do tasks or groups of tasks need to be repeated in certain situations?

As may be evident from the above questions, requirements gathering occurs throughout the workflow project, from developing the business case justification to design through to implementation.

> **Tip** Although a discussion of project management is outside the scope of this book, to give you an idea of what is involved in each stage of a workflow project, some checklists are included in the appendix regarding:
>
> ▶ Gathering Requirements
>
> ▶ Evaluating Return on Investment
>
> ▶ Quality Assurance Design Review
>
> ▶ Building and Testing
>
> ▶ Quality Assurance Implementation Review
>
> ▶ Going Live
>
> ▶ Housekeeping

One other major question is relevant, and that is:

▶ **Why?**

  ▷ Why are we doing this at all?

  ▷ Why are we doing this with workflow?

2.2   Understanding the Business Process

Hopefully the "Why?" question has been asked before you start the workflow but if not, pose it now. This question goes to the heart of understanding the business drivers for the process, and the benefits to be achieved by using workflow on this process.

Not only does this help to ensure that you focus on the parts of the workflow likely to give the greatest satisfaction to the workflow sponsors, but it also helps to warn of any problems you may encounter in building the workflow.

2.2.1 Business Drivers for the Process

Knowing the business drivers for the process will help you assess what are the critical success and failure criteria for the workflow. That is: how do you know when the workflow has achieved its business objective?

Some key questions to ask are:

▶ Is this process currently performed within the company, or is it a new process?

▶ What does this process achieve for the company?

▶ What would be affected if this process did not happen?

▶ What is the financial impact if this process happens or does not?

▶ How often does this process happen?

▶ How many people are or will be involved in a single instance of this process? For example, if a "vacation request" process is built around entering, approving and posting vacation forms, how many people will be involved in processing a single form?

▶ How many people take part in this process in the company overall? For example, everyone puts in vacation forms; therefore everyone in the company is involved in the "vacation request" process.

▶ Does this process affect service level agreements (SLAs) with customers or business partners?

▶ Is segregation of duties (i.e. making sure different people are involved) an issue?

▶ Is sensitive information involved? For example personnel salary details or competitive information.

▶ Is this a self-service process (i.e. do you expect untutored or minimally educated personnel to be involved in the process)?

▶ Are there time constraints on the process?

▶ Must any legal requirements be met by the process?

▶ What else is critical to this process?

▶ When was this process last reviewed or re-engineered?

Sometimes the answers are obvious. Take a "procurement request" process involving procurement requests that are entered, approved, and actioned. Clearly segregation of duties is an issue; you won't want people approving their own purchases. If the procurement requests are entered over the web and are entered by the person who wants the goods, then this is also a self-service process that may affect potentially anyone in the company who needs to buy something. The financial impact of not approving the procurement requests can range from revenue lost when goods critical to production are not purchased in time, to expenses for goods that shouldn't have been bought.

Is This Business Process a Good Candidate for Workflow?

Once you feel you have a reasonable understanding of the business process, it is time for a reality check. That is, is this business process a good candidate for workflow?

Good candidates for workflow usually involve numerous tasks that need to be performed, within given constraints, by numerous people. Often the reasons for implementing the process via workflow revolve around making sure all tasks are performed correctly, all constraints are met, and all relevant people are contacted as efficiently as possible. This is particularly true where communication barriers exist between the people, such as when people are in different locations, different departments, or different companies.

If the process is not a good candidate for workflow, take a moment to consider whether there is a better way to accomplish this task. If you are looking at a process where very few people are involved and there is no particular urgency to the process, perhaps a batch job or report is all that is needed. Spending time to build workflows having few benefits does no one any favors.

Understanding the drivers of the process can help you find the factors to concentrate on during workflow design and implementation. For instance, if a process involves time constraints, focus on deadlines. If a process involves segregation of duties, focus on making sure only appropriate personnel can perform a task. If it is a self-service process, focus on making sure that the tasks performed by untutored users are as user-friendly and self-evident as possible.

Lastly, if the process has not been reviewed or re-engineered for some time, workflow may be the catalyst for some business process re-engineering. You should confirm whether process re-engineering is needed or desired. This will give you an idea of how much flexibility there may be in interpreting the business process for workflow. If you know that business re-engineering is a part of your workflow project, there are a few extra questions you should raise.

▶ Is the process still relevant?

▶ Is the process effective?

▶ What improvements do you believe can be made to the process?

2.2.2 Expected Benefits of Workflow

There are three main reasons why companies implement workflows:

1. To improve the *speed* of a business process
2. To improve the *consistency* of the business process
3. To improve the *quality* of a business process

Any or all of these reasons are usually critical success criteria to the workflow project.

Companies looking to speed up the business process usually want to reduce costs through time savings or hope to retain and expand their current customer base through improved service. To reach these goals, focus on streamlining the process, and making sure that performing the tasks is easy and quick. Aim to automate tasks where possible.

Companies concerned with *improving the consistency* of the business process are usually trying to avoid penalties of some kind, whether financial, legal, or loss of goodwill. If it is important to be able to prove that the correct business process has been followed when examined in retrospect, focus on security, stringent agent determination, and ensuring the workflow is self-auditing.

Companies concerned with *improving the quality* of a business process are usually trying to improve the information provided to decision makers, increase clarity and visibility, reduce errors, and improve acceptance of the process to minimize maverick activity. Focus on ensuring that all tasks are as easy as possible to perform, with good descriptive texts and clear instructions, using attachments to improve communication between people involved in the process, and sending e-mails to people affected by the process.

If the reason for building the workflow is unclear, try asking the following questions:

▶ What's the expected ROI (Return On Investment) for this workflow project?

> **Tip** A checklist is included in the appendix to help you evaluate ROI for workflows.

- Where does the return come from? Increase in revenue? Savings? Increasing customer base? Reducing time to market? Avoiding legal penalties? Satisfying parent company requirements?
- How will this return be measured?
- Are there any other critical success criteria for this project? If they are intangibles, how will their success/failure be measured?

Knowing the critical success criteria for the workflow helps show where particular care needs to be taken in the workflow design. For instance, if off-site access to the process is critical, then which work item delivery method(s) will be used (i.e. how the task is sent to the agent) needs special consideration.

Consider what metrics will need to be gathered via the workflow to prove whether the success criteria have been met. Some metrics that workflow gathers automatically include process start/end times, task start/end times, task execution versus waiting times, and who was involved in performing a particular task. Start/end times can be used to compute the duration of a process or task. Where additional metrics are required, consider having automated steps in the workflow that gather the appropriate data.

As well as proving whether criteria such as expected total processing time have been met, these metrics are useful to help further improve the process in practice. For instance if agents are slower than expected in performing a particular task, perhaps more or better information needs to be presented to them. Monitoring can also show whether the tasks are adequately distributed between agents, or help to identify bottlenecks.

2.2.3   How Does the Process Work in Theory?

If the process is already defined in a business procedures manual or document, now is the time to look at how the "official" process operates. When is the process triggered? How do we know when the process is complete? If the process currently involves paper or electronic forms, try to obtain copies or printouts, since these are often useful when considering what data is needed by the workflow. Look for clues as to which agents are involved; i.e. must the task be performed by people in particular positions or with particular skills.

Note any references to related processes that are affected. Check whether the workflow needs to cater for the related processes in any way, such as notifying or passing information on to personnel involved in the related process. Ask whether the related processes currently use workflow or may be implemented with workflow at a future time.

Watch out for parts of the process that are inherent to the way the process is currently being performed. For instance, paper-based processes often require signatures. Ask whether signatures are still needed, or whether we can confirm the correct person is doing the work by checking their user ID and password?

Understanding how the process is supposed to work lets you move onto the next stage: What actually happens in practice?

2.2.4 How Does the Process Work in Practice?

If you can, speak to the people who actually perform the work. Find out how the process works in practice. How does it differ from how the process works in theory? Why is there a difference? Does the theoretical process not cover some practical situations? Is the theoretical process out-of-date? Has the process not been communicated equally to all affected personnel? Why not? What works well and why? You need to make sure that you retain the ease and quality of those parts of the process.

How are the tasks performed, manually or on the system? If on the system, what transactions and/or reports are used in the process? Can any of the tasks be automated to improve efficiency and reduce workload on the agents? Of all the data available on those transactions and reports, which data is critical to performing the task? Of all the functionality available on those transactions and reports, which functionality is critical to performing the task?

At this stage, you are not restricted to using those same transactions and/or reports within your workflow. Often routines such as BAPIs (Business Application Programming Interfaces) or techniques such as batch input may be more suitable in the final workflow. However, knowing what functionality is currently used will help make sure all necessary functionality is included, and is a starting point in searching for appropriate routines.

How good is the data quality? Poor data quality is usually an issue with paper forms. What is the cause of any data quality problems? Look for opportunities to improve data quality by providing help or validation for common data mistakes.

How easy is it to find out who is responsible for performing each task? Are there situations where no one is willing to take on a particular task? Why not? Is the task difficult or unpalatable? Is there confusion over responsibilities? Is lack of training an issue? Is it a rote task that could be automated wholly or in part?

Do all agents have a similar level of skill in performing the tasks? What information is needed by an experienced/inexperienced agent to complete the task successfully? What information is most critical for an experienced agent to complete the task swiftly?

Is the work fairly distributed across agents? How is the work distributed across agents now? Would distributing the work differently help agents to perform tasks quicker and/or more accurately, for example by giving an agent related tasks such as all procurement requests for the same material group?

Are there many delays? What causes the delays? What happens when an agent is away? What happens when an agent changes position or leaves the company?

What are the average, fastest, and slowest times taken to complete the process? You want to make sure workflow can improve on the average and fastest times if possible, and at least not make the process any slower. How is this measured? Anecdotal process times are unreliable, so you might want to gather some actual start/finish times to let you show later whether total processing time has been improved or at least made no slower.

What do people complain about most with this process? What is frustrating about the current process? Look for opportunities to improve the process where you can. Try to find quantitative measures for any problem areas so that you can plan to measure, monitor, and compare these against the workflow to show what improvements have been made.

Even if the process is new, and there is little practical experience with it, many of these questions are still relevant. You should at least make sure likely exception situations have been included, and potential problems considered.

2.2.5   Unions and Workers Councils

If unions or worker's representatives have a say in how work can be organized, they have to be involved right at the very beginning of the planning stages, especially if this is the first time that workflow has been used by the company. There are customizing settings to help you conform to local rules, but this does not mean you can skip a face-to-face-consultation. Listen to what they have to say, and make sure that this advice is followed.

Because of the positive feedback that the initial users will give, the second workflow is generally far easier to plan and install.

2.3 Gathering Object Data

Gathering the data for a manual business process sometimes seems to be limited to data needed to create paper or electronic forms. Often the data needed is not formally specified in the business procedures manual, and is known only to the people performing the task. With workflow, you need to be much more rigorous about identifying every piece of data, since this needs to be explicitly made available to the workflow.

Many individual pieces of data may be used across a workflow, but there are often close relationships among them. In particular, much of the data is related directly to the entities involved in the business process. Using workflow terminology, you would call these entities *business objects*. By knowing the key of the business object, you can derive all sorts of related data.

Take a workflow that controls follow-on processing of a sales order. It is likely that you will need to use a lot of data related to the particular sales order being processed. By knowing that the key field *order number* identifies a particular *Sales order*, we can use the order number to derive all sorts of related information about the order.

> **Tip** Object data includes table-based data, such as the *order creation date, who created the order*, the *customer number* on the order, and calculated data such as *age of the order*.
>
> You can also include extended relationships. By knowing the *customer number*, which is the key field of the *Customer* business object, you can then access the *customer name* and *customer address*.

However, before you start collecting your data into business objects, you first need to determine what data is needed by your workflow.

2.3.1 What Data is Needed by Workflow

Data may be used for a variety of purposes in a workflow including:

▶ **Data used in performing tasks**
When a workflow is started, the triggering mechanism usually passes some key information to the workflow, for example an order number to a workflow dealing with follow-on processing of an order. The workflow can then pass this information on to each task to be performed. For example it can pass the order number to one task that displays order details and another task that updates the order.

▶ **Data used to determine who should perform the task**

If, for example, you decide that the person updating the order is chosen based on the type of sale (retail/wholesale) and the total order value, then you need to make both *type of sale and total order value* available to the workflow.

▶ **Data used to determine escalation times**

For example, if the workflow must be completed within one week after order creation date/time, *order creation date* and *order creation time* must be made available to the workflow.

▶ **Control data**

Examples are the maximum number of times a sub-process can be repeated before alternative action is taken, or the result of an approval/rejection decision.

▶ **Data used for texts**

Examples are instructions to the person performing the task. For example the name of the person who has created the order, and the name of the customer for whom the order was created. These are often not thought about until late in the workflow development, resulting in frantic last minute development work.

> **Tip** Encourage early thought about what data should be presented to agents. In particularly make sure that data is meaningful (names not just numbers, descriptions not just codes), and useful (aids quick execution of the task, puts forward salient details necessary for decision-making).
>
> This is also a good time to start thinking about how the texts will be worded. Too many instructions created at the last minute or without much thought are abrupt or technical. Encourage prompt action by polite, tactful, and considerate instructions. Ensure the most important information appears towards the start or top of the text so experienced agents can act quickly.

Don't worry about data that is already a part of the transaction (or routine) that is used to execute the task, unless you also need to show this in your instructions to the agent. You do, however, need to make sure that the texts and instructions to the agent, plus whatever is shown by the transaction (or routine), give enough information so that the agent can make decisions and complete the task.

2.3.2   Where to Look for Data

Examine any documents used in the current process, such as paper or electronic forms. These show what information is currently presented to agents, which is a useful starting point. Talk to current and/or potential agents. Ask what data they need to make appropriate decisions and complete tasks. Ask if that data is currently available on the system, e.g. as part of a table, transaction or report. Particularly watch for key data that identifies the entities involved in the process, such as the order number of an order. A lot of data can be derived. For instance if we know an order number, we can find out who created the order, what was ordered, when it was ordered, for which customer.

2.3.3 What Data Already Exists

Workflows provide some data by default, including:

▶ Workflow "system" information (fields on the WFSYST structure), such as the workflow initiator, that is, who triggers the process.

▶ Details of tasks just executed, such as who executed it, start and finish times.

▶ Attachments for e-mails.

Within SAP components, many business objects have already been created, and both table-based data (from the ABAP Dictionary) and calculated data are included in them. Existing business objects can be readily reused and extended in an upgrade-friendly manner. Or you can use them as examples for creating your own completely new business objects.

2.3.4 Making the Most of the Data Collected

Collecting data into business objects is more than just a matter of convenience; it is a matter of principle. Many parts of workflow, particularly business objects, are based on object-oriented theory, whose fundamental benefits include consistency and reusability.

When you are planning to put together workflows, consistency and reusability are very important considerations. Throughout a company, business processes tend to mirror one another; they work in patterns. Instructions and information are presented in similar formats. Escalation processes tend to operate the same way. E-mail notifications are worded in a similar way. Tasks such as approval/rejection decisions are performed in a similar way.

Workflow tends to emphasize these similarities and often directly contributes to them. From a company's perspective, this is highly desirable. Maintaining similarities:

▶ Reduces training requirements and costs

▶ Simplifies maintenance of data supporting the process

▶ Improves speed in performing tasks since the agent knows what to expect

- ▶ Increases consistency in the way tasks are presented and performed
- ▶ Increases consistency in the way outstanding tasks are escalated
- ▶ Reduces errors and simplifies troubleshooting

From a data perspective, consider that when performing a task related to a particular employee, you often want to see not just their user ID or personnel number but their name, address, and contact details. When performing a task for a customer or vendor, you want to see name, contact details, and contact person. Whenever a code or ID is used, you want to see the matching description. When viewing amounts, you want them displayed in the same way, plus or minus sign on the same side, commas and decimal points in a consistent manner, currency shown in a consistent manner.

Using business objects to collect data helps to encourage consistency, and ensures reusability. The more you follow object-oriented rules when collecting your data, the better the consistency and reusability. Again, the important thing to remember is to attach pieces of data to the object with which they have the strongest relationship.

Take a workflow that creates new customer records and assigns them to an appropriate contact person (for example an account manager) in your company according to company policy. Two Business Object that you want to use are "customer" and "employee". You have discovered you need the following pieces of data for your workflow:

- ▶ Customer ID
- ▶ Customer name
- ▶ Customer phone number
- ▶ Employee ID
- ▶ Employee name
- ▶ Employee phone number
- ▶ Contact person

To which object will you assign the pieces of data?

It is easy to see that "customer ID", "customer name", "customer phone number" should be attached to the customer object, and "employee ID", "employee name", and "employee phone number" should be attached to the employee object.

What about "contact person"? Does it belong with the customer or with the employee object? At first glance it could be either or both. After all, the contact person is an employee, but the contact person is assigned to the customer. So which is the stronger relationship? You need to examine the relationship from the point of view of each object.

▶ Employee:
  ▶ Is every employee a contact person? No
  ▶ Are most employees assigned as contact persons? No
  ▶ Is every contact person an employee? Yes
▶ Customer:
  ▶ Does every customer have a contact person? Yes

In this case, the customer object has a stronger relationship to the contact person. However the contact person is still an employee. What happens when we want to know the contact person's ID and name? You solve this by attaching the contact person to the customer, but not just as a piece of data. Instead you attach the contact person to the customer object as a relationship to the employee object. Then when you want to find the name of the contact person assigned to the customer, you can reference the employee name via the customer-to-contact relationship.

What about multiple relationships? For instance a customer can have multiple sales orders open. You attach a "multiline" relationship, that is, a list of order relationships to the customer object. This allows your workflow to process all open orders attached to a customer.

What about the relationship between an order and its items? Is "order items" part of the "order" business object or not? Think of it this way: do they share the same data? Do you treat them the same way when performing tasks? No, you don't. Take a simple example—quantity and value. An order item has a quantity, a price and a value derived from them. An order has a total value derived from adding all the item values. Quantity doesn't make sense at an order level since you might have several items in the order dealing with completely different goods or services. This means "order" and "order item" are two distinct business objects. Of course, attached to the order you will probably want a multiline relationship to the matching order items, and attached to the order item you will probably want a relationship to the matching order so that the two objects can refer to each other.

Each SAP component already provides many business objects with many attached pieces of data, and each upgrade adds to this. All of which you can not only use in your workflows, but take as a guide to what data should be connected to which business object.

Does every piece of data need to be assigned to a business object? No. Control data such as the number of times a sub-process is repeated before alternative action is taken, or the result of an approve/reject decision, is usually not created against a business object but exist independently within the workflow. However, whenever data has a clear relationship to a business object, and there is any possibility, now or in the future, that this data might be reused by another workflow, you should try to attach it to a suitable business object. Why? Over time a considerable amount of data will be set up. When you come to build the next workflow, there will be less data to set up and fewer decisions to make about how that data should be attached to existing business objects. This saves time and effort, makes it quicker to implement future workflows, and increases consistency between workflows.

2.4   Determining the Agents

How agents are determined will be dealt with in detail in chapters 5, *Agents*, and 9, *Agent-Determination Rules*, but we will include a summary here because this is an important part of requirements gathering. It affects directly what can be included in your project and what is out of its scope.

Before you can decide how agents should be found, you need to know and be able to explain to your company how an agent interacts with workflow. For an agent to perform a task, you need to send them a runtime copy of the task that includes the relevant data to be actioned. In workflow terms you call this a work item. To an agent a work item is superficially similar to an e-mail. It has a title, descriptive information, may contain other documents as attachments, and agent can receive it in their inbox. The big difference between a work item and an e-mail, from an agent's perspective, is that an e-mail can only tell you there is some work to be done, whereas a work item brings the work to you. Depending on how the work item is delivered to the agent, the agent usually only has to click one button or hyperlink to start actioning the data.

From a process or workflow designer's perspective, there is one other important difference between e-mails and work items to keep in mind. When an e-mail is sent to multiple people, each person receives a separate copy of the e-mail. Once they have read the e-mail it is up to them to remove it from their inbox. When a work item is sent to multiple agents, you usually only want the data to be actioned once, so all agents view the same work item. Once one agent has executed the work item and actioned the data, the work item is automatically removed from all the agents' inboxes. To an agent this means that they know all the work sent to them by a workflow has been completed when they have no work items left in their inbox. The converse of this is also true—a workflow is held up until the work item is executed but an e-mail notification allows the process to continue without pausing.

2.4.1   Who are Your Agents?

Agents include:

▶ The person who starts the workflow

▶ People who perform the tasks

▶ People who escalate the process

▶ People who troubleshoot problems with workflows, particularly those caused by bad or poorly maintained data

The person who starts the workflow is a special agent, called the workflow initiator. Most workflows include communication between other agents and the initiator throughout the business process. The initiator may not be directly involved in executing work items—in fact they may only create the trigger for the workflow indirectly—but they are often involved in escalation and usually need to be notified of process milestones or when the process finishes.

People who perform the tasks must be able to view relevant texts and instructions as well as to execute work items. They must also have access to the underlying transactions or routines used during execution. The person performing the task should be the person with ownership and responsibility for the work. You want agents to act promptly and that's more likely to happen when they feel ownership for the work involved. Consider the workload on each agent. Are there enough agents to process all the work items created? Keep in mind that executing assigned work items is usually only a small part of a person's daily work.

People who escalate the process may be able to view outstanding work items but not be able to execute them. It is common for the escalator to be the workflow initiator, since they are often the person most interested in having the process completed quickly. This is particularly true of "self-service" functions such as vacation or purchasing requests.

People who troubleshoot problems may be workflow administrators or may be specially trained functional personnel. These are the people who handle reprocessing of documents when automatic processes have failed, and re-routing of outstanding work items where agent determination has failed.

Try to cut out the 'middlemen' of the process, since at best they lengthen the workflow, and at worst they can become bottlenecks. Of each potential agent, ask whether they really do anything, and whether what they do is critical to the subsequent tasks. Can they just be notified by e-mail?

Be aware that all agents must have system access, i.e. login and password, so that security can be checked. An important part of any business process is ensuring that only those people who are permitted to do so take part in the process; this is particularly true of approval processes.

People notified throughout the workflow do not need to be agents. This is particularly of interest when dealing with external partners. It is enough to be able to identify an e-mail address, so that an e-mail can be sent to them.

2.4.2 Criteria for Finding Agents

How do we find the agents in a business workflow? People change jobs and positions over time, so we need a reliable way of identifying the current agent(s) responsible for doing the work. This is usually done using attributes or job functions that point to an agent, e.g. the material group for an item in a purchase requested is used to identify the buyer responsible for this material group. Of course both the attributes and the criteria and the relationship between the attributes and the agent must already be defined in the system.

The possibilities opened by workflow automation present an overwhelming temptation to build complex matrices of criteria for determining agents. This seems to be particularly tempting where approval processes are involved. *Resist the temptation!*

Instead, consider clarity of ownership when deciding how to select agents. Agents need to know why they are doing the work. When they do, they will take more responsibility and be on the look-out for work items they should have received but didn't, and work items they receive erroneously. If it is too hard to understand why they are receiving the work items, agents are likely to react slowly or not at all, but if it is clear whey they receive particular work items, they will resolve mistakes and problems effectively.

Clear and appropriate criteria for selecting agents are important for process audits, as well. Auditors need to confirm that the business process is working as expected, and indeed everyone involved in the workflow must have confidence that the business process is working as expected. If the criteria for finding agents are too complex, proving that the business process is working properly will take a long time and confidence in the process will be lowered.

Consider the maintenance burden, both for maintaining the data and for maintaining the programmed rules that select the agent. Both the criteria being used and the relationship between the criteria and the relevant agent(s) need to be maintained. If there is a lot of data to be maintained, this increases the likelihood that no agent can be found or the wrong agent is will be selected, due to delayed or neglected maintenance. Each agent determination error results in delays while the error is being found and corrected, and the workflow restarted. It is even worse when the problem is not found, i.e. when the system selects the wrong agent to execute the work item, or the work item sits in limbo because no agent could be assigned.

A good test of your selection rules is to see if you can work out who will be the agents for a few test cases in your head in a few seconds. If you need to use paper, or it takes longer than a few seconds the criteria are too complex. A quick way to convince management of this is to show how much maintenance will need to be done if the complex selection criteria are retained. One company had a plan involving four criteria, which worst-case involved 12000 entries to be maintained, and in the best case was still close to 1000 entries. Needless to say, a look at the maintenance burden caused a rapid rethink.

Usually two to three (2-3) criteria are more than enough.

Easy ways to determine agents include:

▶ PD-org evaluation paths
▶ Distribution lists
▶ Tables of criteria values matched to agents
▶ Responsibility rules matching criteria values to agents

Responsibility rules usually have the edge on tables. As well as being able to show abstracted relationships easily, for example the user ID of the person assigned to a position that is assigned to the criteria, they can also specify priorities on the relationships. For example, if the agent is selected according to the material group, priorities can be set to look for agents assigned to specific material groups, but if the material group has not been assigned, fall back to a lower priority, 'default' agent.

> **Tip** Avoid programmed rules if you can, since these can add significantly to development time.

Other options include picking agents dynamically, i.e. having a step in the workflow where someone chooses who will be the agent of a subsequent work item.

You can have multiple agents for the same task. It is important to recognize the difference between:

▶ Tasks distributed to a pool of agents to spread the workload, such that one work item appears to multiple agents, but only one agent will execute the work item.

▶ Tasks to be executed by multiple agents, where separate work items must be sent to each agent.

Consider whether you want to allow work items to be forwarded from the chosen agent to another person. If you do allow forwarding, ask whether the recipient's access privileges need to be checked. Consider substitutes when the current agent is absent or unavailable. Who are acceptable substitutes? Substitutes must have access to execute work items sent to them, even if they are only executing the work items on a backup or temporary basis.

2.5   Determining Work Item Delivery Routes

Once you know who the agents will be, you can start to consider how work items will be sent to them. This is an important decision that will be dealt with in more detail in chapter 4, *Work Item Delivery*. However, it is an important step in the requirements gathering process, so a summary of the alternatives is presented here. Your decision will also influence resource planning for rollout and in some cases it will even have repercussions for development planning.

This decision needs serious and in-depth thought for the first workflow implemented at your company. After that, you will most likely use the same work item delivery route in future workflows. However, it is worthwhile revisiting this decision at least briefly in the light of each new workflow design to ensure that the route chosen is still appropriate.

Consider the agent's environment and work habits:

▶ What hardware do they use? PCs? Laptops? PDAs?

▶ What software do they have access to? Web browser? SAP Workplace/Portals? SAP GUI?

▶ What e-mail system do they use? SAPOffice? Microsoft Outlook? Lotus Notes? Other?

▶ How often do they access their e-mail? This is particularly important when agents belong to higher-level management and may only access e-mail once a day or less.

- Do they sit at a desk with permanent access to the network? Or do they work in the field and connect to the network only at certain times? How often do they connect to the network?
- Do they regularly access your SAP component for non-workflow needs?
- Do they have Intranet, Extranet or Internet access to your network? This is particularly important if the agent is a customer, reseller, vendor or service provider.
- What access do they have to training, online help and help desks?
- If they are agents of existing workflows, how do they currently receive work items?

Don't forget to factor in the needs of the business process. Such as, for the business process to be successful, how quickly agents must respond for the business process to be successful? Does the business process require any particular type of access, for example Web access?

2.6 Confirming the Workflow Design

Workflow design is usually iterative. You start with an initial design, and as you start to gather your requirements you refine it. As you gather more information, you refine it further; then you gather the answers to more questions, refine it again, and so on. One danger with this approach is that the original success criteria of the workflow can be forgotten. It is worthwhile going back to your notes on the business drivers for the process and the success/failure criteria for the workflow to make sure the workflow is still on track.

It is helpful to draw up flowcharts showing the workflow design. Most people are visually oriented and can make sense of graphics more quickly than words. The flowchart can be drawn on paper, via a graphics tool, or in the system using the Workflow Builder[1]. The advantage of using the Workflow Builder is that your model then becomes a starting point for the actual workflow implementation. Make sure that the flowchart is easy to read, with clear and meaningful descriptions for each task.

For complex workflows consider breaking up the process into multiple flowcharts. For example, you might draw separate flowcharts for before-versus-after approval processes, for the escalation process, for exception processes, and for the main process.

---

1 Task TS30100074 can be used as a generic Step in the workflow.

Will the workflow achieve the expected benefits? Does the workflow make sense?

Time for a reality check:

▶ Will the workflow achieve the expected benefits?

▶ Does the workflow make sense?

Check for:

▶ **Consistency**
Are all tasks equally easy to use? Do different tasks sent to the same user work in a standard way? Is information in tasks or e-mails displayed in a consistent manner? Is escalation implemented in a fair and consistent manner throughout the workflow?

▶ **Sequence of Steps**
Make sure you are not trying to perform tasks on data that's just been deleted. Watch this particularly with workflows based on HR infotypes. Since infotypes include the lock indicator in the key, locking or unlocking an infotype results in deletion of the current infotype and creation of a new one.

▶ **Waiting for Outside Activity**
Make sure the workflow won't hang if something is done outside the control of the workflow. This is particularly important if the initial implementation of your workflow will only cover part of the process, or will operate in parallel with a non-workflow version of the process. For example, a "procurement request" process that involves entering, approving and actioning procurement requests, may need to know if the procurement request has been deleted so that the workflow can be cancelled.

▶ **Performance Drains**
Is your workflow triggered many times when the business conditions for using this workflows are not met? Will many workflows be closed immediately after they have been started? Here's a classic scenario suggested by one company: "Create a workflow to notify the goods receiver if an invoice has been received but goods receipt has not been made within x days of the invoice being entered."

   ▶ Workflows would thus need to be started for every invoice with goods receipt outstanding. Most would be closed when receipt is done promptly, which would normally be the case. That is a lot of workflow activity doing not very much to catch a relatively infrequent exception situation!

A better approach is to create a daily report that first identifies invoices greater than x days old where outstanding goods receipts still exist, then only trigger workflows for the invoices identified.

Finally, confirm whether the process is still suitable for workflow. It is important to take future plans into account. Many first iteration workflow designs are close to being mere reports, but future plans make workflow clearly the way to go. Remember, business processes change over time, and coping with that change is where workflow shines.

2.7   Workflow Administration

Consider building error handling into your workflow to cope with most common errors. For instance, if the agent determination fails, have the workflow send the work item to an administrator or specially trained personnel with the power to forward it on to the correct agent and get the appropriate data fixed. If a task performed by the system in the background fails, have the workflow retry it some time later, then if it still fails, send it to be processed manually by specially trained personnel.

> **Tip**   At the very least, plan your 'escape' routes in advance. What will you do if a background task fails; if an agent has left the company and still has work items outstanding? Can you kill the workflow and complete the process manually if need be?

It is worthwhile including your workflow administrator in quality assurance reviews of new workflows. This gives early warning to the workflow administrator of possible problems with the new workflow, and how agent determination works for that workflow.

2.8   Planning for Production Start

Right from the word go you should take into account the infrastructure that will be needed after the project goes live and in the roll-out stage immediately before going live. If this is not the first workflow project in the company, there will probably be an infrastructure in place to deal with:

▶ Security issues

▶ Naming conventions

▶ Documentation

▶ Workers councils, unions

- ▶ Training
- ▶ Help desk and Administration
- ▶ Archiving

These issues are dealt with in detail in the following chapters, but for your resource planning it is worth thinking about them right at the beginning. If your company is small or the scope of the project is small, then you may be able to reduce some of these issues to a minimum. However if you are breaking new ground in a large company you may find dealing with the bureaucracy within the company a full time occupation, but it will be worth the effort once the project goes live. Even if there is no formal written procedure in place, you may well discover colleagues who have seen how things are done and are willing to share their experiences with you. It is important to learn from other people's mistakes, and every company and every department has it is own culture which cannot be overlooked.

Archiving, in particular, is often ignored until the disks are almost full and database indexes are clogging up the system. By estimating in advance how often archiving needs to take place, and what data needs to be extracted from the workflows before archiving takes place you will be in a good position to deal with this before a crisis is imminent. It will be much easier to set up the archiving with the same team that blueprints the business processes and develops the workflows than it will be two years down the road, when archiving is necessary but the skills and know-how have evaporated. For global implementations it is useful to request and document retention periods for workflow logs while developing the specifications for the workflow, and include business controls in the sign-offs.

This can affect design decisions. For instance, if there are multiple geographies implementing a common workflow solution, but the country requirements dictate variable retention periods due to audit requirements, it may be necessary to create identical workflow templates by geography to allow the necessary flexibility for retention periods when archiving. There is good documentation and user feedback about archiving on the SAP's WebFlow service portal.

2.9 Planning for Future Enhancements

Ensuring your workflows will stand up to future change is essential, since being able to change your workflow as your business process changes is one of the key benefits of implementing workflow. Having said that, planning for future enhancements is mostly a matter of commonsense.

Build your workflows using patterns, i.e. use the same approach to common subprocesses such as escalation, approval/rejection, notification of completion of a process, retry of background processes, etc. Common patterns make for easier troubleshooting, and reduce development time for new workflows. Wizards are particularly useful in gaining consistency in workflows. When you upgrade, make sure you re-evaluate the patterns to take advantage of new release functionality.

Follow standards recommendations, such as to create standard tasks (not customer tasks) and workflow templates (not workflow tasks).

> **Tip** Revisit SAP Note 152871 regularly to check on any other requirements of release upgrade.

Don't let your current workflows become out-of-date. Workflow can be an instrument of change.

Regularly review the effectiveness of your current workflows.

Use workflow reports to back up your arguments, for example arguments about bottlenecks, unreasonable workloads on particular agents, number of workflows in error, types of errors occurring, speed of process.

Have a forum or contact point where agents can make suggestions to improve the process. This may include anything from improved instructions and texts, to suggesting better underlying transactions or routines, to suggesting ways to reduce bottlenecks.

Finally consider change management. When you implement changes to existing workflows, at the very least create a new workflow version. This allows data currently being processed by the old workflow version to complete using the old process, while any new data triggers the new process. If the workflow or business process has changed significantly, it is worthwhile creating an entirely new workflow and decommissioning the old workflow. As well as assisting with troubleshooting any issues with the new versus the old process, this also allows you to report the new and old process separately, so that their speed and effectiveness can be compared.

3   Configuring the System

Customizing the system is the very first step that you will take when you plan to use workflow. There are default values for most of the steps, but you can always go back later to fine-tune the system.

Unlike most consultants, workflow consultants actually get a thrill out of visiting a system that has not been set up for workflow. You'll recognize such a system by calling up workflow customizing (transaction SWU3) and seeing row after row of red crosses, signifying customizing activities that have not yet been performed. Does this sound daunting? Not at all! Press the single button *perform auto-customizing (⬤)* and presto, a few seconds later the red crosses in the run-time list have been transformed into green ticks (as shown in figure 3.1). All systems go.

As you will see in the next section, the list of green ticks shows that your system is now set up well enough to allow workflows to run. However, this is just half the story. Enabling the system to run workflows is just the first step. Not surprisingly, you cannot set up complete workflows or transport them into the production system complete with the user assignments for each step by hitting a single button.

Unfortunately, customers often push the workflow development into the implementation stage of the project, thinking that it is enough to say, "we will use workflow" in the design stage. You should be aware that this is not the case. Quite apart from the fact that you have to determine the best method for assigning agents to the tasks, there is also a human aspect of workflow management that cannot be underestimated. Getting the users on your side is key to the success of the project and this is best done if they are involved in the projects early on. They can do this on a part-time basis, spending the rest of their time carrying out their normal duties.

The complete path to getting a successful workflow running is:

1. Configuring the workflow system (primarily auto-customizing).
2. Setting up workflow-specific customizing for the workflow that you intend to use, assuming it is an SAP delivered workflow.
3. Creating new workflows (only if necessary) or copying and changing a SAP delivered workflow (only if necessary). Workflows are assigned to packages and this part of your project is indeed development, not customizing.
4. Setting up any additional configuration necessary in the IMG.

5. Setting up the organizational management structures or whatever other method you are using to assign the users to tasks.

6. Transport and Quality Assurance testing.

We will only deal with points 1 and 4 in this section. An example of point 2 is given in chapter 17, *Setting up an SAP-Provided Workflow*. Point 5 is covered in chapter 5, *Agents* and chapter 9, *Agent-Determination Rules*. Point 6 is dealt with throughout the book.

3.1 Quick Start: Configure SAP's WebFlow Engine in seconds

3.1.1 Automatic Workflow Customizing

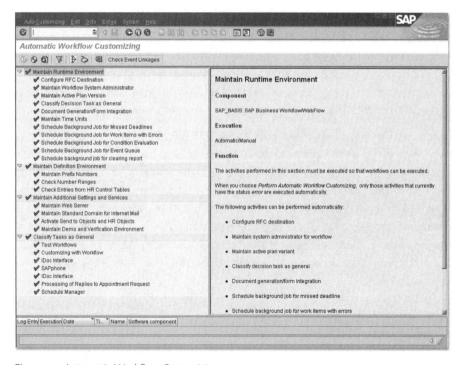

Figure 3.1 Automatic Workflow Customizing

SAP's WebFlow Engine requires certain system settings and system activities, which are to be carried out on a client-specific basis.

When you choose *Perform Automatic Workflow Customizing* (⊕), only those activities in the selected branch[1] that currently have not been configured (red crosses) are executed automatically, to prevent overwriting previous customizing activities.

Some activities that affect the definition system (used when you want to build your own workflows) can only be carried out manually. However, the run-time engine does not require manual activities.

> **Tip** It is essential that you have authorization to execute this task and to perform the individual activities such as job planning or creating the WF-BATCH user in the background. To avoid disappointment and to save wasted time when you arrive at a company's site, make sure in advance that either you have the required super-administrator authorization or that you have the telephone number of a system administrator who can perform this task with you when you arrive.

You can execute all activities manually with the Execute button (⊕) as well, if you wish. This way you can check what the automatic customizing has customized and adjust it as necessary. Some activities can only be executed manually, such as assigning prefix numbers to new custom workflows.

All activities that you perform, either manually or as part of auto-customizing, are logged under your name. These logs are stored in the database and are very useful when you are in a system where several independent workflow teams are at work, which is often the case. By viewing the logs you can avoid the typical tugs of war that take place when different teams tweak the settings independently. The logs are displayed in the bottom frame of the screen and can also be read from the database using the menu option **Extras · Logs**.

Start Verification Workflow

The proof of the pudding is in the eating, and at this point you might be eager to create your own mini-workflow to check that the system really is ready for workflow. However, there is no need to do this because a simple verification workflow is delivered as part of the system. Pressing this button (⚙) configures this workflow (in the background) and triggers it.

---

1 Prior to Release 6.10 the Automatic Workflow Customizing is executed for all activities. Selection is not possible.

> **Tip** This is the fastest way of triggering a workflow to demonstrate what a workflow is and how the logs, inbox and other basic workflow features are used out of the box to improve efficiency. Although there is no business scenario for this example, it is easy for anyone to follow and understand.

Once you have triggered the workflow you will see a message that confirms that the workflow has been triggered. Viewing the long text of this message, you will see instructions about what to do next.

1. Go to the Business Workplace (). You should see a work item here.

2. Execute the work item. You will be faced with a decision. *Execute immediately* or *execute in one minute*. Select *Execute immediately*.

3. You will now receive a mail message that the first work item has been executed successfully and a second mail message confirming that the workflow has completed successfully.

Repeat the process, selecting the second option (*Execute in one minute's time*) and you will again receive two mail messages; however, you will have to wait for one minute before the second message is delivered, because the workflow uses deadline management to create the second mail.

This verification workflow verifies that several of the more complex parts of the workflow run-time engine have been set up properly. These include:

▶ Work item delivery
▶ Background processing
▶ Event generation
▶ Event linkage
▶ Notifications

If at any time you are worried about what appears to be inconsistent behavior in the workflow engine you can call the transaction SWUI_VERIFY that triggers other more complex verification workflows. In practice, this transaction is used only developers at the SAP development laboratories. But it is a useful source of demonstration workflows for understanding a range of workflow techniques.

3.1.2   What Auto-Customizing Does

The automatic workflow customizing sets up the system using defaults so that you are ready to use the system as quickly as possible. You can go back and override the defaults with your own customizing manually later. All the customizing activities are described in detail in the IMG (transaction SPRO). The most important activities are described below.

Maintain Active Plan Version

The automatic workflow customizing chooses the active plan version but you can do it manually, too.

Only one of the plan versions created in the system can be active. This plan version (with its contents) is seen by the workflow system as the only valid plan version. All SAP Workflows supplied automatically become part of the plan version that has been selected as the active plan version .

If you carry out this activity automatically, 01 is set as the active plan version.

If a plan version has already been set, do NOT change it. This has severe repercussions on the workflow definitions that you have created (they will become invisible) as well as on the organizational management structures, including those that are not used in workflow.

> **Caution** In early releases setting the plan version also switches on the link between Personnel Development (PD-org) and Personnel Administration (PA-org), which can cause side effects. In more recent releases this is set with a separate switch.

Configure RFC Destination

The workflow runtime system always executes its tRFC (transactional RFC) calls via the logical destination WORKFLOW_LOCAL_xxx (xxx stands for the three-digit number of the client that you are working in). If this is not configured, the workflows will not run. The workflow runtime system is client dependent, i.e. a single workflow instance normally executes within one client. The naming for the logical destination guarantees that these names are unique across the system.

If you carry out this activity automatically, the logical RFC destination WORKFLOW_LOCAL_xxx is created if it does not yet exist. Background tasks are executed through this RFC destination and performed through the generic user, WF-BATCH, who is assigned to the RFC destination. The user WF-BATCH is automatically created as a non-dialog user, inheriting the maximum authorization of the current user (SY-UNAME)—no more and no less. However the background user

---

2 If you are uncertain, check the PLOGI entries in table T77S0. If the integration switches such as PLOGI ORGA or PLOGI QUALI are set, this shows there is a link between PD org and another HR area. In such cases, speak to an HR expert before configuring the plan version with auto-customizing.

must have the authorization SAP_ALL if the workflow system is to function without problems, so it is essential that the user executing the automatic workflow customization have this authorization. If necessary, get the system administrator to press the button.

> **Tip** Some high-volume installations have fine-tuned the RFC settings[2] so that the check returns an error even though the RFC destination works correctly. If this check displays an error but the rest of the settings appear correct, then you should inspect the RFC destination definition first, before deciding whether or not to execute auto-customizing again to correct the apparent error. You might well find that the RFC description says that the transaction SWU3 check will fail, but that this should be ignored. The verification workflow will confirm whether or not the RFC destination is working properly.

You may well need to reassure the system administrator about this authorization. First of all this user is set as a background user, which means that no dialog login is possible. Secondly, special authorizations prevent this RFC destination from being used by programs other than the WebFlow Engine. If you generate the RFC destination and user with automatic workflow customizing (recommended), then the user cannot be used with other RFC destinations because the password is not known by anyone, having been generated randomly.

Automatic execution to create this RFC destination and background user is recommended. A subsequent automatic customizing execution does *not* overwrite this entry once it has been created successfully (assuming that the authorization SAP_ALL has also been assigned successfully too). If you carry out this activity manually, you can maintain a different background user (however, in practice this tends to create problems because every workflow consultant, developer and administrator will expect you to use the standard WF-BATCH user) or your own predefined password (not recommended for the security reasons described above). The only manual maintenance of WF-BATCH that is necessary is to assign the user an e-mail address so that e-mails can be sent in the background (e.g. notifications to external participants). In this case, you might want to maintain the system administrator as an office substitute for WF-BATCH, so that replies to the e-mails can be periodically scanned.

---

3 You can configure the RFC destination to point to a dedicated application server so that the background processes do not hog dialog processes on the normal application servers.

Maintain the Default Workflow Administrator

The automatic workflow customizing configures this setting, naming you as the default workflow administrator. As such you will automatically receive workflow system error messages, should they arise.

Although it is very convenient to let automatic workflow customizing set this up for you, you should return later and manually re-assign an organizational unit (such as a job or organization) to this setting. This enables several users to act as default administrators at the same time. You should make sure that there is one user for each area where workflow is used, to ensure that a relevant person is notified of errors immediately. If you do not have one central contact person for all workflow issues, then this assignment documents who needs to be informed of any system-wide changes made to the workflow system.

Schedule Background Job for Missed Deadlines

You can plan this to run dynamically, every time a deadline is due instead of at regular intervals. However, this will lead to serious performance degradation in the whole system if many work items with deadlines must be monitored. If in doubt, play safe and use the regular time interval method.

> **Tip**   Deadlines being monitored are not escalated until the deadline job runs.

Prefix Number for Tasks

The three-digit task prefix number must be unique for every client in every system where workflows are developed. This is checked by the global TADIR mechanism. Do not try to override this. If two systems have the same prefix, there is a danger that workflows developed in the one system will receive an identical task ID to workflows developed in another system or client. If workflows from both systems are transported into one system, or if two systems are merged, one of the work-flows will overwrite the other one. The technical IDs of the workflows developed must be unique.

The same applies to the prefix numbers used in organizational management to define the organizational objects, such as positions or jobs.

3.1.3 IMG-Activities for Authorization Management

This section covers the following activities:

▶ Assigning *roles* to users for working with SAP's WebFlow Engine.
▶ Creating structural authorization profiles with which you can create detailed authorizations for Organizational Management objects.
▶ Assigning the structural authorization profiles to users.

The specifications you make in this section concern both workflow authorizations and Organizational Management authorizations.

Maintain Roles

Roles contain authorization objects for specific task areas. With this activity you generate authorization profiles assigned to users based on roles. Refer to the SAP Library and IMG documentation on role maintenance (transaction PFCG).

The following roles are implemented for SAP's WebFlow Engine:

Role	Description
SAP_BC_BMT_WFM_ADMIN	Workflow system administrator
SAP_BC_BMT_WFM_CONTROLLER	Process controller (reporting etc.)
SAP_BC_BMT_WFM_DEVELOPER	Workflow developer
SAP_BC_BMT_WFM_PROCESS	Implementation team
SAP_BC_SRV_USER	User for workflow, communication, etc

Table 3.1 Workflow Roles

Names for your own roles may not begin with the prefix SAP.

Authorization Profiles

If you are working on old releases where authorization profiles are used, these are the primary profiles that you will need to work with.

Role	Description
S_WF_ALL—All	All workflow authorizations
S_WF_PROCORG	Workflow developer
S_WF_USER	Workflow agent
S_WF_ADMIN	Workflow administrator

Table 3.2 Authorization Profiles

Structural Authorizations

Structural authorization allows you to give users in different organizational units different access rights. You may want to read up about this in the IMG if this sounds relevant to your installation.

3.2 Workflow-Scenarios: Task Specific Customizing

As far as possible in the technical and business sense, the SAP-provided workflows can be run directly without any modifications. However, there are always some settings which must be entered in your system and which cannot be supplied by SAP.

3.2.1 Maintaining the Organizational Plan

The company-specific organizational plan describes the organizational assignment of an employee. This allows the responsibilities of employees for performing individual business activities to be defined in the form of activity profiles.

Whether or not you use it is up to you. It is included in the SAP Web Application Server license so we strongly recommend that you take advantage of it, especially if other teams have already set it up for use elsewhere.

3.2.2 Agent Assignment for Tasks

From an organizational point of view, tasks must *always* be linked to their *possible agents*. This means it will often be the case that several employees with the same authorization on an organizational basis are offered the same task for execution. One of these employees assumes responsibility for and processes the work item. This assignment principle supports automatic load distribution within work groups with the same activity profile. For a detailed discussion of this, together with the organizational plan, refer to chapter 5, *Agents*.

3.2.3 Activating the triggering events for a workflow or a task

Workflows and tasks can be started via events, as we will see later in chapter 10, *Business Interfaces*. A workflow or a task can have several triggering events. Every time *one* of the triggering events is raised in the system and satisfies the start conditions, then the relevant workflow is started (i.e. it is a logical "OR" operation between the different start events). The triggering events for a workflow or a task are entered in its definition. If you activate the triggering events, the system automatically activates the associated type-linkage.

If the SAP provided workflow scenarios are to be started via triggering events, this is mentioned in their online descriptions in the SAP Library help. If this is the case, the linkage between the triggering event and the workflow (or task) must always be activated in order to activate the process scenario. The ease with which you can switch the process on and off or use the event activation to swap one process definition for another is a big advantage of using events to trigger workflows. Event activation is usually carried out in the customizing phase.

3.3 Transport and Client Copy

3.3.1 Transport of Cross-Client Tasks

Cross-client transport objects, for example standard tasks (type TS) and workflow templates (type WS), are connected to the transport system. They are automatically included in transport requests, if the client settings allow changes to cross-client objects and if you do not designate the objects as local objects.

3.3.2 Transport of Client-Specific Tasks

Customer tasks (type T), workflow tasks (type WF) and the *general task* attribute for standard tasks (type TS) are included automatically in a transport request in a particular client only if *automatic recording of changes* is set for this client. In other clients, you can include customer tasks and workflow tasks in a transport request manually.

> **Caution** Using customer tasks (type T) and workflow tasks (type WF) for workflow is very heavily discouraged. Instead, standard tasks (type TS) and workflow templates (type WS) should be used for workflow; customer tasks (type T) should only be used as part of HR.

3.3.3 Transport of Settings for Tasks and Workflows

You maintain the following settings for tasks on a client-specific basis:

- ▶ Assignments to their possible agents
- ▶ The *general task* attribute or a task or workflow
- ▶ Type linkages and their activation
- ▶ Workflow configuration

The system automatically includes these settings in a transport request if *automatic recording of changes* is set for a given client.

Tip Once you have got organizational management set up in the production system, either via transport, ALE or customizing, it is a good idea to block the import of agent assignments into the system. This can be done via the IMG. Setting this, you eliminate the risk of overwriting a production organizational model with one that has been set up in the QA (Quality Assurance) system purely for test purposes.

3.3.4 Transporting a Workflow Definition

If a workflow definition is transported to another system, only the active version is actually copied. If a workflow definition exists in the target system, but no executing workflows executing are based on this version, then the existing definition is simply overwritten by the imported version. If there are active workflow instances, then the transported workflow definition is imported with a new version number. This allows the existing workflow instances to continue to execute using the old version of the workflow definition, which is necessary to ensure the non-stop operation of the process.

The transported workflow definition becomes the active workflow definition in the target system. The workflows that are started after the import follow the path dictated by this new version of the workflow definition.

3.3.5 Client Copy

With a client copy, the assignments between tasks or workflows and their possible agents and the event receiver linkages are copied. The type linkages are always deactivated in the target client after copying. If you want to copy the activation indicator of each individual type linkage as well, you must specify this explicitly as a parameter option for copying tables of class A.

3.4 Overview: Customizing for SAP's WebFlow Engine

Activity	Automatic	Always Required?	Default Used
Set active plan version	✓	✓	01
Maintain Prefix Numbers	–	✓[4]	
Configure RFC Destination	✓	✓	User WF-BATCH

Table 3.3 Overview of Customizing Activities

---

4 If you are creating new workflows in this system/client.

Activity	Automatic	Always Required?	Default Used
Maintain the Default Workflow Administrator	✓	✓	SY-UNAME Your own user ID
Classify Decision Task as General	✓	–	
Maintain Standard Domain for Internet	–	–	
Activate Send to Objects and HR Objects	✓	–	
Maintain Demo and Verification Environment	✓	–	
Schedule Background Job for Missed Deadlines	✓	✓	
Schedule Background Job for Work Items with Errors	✓	✓	
Schedule Background Job for Condition Evaluation	✓	✓	
Schedule Background Job for Event Queue	✓	–	
Schedule Background Job for Clean-up Report	✓	✓	

Table 3.3 Overview of Customizing Activities (cont.)

4 Work Item Delivery

Choosing the best work item delivery scheme for your different user groups not only determines how easy it is for them to take part in the process, but also what ad hoc features they can use to enhance its efficiency. This chapter describes the different inboxes and delivery schemes along with their individual advantages.

4.1 The Human Factor

Having activated a workflow so that the optimum process definition is followed and the best possible agent for the task is selected, it is very easy to lean back and believe that the important work has been done. This is far from the truth. Although it takes very little effort to choose a task-list environment for your agents, this choice is one of the most critical success factors for your workflow. By choosing the correct environment and making sure that the agents are comfortable in it, you will ensure a good throughput of work and increase the motivation and quality of the agents' work.

The importance of good task-list environments is not conjecture; it was learned during site visits by SAP development that took place after SAP customers' workflows had gone into production. These visits lead SAP to completely rethink and redesign the principle inboxes in Release 4.6b. The success of the redesign has been praised time and time again at user group meetings, in particular the reduced administration necessary, now that users can track the progress of workflows in their outbox.

Think of it this way. The benefit of workflow is at its highest when coordinating the work of different people, either within one company or within a collaborative scenario spanning the Internet. Humans are doing the job because only they are capable of making the complex decisions or manipulating the data that is involved in the task. If this were not the case you would be better off simply gluing the steps into a single transaction without human intervention.

Here are some of the features that an inbox can provide in order to make the workflow a bigger success:

▶ Easy to access
▶ At-a-glance view of what tasks need to be performed and which tasks need to be tackled first
▶ Clear instructions about how to perform the task

- ▶ Overview of all the relevant data that the user needs to know to perform the task well
- ▶ Mechanisms for letting the user initiate dialogs with other users so that these dialogs are transparent to everyone involved in the process
- ▶ Alert mechanisms so that a user can pull the emergency cord when she notices that things are not proceeding correctly
- ▶ Logs to see what has happened so far and who has participated in the process so far
- ▶ Graphical overview to show where the process is going next and to make ad hoc changes
- ▶ Outbox for researches and to provide positive feedback about the work that an agent has accomplished during the course of the day

This list is long and by no means complete, but it gives you an idea of how critical the human aspect is. It also makes it clear that there is going to be no perfect inbox that provides all these features with the correct user interface for every type of workflow agent. In practice you can distinguish between two different groups of agents:

- ▶ The occasional workflow participant
- ▶ The power-agent who concentrates on one set of duties

Usually these two groups of users will mix within a workflow process, so you will have different participants using different inboxes. This is not an issue with SAP's WebFlow Engine because the workflow definition does not need to be created for one specific inbox. Indeed, an agent can access the same work item from several different inboxes if she chooses. Making the workflow definition independent of the inboxes used by the agent is part of the tool's philosophy. In practice work items are not usually enhanced for one particular type of inbox, although this is starting to occur more often and can yield major benefits if done properly. For example, SAP Markets' Enterprise Buyer Professional (EBP) inbox was developed as a portal to purchasing processes, providing exactly the features that are needed in this scenario (see chapter 15, *WebFlow in Enterprise Buyer Professional* for more details). However, for the majority of tasks the generic work items are better because they allow you to take advantage of changes in the operating environment without having to touch the workflow definition.

Examples of typical changes in the agent's operating environment are:

- ▶ Migrating from one groupware product to another
- ▶ Migrating from SAP GUI for Windows to a Web Browser
- ▶ Migrating from a groupware client to an Enterprise Portal

These migrations are typically forced by a company decision made at the very highest level, so it is a good idea to set things up so that you are in a good position to comply with future changes (of which there will be no shortage) with a minimum of effort.

On the other hand, some companies will want to have as tight integration with their current mail system as possible. SAP's WebFlow Engine supports this too, but the individual tasks may need to be customized to fit this environment, and this will require additional development work.

Before we move on to look at the different factors affecting your choice here's a list of the major inboxes supported:

▶ Business Workplace
▶ Manager's Desktop
▶ IAC Web Inbox
▶ Enterprise Buyer Professional (EBP) Inbox
▶ mySAP Enterprise Portals Universal Worklist iView
▶ mySAP Workplace Workflow MiniApp
▶ Microsoft Outlook
▶ Lotus Notes
▶ CRM task-lists
▶ Transport task-list
▶ Transaction SOO1_old (or SOO1x)—the original R/3 inbox

The same work item can appear in all inboxes simultaneously, but not every inbox supports all features. For these reasons you should decide carefully which group of users should use which inbox to get the optimum results. To make this decision you need to be aware of which workflow features are available and how the agents can use them to enhance the business process. Having made your decision, you should also make sure that the users understand these functions and know how and when to use them. This is not as complicated as it sounds. Usually you can limit yourself to two inboxes, one for occasional users and one for power-agents, and often you will find that one alone is enough.

4.2   Inbox Features

Before describing the inbox features, it is worth reminding yourself of the major differences between a work item and an e-mail.

An e-mail tells you what work needs to be done. A work item brings the work to you.

If you want to remove an e-mail from your inbox, you simply delete it. The only way for you to remove a work item from your inbox is to complete the work, or forward it to another agent (and forwarding can be prevented).

From the modeling point of view, if a workflow sends an e-mail it immediately continues to the next step. However, if it generates a work item it will be held up until the work item completes.

The other difference is that an e-mail is usually copied by the mail system when it is sent to several addressees. When one addressee deletes their e-mail, copies of the e-mail remain in the other addressees' inboxes. However, although a work item can be (and usually is) assigned to several agents, as soon as one agent reserves or completes it, it automatically disappears from the other agents' inboxes immediately. It also disappears when an alternative branch makes this step obsolete or the workflow is cancelled. It is also worth bearing in mind that as a workflow developer, you can have the workflow itself remove the work item from the agent's inbox if it is no longer required (e.g. using modeled deadline monitoring—refer to appendix A, *Tips and Tricks*).

Last, but not least, the work item brings with it a host of other information such as the workflow logs.

4.2.1   Work Item Text

The work item text is easy to set up and if written carefully, it can have a dramatic influence on the success of the process and on the amount of administration needed to cope with exceptional circumstances. Typical exceptional circumstances are:

▶ Agent leaves the department to take on a new job

▶ New employee arrives

▶ The process flow is changed

▶ Teething problems within the first few weeks of going live

▶ Employee absent without configuring a substitute

As you can see, these "exceptional circumstances" are likely to occur quite often and can cause lots of additional administration if not handled properly. Particularly the trend for employees to spend less time in one job before moving to a new department or company means that the first two exceptional circumstances are going to occur more frequently in the future.

The work item text comes in two parts:

1. Short text—one line which should include variables
2. Task description—several lines with sophisticated formatting and variables.

Both of these texts are maintained in the workflow task rather than the step, with the exception of the generic decision step. Both of these can be maintained in your system, even if you are using tasks delivered by SAP. The SAP task description and short text is simply a default and should be re-written in the company's system (this is not a modification).

The short text will always be read, whether or not the inbox is used.

The task description can always be read but it is not always displayed as a default. For example, the Business Workplace displays the description in the preview pane (lower right hand corner of figure 4.1) and it can also be transmitted automatically as an e-mail to notify an agent that they have work to do. However it is not displayed in the mySAP Workplace or the EBP inbox unless explicitly requested by the agent receiving the work item. If the agents are working in the Enterprise Portal you cannot assume that they will view the description. However if the information contained in the description makes it easier for the agent to perform the task, they will be coaxed into viewing the description before executing the task.

A description of what has to be done and how to do it will not be very interesting for an experienced user, but a summary of information relating to the process, which could be obtained otherwise only with complex navigation, is a boon. If the task is simple to perform and all the information that the user needs is displayed when the agent executes the task, then you can assume that the task description will only be used when something goes wrong or when someone new joins the team.

A typical task description contains:

▶ A description of how to do the task. This includes not just a description of which buttons to press but also a description of how to arrive at a good result. For example, a decision task will describe what are the important factors that need to be taken into account.

▶ A summary of the data involved. There is no limit to the number of variables that you can use.

▶ A statement showing why the agent received this work item, e.g. "You are responsible for orders issued in plant 1000."

▶ An address or help desk contact when things go wrong or questions arise.

▶ A URL to an intranet site where additional information is kept, for example, about how to set up a substitute or a FAQ for standard inquiries.

You may even decide to set up an internal forum to deal with process-specific questions such as "Does anyone know how to find out if we can transport phenol-phosphoride-5 through France without special dispensation?". It is a trivial matter setting up a web forum and the benefits are obvious.

Care should be taken with URLs. If they are too long, they may be split in two by SAPscript or the mail system if the task descriptions are sent by mail. You can avoid this by setting up short aliases (redirecting to the full URL) on your web server or by changing the settings in your mail system to allow longer lines in your mail message (e.g. configuration in Microsoft Exchange). Embedding links and images in your work item text is described in appendix A, *Tips and Tricks*.

To get an idea of how the short text can be displayed to the user in the Business Workplace preview pane, take a good look at figure 4.1. You can see that the first part of the description is the most important part and that typically the attachments and other information are displayed alongside the description.

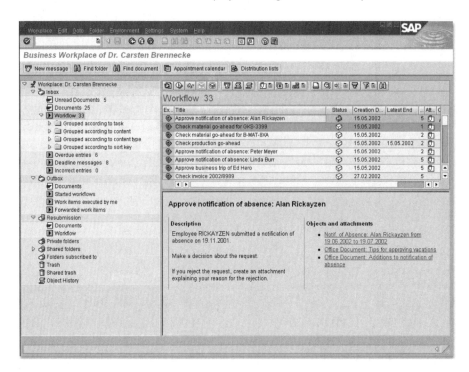

Figure 4.1 Preview Pane in the Business Workplace

The short text has to be handled differently because the text is short but visible to everyone. Make sure you include variables so that the agent can pick the most important tasks first. The most important variable should appear first because most inboxes do not support individual columns for workflow variables (e.g. one column in the mail inbox displaying the cost center associated with the work item), so sorting on the complete short text is the only way of sorting. The variables are also useful when the agent needs to search for a particular work item when someone phones to ask about it.

4.2.2 Attachments

Any agent can add attachments to the work item. These attachments are collected after the work item has finished and appended to a list of attachments linked to the workflow. This means that any attachment added is visible to all other agents in the process, even when that particular step of the workflow has finished.

Three types of attachments are generally used:

▶ A text attachment written in an SAP editor (e.g. SAPScript) by the agent

▶ A PC document which is uploaded to the workflow

▶ A reference to an SAP Business Object

The text attachments are the most commonly used. The agent creates a new attachment to describe how a particular decision was reached or to include useful information for the agent next in line. Either RAW or SCR texts can be created. Links to web sites can be similarly attached using document type URL.

> **Tip** Attachments are also useful when an inexperienced user needs confirmation or help from an experienced user. This is described in detail in section 4.2.8.

The PC document can be a word-processor document, a spreadsheet, an image file or any other PC document supported by the Windows COM interface. When the agent next in line views the document by clicking on the attachment the corresponding PC program is started. Bear in mind that if exotic document types are used there is a good chance that not everyone will have the viewer program installed, and so some of the agents will not be able to view the attachment. Similarly, if some of the agents use a Web Inbox, the appropriate viewer plug-in has to be installed. If the workflow process is a collaborative scenario involving external agents accessing the work items through the extranet, you may need to forbid the use of PC document attachments unless you are sure that the external agents have the viewing programs, too.

You can also attach references to business objects to a work item. So, for example, if an agent feels that one particular material master is related to the purchase order that he is processing, he can simply use the input help to locate the material master and attach a reference to it. Anyone subsequently receiving a work item or viewing the workflow log will be able inspect the material master, authorization permitting, in as much detail as necessary. The beauty of this is that when someone searches for workflows related to this material master, this purchase order workflow will also appear, even though material masters are not part of this workflow definition.

> **Tip** The attachments are stored in the workflow element _Attach_Objects. These are always passed to the work item container. When the work item has finished, any new attachments are appended to the workflow container. This means that it is impossible to remove attachments using customer-code within a task unless the code simultaneously removes references to the item from the workflow container and deletes the attachments, too.

Users may delete attachments created themselves, but they may not delete other people's attachments.

Attachments are very useful in workflow but are all too often neglected. They can document why a decision was made, especially if a manager wants to explain why he has rejected an employee's request. Try to make sure that the users use attachments, because the alternative is often e-mail or telephone. E-mails and telephone calls are lost from the audit trail and cannot be referred to later by new participants in the business process. The attachments on the other hand are visible to everyone.

Of course, a good alternative to attachments is to model the workflow so that it forces the user to create a note as a workflow step. However, this is not always possible or desired. The blocked FI document workflow does not contain such a step, so if you do not add your own step you should make absolutely sure that all participants know how to create an attachment, and how to read them. For the same reason, it is a nuisance if the agents are forced to document what they are doing at every step. Once the agents are disciplined enough to write and read attachments, you will find that they are thankful for having the opportunity to use them.

4.2.3   Reserving and Replacing a Work Item

By reserving a work item, an agent causes it to disappear from everyone else's inbox. This is useful if there are experts in the pool of users. When you start to execute a work item, you will automatically reserve the work item. Canceling the execution will cause the work item to remain reserved in your inbox. Replacing the work item will cause the work item to reappear in other people's inboxes. It will reappear to all agents that have either received the work item initially or have been forwarded it by someone else. In other words, if you are forwarded a work item that you cannot process, you simply reserve and replace it so that it reappears in all the inboxes of the originally selected agents.

> **Tip** To find out who currently has a work item waiting in their inbox, you simply navigate to *selected agents* from the work item display or the workflow log.

4.2.4 Executing a Work Item

Executing the work item is straightforward in all the different inboxes. Once the agent has executed the work item, they will find themselves in the relevant SAP transaction, Web service or whatever else has been configured for this workflow task. Generally speaking they can abort the method at any time (*cancel* key), returning to the inbox to continue processing at a later time.

By executing a task, the agent automatically reserves the work item for herself so that the work item disappears from all the other inboxes. If the agent decides to leave the work item for someone else to do, then she must release the work item by clicking the replace button in her inbox. Reserved work items are displayed with a special status symbol (processing started) in most types of inbox. It is important that the agents know about this and know how to release work items, otherwise they will block other users from seeing (or executing) the work item. When an agent leaves the department she must release all her reserved work items, otherwise the administrator will have to do the clearing up for her.

To make life even more comfortable for the agent, you can provide workflow features that can be called up directly from within the transaction being executed (assuming it is a method executed in an SAP component). This is done by calling the workflow toolbox (shown in figure 4.2), which allows the user to perform the following functions without having to return to the inbox first.

▶ Forward the work item to someone else

▶ Read the task description

▶ Read the work item attachments

▶ Create a new attachment

▶ View the workflow log

▶ Resubmit the work item

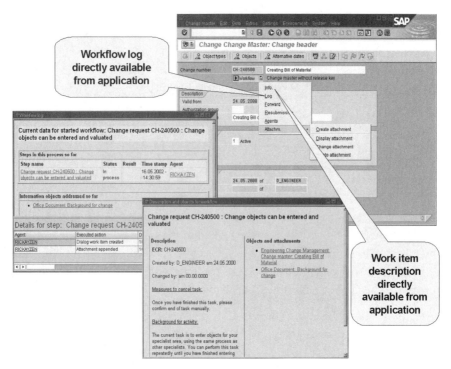

Figure 4.2 Work Item Toolbox in an Engineering Change Request

Chapter 13, *Custom Programs,* describes in more detail how to develop transactions so that they include the workflow toolbox.

Having executed the work item, the outcome will depend on the underlying method and the details in the step definition. If the step has been configured as requiring manual confirmation, then the user must confirm that the step is finished before the workflow continues. This is useful in display or edit tasks where the workflow system cannot determine automatically whether or not the task is finished or whether the agent needs a chance to review what they have done before the workflow finishes. The confirmation button appears as a popup dialog after the work item has finished, or alternatively it can be set directly from the work item list.

If the task is an asynchronous task there will be a slight delay before the terminating event completes the work item. This delay can be of the order of a few seconds at peak times, so if the inbox is refreshed immediately after the work item has been executed the work item may still be visible. The agents should be aware that there may be a delay (e.g. from training, work item description or FAQ), otherwise the help desk will get many unnecessary calls. Asynchronous tasks are described later in this section.

You should also make the agents aware that the work item is completed immediately after it has been executed. Refreshing the inbox simply updates the inbox display and has no effect on the work done by that agent. Some inboxes refresh automatically.

There are two other features, which are relevant to executing work items:

▶ **Synchronous Dialog Chains**
In which a sequence of work items appears one after the other without the need to revisit the inbox

▶ **Multiple-execution**
In which several work items are selected for execution simultaneously and the first result that is reached (e.g. approved) is applied to the rest of the work items without the need for additional dialog.

The next section explains both of these in more detail.

4.2.5   Synchronous Dialog Chains

The term *synchronous dialog chain* has nothing to do with the terms *synchronous tasks* and *asynchronous tasks,* which will be explained later in the book.

A synchronous dialog chain can be defined in a workflow to allow a user to execute several work items one after the other without returning to the inbox between work items. For example, suppose a manager has to explain why she has rejected a request but does not need to explain why she approved a request. You could use workflow to prompt for the explanation by following the approval/rejection step with an explanation request if the request is rejected (as illustrated in figure 4.3).

Without the synchronous dialog chain the agent would receive the approval work item in her inbox and select *reject*. The work item is now finished and when she refreshes her inbox she gets a new work item asking for her explanation. This would be cumbersome for the agent because she has to return to the inbox unnecessarily. To avoid this, you define the first step as a synchronous dialog, chain using the corresponding flag in the step definition[1]. Now when she makes the rejection, the next work item is executed automatically and she now sees the screen where she can enter the reason for the rejection. In other words, she is taken directly into the next step.

---

1   This can also be done at the header level in the workflow definition.

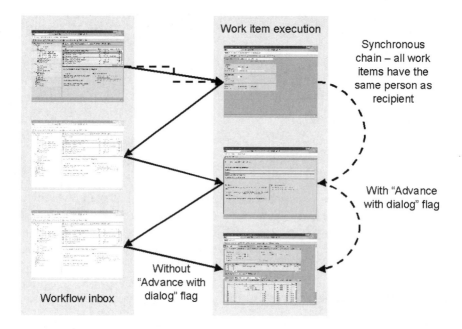

Figure 4.3 Synchronous Dialog Chain Example

This has a number of repercussions:

▶ In order for the synchronous dialog chain to work this way, the agent must be a recipient for all the steps in the chain. If she is not the recipient for one of the steps in the chain, then the dialog chain will break and the work item will land in someone's else's inbox. This is only logical. In fact, any of the steps can be assigned to a pool of agents without breaking the chain, as long as the user is a member of this pool.

▶ This feature is only supported in the Business Workplace inboxes, not the e-mail clients or Web inboxes.

▶ The agent can at any point interrupt the chain by pressing the escape key. The aborted work item will land in her inbox, ready to execute later.

▶ The agent will usually only get a chance to read the task description of the first work item because all subsequent work items rush past without stopping. Bear this in mind when creating the workflow. You can either include all the relevant information in the very first task description in the chain, or you can use the workflow toolbox to allow the user to jump to the description from within the transaction that has been called. The same applies to attachments. But the attachments will not change during the chain unless the agent adds attachments herself.

▶ This technique can also be used for tasks without dialogs. You will see later how this can be used to have actions logged under the agent's name without the agent having to lift a finger to perform the action.

4.2.6 Multiple Execution

Multiple execution allows you to select several work items and execute them all in one go, providing that the task's method, which is called by the work items has been programmed accordingly.[2] This allows the dialog to be shown only once, and the results are applied to all the subsequent work items that have been selected. Prior to Release 6.10, multiple execution simply executes the steps one after the other without suppressing the dialog for any of the work items.

This feature is not available in many of the inboxes, specifically not in the group-ware inboxes. However, multiple-execution is very useful, especially when it avoids repeating complex navigation (such as setting a status). Because the adapted methods will continue to run properly in all inboxes (but without suppressing dialogs in all of them) there is no harm in implementing it, especially if the agents are given a choice of which inbox to use. Clearly if all agents are forced to work in an inbox that does not support multiple execution, then you would be wasting time developing the methods to use this option.

4.2.7 Executing a Work Item Outside the Inbox

This may seem an unusual request; after all, the inbox provides the work item list, together with all the additional bells and whistles. However, some applications, such as R/3 quality maintenance, have their own task list and some tasks are par-ticularly prone to being performed without the user accessing the inbox. For example, this can happen when a senior manager phones and demands that a particular blocked record be released immediately.

If this is the case, make sure that you use asynchronous tasks. Asynchronous tasks terminate in such a way that the work item disappears from the inboxes irrespec-tive of whether the work was done by executing a work item or by navigating to the transaction directly, without accessing an inbox or work item. This prevents the workflow getting stuck, waiting for something to happen that has already happened.

We will not go into detail here, but this should give you an idea of how deeply workflow is integrated into the Basis platform on which the mySAP.com compo-nents and R/3 are built. Chapter 8, *Business Objects,* describes asynchronous tasks in more detail.

---

2 Available from Release 6.10.

4.2.8 Forwarding

Forwarding a work item to another agent will send it to that agent's inbox and remove the work item from all other recipients' inboxes. For this reason the agents should only use this function when either that agent is the only selected agent or that agent wants someone specific to execute the work item. You can even forward the work item to a user who has already been assigned the work item. This will simply remove the work item from everyone else's inbox. If you receive a forwarded work item and replace it, the work item will reappear in all inboxes of the originally selected agents (including the agent who forwarded it) and will remain in your inbox too, even if you were not one of the originally selected agents. In other words forwarding also extends the number of selected agents.

You can configure the task so that it:

▶ Cannot be forwarded to anyone

▶ Can be forwarded to anyone

▶ Can only be forwarded to a possible agent[3]

In fact, forwarding the work item does not so much forward it as reassign the selected agents. Agents working in a groupware mail client should *not* use the mail-client forwarding because this will not work with a work item—the work item will reappear in their inbox because it has not been reassigned. Instead, they should display the work item and use the *forward item* in the work item menu.

When you look at the list of selected agents, you will see who received the work item initially and to whom it was forwarded later.

The principal use of forwarding is when:

▶ Somebody changes position and wants to pass on the work items currently in their inbox to someone else.

▶ The agent determination has failed or is incorrect and the work item needs to be forwarded to another possible agent.

▶ The agent is new to the job and wants someone with more experience to check the work before releasing it. The freshman agent can create an attachment explaining what needs to be checked, and then he can delete this attachment after receiving it back again. Make sure that the workflow step is configured as needing manual confirmation in order to work. You may want to encourage this during training. It makes the users much more comfortable.

---

3 The meaning of the term *Possible agents* is described exactly in the next chapter. For the time being you can think of them as the agents authorized to perform the work.

4.2.9 Priority

Changing the priority of the work item only affects the sorting order in the inbox. It does not affect the priority of the rest of the workflow. The priority can be set in the workflow definition, passed to the workflow dynamically in a binding or manually changed from the work item display or inbox.

Work items with the highest priority (priority 1) will cause an express mail popup message to occur if the user is logged into an SAP component, irrespective of which transaction the agent is using, but depending on which user interface is being used.

4.2.10 Resubmission

If the agent does not want to deal with a work item immediately, she can resubmit the work item by dispatching it to the resubmission queue for several days (or hours). It will automatically pop back in the inbox once the period has expired.

If the agent wants to execute the work item before the resubmission time has elapsed, they can go to the resubmission queue and cancel the resubmission so that it pops back into the inbox queue.

4.2.11 Queries

When an agent creates a query, an SAP mail is sent with an attachment to the person the enquiry is addressed to. This allows the person receiving the query to view the work item, including all the attachments, the log and related objects, providing them with all the information needed to answer the query.

The reply goes back to the work item, rather than the user, so that the query and answer are linked to the workflow for future reference.

A nice touch is that if the agent pops the work item into the resubmission queue while waiting for an answer, it will automatically pop back out of the queue as soon as an answer is received.

Agents must be careful using this feature in the work item display because the forwarding icon ( ) is similar to the query (mail) icon. The bubble text helps to distinguish between them.

4.2.12 Logs

Many different views of the workflow log are created automatically when the workflow runs. These logs can be referred to while the workflow is running to see what has happened so far or what is about to happen next. They can also be used as an audit trail once the workflow has finished.

There are several reports which allow you to access the logs, but you can also view the log from the work item inbox, the work item outbox and usually from the transaction displaying the business object involved in the workflow. It is the generic object services that activate the link to the transactions, and these are described in more detail in the chapter 10, *Business Interfaces*.

All the details are stored in the logs but only the technical log displays the complete detailed view. The technical log is useful when developing a workflow and is very useful when tracking down an error. However the amount of detail is far too much for the average agent, and so her view filters out most of the technical information. You can even configure steps of the workflow so that these technical steps are omitted from the main logs (but they are always displayed in the technical log, see figure 6.5).

The user logs show three views of the history of the workflow:

1. **Chronological view**
   This displays the non-technical steps in the order that they are carried out. You can expand the display to see more details about each step, including the agents who received the work item initially and who added which attachments (see figure 6.2).

2. **Agent-oriented view**
   This displays a list of agents who were actively involved in the workflow. You can expand the display to see exactly what each agent did, which steps they were involved in and which attachments they added (see figure 6.3).

3. **Object-oriented view**
   This displays a list of objects involved in the process. This includes the business objects (such as the parked FI document and the posted FI document) and the ad hoc objects such as attachments that have been added. You can display the objects and view where each object was used within the process. This is particularly useful for processes where several basic business objects are used and the agent needs to refer back to a previous object (providing she has the authorization needed to view it).

You can navigate to the graphical log (see figure 6.4) from any other logs or from the work item directly. This shows the progress of the workflow in graphical form. Clicking on the step shows detail about who executed the step. This log is especially useful when an agent wants to see where the workflow goes next or wants to debug a workflow that contains many parallel branches or loops. Agents use the graphical log to make on-the-fly[4] changes to the process as it runs. This log is not normally available in the Web Browser (Release 6.10), but EBP does have its

---

4   These ad hoc capabilities are described later in the book.

own simplified version of the graphical log, which shows simple sequential processes including branches but not loops. If you are curious about what this looks like take a peek at figure 15.1.

The workflow summary log (fig. 1.5) shows a simple overview of who has done what in the workflow so far and a short list of the attachments and business objects used in the workflow. This log can be viewed from the Business Workplace Outbox or from the generic object services (fig. 10.3) when viewing a business object that has been used in a workflow.

Navigation between a work item and its logs is very flexible, and as you can see there is a good selection of different views that can be reached. To make life easier for your agents, select the most useful views and include them together with a description of how to reach the view in your FAQ for the process. Spread awareness that there are logs, so that the agents themselves can follow up on such common questions such as "What is the workflow doing right now?" (Answer: "Inspect the log from the workflow outbox"). This will drastically reduce the number of help desk calls and bolster the agents' confidence in the system. Bear in mind that the administrator will use more views and has been better trained than the agents.

4.2.13   Preview Mode

The preview pane, shown in figure 4.1, displays the task description in the Business Workplace. You can even create tasks that execute in the preview pane, but if not all tasks execute in the preview pane this can be confusing for the users. If you do have a work item that executes in the preview pane (such as the generic decision) and you want to disable this, then simply remove the preview function module from the workflow step definition (*work item* tab strip).

4.2.14   Enhancing the Work Item Display

The workflow system offers a standard display showing the task description, deadline information, ad hoc attachments and additional useful information for the agent. If you prefer, you can develop your own display for any step in the workflow. You can use this to highlight process-specific information or to show a graphical log of the process. This customized display is automatically shown as the preview screen in the Business Workplace and as the first tab strip when the work item is displayed. This allows the user to jump to the standard display (the next tab strip) if they want to see additional information.

If you want to add enhancements to the standard display, there is an alternative user exit for doing this, too. This 'light' enhancement has the advantage that it preserves the information displayed in the standard display without any additional development work.

Bear in mind that these enhancements are best suited to the Business Workplace and may not show up directly in the other inboxes.

4.2.15 Outbox

The outbox displays the work items that you have already been involved in.[5] These include the workflows you have started, work items that you have executed and work items that you have forwarded elsewhere. The display of the work item will vary slightly according to which of these folders you view. You can use the outbox to follow the progress of the workflow, as it is just one click to navigate to the workflow log from the work item display.

The workflow outbox is not available in all inboxes, but it is very useful for advanced users. At least one expert user should know how to use the outbox in the Business Workplace, even if this is not the standard inbox used. This will help with inquiries from the other agents of the type "What has happened to the workflow that I worked on yesterday?"

Some users like to look at the outbox at the end of the day to see how many work items they have processed. Do not underestimate the effect on the agents' motivation to perform better by getting this immediate feedback at the end of the day.

4.2.16 Rejecting Work Items

Rejecting work items is not the same as canceling work items. When a work item is aborted by the administrator (not to be confused with simply canceling out of the work item processing), the whole workflow is cancelled. This is usually something that the administrator needs to perform infrequently. Rejecting a work item is much 'softer'. Anyone who receives a work item can reject it (if *Processing can be rejected* has been enabled for that step) if they believe that the task is no longer necessary. For example, if the agent recognizes a scanned document as being a duplicate, they can simply reject it.

When the work item is rejected, the process follows a different path from the normal flow. You can add new steps to this path to tie up any loose ends after the rejection. For example, you can force the person rejecting the item to create a

---

5 Prior to Release 4.6B, the outbox only displayed workflows that you had started yourself.

note explaining why it was rejected and you can send notifications to the workflow initiator or anybody else involved.

The *reject processing* button (⊞⌐ or ⊞ → *Reject execution*) is only displayed when this option is selected in the workflow step definition.

4.3 Table of Features Available in the Principle Inboxes

	Business Workplace	IAC Web Inbox	Outlook Inbox	Lotus Notes Inbox	Enterprise Portal iView
Execute	✓	✓	✓	✓	✓
Attachment: Add/Read	✓	✓	✓	✓	–
Resubmit	✓	✓	✓	–	–
Substitution	✓	✓	✓	✓	✓
Setup Substitution	✓	✓	–	–	–
Outbox	✓	✓	–	–	✓
Auto-Refresh	–	–	✓	✓	✓
Forward	✓	✓	✓	✓	–
Query	✓	–	–	–	–
Graphic Log	✓	–	–	–	–
Logs	✓	✓	–	–	–
Number of Users	Unlimited	Unlimited	200	200	Unlimited
Spans Several Systems	–	–	✓ (Different Folders)	✓	✓
In Place Generic Decision Task	✓	✓	✓	✓	–
Offline	–	–	✓	✓	–
Desktop Installation	SAP GUI (Windows or Java)	Web Browser	SAP GUI + SAP Outlook Integration	SAP GUI + SAP Lotus Notes Integration	Web Browser

Table 4.1 Features Available in Workflow Inboxes

4.4   Successful Strategies for Work Item Delivery

In planning work item delivery, the main thing to bear in mind is that you do not need to limit your users to one inbox. The work items will be visible in all the different inboxes simultaneously. However, you should not expect your users to pick and choose at will which inbox they use. You need to offer training (at the very least online) and you need to make sure that a common set of features is supported by the different inboxes. It is no good if one agent uses the query function but the recipient of the query cannot process it.

Bear in mind that the agents will be involved in different processes organized by different departments. For example, as well as handling the daily tasks as part of her job, the agent may well also need to process Employee Self Service (ESS) tasks such as vacation requests. You will make life a lot easier for your agents if you can agree on a common strategy across the complete corporation.

As a rule of thumb, the following selections have proved themselves very successful within the majority of companies using SAP's WebFlow Engine:

▶ Business Workplace for administrators, power users and heavy-duty users

▶ Specialized inboxes such as EBP or CRM task lists where these are available

▶ Web Inbox for occasional users. This can be either the IAC Web transaction or the Enterprise Portal iView (or equivalent) depending on what employee Web portal the company is using

▶ E-mail notification on a subscription basis for occasional users or occasional processes

4.4.1   E-Mail Notifications

The e-mail notification is provided via the report[6] RSWUWFML. This polls the work items periodically, sending e-mail notifications to all users who have configured an auto-forward address. This auto-forward address will be their normal e-mail address, which can be reached through a SMTP connection, Exchange integration or the Lotus Integration for SAP Business Workflow. If a user elects to delete this auto-forward setting, they will not receive these e-mails. This 'subscription' algorithm is useful for users who get many work items every day and do not want to be bombarded with e-mails.

Starting with Release 4.6C you can define a *home* mail address for every user using transaction SU01. This home address is the address to which all mails addressed to a particular user are routed. When home addresses are defined, the

---

6   EBP has its own variant of this report.

notifications are forwarded to the *home* address, rather than the address defined in the office auto-forwarding settings. However, if no office auto-forwarding is defined, no notifications are generated for this user.

You can configure the report to ignore certain tasks or workflows and you can plan the report to run simultaneously with different configurations so that notifications for mission critical tasks are polled more frequently than the run-of-the-mill tasks.

The notification is only sent out once (repeated notifications are just plain annoying and often ignored). You can configure the notification to be sent out on a once-per-work-item basis or a summary basis (e.g. "You have 3 new work items").

This report is available as standard from Release 4.6A and as a pre-release feature described in SAP Note 131795.

4.4.2 Groupware Integration

Some companies use Microsoft Outlook and Lotus Notes groupware, particularly for managers who do not like using any other interface or for nomadic users for whom the off-line capabilities are paramount. However, because additional client software is needed and because the number of users supported is limited, most companies avoid either of these solutions.

Some companies regard work items as mails and have a strict code of operation that forces work items to be accessed within the mail inbox. Point out that SAP Mail can be deactivated via authorizations and office settings so that it does not clash with the company's modus operandi. If the company cannot be convinced otherwise, you may be forced to use Microsoft Outlook/Lotus Notes integration. The company should still give the administrators access to the Business Workplace to prevent their work being hampered.

4.4.3 Portal Integration

If mySAP Enterprise Portals is used, then the workflow iView (shown in figure 4.4) is the obvious choice. It is not only seamlessly integrated into the mySAP Enterprise Portal at the technical level; it also completely redesigned to match the Enterprise Portal philosophy. The three principle features are:

1. Very simple user interface
2. Auto-refreshes the list of work items every 10 minutes or so
3. Displays the work items from all the SAP components in one list.

This means that absolutely everyone can see at a glance whether or not they have work items by scrolling down to the workflow iView. The auto-refresh feature means no delay whatsoever, and this makes it popular with busy managers.

Although some companies do use the Business Workplace (transaction SWBP) within the portal, this is definitely not to be recommended because it will be slow and several features may not work in the SAP GUI for HTML

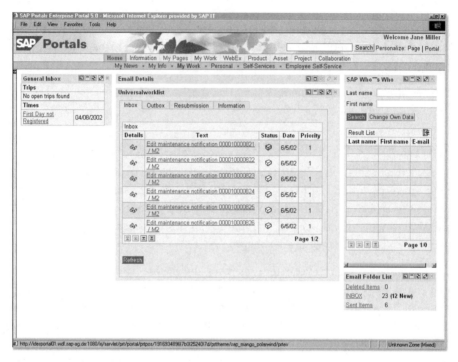

Figure 4.4 Universal Task-List iView Showing Work Items from Different Components in One List

4.4.4 External Users

External users are partners, customers or vendors who your company works with on a regular basis. Examples of such collaboration would be an external supplier in a Supply Chain Management (SCM) process or an engineering process. The integration of partners into the workflows is often a crucial factor for the speed of the process. There is not a lot to be gained in automating a process if the internal portion of the process runs through in one day, only to be held up for several weeks waiting for a response from a partner. Worse still, if the partner is not integrated by workflow, all the ad hoc communications that take place will be lost. Contrast this with a workflow-enabled process where all the attachments are visible to everyone downstream, so anyone can see at a glance what the rest of the people involved have done so far, including, for example, the justification of why they have reached their decisions.

External users will need an SAP user ID in order to participate in the process. The user ID is written to the workflow logs and used to check the authorizations. If you make do with just one group user ID for a number of agents then you might as well publish the password in the newspapers because you will very soon discover that you have no security left in your system at all. In fact, you have to be far more careful about the security of external users than internal users because you have less control over them and command less respect from them than from your own employees. Make sure that they switch passwords frequently and check regularly that they still exist. You could even build your own workflow to verify this, using e-mails.

The only time you would make an exception to the group user ID is when an external user has to request a user ID for the very first time, and this itself is handled by a workflow. You can either trigger this process from inside your company, creating a user ID and forwarding the ID and initial password in separate e-mails, or you can allow the user to trigger the process themselves using an anonymous user. If you select the latter, then the requestor must supply the name of an employee within your company who can vouch for this user. We will call this user the 'referee'. One step in the process will be that the referee approves the issue of the new user ID.

The only solution for your partners will be a Web inbox so that no local installation is necessary. The IAC Web Inbox (shown in figure 4.5) is a good choice because it runs in all commonly used browsers and the template can be adapted easily to fit your company's Web appearance. This inbox also supports SAP mail, which is used for the ad hoc communication that takes place during the process. The users can set up substitutes using this inbox and access all the facilities that they would normally need to use to get the most out of the workflow automation. This inbox lacks the heavy-duty features of the Business Workplace, such as sorting and filtering, but is ideal for work lists that contain just a few work items.

The other choice is the workflow iView inbox in the mySAP Enterprise Portal.

Both these inboxes support the SAP GUI for HTML, so all work items can be executed from the inbox directly. This means that you need no additional development work for your workflow to enable it to work in either of these inboxes. If you do not want to use the SAP GUI for HTML you will have to implement the individual tasks that are to appear in the Web inbox as Web Forms, Business Server Pages or another native Web development language.

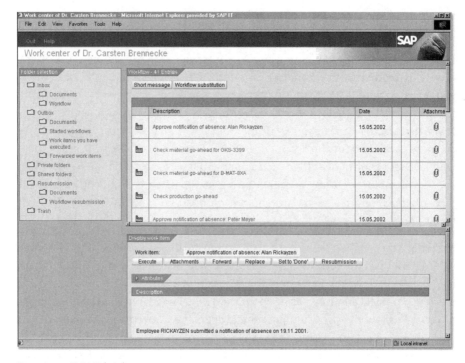

Figure 4.5 IAC Web Inbox

Generic decisions are distributed as Web forms as part of the SAP component, so no additional development is required for workflow decisions, even when the SAP GUI for HTML is not employed.

Bear in mind that synchronous dialog chains and secondary methods are not supported by the Web inboxes.

Whichever inbox you select for your extranet users, you will have to make sure that the agents receive e-mail notifications with the URL to the inbox. You cannot expect them to check the inboxes on a regular basis without prompting.

4.4.5   E-Mail Decisions

There are managers who are reluctant to use any sort of software, be it Web browser or custom-built user interfaces. E-mail on the other hand is acceptable to managers because they have recognized its advantages in speed, privacy and, not least, the chance to communicate with friends and relatives.

Enterprise Buyer Professional supports decisions made by e-mail, and the way this is done is described in appendix A, *Tips and Tricks*. It does involve significant development work, but when all else is rejected, this may be a serious option.

4.5　Other Considerations

One final warning: Just because your main 'customers' are the agents involved in the workflow, do not neglect other employees who are not integrated into the workflow definition but whom the process affects.

No workflow definition will ever cover everything, so rather than spending years implementing the perfect workflow, make sure you reach all the affected users at least indirectly. For example, some colleagues will be very grateful to be notified when a phase of the process has been reached (as opposed to being at the 'requested' stage). Similarly, other colleagues will be grateful to know when the part of the workflow that affects them has been completed, even if the complete process is still progressing. In both cases, you can do your colleagues a favor by setting up the workflow to send notifications when the relevant stage has been reached.

Even though such employees have not been included directly into the workflow definition, they will still have the advantage of getting the timing right, so that they can proceed with their work using traditional methods. For example, if an order exceeds a certain amount, the key account manager would be only too glad to hear when it has reached the transportation stage because this gives her the opportunity to phone the customer, confirming personally that the goods are about to ship.

Do not overdo the messaging. Often enough during your reality check you will find that some notifications can be eliminated or implemented on a subscription basis.

5   Agents

Getting the work items to the correct agents is half the story. Having a strategy to keep this working, despite organizational changes and personnel fluctuation is the other half. This chapter shows you the path to success.

Every work item must be processed by either:

▶ The WebFlow Engine, i.e. using the system user ID WF-BATCH or

▶ An agent

Agents are the people who do the work within the workflow. They do the work that cannot be done (or that you do not want done) automatically by the Web-Flow Engine. *That is, Agents are the decision makers in your business process!*

That is why finding the right agent for a particular work item is so important. You want the right person to make the decision, the person who understands the impact of the decision on the company—especially if that decision is going to have financial and/or legal implications, such as approving the purchase of new equipment or hiring a new employee.

One of the most interesting and often time consuming parts of workflow design is deciding how to determine and assign the correct agent(s) for a particular work item. From a business perspective this is a non-trivial issue, particularly if the process is new and no one has done this sort of work before. Once the business issues have been resolved, you need to decide how much configuration and/or development needs to be done to determine the agents. If you cannot automatically determine the agents, you can still use your workflow to help someone dynamically choose the correct agent for a subsequent step of your workflow (e.g. using the "Choose Agent" wizard described in appendix A, *Tips and Tricks*).

But before you can do any of that, you need to understand:

▶ How an agent receives, views and completes work items

▶ The different ways in which workflow assigns agents to a work item

▶ How agents are identified in the system, via user IDs and organizational objects

> **Tip** Even if you do not have mySAP HR, (Human Resources) you will still have access to create organizational objects, since the basic organizational management (which is all you need for workflow) is included with each SAP Web Application Server[1].

▶ The different techniques that can be used to determine the correct agent for a work item, i.e. the right person for the job.

5.1 Understanding Agent Assignment

The main function of any agent is to complete the work items sent to their workflow inbox by the workflow as quickly and accurately as possible. Clearly, a lot of care must be given to ensure that the correct agents receive the work items.

For each work item the rival claims of several groups of agents may need to be considered by the WebFlow Engine in order to select the correct agents. When you are designing, implementing and maintaining your workflow and related data, you need to understand how the workflow views these different groups of agents if you are to ensure that the workflow comes to the correct decision.

The groups of agents include:

▶ **Possible agents**
Who is allowed to do the work

▶ **Responsible agents**
Who should do the work in this case

▶ **Excluded agents**
Who should *not* do the work in this case

These three groups can overlap and intersect for each work item, as you can see in figure 5.1. The recipients only be determined correctly by evaluating all three (assuming all three are required).

Recipients (also known as the *selected agents*) are the agents who actually receive work items in their workflow inbox automatically, i.e. they are the initial recipients. If they are permitted to do so, recipients can opt to forward work to other possible agents. So the system needs to check both possible and excluded agents for a work item before it decides whether a particular agent is able to do the work. Finally the person who has actually executed and completed the work is called the *actual agent*.

---

1 And the predecessor—SAP Basis.

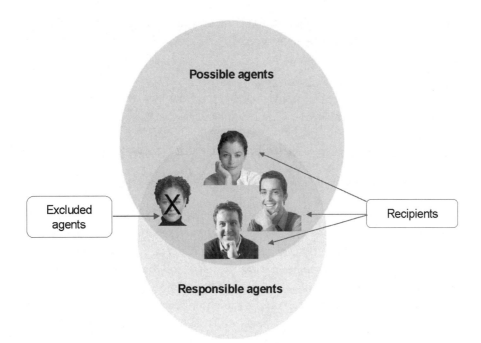

Figure 5.1 Recipients of a Dialog Work Item of a Workflow

Every agent must have a user ID, even when accessing the work item via an external workflow inbox, such as Microsoft Outlook or Lotus Notes. As well as identifying who is executing or has executed a work item, the user ID controls the access the agent has to the work item and, of course, to your system generally.

5.1.1 Possible Agents

Possible agents are the people who are allowed to execute work items based on a particular underlying task. Possible agents are always assigned to a task on which many work items may be based, not to the work item itself. Another way of looking at this is to think of possible agent assignment as a way of securing runtime access to particular tasks. In fact, usually the best way of assigning possible agents is to tie tasks directly to *security roles* (i.e. profile generator roles, previously known as "activity groups").

> **Tip** Making someone a possible agent of a task does not automatically give them access to any data or routine (e.g. transaction, or report) called by the task. You still need to ensure the agent has sufficient authorization to complete the work. That is why it makes so much sense to use security roles to keep the task access, data access, and routine access synchronized.

If you are not a possible agent of the work item you cannot execute it. Likewise, if no possible agents have been assigned to a task, no one can execute any work items based on that task!

> **Tip**   There is one exception to this, namely the workflow administrator, who is able to execute any work item in an emergency via the "Execute without agent check" function, specifically to fix problems where possible agent assignment has been forgotten or neglected. Refer to chapter 6, *Workflow Administration*, for more details.

You can also mark a task with the attribute *general task* instead of assigning specific possible agents. A general task effectively has *no* security over it. That is, anyone can execute the task. Be *very* careful when marking a task as a general task. People who are new (and sometimes not so new) to workflow sometimes set a task as a general task to simplify the agent determination. That is okay in a development environment, but if you do the same thing in a production environment you can create performance problems as well as a serious security breach.

For example:

1. An employee requests some items to be purchased, which starts a workflow.
2. The workflow sends a work item requesting approval of the purchase to the employee's manager.
3. The manager needs more details before a decision can be made, adds an attachment to the work item asking for more details, and forwards the work item to the employee.
4. If the approval task has been marked as a general task, the employee is then able to approve his or her own purchase!

If the task had been properly assigned to possible agents, the manager would have been warned on attempting to forward the work item that the employee is not allowed to execute it, and, depending on the task attributes, may also be prevented from forwarding it.

> **Tip**   A better way for the manager to contact the employee would be by using the query function, which links an e-mail to a view of the work item, and returns the reply back to the work item itself.

Therefore you should make sure that you only mark tasks as general if you really want anybody to be able to execute work items based on that task. Good examples of general tasks might include:

▶ Edit rejected purchases—you might want anyone to be able change and resubmit any purchases they requested that have been rejected.

▶ Respond to proposal—you might want anyone to be able to respond to a proposal that has been sent to them.

There are a number of places where possible agents can be assigned to a task, these include:

▶ In the IMG (implementation guide), in the relevant workflow configuration section.

▶ When displaying a task via menu option **Additional Data · Agent Assignment · Maintain** (transaction `PFTC_DIS`). The attributes of the task, such as general task, can also be assigned here.

▶ From the "task profile" section of an organizational plan.

▶ From the profile generator (transaction `PFCG`) in the "workflow" section (note this is only available in Release 4.6 and higher environments).

▶ From the Workflow Builder: the step definition has a button to assign possible agents where possible (i.e. for dialog tasks), and basic data allows you to assign possible agents to the workflow itself to enable the agents to start the workflow manually (e.g.from *generic object services* for testing purposes).

> **Tip** No possible agents are assigned initially to tasks or workflows supplied by SAP. You must always do the possible agent assignment yourself, e.g. using *Task-Specific Customizing*.

For each task the list of possible agents assigned can be quite long. You need to assign everyone who might need to execute work items based on that task. You use responsible agents and excluded agents to narrow down the list of all possible agents to those who that you want to receive a particular work item.

5.1.2 Responsible Agents

Responsible agents are the people you want to execute this particular work item. That is the agent who is responsible for doing the work in this particular case. You can understand the difference between possible and responsible agents with a simple example:

- ► Possible agents—All managers approve requests from employees to attend training courses.
- ► Responsible agents—Your manager is responsible for approving requests to attend training courses that have been submitted by you.

Responsible agents are usually assigned at the workflow step level, but they can also be assigned at the task level via the default agent determination rule option in the task definition.

> **Tip** The default rule is only used if no responsible agents have been entered at the workflow step level or if the step's agent determination rule fails. It is also used if a task is executed without a parent workflow, i.e. as a standalone single step task.

It is possible to assign organizational objects (such as an organizational unit, job or position) as responsible agents, but this option is rarely used in production systems. In most cases an expression or rule is the best way to determine agents.

With an *expression*, the agents (responsible, deadline, or notification depending are the context) are predetermined. For instance if you want to send rejected requests back to the person who created the request, at the start of the workflow you save the person who created the request (the initiator) to a container element. Later you can use an expression to assign the value in the container element to the agent assignment of the workflow step for sending the rejected request. That way, the rejected request is returned to the same person who created it.

With a rule, the agents are calculated dynamically when the work item is created. You can bind data from the workflow to the rule and the rule will then calculate the agents based on that data. For instance, you might have a rule to calculate the manager of an employee using the employee's user ID and the organizational hierarchy. By passing your user ID at runtime, the rule will find your manager. If you do not assign responsible agents explicitly, by default all possible agents are assumed to also be the responsible agents, unless a default rule has been linked to the task itself.

Note that the responsible agents should also be possible agents. If you identify responsible agents who are not possible agents, the workflow will not send these work items to them. There's no point in doing so—they do not have proper access to do the work. If the organizational object, expression or rule includes some agents who are possible agents and some who are not, only the responsible agents who are also possible agents will receive the work items. A thorough treatment of how to calculate responsible agents is given in chapter 9, *Agent-Determination Rules*.

5.1.3 Excluded Agents

Excluded agents are the people that you do *not* want to execute this particular work item, even though they are a possible or responsible agent. For instance, all agents in a shared services center can approve requests for payment of employee expenses. Normally employees outside the shared services center enter the requests for payment. However, if one of the employees within the shared services center has requested payment of their own expenses, they should not be able to approve their own payment request. Otherwise they could (deliberately or accidentally) defraud the company by receiving payments to which they are not entitled.

Excluded agents are also useful for segregating duties within business processes. Consider, for instance, a proposal that has to be reviewed by at least two agents within a proposal review team. You send the first "review proposal" work item to all agents in the review team. Once the first work item is completed, you set the actual agent of the first work item as the excluded agent of the second work item. That is, the second "review proposal" work item is sent to all agents of the review team except the agent who has already reviewed the proposal. Because the first reviewer is an excluded agent of the second work item, they are not able to review the proposal twice.

Excluded agents are always assigned by an expression to the workflow step. That is, you put all agents to be excluded in a list (a multiline container element) and then use an expression to assign the list to the workflow step.

> **Tip** An excluded agent does not have to be a possible or responsible agent. This covers the situation where the person who needs to be excluded is acting as a substitute for another agent.

5.1.4 Recipients

Recipients are the people who automatically receive a work item in their inbox when the work item is created by the workflow. They are also known as *selected agents*.

Recipients are:

1. The possible agents of the task
2. Restricted to the list of responsible agents for the work item
3. Not members of the list of excluded agents

You should, however, note the following:

▶ If there are no possible agents, no one receives the work item!

▶ If no responsible agents are defined for a step, the system checks for a default agent-determination rule in the task definition. If there is none, all the possible agents, barring excluded agents, are recipients of the work item.

Recipients can forward work items to other agents if allowed. However only possible (but not excluded) agents can execute a forwarded work item. The agent who is forwarding the work item is warned if the new agent is not a possible agent. Whether a work item can be forwarded, is determined by the attributes of the underlying task. Relevant options are:

▶ **General task**
Work items can be forwarded to any user (and executed by any user)

▶ **General forwarding**
Work items can be forwarded to any user

▶ **No general forwarding**
Work items can only be forwarded to possible users

▶ **No forwarding**
No forwarding allowed (from Release 4.6D)

5.1.5   Actual Agent

While the work item is still being processed, the actual agent is the user currently processing the work item. Once the work item has been completed, the actual agent is the user who last processed the work item. It is useful to be able to know who was the actual agent of a completed work item. Not only can you tell people who made a particular decision in a subsequent step of your workflow, but you can also evaluate who is actually making the decisions in your company.

5.1.6   Assigning Multiple Agents per Work Item

Many agents can be assigned to a single work item. If you send an e-mail to more than one person, every person receives a copy of the e-mail; they can view and delete their own copy of the e-mail whenever they like. That is fine for e-mails because they simply bring information to the recipients. However, when you send a work item to many agents, you are sending work along with the information. Usually the work only needs to be done once. As soon as one of the assigned agents executes and completes the piece of work (or simply reserves it), the work item is no longer needed and the WebFlow Engine removes it from all agents' inboxes.

Another way of understanding how work items appear to several assigned agents is to think of all the work to be done being collected in a huge pile, each piece of work being represented by a work item. Agent determination is simply a way of sharing out the pile of work to be done.

Sometimes there is only one suitable person to do a piece of work, and therefore only one agent for the work item. In this case, the work will not be completed until the single assigned agent has done it. If that person is sick or attending a training course, the work waits until the agent returns. In other cases, there are several people who can do the same work. They might even work together, such as at a helpdesk or shared services center. The work items that can be done by these people are given to all of the agents. Each agent selects a piece of work and does it. Because the work to be done is shared out, it is completed much more quickly than it could be by a single person. If one agent is sick or attending a training course, the rest of the agents will still be getting the work done in their absence. No single process will be held up until the agent returns.

Sometimes you really do want more than one person to act on the same piece of work. For instance, you might want several people involved in deciding whether an expensive piece of equipment can be purchased. To do this, you simply create one work item per agent. There are many ways you can create multiple work items without complicating your workflow. For instance, you can use a list (a multiline container element) assigned to a step in your workflow to create multiple work items, one for each item in the list.

If you want to make sure all agents are doing their fair share, it is worthwhile tracking how many work items each agent processes and how much time they spend on the items. You could use this to inspire and reward agents to be even more productive, company's culture and customizing settings permitting. For suggestions on how to measure and report on work items, turn to chapter 6, *Workflow Administration,* and chapter 13, *Custom Programs.*

5.1.7 Deadline and Notification Agents

In most workflows, agents are the people assigned to actually perform tasks via work items. However, as a workflow developer you may also want to assign:

▶ Deadline agents
   People who receive escalation work items when a deadline has been exceeded. Deadline agents are usually entered on the relevant deadline tab (latest start, requested end, or latest end) of the workflow step.

▶ **Notification agents**

People who are notified via an e-mail when a work item has been completed. Notification agents are usually entered on the notification tab of the workflow step.

Deadline agents may receive deadline work items, which consist of a reminder to escalate a task and a "Done it" button. If they fail to act, the workflow can still continue. Often you do not even need to send them a work item; a simple e-mail may be enough. Note that deadline agents are recipients of work items just like the agents who actually perform the task, but it can be helpful to think of them separately. Of course, you are not limited to simply notifying agents. As you will see in chapter 7, *Creating a Workflow*, you can introduce deadline and escalation procedures into your workflow that are far more sophisticated than simple notifications.

5.2   Agent Assignment Using the Organizational Structure

Every workflow agent must have a user ID. So when you are assigning agents to a work item, whether via possible agents, responsible agents or excluded agents, you are essentially assigning user IDs.

Unfortunately, assigning user IDs directly is very maintenance intensive. People join, change positions and roles, transfer between departments and leave your organization continuously. Keeping up with the current agent assignment is hard enough. As you add more workflows the task becomes nearly impossible.

There has to be a better way of identifying agents—and there is. It is called the organizational plan.

> **Tip** The organizational plan is sometimes used for possible agent assignment, but can also be used for assigning responsible agents either directly or in conjunction with agent determination rules.

People often think the organizational plan is part of mySAP HR and is therefore only available if you have mySAP HR installed. That is incorrect. Every SAP Web Application Server also includes a basic organizational plan that has everything you need for workflow. If you do have mySAP HR, you have access not just to the basic plan, but also to the extended plan. The extended organizational plan still has everything needed for workflow, but it includes a lot more features. Some of the extended features can also be used in your workflows, e.g. assigning agents to perform a task based on their formal qualifications to do the job.

5.2.1 The Basic Organizational Plan

The basic organizational plan consists of relationships, represented as a hierarchical organizational structure, between different organizational objects such as:

▶ ☐ **Organizational units**
Each unit represents a group of people such as a team, section, department, work area, laboratory, helpdesk, or shared services center.

▶ 🖳 **Jobs**
Each job describes a functional role within the organization. They equate to a job description. They may represent a full time or part-time role in your organization.

▶ 🧑 **Positions**
Each position represents a headcount placement, e.g. a physical desk or vacancy.

▶ 🖳 **Users**
Each user is the actual user ID of a person in your organization.

> **Tip** You can build an organizational hierarchy without using jobs, which makes it easier to deploy in mySAP HR where *jobs* are used for more specific purposes (e.g. where jobs are directly associated with a salaries scale).

Most organizational objects and relationships have validity periods. By default the validity period is usually set to start on the date on which the organizational object or relationship is created and finish on 31st December 9999; however, the validity period can be changed. Restricting the validity period is useful to indicate temporary relationships, for example when a user holds a position on a temporary basis such as "acting supervisor", or to show that a person no longer holds that position.

Organizational objects and relationships are maintained via Organizational Management transactions such as PPOM (Organization and staffing), PPOMW (Organization and staffing—Workflow view), or in an EBP/CRM system PPOMA_CRM or PPOMA_BBP (Organization, staffing and attributes). Use of these transactions is described in detail in the SAP Library help documentation. Within these transactions you can find organizational objects by ID, description, and hierarchical structure or by relationship to other organizational objects. For instance, by finding a position you can view all users assigned to that position. Several views of the organizational plan can be displayed. For example, you can display both top-down hierarchies (org unit to positions to users) and bottom-up hierarchies (users to positions to org units), depending on your starting point. You can also create new objects and relationships (also known as "assignments"), edit, copy, move, reposition, delimit and delete them. You can display and maintain details of objects (e.g. organizational units have addresses) as shown in figure 5.2. You can start the display and maintenance of organizational objects at any part of the organizational plan.

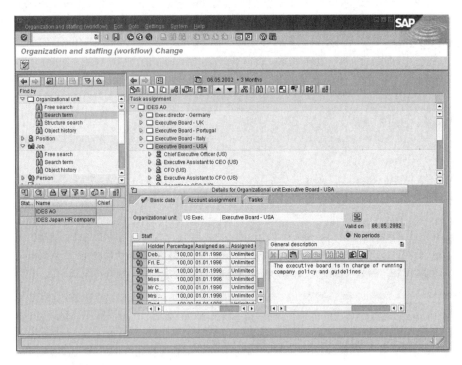

Figure 5.2 Organizational Plan Maintenance

Common relationships between the different parts of the organizational plan include:

▶ ☐ **Organizational units** can be hierarchically linked to other ☐ **organizational units**, giving you an organizational hierarchy, e.g. teams within sections within departments.

▶ An ☐ **organizational unit** may be linked to several ⚏ **positions**, where the positions represent employees belonging to the team, section, department, etc. Note that these relationships are inherited by hierarchically higher organizational units. For instance, the positions within a department include all positions assigned directly to the department's organizational unit, plus all positions assigned to the organizational units of sections and teams hierarchically below the department.

► A 🯁 **position** may be linked to 🯇 **jobs**, where the job describes what the person in the position does. One job may be linked to several positions, for example when several people perform similar activities.

► A 🯈 **user** may be linked to a 🯁 **position**, where the user ID is that of the person currently holding the position. One user may hold several positions (hopefully, each on a part-time basis!).

► Workflow tasks may be linked to one or more ▢ **organizational units,** 🯁 **positions,** 🯇 **jobs,** or 🯈 **users**.

By assigning a workflow task to a job you are specifying all of the users who are linked to all of the positions linked to that job as agents for that task. E.g. if *manager* is a job and *approve leave request* is a task, then assigning the task *approve leave request* to the job *manager* means all managers are able to approve leave requests. You can change the users and positions linked to that job and know that all users/positions currently linked to the job will be able to execute the tasks assigned. By assigning a task to a position you are making the user or user(s) who are linked to that position agents of the task. E.g. if *Financial Business Process Owner* is a position and *approve changes to financial processes* is a task, then the user or users holding that position are able to approve changes to financial processes. You can change the users linked to the position and know that all users currently linked to it could perform the tasks assigned.

If in doubt, it is a good idea to assign a task to a job, or to a task group, which is in turn assigned to a job or organizational unit as shown in figure 5.3.[2] This is a logical extension to the organizational management model. Looking at it the other way round, the job is a collection of tasks. As a bonus, using this strategy you can see online which tasks are assigned to a job, which makes the job description transparent in the system and hence easier to maintain.

You can create several organizational plans in different plan versions. This lets you depict different views of your organization in different plan versions. In one plan version, you depict your currently valid organizational plan, i.e. the one you use for your current business processes (evaluations, workflow, personnel planning, for example). In additional plan versions, you can depict organizational plans as planning scenarios (for Business Process Re-Engineering, for example).

Note that WebFlow *always* uses the current plan version.

---

2 You can also use a security role to collect tasks, if you want to avoid using jobs—see section 5.2.3.

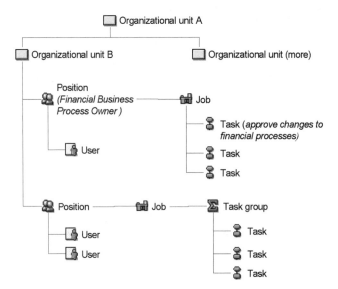

Figure 5.3 Relation Between Tasks, Jobs and Agents

5.2.2 The Extended Organizational Plan

If your system includes mySAP HR, then you can use the extended organizational plan. In this case you have access to additional features above and beyond the basic organizational plan. The most obvious difference between the basic and extended organizational plans is that the extended organizational plan includes *personnel numbers*.

▶ A 👫 **Person** represents the personnel number assigned to an employee.

▶ A 👫 **Person** may be assigned to one or more positions.

▶ A 🧍 **User** is assigned to a 👫 **Person** by setting up a "communication" relationship (otherwise known as infotype 105).

Whenever you assign a 🧍 **User** to a position, job, task, or organizational unit in a system with an extended organizational plan, by default the system will replace the object to 🧍 **User** relationship with an object to 👫 **Person** to 🧍 **User** relationship. From a workflow perspective, apart from the additional *person* organizational object, using mySAP HR provides the following benefits:

▶ Much more data is held describing organizational objects and relationships that can be used in workflows. For example, if the qualifications held by employees are stored, a rule can be built to identify the responsible agents of a work item as those agents with current qualifications to perform the work.

- Evaluation paths can be custom-built and used as rules for determining responsible agents. Evaluation paths describe a way of moving across the organizational plan to find organizational objects. For instance, the evaluation path SAP_TAGT describes how to find workflow agents belonging to any organizational object, i.e. how to find users from an organizational unit, job, position or person. (Note that some evaluation paths, such as SAP_TAGT exist even in systems without mySAP HR, but there is usually no reason for building custom evaluation paths unless you use mySAP HR.)
- Additional security can be provided over tasks using structural authorizations.

> **Tip** If your system includes mySAP HR, be careful that your use of the organizational plan in your workflow fits with your overall HR strategy.

5.2.3 Doing without an organizational plan

Maintaining an organizational plan can be a burden, particularly if there is no specific section or department dedicated to its maintenance. This begs the question, *Do you need to use an organizational plan for workflow*?

In fact, you do not. There are alternatives so long as you keep your agent assignments simple using responsibilities built into the SAP component, office distribution lists, or your own custom tables and function modules as described in chapter 9, *Agent Determination Rules*. However if you want to build sophisticated relationships between tasks and agents, particularly for possible agent assignments, then an organizational plan will give you significantly greater flexibility and choice.

The alternatives to using an organizational plan for possible agent assignment include:

- Setting tasks as general tasks in the task attributes. This allows all users to execute work items based on the task. Remember however that this effectively means you have *no* security on your tasks.
- Assigning security roles (i.e. profile generator roles, formerly known as "activity groups") as possible agents of tasks. This allows all users with the security role to execute work items based on that task. Note that this option is only available in SAP Basis systems 4.6 and above. Task to security role assignment can be made either via the usual task agent assignment (e.g. via transaction PFTC_DIS, menu path **Additional Data · Agent Assignment · Maintain**) or via the profile generator (transaction PFCG).

Any of the responsible agent determination options such as responsibility rules or evaluation paths can also be linked directly to user IDs rather than to organizational objects if you wish.

5.3 Agent Assignment Using Task Groups

Σ **Task groups** are literally that—a way of grouping workflow tasks together. You can choose how you group tasks into task groups. One task can be assigned to many task groups. You can create a task group using transaction PFTC, just like any other task. You enter a description for the task, and list the tasks assigned to the task group.

One option is to use task groups to group together tasks based on similar content, for example all tasks based on the same business objects, so that you can quickly find all tasks concerned with the same business object. You can use task groups to delimit the search range when calling the Workflow Explorer or within the "My workflows and tasks" area of the Workflow Builder. You can also use the where-used list option in the Business Object Builder (transaction SWO1) to do this.

Another option is to collect all tasks involved in the same or similar business processes into the one task group, again to simplify searching for related tasks. Of course you can also use the Diagnosis Utility (transaction SWUD—test environment) to get a quick overview of all tasks in a workflow.

However, you can also assign task groups to organizational objects such as organizational units, jobs, or positions, using the usual agent assignment options (e.g. transactions PFTC_DIS and PFCG). This means you can also collect tasks into task groups for the purpose of agent assignment. For instance, you could create a task group called "common management tasks", assign all tasks that all managers need to perform to it, and then assign the task group to the manager job or security role. Then, any time a new task for managers is created, you can add it to the task group, thus assigning all managers as possible agents of the new task (from transaction PFTC, menu path **Extras · Agent Assignment · Maintain**.)

You can also collect task groups into other task groups. So you could create task groups for different job functions and add them together to create a task group for a specific job. For example, combine the "common management tasks" task group with a "senior management tasks" task group for a senior manager.

5.4 Implementing and Maintaining the Structure in Practice

5.4.1 Strategies for Organization Plan Maintenance

Often the most contentious issue for organizational plan maintenance is deciding who will be responsible for updating the organizational plan. The basic rule of thumb is:

▶ If you have an HR section responsible for updating the organizational plan for other reasons, they should also update the organizational plan for workflow requirements.

▶ If the organizational plan is only used for workflow, persons in the workflow team, e.g. business process owners, should be responsible for updating the organizational plan.

Of course, if you start by using the organizational plan only for workflow, and then decide to use it for other purposes, you can reassign who is responsible for keeping the organizational plan current.

Another option is to have the HR section maintain the organizational plan, but have workflow personnel update rules, e.g. responsibility rules. However, this requires good communication between the HR section and the workflow personnel to ensure that changes to the organizational plan and the rule data are adequately synchronized.

Regardless of who actually maintains the organizational plan, it is important that the people doing the maintenance:

▶ Understand the potential impact of their changes and any delay in making those changes on your workflows.

▶ Communicate with the relevant workflow people, especially the workflow administrator.

▶ Allow relevant workflow people, especially the workflow administrator and business process owners, the ability to check and review *at any time* what has been done, in case of problems. The ability to check at any time is essential, as problems often do not appear immediately.

One final point: If a user is to be removed from the system, to ensure that work items being generated do not end up orphaned (i.e. with no valid agent), it is usually best to assign the new user to the workflow, then delimit the old user assignment so that it is no longer valid from this date.

> **Caution** Do not delete the old user, otherwise you will lose valuable auditing and reporting information.

5.4.2   Transporting Organization Plans

It is possible but potentially problematic to transport organizational plans. You need to be clear about exactly what part(s) of the organizational plan you will transport and what part(s) will be maintained directly in the production environment. Keeping an organizational plan clean, i.e. well structured, in a development environment is difficult since configurers and developers often need to change the organizational plan to test their settings and programs. So the organizational plan may not be ready to transport to a production environment. One way of keeping the organizational plan clean is to create it in a separate client put aside for this purpose, for example a configuration master client.

Even if the organizational units, jobs or positions are transportable, often the relationship between position and user can only be created in the production environment, as most users will not exist in a development environment.

Similar complications ensue when transporting organizational plans across different SAP components, e.g. an R/3 system and an EBP system. A user may not exist in the R/3 system but does exist in the EBP system or vice versa.

Usually, only the organizational plan is transported (or the units within the organizational plan), and not the assignments to actual user IDs. However if you do want to transport user IDs also, then Central User Administration (CUA) is one option for keeping the user IDs synchronized across multiple systems. Some systems, such as EBP, also provide mass user creation programs to help assign user IDs to the transported organizational plan.

There are a number of options for transporting the organizational plan:

▶ Automatic transport of all organizational plan changes. Table T77SO, entry TRSP.CORR is set to space.

▶ Manual transport of organizational plan changes, by manually selecting what part of the organizational plan is to be transported. Table T77SO, entry TRSP.CORR is set to 'X'. Program RHMOVE30 performs the transport.

▶ Transport via an object lock by using a change request. Table T77SO, entry TRSP.CORR is set to 'T'. Program RHMOVE50 performs the transport.

All options require an ALE (Application Link Enabling) distribution model to be created for the HR master data. The model allows IDOCs of type HRMD_A to be transported from one system to another. Within the model, you then specify filters determining which infotypes will be transported.

Within the organizational plan transactions, change pointers are used to detect what objects have changed in the source system, and therefore what objects are suitable for transport.

Entries in table T77TR (*Transport Lock for Infotype and Subtypes per Object*) in the target system can be used to block objects from being transported into the target system. This prevents locally maintained objects and relationships from being overwritten by incoming transports.

Customer exits for the HRMD_A IDOC allow outgoing and incoming data to be adjusted if necessary.

Further documentation on this topic can be found in the SAP Library help.

5.4.3   Reassigning Work Items from One User to Another

If a user changes their job or position, they may have existing work items assigned to them that need to be reassigned to the person taking over their old job or position. This is particularly necessary where changes in the job or position include changes in a user's security, so that they are no longer able to execute the work items assigned to them. Reassigning work items is usually only necessary where work items have been reserved by the user, in other words selected but not completed, or where the user is the only recipient. If other recipients exist and a work item is still in READY status, there is no need to reassign it.

Users should be encouraged as much as possible to replace reserved work items, which returns the work item to READY status prior to the move.

You can find outstanding work items for a user by using the *Workload Analysis* (transaction SWI5) report with the *To be processed by* option. This report should be run BEFORE moving the user.

To find orphaned work items after the move, report *Work items without Agents* (transaction SWI2_ADM1) is helpful. To reassign the work items simply forward the work item to an alternative agent. When someone leaves the company, an alternative is to lock the defunct user ID and use user substitution to allow her replacement to execute all outstanding work items sent to the ex-employee.

5.4.4   Substituting Users

If you want to substitute agents on a temporary basis, e.g. while the original agent is ill or attending a course, there are two ways of doing this.

1. **The HR substitution relationship A210**

   You can create a substitute for a position by creating an A210 relationship between the position and the substitute, e.g. another position, person or user ID. All work items assigned to the original agent *based on that position* are then made available to the substitute. You can further refine which work items are assigned to particular substitutes by specifying a task classification. By default the classifications *Disciplinary*, *Professional*, *Personal* exist. If you do use classifications they need to be defined both against the task underlying the work items to be assigned and against the A210 relationship.

2. **User substitutions — table HRUS_D2**

   Usually the HRUS_D2 entry is created by the original agents via their inbox, such as from the *Business Workplace* transaction (SBWP) or the equivalent *Web Inbox* Internet service (BWSP). However, if you want to maintain this table centrally, this is one of the few cases where the table is sufficiently straightforward and independent of other tables that creating your own maintenance view of the table is a reasonably safe option. You can create a substitute for a user by creating an entry in table HRUS_D2 that identifies another user to act as the substitute. All work items assigned to that user ID are then made available to the substitute.

> **Caution**   This table is not an open interface, and could change from release to release.

Make sure when creating substitutes that you create a workflow substitute, not an inbox substitute, as an inbox substitute simply receives the original agent's e-mails, not their work items.

Substitutions can be active or passive. Active substitutions are similar to auto-forwarding — all work items sent to the original agent automatically appear in the substitute agent's inbox. Passive substitutions (called *adopt substitutions*) require the substitute to explicitly choose to see the original agent's work items via the appropriate inbox option. Active substitution is more suitable when someone is absent. Passive substitutions can be useful when someone is a regular backup for the original agent. The substitution can then exist for a long time, but is only be used when the substitute is acting as a backup.

Workflow substitution gives the substitute the permissions to view and execute the work item, but it does not give the substitute permission to access underlying transactions and routines used by the work item. So it is usually best to encourage substitution at the same level of the organization, e.g. substitute from one manager to another, rather than from a manger to subordinates.

5.4.5   When Do You Choose to Refresh the Org Environment?

A continual issue with maintaining an organizational plan is buffering. Buffering means that the system holds temporary views of the organizational plan for use at runtime. Even if you change the organizational plan, it will not be used at runtime until the relevant buffer is updated. The main benefit of buffering is improved performance. However the delay between the time when an update to the organizational plan is made and the time when the changes take effect can be very confusing and cause unusual problems—especially when some buffers may be updated before others. This is particularly relevant in development systems, where frequent changes are made for testing purposes.

Under normal operation, all the buffers relevant to the organizational plan are updated at midnight system time. So one strategy for avoiding buffering problems is simply to update the organizational plan the day before the changes will be used.

Another way to prevent buffering problems is to manually trigger refreshing of buffers. Transaction SWU_OBUF is provided specifically for this purpose. It provides a *refresh* option that resets the timestamp on the HR buffers, thereby invalidating existing buffers, so that all organizational plan data is read from the database and the buffers refilled with this fresh data. You can refresh as often as you wish, remembering that the system will perform a little slower when buffers are being refilled.

If you want to create your own program to refresh the buffers, e.g. so that only those objects changed are refreshed, then the following function modules are worth knowing:

▶ RH_WF_OM_INDICES_TIMESTAMP_RFS
  Resets the timestamp on all HR buffers

▶ RH_TASK_INBOX_VIEW_REFRESH
  Refreshes the buffer for the current user only

▶ RH_TASK_AGENTS_INDEX_REFRESH
  Refreshes the buffer for a particular task ID only

Note that it is not a good idea to refresh the buffers if no changes have been made, since this simply degrades system performance for no benefit. For example, creating a background job to reset the buffer timestamp every hour would be counter-productive, as the benefits of buffering would be lost.

5.4.6 Training and Encouraging Agents

Agents are generally very sympathetic towards workflow if it is presented to them properly. They see it as a helping hand, making sure that they know what to do and are presented with their tasks rather than having to fetch them themselves. Usually you will not have a chance to train all the agents, so make sure that you have power users or change advocates to support the rest of the agents, and make sure you have a good roll-out (e.g. by having power users train each other in a snowball effect) so that everyone feels comfortable. Emphasize the benefits the individual agents will see rather than stressing the advantages to the corporation, and allow the agents to monitor their own performance so that they can see how they improve (e.g. via the outbox). Make it clear that these statistics will not be used to compare individual users with each other.

Try to anticipate the problems that the agents will have (e.g. the workflow appears to have disappeared) and provide solutions. Often these problems will become apparent during train-the-trainers sessions, so be especially careful to take notes when an exception occurs.

Make sure all agents understand the difference between a mail (copy delivered to every recipient) and a work item (shared by the recipients), and make sure that they do not see the WebFlow Engine as an infinitely powerful mechanism that can do everything on its own. The fact that the workflow can have limited embedded intelligence and can perform some actions in background steps does not mean that it can compensate for users' mistakes. It helps if the agents have a rough idea of the complete process in which they are involved. Not only does this heighten their awareness of what is going on in the company they work for, but it also helps them understand why the quality of their work is as important as the speed with which they complete it. Many a user has been surprised when shown the scope of the process and the number of people involved even after they have finished doing their bit.

6   Workflow Administration

The administrator plays a key role in the success of the workflow and on publishing this success to the stakeholders. Although very little time needs to be spent on these duties, awareness of these duties is important and they must be taken seriously. If a problem does arise, the administrator will need to resolve it quickly and confidently.

6.1   Introduction

Feedback from user groups has consistently shown that administration for SAP's WebFlow Engine is far less time consuming than for third party software that attempts to integrate with the mySAP.com components. This not only affects the day-to-day running but also ease of upgrade and the overall stability of the system. This is without doubt due to the fact that SAP's WebFlow Engine, rather than trying to influence the system from the outside, lies at the heart of the system. Similarly, the release cycle of the mySAP.com components exactly matches that of the engine so that the engine, the business applications and the workflow templates stay in step with each other during development, rather than having to be coaxed back into shape at the company's site during upgrade.

Nevertheless, there is no getting round this simple rule of thumb: *If you use a system, you need a system administrator. If you use a workflow, you need a workflow administrator.*

> **Tip** For workflows using web functionality, assistance may also be required from the Web server/ITS administrator to resolve errors and monitor performance.

Once a workflow is activated, experience has shown that any problems with any part of the business process are likely to be blamed on the workflow, whether or not this is justified. This is a very natural reaction on the part of people involved with the business process, as the workflow:

▶ Controls their view of the business process
▶ Controls their access to the business process
▶ Controls the flow of the business process between them and other users
▶ Automatically performs parts of the business process that they are not able or not expecting to have to perform manually

Great benefits can be achieved when a process that is critical, essential or high volume is automated As a workflow administrator one of your tasks may be to develop and execute reports to:

▶ Prove that benefits have been achieved

▶ Justify workflow implementation and support costs

▶ Prove the business case for changing the business process and/or the workflow design

▶ Prove that changes in the workflow have had the desired effect

▶ Prove that users are performing tasks efficiently and promptly

6.2   Reporting on Workflows

There are many reports provided as standard with WebFlow, and many more that can be created with tools such as Workflow Information System (WIS), or Business Information Warehouse (BW). If there is no standard report available in the system, you can of course create your own. Refer to chapter 13, *Custom Programs*, for more details on custom reporting.

You should find the reports listed here a useful starting point, but look around for other reports. Often where standard workflow templates have been built around particular transactions or data, special workflow reports exist for them.

All standard reports provide access to see the work item display, the workflow log using the 🖳 option, and common reporting functions such as sort, filtering, change layout, etc. When selecting a workflow instance, most reports show the major steps executed so far and their agents, and the major object instances used so far. Most standard reports include selection criteria to restrict the list to a particular task, task group, component, selection period (today, last week, last month, last year, all) as well as by active and/or completed instances.

When you are assessing workflows it is useful to know what the different workflow and work item statuses mean. A complete list is shown in chapter 13, *Custom Programs,* but here are the statuses that you are most likely to see:

Technical Status	Meaning
READY	Usually applies to work items. The work item has been created and is activated but has not been executed yet. E.g. It is sitting in a user's inbox but they have not opened it yet.

Table 6.1 The Most Significant Work Item Statuses

Technical Status	Meaning
SELECTED	Appears in the work item display as IN PROCESS. Usually applies to work items. The work item has been opened or reserved by a user but has not yet been executed.
COMMITTED	Appears in the work item display as EXECUTED. Usually applies to work items. The work item has been executed, but is waiting for the user to manually confirm the end of processing. E.g. via a *Set to Done* option.
COMPLETED	The workflow or work item is completed. No further changes can be made once completed.

Table 6.1 The Most Significant Work Item Statuses (cont.)

6.2.1 Reporting on Workflow Progress

Usually the most interesting question for anyone involved in a business process is "what's the current status of the workflow".

Useful reports for finding this include:

▶ **Workflows for Object**
Choose **Runtime Tools · Workflows for Object** (transaction SWI6). This report shows all workflow instances linked to a particular object instance, such as a particular purchase order. Note that to use this report in releases prior to 6.10, the business object must have interface IFFIND implemented.

Tip This is one of the most useful reports for general tracking, not just by the administrator but also by all other users of the workflow.

▶ **Workflows for Object Type**
Choose **Runtime Tools · Workflows for Object Type** (transaction SWI14). This report shows all work items and workflow instances for all object instances of a business object type. E.g. Workflows related to all purchase orders.

6.2.2 Reporting on Workflow Performance

When you are reporting on workflow performance you need to look at both the frequency of work items/workflow instances as well as the time taken to realistically assess the behavior of the workflow over time.

Every workflow instance and work item records creation time, start time (when the work item was first opened) and end time (when the work item was completed). If deadline monitoring is used, the work item also records the relevant deadline times.

The best standard report to give a consolidated view of this is *Work items by processing duration* (transaction SWI2_DURA). However, this is one area where it is very useful to create your own custom report via WIS, BW or if neither of these is available, by writing your own program.

When evaluating performance time it is important to consider not just total elapsed time, but also the wait and process times. For instance, the workflow may have taken five days from start to finish, but four days may have been spent just waiting for the first agent to act. If you need to speed the process further, you need to know whether you should focus your efforts on improving the workflow design or improving user behavior.

Wait times can result from a number of factors such as:

▶ Agent was sick, taking a course, in a meeting, or on vacation, and there was no substitute

▶ Agent was not aware of the work item (perhaps they check their inbox infrequently)

▶ Agent wasn't sure how to execute the work item

▶ Agent needed to consult with others before completing the work item

You should never assume that a long wait time means that the user is acting inappropriately, but always investigate the cause of the delay.

If you have deadlines on your work items, more detailed analyses can be made, for instance by using the standard report *Work items with Monitored Deadlines* (transaction SWI2_DEAD).

If you want to know the number of work items processed per period, use report *Work items by task* (transaction SWI2_FREQ).

6.2.3   Work Items by Processing Duration

Choose **Reporting · Work Item Analysis · Work Items by Processing Duration**.

This report gives information on the processing duration of work items of the specified type or for the specified tasks that ended in the period, sorted by task. Provided there are appropriate work items, the current period is compared with a prior period of the same length. The variances and differences are shown.

The process duration of all work items for one task is displayed as standard with threshold values (10% threshold, 50% threshold, 90% threshold). The threshold values should be interpreted as follows: The process duration for the x% threshold means that x% of all work items for this task were processed within this period or a shorter period. You can switch mode to show the *wait time* (i.e. wasted time), *processing time*, or *total time,* which is often more useful than the threshold times. You can also look at times for particular work items. For example, if most work items were completed in seconds but a few work items took several days, you might want to look at the work item, find who was the agent and discuss with them why the task took so long.

6.2.4 Work Items with Monitored Deadlines

Choose **Reporting · Work Item Analysis · Work Items with Monitored Deadlines** (transaction SWI2_DEAD).

This report shows work items that are subject to deadline monitoring. This report is especially useful for seeing whether deadlines are being met or exceeded, as all missed deadlines are shown, whether or not the work item has now been completed. For each missed deadline, the current status of the work item is shown. Since the missed deadlines are shown grouped by task, you can quickly see whether any tasks are repeat offenders. This may indicate that the deadline time is unrealistic, or that further training, on-line help, etc. is needed.

6.2.5 Work Items per Task

Choose **Reporting · Work Item Analysis · Work Items per Task** (transaction SWI2_FREQ).

This report shows the number of work items created in the specified period. The list is sorted according to task.

6.2.6 Reporting on Agent Behavior

Apart from monitoring how quickly agents act on their work items, it is worthwhile evaluating the workload on your agents, especially if the agents complain that they are receiving too many work items. You can analyze both past workload, i.e. what the agent has been processing over a given time period, and future workload, i.e. what they currently have in their inbox that has not yet been processed.

To call workload analysis, choose **Reporting · Workload Analysis** (transaction SWI5).

Workload Analysis for the Past

This report is particularly useful for assessing workload over particular time periods, such as end of month, or end of financial year. To determine the past workload, select the option *Completed since* on the selection screen *Workload analysis*. The report lists work items completed before the specified date.[1] Only completed dialog work items are shown, and the work items must have an actual agent who is a user assigned directly or indirectly to the organizational object specified in the selection criteria.

You can also opt to see further statistics on the number of work items completed by employees linked to an organizational unit, agent, task or completion date.

Workload Analysis for the Future

This report is particularly useful for reporting on the type and frequency of tasks being sent to an agent.

To determine the future workload select the option *To be processed by*. The selection produces a list of work items that must be processed by the members of the organizational object by the date entered.

> **Tip** When no date is specified, a user's workload is the contents of their workflow inbox. Work items in error will not be shown.

The list of work items is grouped according to actual agents and tasks. At the end of the list, the work items and tasks for which no actual user exists are displayed under the header *Not reserved by an agent*.

6.2.7 Identifying and Justifying Potential Improvements

Consider not just the workflow but also the process as a whole. While much can be done in the workflow to help improve the business process, simple considerations such as checking that all agents have received workflow training, or sending e-mail notifications to agents of outstanding work items, or an intranet based FAQ list, can be used to improve the process without needing to change the workflow itself.

The most useful tools for justifying potential improvements are the error overview and performance reports.

---

1 In countries where reporting on individuals is not permitted, the system should be configured to prevent the display of user Ids.

The error overview can be used to show which errors are recurring frequently. In particular, frequent failures in determining agents can lead to more robust rules for agent determination, or to tightening of procedures for agent maintenance by human resources and security personnel.

Workflow performance reports show tasks that have long wait and process times. This can lead to changes to the process such as:

▶ Improving the online help

▶ Making the most important details for the decision more prominent when displaying and executing the work item

▶ Improving training and checking that all agents have received training

▶ Sending e-mail notifications of outstanding work items to the agent

▶ Setting up substitutes

▶ Improving the escalation process by notifying someone when an agent has not performed a task in time, or by automatically redirecting work items to a new agent after a deadline has passed

It is a good idea to give agents and others involved or affected by the process an opportunity to provide suggestions for improving the workflow, for example, via a Web-based suggestion box. If many agents are asking for similar improvements, that in itself may be sufficient justification for changing the workflow.

6.3   Error Resolution

When a process that is critical, essential or high volume fails, the organization suffers. Prompt error resolution is vital if confidence in both the business process and the workflow are to be maintained.

You may know the saying: "If you fail to plan, you plan to fail". As a workflow administrator, the worst mistake you can make is to fail to plan for failures.

The most likely time for failures to occur is immediately after the workflow is activated, or after changes to the workflow are activated. This is also the most critical time for building confidence in the workflow and the business process. You need to make sure that as a workflow administrator you know how important the process is, who will be impacted by the failure (so you can reassure them that the problem is being handled), what to do and who to contact to make sure any errors are resolved quickly and confidently.

This is particularly true of the very first workflow activated in your organization!

There are three parts to any error resolution process:

1. Diagnosing the problem
2. Fixing the problem
3. Preventing the problem from happening again

A considerable number of tools are provided to help you diagnose errors. These tools range from simple reports to detailed technical traces to complex graphical displays. These error diagnosis tools are heavily used by workflow developers testing their workflows, and as needed by workflow administrators diagnosing errors. Due to the large number and variety of tools, diagnosis is a separate topic in itself that will be covered in chapter 14, *Advanced Diagnostics*. If workflow administration is new to you, you may want to get some assistance from your workflow developers in diagnosing errors. Watching a developer solve a workflow problem can be a very effective way to learn how to diagnose workflow errors.

However, when a workflow developer diagnoses a problem, they usually just abandon the failed workflow instance, make some changes and start a new workflow instance. In a production environment, you do not usually have the luxury of ignoring failed workflow instances. You actually have to fix the problem. So in this chapter the focus is on how to resolve the error once you have diagnosed it, i.e. how do you fix it, and stop it from happening again.

The possible runtime problems can be grouped into the following categories:

▶ **Agent determination errors**
I.e. the wrong agent or no agent was found for a dialog work item.

▶ **Buffering errors**
These usually manifest themselves as an inability to access work items despite the maintenance of the agent determination and security being up to date.

▶ **Work item errors**
These are usually caused by an incorrectly modeled workflow or rushed transport. For example, the workflow does not take into account incomplete data extracted from legacy systems, or exceptions in object methods are not trapped.

▶ **Event linkage errors**
These are usually caused by changes in the application customizing or incorrectly modeled workflows. Symptoms are that the workflow didn't start at all because the triggering event was not raised or failed to start the workflow, or the workflow hangs in the middle of the process waiting on a terminating event that never happens.

As you can see, the majority of errors are preventable by good workflow design and thorough testing (e.g. are the exceptions trapped?). However, despite the best efforts of developers, some errors will always occur unexpectedly, because of time pressures, inexperience, or changes made by personnel who don't understand their impact on workflow.

Make sure that people involved in the business process are aware that problems need to be reported promptly. Anecdotal evidence that a process has failed is often very hard to match with the offending work item. So encourage people to report object keys (e.g. if the work item was based on a financial document, give the company code/document number/fiscal year of the document), and dates the process started or when they first noticed the problem. As stated earlier, processes that have been put into workflows are nearly always critical, essential or high-volume. So if an error does occur you need to act promptly and fix it fast!

6.4 General Techniques for Resolving Runtime Errors

Reading Tip Although the information in this chapter is invaluable for a workflow administrator, if you are not yet at the stage of delivering workflows in your production environment you may find this section dry reading. You will also find that some of the error analysis assumes knowledge which is not described in detail until later in this book. For this reason you might want to skip forward now to section 6.8 and return later when you need more detailed support.

In this section you will find the basic settings used to assist error monitoring, as well as some generic techniques for finding and diagnosing work items or workflows that are in error.

Many of the more specific techniques need you to be aware of some basic techniques. In particular you should know:

▶ How to access and read a workflow log

▶ How to access, read and change a work item

6.4.1 Basic Settings for Error Monitoring

There are a few workflow runtime environment settings that are particularly important for runtime error monitoring. Most are mentioned in chapter 3, *Configuring the System,* but you can refer to the IMG for more details.

The most important configuration setting determines who is a workflow administrator so that erroneous work items can be proactively dispatched to the administrator's inbox. If you are a workflow administrator, you must check your inbox regularly.

6.4.2 Finding and Fixing Work Items

The best report for reviewing the status of workflows is the Work Item Selection report (transaction SWI1 or **Utilities · ?Work Item Selection**). It lets you select and display work items of all types according to various criteria. In particular, you can use this function for "lost" work items that do not appear in the expected inbox. Once you have found your work item this report also gives you a number of options for fixing work items in trouble. This report is also useful if you want to get a quick overview of certain types of work items, for instance to examine background work items (enter work item type B) to check that they are all completing promptly. You can select work items either by criteria such as type, status, task/task group ID, date/time created.

> **Tip** The task ID must be appropriate to the work item type selected. Work item type W represents tasks (ID TSxxxxxxxx). Work item type F represents workflows (ID WSxxxxxxxx).

By default the selection criterion is set to show all work items that have occurred in the last hour.

When specifying intervals, ensure that the second entry is later than the first. For example, do not use intervals such as "from 13:05:00 to 00:00:00", instead use "from 13:05:00 to 23:59:59".

You can also select a single work item by its ID number.

> **Tip** If you enter an ID as a selection criterion, the system ignores all other selection criteria.

Setting the *Output Options* flag adds the columns: *workflow definition number, workflow definition version, workflow administrator* and *executed by*.

▶ From the resulting list of work items you can navigate to the work item display if the entry is *not* type F, or the workflow log if the entry is type *F*.

To fix work items in trouble, a number of options are available under **Edit • Work item** or through the administration reports, which are available in the administration menu. These include:

▶ **Restart after error/Execute without check**
With these you can execute a work item. If the work item is in error, use *Restart after Error*. If the work item has no valid agent and you still need to execute it, use *Execute without check*. This option allows you to execute work items unhindered by access restrictions, so authorization to use this option should only be given to the workflow administrator in a production environment.

▶ **Complete manually**
With these you can complete a work item without re-executing it.

▶ **Replace manually**
If a work item has been reserved by a particular agent, you can use this to un-reserve it, i.e. to allow all recipients to see the work item in their inboxes.

> **Tip** If you are restarting a work item after error, make sure you restart using the administration report *restart after error* (transaction SWPR) to ensure that both the work item and the top level workflow are restarted. You should always check that the workflow has restarted correctly in case an error occurs (it could even be a new error) before the workflow has a chance to continue.

6.4.3 Working with the Work Item Display

You can enter the work item display from most workflow reports, including work item selection. The work item display shows detailed information about the work item and also lets you fix certain problems.

In particular in the standard display (see figure 6.1) you can:

▶ Forward, i.e. send the work item to another agent

▶ Replace work items that are held by one selected agent so that other recipients can see them in their inboxes

▶ Reject the work item (the workflow follows the reject path that has been defined in the workflow builder)

▶ Change deadlines

▶ Add attachments. For example, you might want to explain why it was necessary to execute a work item without agent check for the benefit of future audits

You can choose between a standard and a technical work item display. The standard view is aimed primarily at end users. The technical display has some extra options for developers and administrators. You can pre-set which display variant you want to use in your personal workflow settings, or use the menu options, e.g. **Goto · Technical Work Item Display** to move from the standard display to the technical display.

Standard View

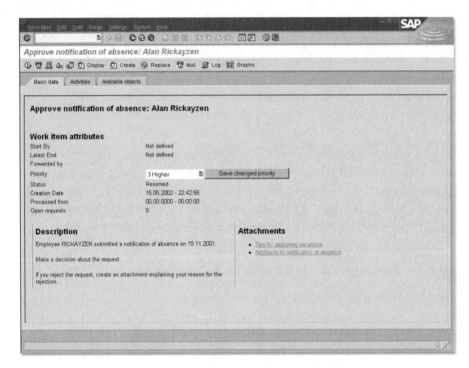

Figure 6.1 Work Item Display Standard View

The standard work item display (shown in figure 6.1) shows the information about dialog work items concisely. It contains details about deadlines, statuses, agents, attachments and linked objects for a work item. It is worth familiarizing yourself with all the features available in the work item display. If the work item execution has failed, the *Messages* (Display Last Message) function will display the error message or return codes for executed work items.

All objects that are related to the work item, including the formal process objects and the ad hoc attachments, are displayed in the list of available objects on the tab page *Available objects*. Of particular interest are:

▶ The object currently being processed (container element _WI_Object_ID of the task container)

▶ The object added for grouping purposes (container element _WI_Group_ID of the task container)

You can display each object referenced in the work item container with its default attribute. If no default attribute was defined for the object type, the key fields of the object are displayed. The default method of each object can be executed upon request.

> **Tip** Most objects set the `Display` method as the default method. So when you want to check on the details of the object, for example to help diagnose an error, you usually do not have to worry about finding the transaction needed to view it.

You can extend and process the list of objects, i.e. create, display and remove them. The main purpose of this is to make extra information available to the agents of the subsequent steps in the workflow, such as why you have forwarded this work item. When you are trying to resolve agent determination problems or just trying to find who has a particular work item **Goto · Agent · ...** is the most useful work item function. You can see the different categories of agents. An icon is used to highlight the users that have the work item in their inboxes.

Technical View

All information from the displayed work item is shown in the technical work item display. The technical work item display is particularly aimed at workflow administrators.

The following specifications are displayed depending on the work item type:

▶ Work item ID and type

▶ Work item status

▶ Actual agent of a dialog work item (after it has been executed)

Additionally, attachments and mails are displayed for the work item. If an error message was generated when the method was executed, you can display this by choosing ▨ **Message** or **Extras · Display return value**.

You can find the current dates/times as well as the deadlines that are monitored by the runtime system (requested and latest start and end deadlines).

Current Date/Time	Meaning
Creation date	Date when the work item was created by the WebFlow Engine with the status READY or WAITING (if a requested start was used).
Start date/time	Date and time when the status of the work item changes from READY to SELECTED or STARTED for the first time, e.g. when a recipient executes the work item.
End date/time	Date and time when the status of the work item changes to COMPLETED or CANCELLED.
Requested start	Date when the WebFlow Engine changed the status of the work item from WAITING to READY (if a requested start deadline was used).

Table 6.2 Work Item Timestamps

A highlighted monitored deadline shows that it has been missed. If the 🔔 symbol is displayed as well, an escalation action was triggered by the deadline background job.

As well as the functions available in the standard view of the work item display, there are additional functions available via the technical view (**Goto · Technical work item display**).

You can go to the definition of the instance linkage for terminating events or wait step work item by choosing **Extras · Instance linkage**. There you can see which event (identified using an object type and event name) is expected by which object (identified using an object reference). This is useful if the work item has been executed but is waiting on a terminating event, as this function lets you see exactly what terminating event and event values are expected.

Choose **Extras · Container** to display the content of the work item container.

The **Edit · Change** option lets you:

▶ Change the work item container (e.g. if binding errors caused the wrong data or incomplete data to be passed)

▶ Logically delete the work item (i.e. mark it as cancelled, no longer required)

▶ Manually complete the work item without re-executing it

▶ Lock/Unlock the work item to prevent someone from executing it or to give them access to it.

In the following work item types, you can display additional details by choosing **Goto · Type specific data**:

▶ For *work queue work items*, the objects and tasks contained in the work queue are listed.

▶ For *wait step work items*, the system specifies how many events are expected and how many events have already been received.

6.4.4   How to Work with the Work Item Container Display

The contents of the container for the relevant work item are displayed in an overall view. You can see the current, runtime-specific data on the specific work item. If you are looking at a dialog or background work item, the container belongs only to that work item. If you are looking at a workflow work item, the container belongs to the whole workflow instance.

The container holds:

▶ System fields relevant to the workflow
▶ ABAP Dictionary based container elements
▶ Object based container elements, i.e. object references

Object references are always prefixed with the logical system ID. This is followed by the ID of the object type and the concatenated key of the object.

If you need to change an object reference, always use the input help on the object reference field. This enables you to fill in the object key correctly, works out the appropriate system/client references for you, and checks that the object exists.

6.4.5   Working with the Workflow Log

At runtime, a workflow has its own work item (of type F) that represents the workflow instance. You can use work item selection and similar reports to find the workflow work item for your workflow. However, the work item display will only show you limited information about the workflow instance. The best way to look at the workflow instance is via the workflow log.

The workflow log formats all the information created or collected during the execution of the business process (i.e. the workflow instance) in one place, as shown in chapter 4, *Work Item Delivery*. The standard view (shown in figure 6.2) is intended for agents and process owners who want to get an overview of the steps processed so far. The technical view (see figure 6.5) is intended for developers and workflow administrators.

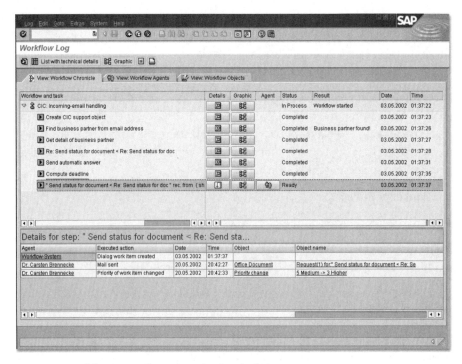

Figure 6.2 Workflow Log—Chronicle in the Standard View

Standard View

Only data for the most significant step types is shown in the standard view. In the workflow definition, you can exclude steps with the above step types from being displayed in the workflow log if you wish. If you want to see the complete log you should switch to the technical view of the log (![icon]).

The workflow log contains the following tab pages:

▶ **Workflow Chronicle** ![icon] (What was processed when?)
The tab page *Workflow Chronicle* shows a hierarchical display of all steps in the workflow that have been processed so far, or are currently able to be processed. If the workflow has a subworkflow structure, the subworkflows are also displayed.

The Details function (![icon] symbol) lists the following information about each step in the lower part of the screen:

▶ Who carried out what detailed actions for these work items and with what results

▶ When this action was carried out

▶ The objects involved

The Agents function (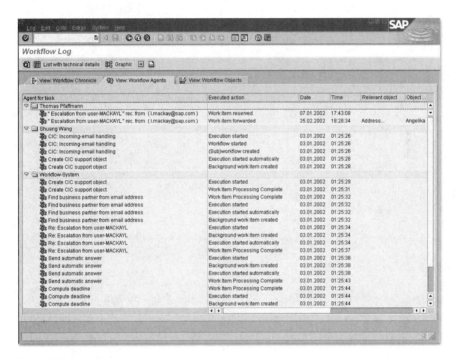 symbol) displays the selected/possible/excluded agents of a step.

▶ **Workflow Agents** (Who processed what?)
The tab page *Workflow Agents* (figure 6.3) shows the agents involved in the workflow up to now. The following is displayed for each agent:

▷ What action was carried out in what step

▷ When this action was carried out

▷ The objects involved

Figure 6.3 Agent log

▶ **Workflow Objects** (What was processed?)
The tab page *Workflow Objects* lists the objects related to the workflow or addressed up to now in the execution of the workflow. This view shows what objects were created and processed, and how. These objects include:

▷ The main object of the workflow

▷ Any attachments and objects added in individual steps of the workflow

The following is displayed for each object:

▷ Who carried out what detailed action for what task

▷ When this action was carried out

In addition you can navigate to the graphical workflow log (figure 6.4), which displays the workflow steps already processed (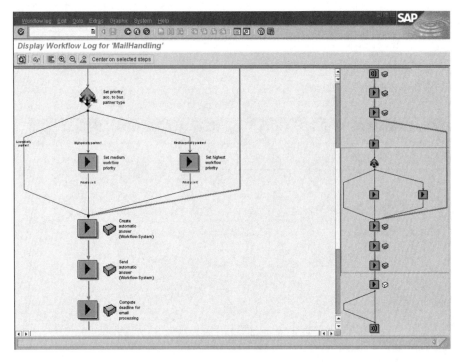) in a graphical representation of the workflow definition.

Figure 6.4 Graphical Workflow Log

The main benefit of the graphical workflow log is that you can see at a glance which 'route' a workflow instance has taken and which activities are processed in parallel to your own within a business process. Unlike the text version of the workflow log, the graphical workflow log also shows the subsequent flow of a workflow instance. This view also allows you to make ad hoc changes to this single workflow instance.

Technical View

The technical view (see figure 6.5) shows technical control information and is therefore aimed particularly at workflow administrators. For a workflow with errors it allows you to see at a glance where the error has occurred and all messages (including warning messages) generated by the workflow. However, it is also a very useful display for determining exactly what happened during the workflow.

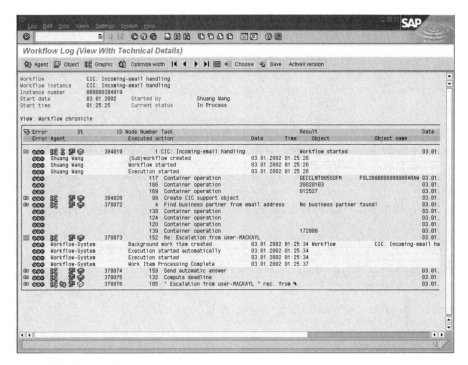

Figure 6.5 Workflow Log—Technical View

The workflow log is displayed as a two-level, hierarchical list. You can adapt the appearance of the list to suit your requirements using layouts.

> **Tip** If you save your configuration as the initial configuration using the SAP List Viewer (ALV) settings control, then this view is displayed whenever you display the technical log. It is a good idea to customize the administrator's initial configuration so that it always shows the task Ids of the work items in addition to the standard columns.

The technical view shows technical nodes and control structures, and makes additional data available, such as container elements (⚏), agent data (👥), and workflow data (⚎). The status of each work item is also displayed.

If the workflow is in status ERROR, the workflow log may contain a hierarchical list of underlying WebFlow Engine function modules that indicate exactly where the error was detected, helping to localize particularly obscure errors.

If you choose *... With subworkflow structure*, you decide whether or not to display any subworkflows and their structure.

Depending on your personalization, you may have to choose 🔲 ... **With error indicators** to view the errors, which are marked in the log with the ●●● symbol. The standard indicator for work items that are not in error is ⊙⊙⊙. This is particularly useful for identifying at a glance work items with errors, particularly in more complex workflows where many work items are displayed in the log.

> **Tip** By clicking on the error symbol associated with the parent workflow item (at the top of the list) you will be presented with a complete error analysis of the workflow, showing the probable root of the problem.

Just as with the standard view you can display a chronicle, agent or object view.

6.5 Resolving Agent Determination Errors

The most probable workflow problem that you are likely to encounter in a production environment is an agent determination problem. That is, a work item is sent to the wrong agents or to no agents at all.

> **Tip** The WebFlow Engine cannot alert you if the wrong agent receives a work item (e.g. agent determination data out-of-date). This is where a good work item description comes to the rescue.

Once a workflow is developed and transported to production it may not need to be changed for some time, and even changes can be planned. With good design and thorough testing you can prevent most workflow problems. However, agent determination relies on data that is usually maintained directly in the production environment and may need to be changed at short notice. Even a relatively minor delay in updating agent determination rules or agent authorizations can have an immediate negative impact on a workflow.

The most common cause of agent determination errors is inadequate maintenance of the agent determination rule or the authorities given to agents. Ensuring timely maintenance of agent determination rules and workflow security can prevent the majority of agent determination errors. Problems can also occur because an agent has left the company, or is absent for some other reason, and has no substitute, or has reserved the work item so that none of the alternative agents can access it.

The good news is that implementing simple strategies such as substitution or default agents can help alleviate agent determination problems. For more details on these and other strategies refer to chapter 5, *Agents*.

6.5.1 Fixing Work Items with No or Wrong Agents

As a workflow administrator, it is usually your responsibility to redirect any work items that were sent to the wrong agent or have no agent at all.

You will probably also need to diagnose why the problem occurred and follow up any maintenance issues with the relevant personnel; otherwise the same problem will boomerang back to you on future work items.

Before you fix a work item with an agent problem, always check that you have identified the correct agent; for example, check it with the business process owner. Do not just take someone's word for it that they are the correct agent; otherwise, you may inadvertently cause a security breach.

The other point to remember about fixing work items with the wrong agent is that you cannot send a work item to a new agent if it has already been completed. So if the wrong agent has already completed the work item, the most you can do is stop the problem from happening again and discuss the situation with the agents and business process owners involved. It is also a good idea to keep a log of what occurred for the benefit of auditors, and/or add an attachment to the workflow explaining why the wrong agent executed the work item.

Diagnosing why agent determination has failed is a topic in itself. Chapter 14, *Advanced Diagnostics,* will walk you through a plan of attack for diagnosing agent determination problems. Knowing the cause will help you solve the problem.

▶ *Problem:* An agent lacks authorization to execute the work item; i.e. the desired agent is not a possible agent of the work item.

▶ *Solutions:*

- ▶ Once the agent's authorization has been corrected, forward the work item to the desired agent.

- ▶ If the agent's authorization is correct but they are still unable to execute the work item, it may be a buffering problem—see section 6.6.

- ▶ If the work item needs to be executed before security can be corrected, discuss the data with the desired agent, and use *Execute Without Agent Check* to execute and complete the work item.

▶ *Problem:* The wrong agent or no agent was found, even though the desired agent has sufficient authority, i.e. the agent determination rule has failed.

▶ *Solution:*

- ▶ If the agent is already a possible agent, but was not excluded or selected, forward the work item to the desired agent.

- *Problem:* The desired agent cannot execute the work item because they are an excluded agent, i.e. they have been specifically excluded from executing the work item.

- *Solutions:*

  - If the agent is excluded, they cannot execute the work item, so you will need to forward the work item to someone else. The business process owner should be able to suggest an appropriate agent. Before you forward the work item, make sure the new agent is a possible agent of the task and *not* an excluded agent.

  - Alternatively, discuss the data with the appropriate agent, and use *Execute Without Agent Check* to execute and complete the work item.

- *Problem:* The work item cannot be accessed from any agent's inbox.

- *Solutions*:

  - If an absent agent has reserved the work item, but there are other recipients available, replace the work item. This will allow other agents to view it. The same is true of work items in someone's resubmission queue.

  - If an absent agent has reserved the work item, and your agents are used to working with workflow substitution, create a substitute for the absent agent. The substitute agent can then execute the work item. Remember that the substitute must still have sufficient authorization to do this.

  - If there are no alternative agents in the selected agent list and you do not want to use substitution, forward the work item to the appropriate (possible) agent suggested by the business process owner.

6.5.2 Preventing Agent Determination Problems from Reoccurring

Once you are confident the immediate problem is solved, you need to ensure that this does not happen again. This may mean:

- Ensuring that administration of security and agent determination is done promptly. If you can't do this yourself, you may need to call on the business process owner and the relevant managers to improve the situation.

- Ensuring that personnel who are able to change values related to the workflow are aware of their impact on the workflow. You may need the assistance of the business process owner to improve the situation.

- Changing the workflow design or the rule determination design. For instance, if you are using a responsibility rule, you may want to turn on secondary priorities so that a default agent is determined when no specific agent is found.

- Setting up workflow substitution for relevant agents.

6.5.3 Support Tools for Agent Determination Problems

Execute Rules for Work Items

Administration · Workflow Runtime · Execute rules for work items (transaction SWI1_RULE).

You can use this function to repeat the step of defining the recipients for a work item. If a rule was used to determine the recipients, the rule will be re-executed.

Work Items Without Agents

Administration · Workflow Runtime · Work items without agents (transaction SWI2_ADM1).

This report finds all work items that have no agent at all, i.e. orphaned work items, for a particular selection period. The list displayed is similar to the work item selection report, and you have the same options available for examining and/or correcting work items.

Execute Work Items Without Agent Check

Administration · Workflow Runtime · Execute work item without agent check (transaction SWIA).

This report enables you to execute work items for which you are not a possible agent. This is therefore a very powerful tool and so should be given only to the administrators in production environments. Using the work item selection, you can select the necessary work items and then execute them, complete them or make them available again to the recipients (i.e. *replace* them).

If you need to use *Execute Without Agent Check* to fix a problem, consider adding an attachment to the work item explaining why this action was necessary and who advised what action should be taken. This can help answer and avoid awkward questions made by auditors or managers who are reviewing business processes retrospectively, long after the problem was solved.

6.6 Resolving Buffering Errors (The Cinderella Principle)

Buffering simply means that the system keeps a copy of certain data in memory rather than reading it from the database. This is done to improve overall system performance, and is particularly prevalent in organizational management related entities such as organizational units, jobs, positions, agents, tasks and relationships between them. Because there are so many buffers used for organizational management related entities, most of these buffers are normally only refreshed at midnight (system time). Unfortunately, out-of-date buffers can have some curious effects on a workflow.

The majority of buffering errors can be prevented by ensuring buffers are updated whenever new agents are added, or when agent-determination rules or work-flow-related security is changed. However, the lack of tools in pre-4.6x Basis environments does make updating the buffer more difficult.

Another way to avoid buffering problems is to habitually set up agent assignments and security at least the day before they are going to be used.

Buffering problems result in apparently impossible situations:

▶ The work item may appear in the agent's inbox, but the agent is unable to execute it.

▶ All the agent administration and security is correct, but the agent determination still doesn't work.

Most frustratingly, you can spend all day trying to resolve this problem, come in the next morning and find that everything is working fine. You could call this: "Midnight Magic" or the "Cinderella Principle", i.e. everything's back to normal after midnight.

6.6.1   Fixing Work Items with Buffering Problems

You can fix buffering problems by refreshing buffers. This can be done by:

▶ Using the *Synchronize runtime buffer* option. This refreshes the majority of organizational management buffers.

▶ Using the *refresh index* option when assigning agents to tasks. This updates buffering of the agent assignment to a task.

▶ Using the *refresh organizational environment* option in the Business Workplace or in the "Start Workflow" function (Transaction SWUS). This refreshes buffers for the current user ID.

If buffering has stopped an agent from accessing a work item, it is enough to refresh the buffers. However, if buffering has caused an agent determination problem, i.e. the work item was not sent to the correct agent, you will still need to fix the agent determination problem on work items created before the buffers were refreshed (see section 6.5).

Sometimes security problems can appear to be buffering problems. For instance if you are in an R/3 system with HR structural authorizations, a lack of appropriate authorizations will result in agents not being able to access their work items. The error messages that appear when attempting to execute the work item are the same or similar to error messages that appear with buffering problems.

6.6.2 Preventing Buffering Problems From Reoccurring

Prevent buffering problems in the longer term by:

▶ Encouraging updates of relevant security, organizational management data, and workflow data the day before it will be used.

▶ Synchronizing the runtime buffer after emergency changes to workflow related security if it needs to be used straight away.

▶ Making agents aware of buffering problem symptoms (e.g. via a web site) and, where possible, give them access to the *refresh organizational environment* option so that they can refresh their own buffers.

6.6.3 Support Tools for Buffering Problems

Synchronize Runtime Buffer

Administration · Workflow Runtime · Synchronize runtime buffer (transaction SWU_OBUF)

You can use this function to initialize the main memory buffers used by the Web-Flow Engine. You can set the current time as the new buffering start time. After the new buffering start time has been set, the system reads the values from the database instead of from the buffer so that the current data is used. As the data is read from the database, it is added to the buffers once more.

> **Tip** You should always refresh the runtime buffer when you have made a change in a task definition or after transporting new workflows or versions of workflows that are to be used on the day of transport.

After executing this function, some workflow functions will initially have lower than optimal performance. This applies until the main memory rebuilds the buffers up to optimal levels.

6.7   Other Support Tools

Here are some more reports and functions that you may find useful in dealing with work item errors:

Diagnosis of Workflows with Errors

Administration · Workflow Runtime · Diagnosis of Workflows with Errors (transaction SWI2_DIAG)

This function displays all workflows with errors and groups them according to error cause (agent, deadlines, binding, or other). This report helps you to assess whether particular types of errors are reoccurring across many workflows, or whether the problem is specific to just a particular work item. You can also fix and restart the workflow from this report.

> **Tip** The system determines highest-level work items with errors, i.e. if a work item is in error status, the work item shown will belong to the highest workflow in error hierarchically above it.

Workflow Restart After Error

Administration · Workflow Runtime · Workflow Restart After Error (transaction SWPR)

This report can be used to display a list of workflows with errors for a particular selection period, and then restart them. The benefit of this report is that it allows you to perform a mass restart of workflows.

Deadline Monitoring for Work Items

Administration · Workflow Runtime · Work Item Deadline Monitoring

Tasks with deadlines have also have deadline monitoring based on a background job. You can change the period duration of the background job, change it, schedule it, display it, or execute it manually (transaction SWWA).

Work Item Rule Monitoring

Administration · Workflow Runtime · Work Item Rule Monitoring

If conditions are defined for the work item start or work item end for steps in the workflow, these conditions must be regularly checked. This task is performed by a report that is controlled by a background job. You can schedule or display the background job. You can also start the report manually using *Execute Work Item Rule Monitoring* (report RSWWICOND).

Continue Workflow After System Crash

Administration · Workflow Runtime · Continue Workflow After System Crash (transaction SWPC)

You can use this report to select and continue workflows that have had the status STARTED for longer than a day. This means that workflows that have come to a halt after system errors can be continued.

6.8 Help-Desk in the Intranet

As you have seen so far, being prepared is the best way of ensuring smooth and efficient processing. However, by distributing responsibility to the workflow agents, you will make the whole process transparent to them and less of a mystery. This allows them to react faster to exceptional circumstances (such as another agent sitting for too long on a work item) and proactively support other agents downstream in the process.

Take a multi-pronged approach.

1. Use a web-based help desk to distribute information and provide generic support.
2. Use the agents to help report and diagnose problems promptly. Give the agents enough information to avoid confusion over what is or is not a problem.
3. Use workflow administrators to deal with problems before they become noticeable to the agents.

6.8.1 Web-based Help Desks

It is helpful to provide a web-accessible (Intranet/Extranet) help desk support site that provides:

▶ Contact numbers for problem resolution.
▶ FAQs—Frequently asked question lists to increase understanding and helps users diagnose and resolve their own problems.
▶ Access to generic training material.
▶ Access to "tips and tricks" for dealing with inboxes, attachments, performing tasks, etc.
▶ Reference documents explaining the business process and workflow, e.g. in the form of a graphical flowchart.

- ▶ Highlight new and soon-to-be-provided workflows.
- ▶ Post interesting results such as: time taken to complete the process before versus after the workflow was implemented; number and frequency of workflows.
- ▶ Provide a 'suggestion box' for ways to improve the workflow.
- ▶ Acknowledge users who have contributed to improving workflow.

In addition, when the business process changes, the help desk is the ideal place to publish information to:

- ▶ Announce that the workflow process definition has changed.
- ▶ Explain why the workflow has been changed and what benefit the changes will give.
- ▶ Explain the differences between the new and old process.
- ▶ Explain what if any affect this will have on users.

6.8.2 Self Help

Encourage agents to understand where they fit into the business process. One way to do this is to give them a copy of the workflow flowchart with the tasks they perform highlighted. Another way is to hand out 'survival packs' or newsletters explaining the workflow flowchart to all users, the expected benefits of the new workflow, and how to access their work items, updating any last minute training information, and showing who to contact if they have any problems.

Send clear, concise and complete instructions with the work item. If possible, have some of the agents read the instructions prior to the workflow being activated, to check that they make sense. Give the agent enough information to help identify, diagnose and fix problems. As well as speeding error resolution, this also helps to build the agent's acceptance of the process.

In each work item, tell the agent why they have received it and who to contact if they believe they should not have received it or if they are having problems completing it. Thus, your agents will see:

- ▶ "You have received this work item because..."
- ▶ "Please contact ... if you believe you should not have received this work item."
- ▶ "Please contact ... if you are unable to complete this work item/access this hyperlink."

Encourage prompt reporting of any problems. Anecdotal problems are often difficult to substantiate, as the work item is often completed and the evidence lost before any diagnosis can be attempted.

Make reporting problems easy. Consider using a simple workflow to do just this. For instance, let the agent enter a text describing a problem, a code for the type of problem found (wrong agent, missing information, cannot execute work item), a code for the process to which it belongs (purchasing request, vacation request, etc.), and user ID/contact details. Have the workflow route the problem reported to an appropriate agent based on the type of problem found and the process to which it belongs. Include an e-mail response directed back to the initiator confirming that the problem has been fixed.

6.9 Day in the Life of a Workflow Administrator

The title of this section is perhaps a little misleading, because, thanks to the high degree of integration of SAP's WebFlow Engine with the rest of SAP's software, the time spent purely administrating (as opposed to development) is of the order of an hour a week, even in large corporations with high workflow volume.[2] Most of this time is devoted to updating the organizational model to deal with staff fluctuation and organizational changes or helping review workflows currently being developed. However, if you have been nominated as a workflow administrator, or you are responsible for resourcing workflow administrators, then you will want to take this responsibility seriously and it helps to have some idea of what a workflow administrator does on a day-to-day basis.

You need to consider:

▶ **Who should be the workflow administrator?**
What sort of skills does a workflow administrator need? Are they technical skills, business knowledge or both? Can the system administrator be the workflow administrator, too? Is it a full time or part-time position?

▶ **Who makes the business decisions in the event of failure?**
Given that workflows are business processes in action, how does the business interact with the workflow administrator if the workflow fails?

▶ **Crisis response**
When a workflow fails, the business process fails. If the process was important enough to be implemented as a workflow, then any failure is equally critical. What does the workflow administrator do in the event of such a crisis?

▶ **Day-to-day monitoring**
What does a workflow administrator need to do on a day-to-day basis, even when there isn't a crisis?

---

2 Metrics from one company with 90 different workflows and 75 000 work items per day: 8 working hours workflow administration per week—mainly organizational management changes such as a user changing job.

▶ **Housekeeping**
How does a workflow administrator help maintain optimal efficiency of your workflow environment?

▶ **Making the most of a precious resource**
How can you make the most of the workflow administrator in your organization?

6.9.1 Who Should be the Workflow Administrator?

Workflow administration usually involves both technical activities and business activities, so it makes sense to have both technical and business personnel as administrators. It is rare to find someone with all the technical and business skills needed to support your workflows, so consider having either a team of administrators who work together, or setting up a contact sequence for support. Both the technical and business people need to have a good understanding of workflow. Bear in mind that there will not be enough workflow administration duties to perform to keep a single person fully occupied, let alone a whole team. So the administrator will pursue other duties too.

There are a number of possible team structures, for instance:

▶ A centralized, dedicated team of technical and business administrators

▶ A centralized, dedicated technical administrator and a decentralized part-time business administrator on an as-needed basis

▶ Regional teams of technical and business administrators on a part-time basis

▶ Centralized system administrators who are part-time workflow administrators, with nominated business contacts for each business process

▶ Workflow administrators who are also workflow developers

The team structure that is right for your organization depends on:

1. The number and frequency of workflows you are running. The more workflows you run, and the more you have in the development pipeline, the more likely administration will become a full-time activity.

2. The number of people affected by the workflow. This includes not just the agents but also people who are relying on the workflow to complete processes for them. The more people affected, the more business administrators will be needed to help educate and explain the workflow behavior. You can reduce this activity by using a web site to help educate and explain workflow behavior.

3. The availability of workflow resources. If you have only a few people skilled in workflow, they may act as workflow developers and workflow administrators. As the number and frequency of workflows grow, you will probably need to separate these roles.

4. How extensively workflow is being used, i.e., whether workflow is regarded as continuous business improvement, where the administrator plays an on-going role in the development of new scenarios, or whether only a few limited processes have been activated.

The basic rules of thumb are:

1. Business people (e.g. supervisors) and/or a web site as the first point of contact for queries about how the process works and for "what do I do now?".

2. A technical administrator available to solve deeper problems.

3. Assign business process owners who can be contacted to make business decisions in case of failure. Make sure you have backup contacts as well; in a crisis you may need to contact someone within a few minutes of finding the problem.

4. Make sure the workflow developer is available to help solve problems especially in the first couple of weeks after a new or changed workflow is activated in production.

The workflow administrator is on the front line when workflow problems happen. Usually it is your critical, essential and high volume business processes that have been worth the cost of implementation as workflows. Therefore, it is vital that your workflow administrator be capable of handling problems as they arise from the very first time a workflow is run in your production environment. Remember that most problems are likely to occur in the first few instances of a new or changed workflow. Above all it is not realistic to give workflow administration to a system administrator and expect them to be able to diagnose or resolve problems without any workflow training.

A workflow administrator needs the following:

▶ An understanding of workflow basics

▶ An understanding of the particular workflows they are supporting

▶ Practice in using the various diagnosis and error resolution support tools

▶ Names of persons to contact when a workflow fails and a business decision needs to be taken

Tip Pick an administrator with good *people* skills (e.g. communication and tact) and preferably with hotline experience too.

6.9.2 Who Makes the Business Decisions in the Event of Failure?

Whatever the cause of a failure, correcting workflows in error is much more than a technical activity. Remember always that the workflow represents the business process, and when you make decisions about how to deal with failed processes you are literally affecting business operations. You need to have a business process owner (and backup — in a crisis you often have to be able to contact people rapidly) who can be contacted to help manage and resolve the failure by assessing:

▶ How serious is the failure from a business viewpoint?

▶ How critical is this particular failure? If it is not critical now, will it become critical if it is not resolved in the next hour, day, week, etc.?

▶ Who needs to be notified of the failure?

▶ If the fault in your workflow affects a customer directly, you may need to notify them. If the fault hinders issuing a payment this may mean notifying a supplier.

▶ Is there a workaround? For example can someone do the work manually until the problem is resolved?

▶ When the crisis is over, how can we prevent it from happening again? Should the workflow be enhanced to cope with this problem? Should procedures (e.g. for maintaining agent data) be updated? Should the helpdesk or Web site include instructions to agents to encourage better and faster reporting of similar problems in the future?

Even if the workflow administrator knows the answers to these questions, most organizations cannot afford for these decisions to be taken by one person alone. Your organization will usually need to be able to show that the correct process has still been followed and that the relevant personnel have been involved in deciding on the actions to be taken. On the other hand, you don't want to delay resolving workflow problems while meetings are being held to evaluate possible remedial actions. As much as possible:

▶ Make sure workflows are designed so that they can be easily restarted in the event of an error.

▶ Build workflows that listen for manual action so that corrective action taken outside of the workflow will not leave the workflow hanging.

▶ Have a plan of action *before* problems happen. Anticipate potential failures and how they will be resolved as part of the workflow design.

▶ After every problem, and particularly after recurring problems, do post-mortems and evaluate what was the root cause of the error and how the process can be improved to prevent the error.

▶ Make sure that problems in the workflow will be quickly highlighted so corrective action can be taken. This means making sure that the workflow reports errors effectively (e.g. by using the standard error monitoring program to notify the administrator).

Here is one real-life example of a workflow designed to handle errors effectively:

1. At one point in a workflow, a background work item updates some data. As other personnel may also be working on the data, locking conflicts can arise. The background work item is designed to report any errors including locking errors. If you designate the error as temporary, the WebFlow Engine will repeat the method execution whenever the locking problem occurs.

2. If the background work item is locked, the WebFlow Engine automatically retries the operation several times after a predefined wait (e.g. 10 minutes).

3. If the retry count is exhausted so that the work item is sent into an error state, the workflow definition sends a dialog work item to a designated agent, asking them to complete the activity manually.

Here is another example:

1. At one point in a workflow, a work item asking for an approve/reject decision is sent to an agent. Maintenance of the agent determination rules is a problem and frequently no agent is found. The agent determination rules are maintained using a responsibility rule.

2. The *secondary priorities* option is turned on for the responsibility rule. This allows specific agents to be maintained at high priority, and default agents to be maintained on a lower priority setting. Thus, when the work item is assigned, the workflow examines the specific agents first, and only if no specific agent is found will it use the default agents. The default agents are trained to determine the correct agent, forward the work item to the correct agent, and update the responsibility rule.

Your workflow developer and technical workflow administrators will probably be able to describe many more examples but it is the business process owner who must decide what suits your organization best. No matter how well designed your workflow, in the event of a failure it is the business process owner who ultimately must decide what corrective action should be taken, and whether fixing the failed workflow is enough to fix the process from a business perspective.

6.9.3   Crisis Response

Crisis response is the most important part of any workflow administrator's job. When a process fails, the pain felt by the business, and thus by the head of the workflow administrator, can be considerable. It is helpful to have a plan of attack for those panic calls. Most of the following plan is common sense.

▶ Gather the symptoms of the problem from the person reporting it.

▶ Use these to identify the workflow.

▶ Check whether the workflow is functioning as designed or not.

▶ If the workflow is working as designed and there is no error, notify the person reporting the problem and the business process owner. Get the business process owner involved in explaining the designed process to the person reporting the error. If appropriate, ask the business process owner to discuss with the person reporting whether the workflow needs to be altered.

▶ If the workflow is working as designed but poor data maintenance is affecting it, notify the business process owner. Get the business process owner to help organize corrections to the data and discuss whether corrective action needs to be taken until the data has been fixed. Notify the person reporting the problem of what caused the problem and what is happening to resolve the issue. Avoid laying blame.

▶ If there is an error, diagnose the error. Notify the business process owner of the problem and discuss possible resolutions. Notify the person reporting the problem of what caused the problem and what is happening to resolve the issue. Avoid laying blame. Resolve the problem. Notify the person reporting and the business process owner that the problem has been resolved.

▶ Keep a log of reported errors. For example, note which workflow, what type of error (education issue, process gap, bad data maintenance, error), who reported it, which business process owner was involved in resolving it.

▶ Hold a post-mortem with the business process owner. This may be a quick chat or a formal meeting, depending on the nature of the problem. Discuss whether the problem could have been better handled, and whether it is appropriate to change the workflow to help.

▶ Use the log of reported errors to demonstrate to management which workflows are causing problems so that corrective action can be taken.

Of course you can additionally create a special workflow to let users report problems. This will help you find and notify the business process owner, and finally update a reported errors log. If the log is kept on the system, then you can easily summarize the data for management.

Often it is not the workflow itself that causes a problem, but an underlying transaction or routine that has failed in a way not anticipated by the workflow. This could be due to any number of causes such as:

▶ Changes that were made to the configuration of transactions or routines without considering possible effects on the workflow. This can include seemingly harmless changes, such as adding a new value for a code.

▶ Changes in values, including master data, used by the transaction or routine that are used for determining agents for follow-on steps in the workflow. This may have the effect that no agent can be determined from the new values.

▶ Users operating transactions or routines in an unexpected way, possibly due to inadequate or ineffective training in the process.

▶ Users involved in the process failing to act in a timely manner, especially where underlying transactions/routines use perishable data.

It is quite normal for many of the reported 'workflow' errors to not be workflow errors at all. Remember that the workflow is some person's view of the business process, and even if the problem is not the workflow itself, make sure you at least help coordinate a response. Thus, the workflow administrator's job is not just diagnosing and resolving errors but also acting as an intermediary to ensure that the process as a whole is running smoothly. This part of the job can easily be split between the administrator and the business process owner. It is worthwhile deciding who will be responsible for what before the workflow is activated in the production environment.

6.9.4 Day-to-Day Monitoring

Even when everything is running smoothly, there are still a few things for the workflow administrator to do. The following are mostly 'health checks' that should be carried out at least once a day. If you are running a large number of workflows you should, of course, make these checks more frequently.

▶ Regularly check your inbox for workflow errors. The error-monitoring job (SWWERRE) will report severe errors such as event linkage errors, binding errors, and rule resolution errors directly to your inbox. This way you may be able to fix a problem before the agents notice it.

▶ Execute the error overview report (*Diagnosis of workflows with errors*, transaction SWI2_DIAG) to see what errors, if any, are outstanding.

▶ Check that the error-monitoring job (SWWERRE) is running correctly.

6.9.5   Periodic Reality Checks

It cannot be stressed enough, how important the human role is in squeezing maximum success out of workflow automation. Having a workflow definition that defines the optimum process is half the story—helping the users to support this process is the other half.

Make sure you periodically check all of your different user groups to see that they are using the workflow the way you had intended, especially in the period immediately after going live. Do not be depressed if the users are not following your guidelines—work with the users to improve things.

Typical things that go wrong are:

▶ Agents print out work items on paper, asking other colleagues to fill in the details on paper. The original agent then types the paper input into the relevant transaction.

Solution: Check the business logic of your agent determination rules.

▶ Agents are not completing the work on time because they need to research additional information before completing the task.

Solution: Try to retrieve this information up front. You could include it in the work item description.

▶ Agents are not completing the work on time because they are being held up by other processes that are not synchronized with this task.

Solution: You can synchronize one process with another using events.

▶ The agent simply does not understand what has to be done (work item description may be missing).

Solution: Update the work item description and provide more background information on the Web.

▶ Deadline notifications are going to the managers but the managers never log on to the system

Solution: It is often more effective sending deadline notifications to the agents themselves rather than the managers.

▶ Authorization problems are preventing an agent from performing a task in the way it was intended.

Solution: Authorization needs to be changed or an alternative method used (such as a form).

Luckily, problems like these are more the exception than the rule, but they highlight the importance of performing these reality checks *after* going live. Most of the common problems are easily resolved, but if they are not resolved they have a big effect on the overall performance of the workflow. Planning one reality check for the period after going live is just as important as planning the user acceptance before going live—there is no excuse for skipping either.

6.9.6 Housekeeping and Archiving

The workflow administrator is also responsible for the health of the WebFlow Engine in the long term. An important part of this job is to ensure that old work items and workflow logs are regularly cleared from the system. If you use data from the work items or workflow logs to create reports via WIS or BW or similar, make sure you have run your reports and summarized the relevant data before the work items and logs are deleted.

Clearing Tasks

Administration · Workflow Runtime · Clearing Tasks

The background jobs of the WebFlow Engine create job logs that need to be regularly deleted. This task is performed by a report that is controlled by a background job. You can schedule or display the background job. You can also execute the report *Execute clearing tasks* manually.

Archiving and Reorganization

Administration · Workflow Runtime · Reorganization

These functions include reports for archiving and deleting work items.

▶ Archive work item
The archive object for work items is called WORKITEM. Archiving is performed using the standard archiving utilities. Only completed or cancelled work items are archived. If the work item refers to a workflow instance, dependent work items are also archived. If the work item is part of a higher-level work item (i.e. if the work item is a step of a workflow) it cannot be archived until the higher-level work item is completed or cancelled. Both work item data and matching log data are archived.

Container references are archived, but the objects they represent are not affected. For example, if a work item has an object reference to a material master, the reference will be archived, but the material master data will be unaffected. Attachments to work items will be deleted even if they have not been archived.

During archiving, data that is no longer required in the system is checked using application-specific criteria and put in an archive file. The data is not removed from the database. After the files to be archived have been completely copied to the archive file, they can be deleted from the database in a separate program run.

All actions or programs are processed in the background. You can schedule the necessary background jobs in archive management.

▶ **Display workflows from archive**
You can use this report to display a workflow for an application object. After the workflow work item determined by the selection criteria is read from the archive, the system displays the workflow log. The functions of the workflow log are not fully available, however.

▶ **Delete work item**
This report deletes work items from tables without archiving. It simply deletes whatever work items you ask it to delete without checking; in other words, you could delete work items from an active workflow! It is primarily designed for clearing abandoned work items from development systems. If you do not set the indicator *Delete immediately*, the report is executed only on a test basis.

> **Caution** This report should not be used in a production system. Not only does it run slower than the archiving report, but if used incorrectly, it jeopardizes the good working relationship you have built up with your colleagues! Authorization controls should prevent its accidental execution, other than with a tested report variant.

In a production system you must use archive management to archive and delete work items in order to ensure data consistency.

▶ **Delete work item history**
This report deletes all workflow log entries relevant to work items (work item history) without archiving. If you do not set the indicator *Delete immediately*, the report is only executed on a test basis.

6.9.7 Making the Most of a Precious Resource

You will want to make the most of your workflow administrator, and keep the job interesting so that you retain your administrator for as long as possible.

Apart from administration itself, your workflow administrator can:

▶ Develop new workflows

▶ Enhance existing workflows

▶ Review new and enhanced workflows (quality assurance)

- ▶ Train agents in using their workflows
- ▶ Educate personnel responsible for data maintenance, particularly maintenance of agent determination rules and workflow related security.
- ▶ Educate new business process owners in how their workflows work and the sorts of problems/error resolutions that can or have occurred for their workflows.

Evangelize workflow to the organization. It helps to use quantitative data produced by reports to show the benefits of workflow. It may also be useful to show how workflows operate in practice, how the various workflow logs and reports show what is happening, and what sort of information can be evaluated after the process has completed.

Part 2
Developing Your Own
Workflows

7 Creating a Workflow

Although you will spend far more time blueprinting a process and developing subsidiary reports and transaction, than developing workflows in the Workflow Builder, it is nevertheless an important tool. Used properly, it offers features that can save weeks of development time and increase the effectiveness of your workflows.

7.1 Introduction

The central tool for creating, displaying, and processing a workflow is the Workflow Builder (transaction SWDD or **Definition Tools · Workflow Builder**). Within the Workflow Builder you can create all components of a workflow, including all the containers you need for getting the data from one step to another.

This chapter will describe the main features of the Workflow Builder, giving a good foundation from which to embark on your own development. However, to describe the main features adequately we have had to neglect further features, that in exceptional circumstances can certainly come in handy. As anyone who has developed a workflow knows, these less common circumstances are bound to turn up from time to time. When you need more information, the SAP Library help describes all the Workflow Builder features, fields, and buttons.

In order to introduce the Workflow Builder, we will first explain how to create a simple workflow and then extend it. Finally, a few advanced aspects are discussed.

It will help understand the main parts of a workflow before you read further, so we will start off with a simple description of them here. Most workflows are started by an *event* (e.g. when data is entered or changed, when an e-mail arrives, when an error occurs, when a document is printed) that happens in a business application. You define which data from this event needs to be passed to the workflow via a *binding*. Events are described in depth in chapters 10, *Business Interfaces,* and 13, *Custom Programs*, which shows how they are linked to workflows and are created by business applications.

You can also start any workflow directly, for example via generic object services (refer to chapter 10, *Business Interfaces*), if that suits your business process. Since events are a major topic on their own, to keep the focus on workflow in this chapter stick to starting the workflow directly, using test tools.

The *workflow container* is used to hold all the data needed by the workflow. Data may be passed from one step to another.

Each workflow has a number of *workflow steps* that execute activities or control the workflow. The activities are handled within *tasks*. You can use the same task in several steps of a workflow (or even in the steps of several different workflows) if you wish.

A *task* has a *task container*, which holds all the data necessary for that task. To pass data from the workflow container to the task container or vice versa you define a *binding* as part of the workflow step.

Every *step* has one or more possible *outcomes* depending on the step type and the underlying task, if one exists.

Expressions are variables used in the workflow to control the workflow (e.g. branches) or to deliver a result (e.g. the agent ID for executing a step). Examples of expressions are simple container elements or the attributes of business objects (as described in chapter 8, *Business Objects*).

Basic Data controls global aspects of the workflow, such as constructor and destructor methods and defaults for the workflow steps. Part of this Basic Data is version-dependent; the other part applies to all versions.

The workflow will have one *end point.* There are no hidden exit points.

7.2 Workflow Builder Basics

7.2.1 Look and Feel of the Workflow Builder

The Workflow Builder provides a graphical view of the workflow definition. Alternatively, you can view an alphanumeric display, which provides a textual view of the workflow definition in a tree format; however in practice most people prefer the graphical view.

The Workflow Builder screen is divided into the following frames (see figure 7.1):

▶ **Workflow**
Here you can insert new steps into the workflow definition and process existing ones. Double-clicking on a step displays the associated step definition.

▶ **Overview**
The overview graphic is displayed here. The part of the workflow graphic displayed in the *Workflow* frame is marked with a green rectangle. Changing the size or position of the rectangle changes the display in the *Workflow* frame.

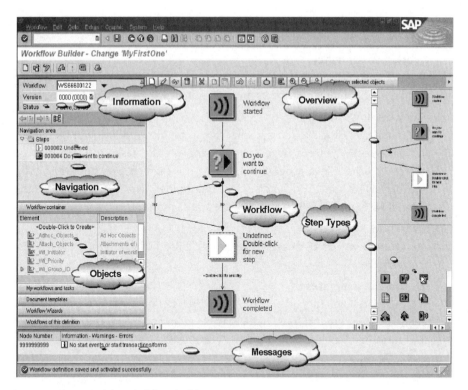

Figure 7.1 Frames of the Workflow Builder

▶ **Step types** (visible only when in change mode)
All step types available in the workflow are displayed here if you are in change mode. To insert a new step into the workflow, click on the step type and insert it into the workflow definition.

▶ **Information**
This displays which workflow is loaded, the status of the workflow, and the version number of this workflow in the original system. To load a different version, simply overtype the version in this frame and press the Enter button. The same applies to the workflow ID.

▶ **Navigation**
All workflow steps in the currently displayed workflow definition are listed here. You can jump directly to the relevant step definition from the list. As with all the frames in the Workflow Builder, you can resize this frame to display the amount of information that you require. The step number corresponds to the number in the workflow technical log (see figure 6.5).

► **Objects**

This frame contains the following trays:

> ► **Workflow container**
>
> All the workflow's container elements are displayed here. You can also define new container elements and generate a where-used list here.
>
> ► **My workflows and tasks**
>
> Tasks and workflows that are displayed can be inserted into workflow definition as activity steps by double-clicking on the task. You can also go directly to the relevant definition. You choose which workflows and tasks are displayed here. Your choice also determines what is displayed in the Workflow Explorer, which is a separate transaction (SWDM).
>
> ► **Workflow Wizards**
>
> All Workflow Wizards available for the definition of your workflow are displayed here.
>
> ► **Document templates**
>
> All the workflow's document templates that can be used in *document from template* steps are displayed here. You can generate a where-used list to find the steps in which a document template is used.
>
> ► **Teamworking**
>
> Here you can search for steps by selected criteria such as who last edited the step in the definition or which steps are grouped together. The result is displayed graphically in the workflow frame.
>
> ► **Workflows of this definition**
>
> Your Workflow Outbox is displayed here, which displays all currently running workflows for this definition.

You may choose whether the last four trays of the list should be displayed or not via your personal workflow settings.

► **Messages**

All messages generated in where-used lists and syntax checks are displayed here. Clicking on a message takes you to the relevant step definition.

7.2.2 Building Your First Workflow

The simplest workflow to build is one containing a single user decision step. In this workflow, you will ask an agent a question and they will choose a response. To keep it simple, you will be the agent. If you have a test system, you are welcome to follow this section online, however this is not necessary in order to understand this chapter. By following a simple example that becomes more sophisticated as the chapter progresses, you will get a good idea of what workflow can achieve.

When the Workflow Builder is called for the first time or you opt to create a new workflow, a newly created initial workflow definition appears (see figure 7.2).

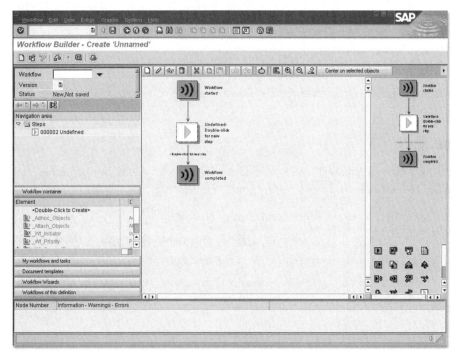

Figure 7.2 An Initial workflow

This initial workflow has the following parts:

▶ The start of the workflow definition is indicated by ⟩⟩ **Start workflow**.

▶ The end of the workflow definition is indicated by ⟩⟩ **Workflow completed**.

▶ The area in which you insert the new workflow definition is indicated by an undefined step with one outcome. Steps are represented by symbols. The name of the outcome is displayed on the arrow leading to the next step in the standard view.

Your first workflow will illustrate how a user decision works. User decisions have their own step type and symbol ▶. When a user decision executes, a question together with a predefined list of answers (the possible outcomes) is displayed to the recipients. User decisions are useful in the following situations:

▶ Only *one of several* possible alternatives should be processed in the workflow at execution time. An agent needs to make a business decision about which alternative is appropriate.

- ▶ An *instruction* (i.e. a user decision with only one outcome) is required to continue the workflow.
- ▶ For *approval*, *release*, or *status change* steps, the recipient needs to choose whether to approve or reject.

On the *decision* tab page, you can make all the entries required to define an executable *user decision*.

At runtime the user will see the *decision title* as the subject text of the work item in their inbox.

Example

In this example, you will create a workflow that asks an agent (you) whether they want to continue, and lets them respond "Yes" or "No".

1. Open the Workflow Builder and choose **New step** 🗅 .
2. In the step type area, choose the ▶ **User decision** step type by clicking on it.
3. Click on the undefined step (to drop the decision into place).

    The step definition of the user decision is now displayed.

4. Enter the title *Do you want to continue?*.
5. Enter the decision texts *Yes* and *No*.

    The outcome names default to the decision texts but you can specify your own names if you prefer.

6. Set the agent to the expression *Workflow Initiator* using the drop down help (but make sure you leave the *excluded agents* field empty).

    Normally you would assign an expression, agent assignment rule, or organizational object (job, position, etc.) to the step, but for the purposes of this tutorial just take the easy way out and use the person starting the workflow.

7. Complete the step by choosing the ✔ **Transfer and to graphic** button.

You have now defined a workflow with a user decision step. However it must be saved and activated before you can use it.

7.2.3   Saving, Activating and Testing

When you choose *Save* (🖫) for a new workflow, you must enter an abbreviation and a name for the workflow. You can change both at any time in the basic data of the workflow. You also have to choose a package for transporting the workflow to other systems. Saving the workflow gives it the status REVISED. The status in the title bar of the Workflow Builder is always visible.

To execute your workflow, activate it by choosing *Activate* ( ), which compiles the definition so that the WebFlow Engine can interpret it. The section on versioning (section 7.5.9) explains why this is necessary.

Before being activated, the workflow definition is subjected to a syntax check. If you only want to check the workflow definition, you can choose *Syntax Check* ( ). All recognized problems are classified as errors or warnings and are output in the message area, together with other useful information. You can process the step in which the error occurs by clicking on the message.

The workflow will only be activated if no syntax errors are found. The status of the workflow is now ACTIVE, SAVED. You can now test your workflow by choosing *Test* ( ).

> **Tip** When you choose *Test* ( ) the workflow is automatically saved, checked, and activated if it is in the *inactive* state and you are in change-mode of the Workflow Builder. There is no need to *check* and *activate* separately.

Example

In this example, you will save, activate, and test your workflow.

1. Save your new workflow. Use an appropriate name and abbreviation.[1]
2. Activate the workflow.
3. Test the workflow by choosing *Test*( ).
4. In the test environment choose *Execute* ( ) to start the workflow.
5. Execute the user decision. Choose *Yes* or *No*.
6. Now return to the Workflow Builder and open the *Workflows of this definition* tray. You can double-click on the new entry to see the matching workflow log.

If you have tried this example in a test system, you may be surprised that when you start the workflow you are presented with the generic decision straight away without having to look in your workflow inbox first. This is because the step is configured as part of the synchronous dialog chain by default (described in chapter 4, *Work item Delivery*). Because the person starting the workflow (you) is identical to the person assigned to perform the first step in the workflow (you), you are presented with the task straight away.

---

1 You must specify a package when saving the task. The system completes the fields *Package* and *Application component* from this. Being cross-client transport objects (transport object PDWS), workflows are always connected to the transport system. If you save the workflow as a local object, you cannot transport it into other systems.

This is very useful in a production environment, but it can be counterproductive when trying to understand how the system works in this tutorial. To stop this behavior simply reset the attribute *Advance with dialog* in the step's *control* tab.

7.2.4   Deadline Monitoring

A major advantage of workflow is being able to monitor workflow steps according to a predefined schedule. You can monitor a number of different date/time deadlines against each workflow step: requested start, latest start, requested end and latest end. If a requested start deadline is active for a work item, then the work item only becomes visible to the recipients after the date/time specified. Background work items are started (*executed*) when the start deadline is reached.

If a latest start, requested end or latest end deadline is active, then the workflow reacts to the deadline when the specified date/time is reached. The standard reaction of the workflow system is to send an escalation mail. However, you can perform more complex escalation procedures by specifying a deadline outcome name. This lets you add steps to your workflow, which are executed after the deadline fails. This is called a *modeled deadline*.

You define deadlines with respect to a *reference date/time*. The system offers the following reference date/times:

▶ The creation date/time of the work item.

E.g. "You have two days to perform this task"

▶ The creation date/time of the workflow to which the monitored work item belongs.

E.g. "You must finish this task within seven days of the workflow starting, regardless of how much time your colleagues have already used for the previous tasks"

▶ A date in the form of an expression, which is derived from the context of the application during execution of the workflow.

E.g. "You have two days for a priority B service complaint but only one day for a priority A service complaint"

Activate monitoring of the relevant deadline by selecting a reference date/time for the deadline. Activated deadlines are marked with 🔔 in the tab page index.

If you choose *expression*, you must define the reference date/time by specifying expressions for the date or time. Use the F4 input help for entering expressions.

> **Tip** The value referenced using the expression must be of data type D for the *date* and data type T for the *time*. If you specify a date but *no time*, the system sets the time to 00:00:01 (requested and latest start) or 23:59:59 (requested and latest end).

Specify the deadline by entering duration and an appropriate time unit (e.g. minutes, hours, days). Negative durations can only be used if you define the reference date/time via an expression.

To notify someone of the missed deadline, specify a recipient on the tab page *Display text*. The message text is displayed in the display area. From here you can go directly to the task definition, where you can change the text on the tab page *Description*. If the deadline is missed, all deadline recipients receive a missed deadline work item in their inbox. The deadline work item is completed when the deadline recipient processes it, or when the original work item is completed, whichever occurs first.

> **Tip** With the standard deadline reaction, the status of the monitored work item is unchanged. The work item still has to be executed by one of its recipients before the workflow can continue. If the monitored work item is to be aborted when the deadline is exceeded, you need to use the modeled deadline reaction. Refer to the section 7.5.2 and to appendix A, *Tips and Tricks* for more details.

Example

In this example, you will add a deadline to your user decision step and test the deadline.

1. Go back to the Workflow Builder and reenter the step definition of your user decision step by double-clicking on the step. In your user decision step, choose the *latest end* tab, and activate the monitoring of the requested end deadline. Choose the *work item creation date/time* as the reference date/time, and add an offset of 5 minutes. Enter the workflow initiator as the recipient of the deadline message.

2. Test your changed workflow (remember saving and activating is performed automatically when you choose the test option from the Workflow Builder).

3. This time do not execute the decision step (cancel out of it if you have not reset the *advance with dialog* checkbox). If you display the work item (without executing it) in the Business Workplace you will see the calculated deadline date/time being monitored.

4. Wait for the deadline to be exceeded and you will receive a deadline message in the Business Workplace.

Tip The background job for deadline monitoring must be scheduled so that the WebFlow Engine can monitor and escalate deadlines. This job is explained in chapter 3, *Configuring the System*. When the deadline job is run, all exceeded deadlines are escalated. If you are running this job periodically, then the actual time of escalation will be delayed until the job next executes.

7.2.5   Creating Container Elements in the Workflow Container

The work item text of the user decision can display current runtime values from the workflow. You can integrate these values by including variables relevant to the decision directly in the work item text. The variables are replaced at runtime with values from the matching Workflow container elements. Of course, this is just one example of how container elements are used in the workflow, but it is one that is very easy for you to try yourself.

Create container elements by double-clicking on the *<Double-click to create>* line in the workflow container tray.

Enter the technical name of the container element in the *Element* field.

You give each container element a technical name (minimum of two characters) that can be used to identify it uniquely. The technical name must begin with a letter, but it can be followed by letters, underscores or digits. It is not case-sensitive. Because the technical name is not translated, it is conventional to use English words in multi-lingual environments.

Under *Texts* maintain the *name* and the *description (optional)*. Both of these can be translated in multi-language environments.

According to the data type reference of the container element, make the following entries on the tab page *Data type*. First check whether your container element is modeled on one of the predefined types. Choose 🗔 and double-click to choose the predefined type. The system carries out the necessary entries for the data type. If you want to create a container element that is not predefined, make the following entries, depending on the data type.

► **Structure or Table**

Choose *ABAP Dictionary Reference*, and enter the table or structure in the field *Type name*.

► **ABAP Dictionary field**

Choose *ABAP Dictionary Reference*, and enter the relevant field of the table or structure in the field *Type name*.

► **Object type**

Choose *Object type*, an object type category, and enter the name of the object type.

> **Tip** Specification of an object type is not mandatory. If no object type is specified, the container element can be assigned a reference to any object type at runtime. However, binding restrictions may limit its use later in the workflow.

> **Tip** A common misconception of workflow is that only one business object can be used per workflow. This is *not* the case. Often cross application workflows use several different business objects and the flow itself forms the link between them. A simple example of such a scenario is the link between a scanned document (for example the object type IMAGE) and the invoice record that is posted to the database (for example the object type BUS2081).

On the tab page *Properties*, select whether the new element is to be an *import* and/or an *export* element. Mark an import element as *mandatory* if applicable.

Example

In this example you will create a simple single-value numeric container element and use it in the user decision step.

1. Open up the workflow container tray and create a new container element by double-clicking on the *<Double-click to create>* line. Create a container element that can hold a number using ABAP Dictionary reference structure SYST field INDEX.

2. In the step definition of your user decision step, set *Parameter 1* to your new container element. Use the drop-down help to do this.

3. Use the variable in your work item text by writing &1 in the text where you want the value to appear. E.g. *Do you want to continue &1?*

4. Save, activate and test your workflow. Notice what number appeared in the work item text—you should see an empty value, i.e. zero.

A Word About the Task Description

Although the short text in the generic decision is part of the step definition (to make things simpler), the long text is part of the task. To create your own long text you can copy task TS00008267 to a new task and write a suitable task description for this new task. You may select your own variables and add these to the task container. Once you have created your task, substitute it into the step's *control* tab in place of task TS00008267. Do not forget that you will need to assign possible agents to your new task.

7.2.6   Changing Container Elements

If you execute your workflow, you will see that the work item text contains an empty value (zero) for the variable. To change this you need to fill the workflow container element. There are several ways of doing this:

▶ **By Initial Values**
You can assign an initial constant value to a container element. When the workflow is executed, the container element will initially be filled with this value. Any changes made to the contents of the container element will overwrite this value.

▶ **By a container operation step**
A container operation step lets you fill a container element with a constant or another container element.

▶ **By bindings in a workflow step**
From any workflow step that can output data to the workflow (such as activity steps, user decision steps, document from template steps, Web activity steps, form steps, etc.) you can transfer data from the task container of the workflow step to the workflow container (or vice versa) via container bindings. Think of bindings as the rules for parameter passing within your workflow.

▶ **By bindings from an event**
Whenever your workflow responds to an event—for example when it is started by a triggering event—data can be passed from the event container to the

workflow container. If you want to pass data from a triggering event to start your workflow, the workflow container elements to be filled from the event container need the *import* flag turned on before the bindings can be defined. Refer to chapter 10, *Business Interfaces,* for more details.

Example

In this example, you will assign a constant value to the container element by adding a container operation step before your user decision step. Container operations are useful for counting operations (e.g. loop ten times) and for setting flags.

1. Create a container operation step by dragging and dropping (as you did for the user decision step) the step type 🔲 **Container operation** onto your user decision step. This will create the container operation step in front of your user decision step.

2. Give your new step a name and make your container element the Result Element using the F4 input help.

3. Assign a constant numeric value to your container element by entering a number in the first *Expression* field.

4. Test your workflow. The number you entered in the container operation step will now appear in the decision title.

7.3 Intermediate Workflow Builder (Steps, Tasks and Objects)

7.3.1 How to Access Data and Activities

To access data, activities and events within your workflows they need to be defined as parts of a business object type. They can then be used in many different workflows, tasks and rules. SAP components contain many predefined business object types. These predefined data, activities, or events can be used as is, or you can create your own.

A business object type describes for a particular business entity the data (attributes), functions (methods), and events used in a workflow. An example of a business object type provided by SAP in R/3 is object type BUS1001, representing material master objects. If you were creating an "accept material master change" workflow, you might want to use data such as the material number and material name, functions such as "display material" or "change material", and events such as "material changed", by using this object type.

Data relating to a business entity needs to be defined as an *attribute* of a business object type before it can be used in a workflow. Attributes are defined as part of the object type to which they are most closely related. For example the attributes *material name* and *material number* would be defined within the *material* object type, but *order number* and *order value* would be defined as part of the *order* object type. In other words, the attributes describe data related to the business object.

Activities to be performed on or using a business entity are defined as *methods* of a business object type before they can be used in a workflow. Every object type has methods that define activities that can be executed on that object or its data (e.g. *create material* or *change material*). Within the method you can call the transactions and BAPIs of the SAP component, your own function calls, or other external applications.

Events are another important component of an object type. The events describe the status changes that an object can undergo (for example, "material deleted" or "material changed"). A workflow can be started, cancelled or resumed (wait step) when an event of this kind is raised. Just like attributes and methods, events need to be defined as part of a business object type before they can be used in a workflow. Events are discussed in chapter 10, *Business Interfaces*.

The Business Object Repository provides an overview of all the object types in your SAP component. You can use or extend the existing object types as well as create new object types, as described in chapter 8, *Business Objects*. During execution of a workflow, individual object instances of the business object type can be accessed, for example material number 3594.

If you want to use workflow to implement a business process, this is a rough picture of what is involved in accessing the relevant data and functions:

▶ First, identify all business entities involved in your business process. You sort out which business functions and events you want to map in your scenario and which data you want to access.

▶ Then check whether the relevant business object types with their methods, attributes and events are defined in the Business Object Repository. The grouping of object types in the application component hierarchy, and the option of searching generically for parts of a name, help when looking for existing object types.

   ▶ If you find an object type whose definition meets your requirements, you can use it without making any modifications.

- ▶ If you find an object type whose definition does not quite meet your requirements, you can extend its definition.

- ▶ If you do not find a suitable object type, you can define your own object type.

▶ Use the methods, attributes, and events of the object type in the relevant parts of your workflow.

Further information on how to create your own object types or extend existing object types can be found in chapter 8, *Business Objects*.

Example

In this example, you will add a container element referencing a flight booking object (using object type SBOOK), and display an attribute of this object in your user decision step.

> **Note** We have chosen the SAP delivered training object type SBOOK representing an airline flight booking for use in this and the following examples as it is delivered in all SAP components. However you should be aware of the following:
>
> ▶ If you execute these examples using the training object type SBOOK , make sure test data has been created for SBOOK (e.g. using transaction BC_DATA_ GEN. Make sure you read the documentation prior to creating the data).
>
> ▶ Any business object type that you prefer can be used in these examples. For instance, you might want to use LFA1, representing a vendor, if you are using R/3, or BUS1006 representing a Business Partner if you are in EBP/ CRM.
>
> ▶ Make sure that whatever object type you use, you have first tested it so that you understand its key, attributes, and methods.
>
> ▶ Make sure you have suitable test data available. For example for BUS1001, you need a valid material ID, for LFA1 you need a valid vendor ID, for BUS1178 you need a valid product GUID, for BUS1006 you need a business partner ID, for SBOOK you need a valid booking number.
>
> Finally, SAP delivers tutorials in the SAP Library help using delivered training object types that you can execute in any SAP component. We strongly recommend that you use these tutorials to increase your understanding of the Web-Flow Engine.

1. Create a new workflow container element (e.g. FlightBooking) referencing the object type representing a flight booking (SBOOK), and set the *import* and *mandatory* flags.

1. Go to your user decision step.

2. Add a second variable in your user decision title, for example *Do you want to continue &1 &2?*, and set *Parameter 2* to an attribute of your new container element (e.g. FlightBooking.FlightDate) using the input help.

3. Test your workflow. You must enter an object key of your business object type before executing the workflow test. In this example you use the input help to find a flight code and booking ID from the *input data* tab on the *Test Workflow* screen.

7.3.2 How to Create and Use Tasks

To execute business functions, you use the business object type methods in **Activity** ▶ steps. However, you do not directly refer to a method of a business object type in the definition of the step. Instead, you use a task that has the object method embedded within it. The task also includes other important information, such as subject text, instructions, and possible agents.

When a workflow is executed and the activity step is reached, a work item is created based on the task definition and the current runtime values.

Your task or an SAP-provided taskcan be re-used in any number of activities in different workflows. In this way, for example, all *user decision* steps refer to the generic decision task (TS00008267) as standard. The step types *document from template* or *send mail* also use tasks to execute their functions.

One way of defining a task is using the *Create Task* option from the activity step definition. Alternatively, you can create the task definition independent of the Workflow Builder using the transaction PFTC. Regardless of how you call the task definition, the same screen for editing the task definition is displayed. You define the activity of the task using an object type method of one of the object types from the Business Object Repository. Only use methods and objects that are in RELEASED status.

The definition of tasks is spread across several tab pages (see figure 7.3). You can make all the mandatory specifications on the tab page *Basic data*. The specifications on the other tab pages are optional.

The basic data is used to identify a task. Each task is identified by the object identifier TS (for standard task) and an 8-digit task number automatically allocated by the system during creation.

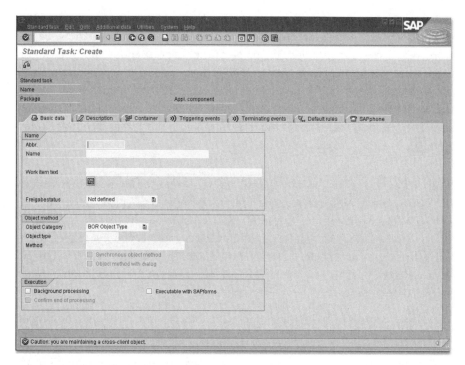

Figure 7.3 The Task Definition

You must specify a package when saving the task in the same way that you specified a package when saving the workflow definition. The transport object in this case is PDTS.

> **Tip** If you also assign your tasks and workflows to a task group, you can use the task group as a logical package for the complete scenario. This is not only useful for documenting which workflows are the active valid workflows (as opposed to test workflows or scrapped versions), but also makes navigation in the Workflow Builder and Explorer easier.

A task has an abbreviation that can also be used in input fields as a search term. It also has a name, which is written to logs for identification. So first of all edit the abbreviation and name of the task.

> **Tip** It is a good idea to decide on a naming convention for task abbreviations to make tasks easier to find. E.g. a specific prefix for all tasks in the project.

Enter a work item text for your task. The work item text is displayed in the Business Workplace, in the work item selection reports and in the workflow log. If a work item text is not specified, the name of the task is used instead. You can use expressions within the work item text. They are replaced at execution time with the current values from the task container. Note that container elements used in the work item text must be filled using a binding. To use expressions in the work item text, position the cursor at the relevant point in the text and choose **Expression** .

> **Tip** If you are looking at an SAP task or a task imported from another system in display mode, you can redefine the task description (which appears in the inbox as the work item text). Choose and enter a new text to replace the original text. Using the redefine option overlays your version over the original task description as an extension rather than as a modification. In an emergency you can even use this technique with your own tasks in the production system.

The *release status* is of an informal nature and indicates the development status of the task or workflow.

Define the activity to be executed by specifying an object type method in the task. The system takes the following from the definition of the object method, as applicable:

▶ Synchronous or asynchronous object method

▶ Object method with or without dialog

You cannot change these. If method parameters are defined for the object method, the system gives you the option of creating matching container elements automatically in the task container. The names of these container elements are then identical in the task container and the method container. You should make use of this option.

> **Tip** Methods that you execute with a task may be synchronous or asynchronous methods. Section 7.3.4 explains the differences and their effect on modeling.

Finally, enter the following information on the tab page *Description* by selecting the text type:

▶ **Task description**
You can describe the task or make notes and recommendations for processing. The task description is displayed in the work item display.

▶ **Notification texts**
These texts are sent as notification to the message recipients for completion or missed deadlines.

Example

In this example you will create a new task to display an airline flight booking and add it to your workflow.

> **Note** We have used the object type SBOOK, since it is available in all SAP components, but (as stated in the example in section 7.3.1) you can use another object type if you wish.

1. Add an activity ▶ step to your workflow, for example, after the *Yes* outcome of your user decision step. If you are having difficulty placing the new step where you want it, read section 7.4.2.

2. Use the *Create Task* option (you will find it in the button list on the button next to *Task*) to create a new task.

3. Enter appropriate texts for abbreviation, name, work item text, and description.

4. Enter the object type SBOOK and method DISPLAY. If you see a message *Transfer missing elements from the object method?*, answer *Yes* (the system is helping you to set up the task container—more on this later).

5. Save (🖫) the task.

6. Set up the security for this task by going to menu **Additional Data · Agent Assignment · Maintain**. Normally you would assign the appropriate security role or organizational objects here, but for simplicity just choose *Properties...* (in older releases *Attributes...*) and make the task a general task.

7. Return to the workflow. The workflow will suggest a binding between the workflow and the task. Accept the binding by choosing *Enter* ✔.

8. Set the agent of the activity step to the workflow initiator expression using the drop down help.

9. Test your workflow. You must enter an object instance of your business object type into the container in the test tool using the F4 input help. In this example you enter a flight code and booking ID, before executing the workflow test by using the *Input Data* tab on the *Test Workflow* screen. If you choose *Yes* in your user decision step, then the booking details of that flight booking will be displayed to you.

7.3.3   How to Create Containers and Bindings for Tasks

When SAP Business Workflow was first released, there was a lot of skepticism about its use of bindings and containers. Surely, some said, it would be simpler to have one global source of data, which the workflow accesses. Simpler—yes, but at the expense of stability, flexibility and scalability. Although it may seem daunting at first, you will soon come to appreciate how powerful the use of binding between containers is. Here are just a few of the advantages:

▶ You can reuse elements in your workflow.

▶ You can make major changes to activities within the process without jeopardizing the process as a whole (or vice versa).

▶ Even when the applications that trigger the workflows are changed from release to release, your workflow is sheltered from these changes.

▶ You can use parallel activities within the workflow without worrying about data reconciliation problems or interference between the activities.

Containers and bindings are explained in more detail in section 7.4.5, but this section gives an introduction to how they are used. All the data needed to execute the method or to display in the task text must be available in the task container. Container elements for the task container are partly generated automatically when you enter a method in the task. The container elements needed for the execution are recognized by the workflow system, and the workflow system prompts you to automatically insert these container elements in the task container. To display workflow data in texts, you create your own container elements in the task container and define a binding between the task and the workflow so that these container elements are filled at runtime.

The task container is edited on the *Container* tab page.

To enable the method to process the data, you may (optionally) define a binding from the task container to the method container. The task object itself (based on the object type entered in the task) is automatically bound to the method container. For other method parameters, the system makes a proposal for the binding that you should check by choosing *Binding Object Method* on the *basic data* tab.

However, it is simpler and there is a performance gain if you do not define any binding between task and method, provided the container element names are the same in both containers. In this case the contents of the task container are matched by element name and automatically copied to the method container (for all elements defined in the method). The same applies to the reverse binding.

> **Caution** The container is only copied for a binding between task and method. For all other bindings you must explicitly define a binding. However, in Release 6.20 you can use the "merge" operator to avoid explicit binding.

Variables used in your work item texts and descriptions are also bound from the task container. To add **variables** while editing your description, choose **Insert · Expression** to choose a variable from the task container. You can add as many variables to the text as you want. You can even add multiline container elements, i.e. tables of data, to the text.

Example

You want to add to your task description some instructions that include the name of the customer.

1. Go back to the task. Make sure you are in change mode.
2. Go to the *Description* tab. Add some text. Put your cursor where you want the customer name to be added, then choose the menu **Insert · Expression**.
3. Expand the container element representing your object type SBOOK (i.e. FlightBooking) and choose Customer. Expand again and choose the CustomerName attribute (i.e. FlightBooking.CustomerName). Do not forget to save your task.
4. Test your workflow again. Notice how your work item description has changed.

To provide your task container with data from the workflow, define a binding from the workflow to the task container by choosing *Binding* (near the task/step name) in the activity step definition. Use the drop-down help if necessary. In this tutorial, you let the workflow generate the binding for you when you added your task back into the workflow step.

7.3.4   Using Asynchronous Tasks

An asynchronous method must be embedded in an asynchronous task in the workflow. A full description of the reasons for using asynchronous methods and the consequences is given in chapter 8, *Business Objects*, but for the time being, just think of them as methods which are not completed until the application itself confirms completion by sending an event to the workflow. From the Workflow Builder point of view, an asynchronous task requires the terminating events to be activated as outcomes of your step. When modeling an activity step, you can bind the results of a synchronous method to a workflow when the method is completed. However, the asynchronous method cannot return information to the workflow via the bindings from method to task, task to workflow. Instead, you define at least one terminating event. You can bind data from the terminating event to the task.

The *terminating events* of a task express the possible end statuses of the task. A terminating event always refers to the specific object for which the event must be triggered. For example, if the work item changes document 123456, then the work item should only be completed when the event "document 123456 is posted" occurs, and not when any other document is posted.

When the work item is created, the WebFlow Engine automatically registers that this specific work item is waiting for a terminating event for the specific object involved. This is called an *event instance linkage* (refer to chapter 10, *Business Interfaces,* for more details). You define the object for which the event must be triggered in the terminating event definition using a container element, referenced to the event's object type, in the task container.

For example, the event DELETED of object type BUS2032 is defined as a terminating event for a task. At runtime, the sales order 123456 is passed via the task container. The work item is now only terminated if the sales order 123456 is deleted and the event BUS2032.DELETED is triggered for that sales order. If another sales order is deleted, the work item is not terminated.

If a work item is terminated by an event, the execution of the workflow is continued by a matching outcome. You must activate this outcome, otherwise the terminating event will be ignored. The method does not necessarily have to have been executed before the event occurs. If a work item is aborted or undefined processing statuses arise, the work item is not terminated since no event is created. Only when the terminating event is received will the work item finish and the workflow continue.

You maintain the terminating events on the tab page *Terminating events*.

You specify a container element of the task container that at runtime will contain a reference to the relevant object. This is generally the task container element _ WI_Object_ID. The fields *Object type category* and *Object type* are filled automatically.

> **Tip** If you are looking at an SAP task in display mode, you can append additional terminating events to the task. This creates an extension of the task definition.

You identify the event by specifying its event name. The event must be defined for this object type. The workflow system creates the event instance linkage required at runtime and activates it. To check the properties of the terminating event, choose ![icon] . The properties of the instance linkage are displayed and can be changed.

> **Caution** If you change the properties of the instance linkage, all terminating events that exist for this task in the workflow system are affected by the change. Above all, do not deactivate the event.
>
> If the event linkage contains a check function module, as in the case of the QM tasks in R/3, then this event linkage must be activated by hand. It will not automatically activate as is the case with asynchronous tasks with no check function module.

7.4 Advanced Workflow Builder—Step Definitions

7.4.1 What Other Step Types Exist?

As well as the step types *user decision*, *container operation* and *activity* shown above, there are other step types available for modeling a workflow. These are mostly used to control the workflow.

Table 7.1 shows all step types available in Release 6.10. The step types *Ad hoc anchor* and *Form* were added in Release 4.6D.

Steps that involve conditions (i.e. logical expressions) may use constants or workflow container elements in the condition, including attributes of objects referenced in the workflow container. The condition editor helps you to create complex logical expressions using the available data. Conditions can include parentheses, logical and/or/not, and existence checks.

Step Type	Symbol	Runtime Function
Activity	▶	Execution of a task or subworkflow. At runtime, data is passed from the task or subworkflow to the workflow container on creation of the matching work item, and vice versa on work item completion.

Table 7.1 Step Types

Step Type	Symbol	Runtime Function
Ad hoc anchor		In the definition, you specify workflows that can replace this step. At runtime, an authorized user can select one of the specified workflows. The steps of this workflow then dynamically replace the ad hoc anchor.
Condition		Depending on the result of the condition, either the true or the false path is followed. In the condition editor you can simulate the results of the condition to make the testing of complex conditions easier.
Container operation		Used to perform arithmetic operations or value assignments to workflow container elements using constants and data in the workflow container. This includes operations on multiline container elements, for example, appending to a list.
Document from template		A PC document is created from a document template using variables in the text which are filled during workflow execution using the workflow container elements. The workflow container receives a new container element that contains the document ID. This is described in more detail in chapter 12, *Forms*.
Event creator		An event is raised. You fill the event container from the workflow container.
Fork		Used for parallel processing. You can define how many parallel branches exist and how many branches must be completed for the fork to terminate and the workflow to continue. Alternatively, simply define an end condition.
Form		A structure-based container element can be displayed, processed or approved as a form. The data is transferred directly from the workflow container and back again. Forms are discussed in chapter 12, *Forms*.
Loop (UNTIL)		A sequence of steps is processed at least once and then repeatedly until the defined termination condition occurs.
Loop (WHILE)		A sequence of steps is processed repeatedly as long as the defined condition is true.
Multiple condition		Based on the value of a workflow container element, one of several branches defined in the workflow definition is processed. Any value not specifically assigned to a branch can be processed in an *Other values* branch.
Process control		This can be used to cancel the execution of a work item or workflow or set a work item to obsolete, so that alternative steps can be taken in the *Processing obsolete* branch.
Send mail		The text entered in this step type is sent as an e-mail. The task required and the necessary bindings are automatically created by the workflow system.

Table 7.1 Step Types (cont.)

Step Type	Symbol	Runtime Function
Subworkflow		An activity that refers to another workflow rather than a task. The subworkflow is called when the activity is to be executed. A binding from the workflow container interfaces with the subworkflow container. You add a subworkflow to the workflow using the activity step shown at the top of the table, but it is represented with this symbol when you inspect the workflow definition.
Undefined step		These can be used as placeholders during development. These steps are ignored at runtime. Undefined steps always have a single outcome.
User decision		The agent is asked a question and given a predefined list of answers. Each predefined answer is a separate branch in the workflow.
Wait for event		The system waits for a specific event. The work item is only completed if the expected event occurs. Data from the event container can be sent to the workflow container using a binding.
Web activity		The selected container elements are posted using the http protocol in an XML or SOAP message. This step can also wait for a message reply. The Web activity is described in detail in chapter 11, *E-Process Interfaces*.

Table 7.1 Step Types (cont.)

7.4.2 How to Insert New Steps

There are several ways of inserting new steps in your workflow. You can either use the step type area, where you can select the step types using drag and drop, the context menu, or the corresponding icon in the toolbar. What you select with the mouse determines where your new step will be placed within the workflow. Table 7.2 gives you an overview:

Where Do You Want to Insert the Step?	What Do You Have to Select?
After a step	The outcome of the step, which is located in the relevant branch of the workflow definition. It is helpful to name the outcome of the existing step first.
Before a step	The step.
As a new branch of a fork	The ⇒ symbol at the start of the fork.

Table 7.2 Inserting Steps into a Workflow

The *My workflows and tasks* tray provides an efficient way of inserting tasks as activities in your workflow. There, tasks and workflows that you have selected are displayed. The selection is made using a search area that provides diverse selection criteria. If you frequently need a group of tasks to define of your workflows, you can put these tasks together in a task group and insert the group into your search area.

Display the contents of the task group in the tray, select the position in your workflow where you want to insert the task, and choose the task by double-clicking on it. An activity step is then automatically created in your workflow that refers to this task.

7.4.3   What Kinds of Outcomes Exist?

There are different outcomes available according to the step type chosen. Some outcomes are optional and others are only displayed by the system if they are necessary as a result of specific settings. Table 7.3 shows all possible outcomes:

The Outcome is ...	The Outcome Exists if ...	Notes and Comments
Event name (terminating event of task)	The task was defined with terminating events.	If the underlying method is an asynchronous method, you must activate at least one event as an outcome.
Value name (possible value of method result)	The synchronous object method is defined with a result for which fixed values are maintained in the ABAP dictionary.	If you deactivate all values of the results, the system activates the `Step executed` outcome instead.
Exception name (method exception)	The object method is defined with exceptions.	Refer to chapter 8, *Business Objects*.
System outcome: `Workflow aborted`	The step is a Web activity step.	The outcome is activated if the step is to wait for an Wf-XML reply document. If the Wf-XML reply has the process status `closed.abnormal-Completed` this outcome is triggered.
System outcome: `Document could not be created`	The step is a document from template step.	This outcome is triggered if document creation fails.
System outcome: `Task executed synchronously`	The step is a document from template step.	Normal completion of a document from template step.

Table 7.3 Step Outcomes

The Outcome is ...	The Outcome Exists if ...	Notes and Comments
System outcome: `Step executed`	The activity refers to a synchronous object method without result. The activity refers to a synchronous object method with result, but no result is selected.	Normal completion of a step.
System outcome: `Processing rejected`	The indicator *Processing can be rejected* is set.	If processing of the relevant work item is rejected at runtime (e.g. using *Reject execution* in the Business Workplace), the steps defined after this outcome are executed.
System outcome: `Processing obsolete`	The work item can be set to obsolete using a *process control* step.	The steps defined after this outcome are executed. This outcome is used to skip steps when modeled deadlines are missed.

System outcome:
`Requested end`
`Latest end`
`Latest start`
	The relevant deadline monitoring is activated and a modeled reaction required.	Within these branches, you model steps to be executed when the deadline is missed. E.g. you can model a *process control* step that sets the work item of this step to obsolete.
		
		You cannot deactivate these outcomes.

Table 7.3 Step Outcomes (cont.)

7.4.4 Containers and Bindings in Depth

Containers are a common way of holding data throughout the workflow instance's lifespan. Use them to interface data between different parts of a workflow and between the workflow and business applications.

The principal containers used in SAP's WebFlow Engine are:

▶ **A workflow container for each workflow and subworkflow**
Only the container elements classified as *import* can be filled when the workflow is started (e.g. from an event container or the test transaction SWUS).

▶ **A task container for each task**
Import container elements are filled from the workflow container and *export* container elements are transferred back.

- ▶ **A method container for each method**

  Import container elements are filled from the task container and *export* container elements are transferred back.

- ▶ **An event container for each event**

  All event containers are *export* container elements only.

- ▶ **A rule container for each rule**

  The *import* container elements are filled from the workflow container (or task container in the case of a task's default rule). The _RULE_RESULT element is the only *export* parameter and this is optional (see chapter 9, *Agents-Determination Rules*).

- ▶ Figure 7.4 shows how the data flows among the different containers in a workflow as a workflow progresses. The *bindings* simply control which data is needed from the source container and how it is mapped to a target element in the target container.

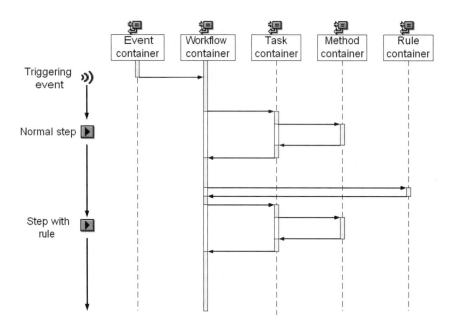

Figure 7.4 Bindings Between the Different Containers

The container holds all data used during execution. The workflow container holds all data values used in control steps (such as *container operation, condition, loop* steps, etc.) and passed from each step to any subsequent steps. The task container holds all data used in work item texts, descriptions, and passed to/from the method. The method container holds the parameters of the function to be executed, including the results of the function. The rule container holds the criteria used, for example, to determine agents. The event container holds data passed from a business application, so that it can be passed to the workflow.

Containers hold named data and object references known as *Elements*. Container elements may hold a single value (including structures) or an object reference, or they can be multiline elements. A multiline element holds multiple values or object references, i.e. a list of values or object references. For instance, the workflow container includes a multiline element for attachments. When an agent creates an attachment, it is appended to the attachment element, so that the list of all attachments created so far can be passed to the next agent in the workflow.

Most containers have standard system elements. For instance, the workflow container has the workflow initiator element. You can also add your own container elements to the container.

Starting with Release 6.10 single value container elements can be based on complex data types containing embedded structures and hierarchies of structures.

> **Tip** In early releases you should generally avoid elements which are structures because these increase the size of the container and cause the performance of the workflow to deteriorate (refer to the online documentation for exceptions to this). However, from Release 4.6D onwards, the structure elements can be stored in their own tables (or XML format from Release 6.10 onwards) to improve performance.

Data can be passed from one type of container to another using bindings. These bindings appear whenever two different types of containers meet. For instance, the workflow to/from task binding appears in the activity step definition that links the task to the workflow. In display mode, only the defined bindings will be shown. In change mode, you may only see already bound items and common or mandatory elements initially. Choose *Show lines* (⬛↓) when binding to see any hidden container elements.

> **Tip** For complex bindings, where simply passing the data from workflow to task or vice versa is not enough, you can use an alternative programmed binding. To reach this, press the **Define Programmed Binding** button (▦) on the binding screen. There are very specific requirements for the definition of the alternative binding interface and code, so you should read the documentation on this in the SAP Library help if you think you need to use this option.

At runtime, the bindings are executed at the appropriate point in the workflow. For instance, for a synchronous task, the workflow-to-task binding is executed as part of work item creation, and the task-to-workflow binding is executed as part of work item completion.

It is worth noting that if you assign the agents of an activity step to a rule, the binding is between the workflow and the rule (not the underlying task and the rule), and the binding is executed just before work item creation. If the rule fails, the workflow can stop and inform the administrator without leaving a half-finished work item in limbo. When the problem has been fixed, the administrator can restart the workflow, and the binding will be executed again.

Depending on the types of containers involved, you may only be permitted to bind container elements with an import or export flag. For instance, to bind data from an event to a workflow, event container elements can only be passed to workflow container elements marked with the *import* flag.

If binding is permitted in both directions (e.g. workflow-to-task and task-to-workflow), make sure you are binding in the correct direction.

Some binding is automatic. For instance, the system container element _WI_ Object_ID[2] in the task container automatically determines the object on which the method is to be applied. Often container elements with the same name in both types of container are automatically passed during workflow execution. However, to avoid confusion, as much as possible you should explicitly define any bindings you need.

Often the system proposes bindings for you. You should *always* check these.

Bindings are optional. For clarity and efficiency, you should only define the minimum bindings that your need. For example, for an activity step linking your workflow to an *Edit Flight Booking* task, bind only the container element holding the SBOOK object reference (i.e. FlightBooking) from the workflow to the task. There is no need to bind the FlightBooking container element back from the task to the workflow because even if you are changing the flight booking details, you are not changing which flight booking is being processed (i.e. the flight code and booking ID will not change).

---

2 The leading underscore is part of the element name

7.4.5 Which Task and Step Attributes Affect Work Item Execution?

You can find the attributes that influence the execution of work items in the task definition and the step definition. You can make the following settings in the task definition:

▶ **Background processing**
Set this checkbox if you want the workflow system (i.e. user WF-BATCH) to execute the work item automatically in background without user involvement. This flag is only available if the underlying method is non-dialog, i.e. it does not require user involvement. The work item will not appear in any inbox, but you can view it via the work item reports or workflow logs.

▶ **Confirm end of processing**
Set this checkbox if you want the user to decide when the work item is complete. As long as this confirmation has not taken place, the relevant work item remains in the inbox of the agent even if the work item has already been executed. The agent can execute the work item again or forward it. You *cannot* assign this indicator for tasks that are to be executed in the background.

> **Tip** Make sure the method is suitable. For instance, there is no problem with displaying an order over and over again, but you would not want someone to create an order for the same data multiple times.

The following settings are allowed in the step definition:

▶ **Processing can be rejected**
Set this checkbox if the user can opt to skip this step. You can model alternative steps to be taken against the matching *rejected* outcome.

▶ **Step not in workflow log**
Work items for this step do not appear in the standard logs, but they will always be displayed in the technical workflow log. The graphical log (fig. 6.4) will not only filter out these steps, but also the outcomes. This means that if a step with several outcomes is filtered out, all the outcome branches and the steps included in these branches will be filtered out of the graphical log, until the point is reached where the paths merge together again.

▶ **Advance with dialog (Synchronous dialog chain)**
If the agent of the previous step is also an agent of this step, this step is executed immediately on completion of the previous step as described in chapter 4, *Work Item Delivery*.

7.4.6 How to Influence the Generation and Termination of the Work Item

A work item is usually generated as soon as the previous step has been completed. However, from Release 6.10 on it is possible to execute the work item dependent on a condition. When the previous step has been completed, the new work item has the status IN PREPARATION. The condition is subsequently checked by a periodic background job until it is met. Only then is the work item set to the status READY and displayed in the workflow inboxes of its recipients.

> **Tip** If a requested start is also defined for the work item and if this has not yet been reached at the time when the condition is met, then the work item is set to the status WAITING. The recipient will only see the work item when the requested start is reached.

You can also set the work item to complete independently of the execution of the method linked to the task by using the *set work item to completed* condition. If the condition is met, processing continues via a separate step outcome.

> **Tip** If this condition is met when creating the work item, the work item is completed immediately and no recipient can execute it; in other words the method execution is skipped.

Each of these two conditions works on the workflow container and is checked by a background job that runs periodically.

Starting with Release 6.20, there is an additional condition to test the result of an execution, and to repeat this if necessary. This condition operates on the task container and is executed once after the method is executed or after a terminating event has been met. If the condition is not met, the work item status is set to IN PROCESS again. The method can then be executed again or it waits until another terminating event occurs.

7.5 Advanced Workflow Builder—Special Workflow Techniques

7.5.1 Reusing Workflows as Subworkflows

Subworkflows can be used to structure a workflow. Subworkflows are workflows in their own right, but usually do not have triggering events since they are only started by another workflow. You can have a workflow call a subworkflow by using an activity step and specifying the subworkflow instead of a standard task. Use the workflow-to-workflow binding in the activity step to pass data between the workflow and subworkflow. You can only bind subworkflow container elements marked as *import* or *export*.

To insert the steps from subworkflows directly in your workflow, you can expand a subworkflow. If there are naming conflicts between the container elements of the existing workflow container and the container elements to be inserted, the system informs you and provides the opportunity to rename these container elements.

If you have a large workflow that you want to split into several subworkflows to make maintenance easier, consider carefully what parts of the workflow will be split into subworkflows. Remembering that subworkflows can be reused in other workflows or multiple times in the same workflow, try to break out logical sections of the workflow that can make the most of this ability. Good candidates for subworkflows include:

▶ Exception handling

▶ Retry handling for background processes

▶ Pre and post decision processing

For example, an approvals process might contain one subworkflow defining the process for making the approve/reject decision, and another subworkflow could define the processing that happens after the decision has been made. If you need to change the approve/reject decision subworkflow you know you will not be affecting the post-decision handling and vice versa. Also you may later want to reuse the post-decision handling in a new workflow that uses a different approve/reject decision process.

One very useful technique, which stabilizes maintenance, is to create a main workflow that simply consists of a call to a subworkflow with parallel branches to take care of exception handling. The branches contain *wait for events* steps so that they are only processed when an event representing the exception is raised, for example by a *create event* step elsewhere in the workflow definition. To a certain extent this is obsolete in Release 6.10 because the workflow itself can react directly to events (specified in the *Basic Data*), but on the other hand, the exception handling itself can be complicated and easier to manage in parallel branches.

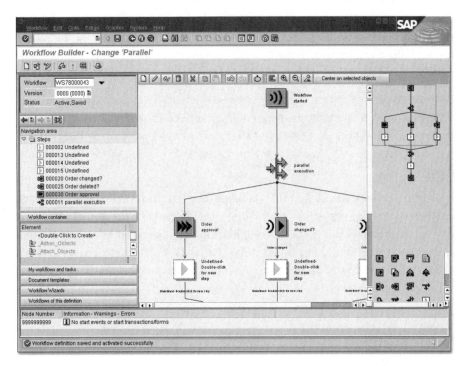

Figure 7.5 Diagram Showing Parallel Branches Waiting for "Order Changed" and "Re-Start Necessary" Events

7.5.2 How to Use a Modeled Deadline?

If you choose the modeled variation as the response to a missed deadline, you get a new outcome, where processing starts as soon as the deadline is missed. In contrast to all other branches of workflow, deadline branches are not joined with the actual workflow. Therefore, it is best only to insert steps here that should be executed for exactly this missed deadline (you can have separate branches for the latest end, requested end, and latest start deadlines).

> **Tip** The time data within the deadline definition normally refers to the time data in the standard calendar, and neither weekends nor public holidays are considered. If you want to use time data that refers to the factory calendar, you use expressions when defining the deadline that refer to a calendar-checking object type that you have created. You can find one way of doing this in appendix A, *Tips and Tricks*.

The two most important examples for modeled deadline monitoring are explained below:

Notify Recipients Via E-Mail That Deadline Has Been Missed

If the notification of the recipients cannot or is not to be implemented as a work item, a missed deadline notification can also be sent as an e-mail or an external document.

1. Maintain the reference date/time and enter a name on the tab page *Modeled*.
2. Model a send mail step in the newly created branch.

> **Tip** Keep in mind that the work item being monitored does *not* yet have the status COMPLETED. The status and agent assignment of the monitored work item are not changed by the missed deadline and notification.

Skip the Work Item If Deadline Has Been Missed

You can terminate the execution of the work item (i.e. mark it as obsolete) if a deadline is missed. This may be necessary if the activity to be executed no longer needs to be carried out or if it is to be redirected to other agents. To do this, insert a *process control* step in the new branch.

> **Tip** You can use the Workflow Wizard *model deadline monitoring* to assist you in the creation of modeled deadline monitoring. Select the step that you want to monitor and choose the Workflow Wizard by double-clicking.

The following settings are required in the step definition of the step for which deadlines are to be monitored:

▶ On the *Outcomes* tab, activate the outcome *processing obsolete*

▶ On the relevant deadline tab page, enter the deadline reference date/time/offset and enter a name for your deadline outcome, e.g. *deadline missed*, on the *Modeled* tab page

Insert a *process control* step in the new branch after the outcome *deadline missed*. In its step definition, specify that the work item of the deadline-triggering step is to be set to obsolete.

In the branch *processing obsolete* you can model alternative steps that are to be executed when the deadline is missed.

> **Tip** A new branch is created in the workflow definition for each missed deadline type activated with a modeled response. Model all steps that are to be executed when this particular deadline type is missed in the matching branch. Model all steps that are to be executed, regardless of the deadline type missed in the branch *processing obsolete*.

Note that when you use modeled deadlines, the recipient for missed deadline is **not** notified automatically. If you want a notification to be sent, you model this in the branch after the relevant *deadline missed* outcome using the *send mail* step type.

7.5.3   How to Implement Parallel Processing

Suppose you have some objects (or values) that can and are to be processed in parallel and independently of each other. This stands in contrast to loops, where one loop does not start until the previous iteration has completed. Table 7.4 compares two parallel processing techniques to help you decide which will best suit your workflow.

Table-Driven Dynamic Parallel Processing	Fork
The objects to be processed must all be of the same type.	The objects to be processed can be of different types.
All objects are to be processed with the same task. This task can be a task with or without dialog, or even a subworkflow.	Each object is processed in a separate branch. Different steps, tasks and even subworkflows can be used in each branch.
All the objects must be processed before the next step in the workflow can be executed.	Not all branches have to be processed (*n* from *m* or condition logic) before the workflow continues.
The number of objects to be processed is not known until runtime. E.g. the list of objects consists of order items, and the number of items varies from order to order.	The number of objects to be processed is known at definition time.
The list of objects is available at runtime in a multiline container element.	The objects are available at runtime in separate container elements of the workflow container.
At runtime, a dialog, background or workflow work item is created for each object in the list. This work item is processed in the normal manner.	At runtime, an appropriate work item is created for each step within the fork. This work item is processed in the normal manner.

Table 7.4 Comparison of Parallel Processing Techniques

Table-Driven Dynamic Parallel Processing	Fork
Deadline monitoring, rules for agent determination and binding can be defined once and then applied equally to each work item created.	Deadline monitoring, rules for agent determination and binding are defined individually in the normal manner.

Table 7.4 Comparison of Parallel Processing Techniques (cont.)

How Do You Implement Table Driven Dynamic Parallel Processing?

Suppose you have defined a multiline container element in the workflow container, which contains a list of values of the same type at runtime. The exact number of values is not known until runtime. For each value in this list, the same task (or subworkflow) is to be executed as a step in the workflow. For example, the materials connected with an order are stored in a multiline container element in the workflow container. Stock is to be checked for each material.

> **Tip** It could also be a list of agents needing to approve an object. All approvals are to be made in parallel. The number of approvers is not known until runtime. (There are a choice of wizards in the Workflow Builder to help you build robust approval processes.)

A multiline container element is created with one data type reference and can therefore only include a list of values that refer to the same data type reference. This could be a list of object references. The multiline container element can be filled with a list of values by:

▶ **Binding from an event**
E.g. from triggering event, to the multiline import container element in the workflow container when the workflow is started.

▶ **Binding from a task**
E.g. from a multiline container element in a task container (result or return parameter of a method) to the multiline container element in the workflow container.

▶ **Repeated binding**
E.g. in a loop, from single value container elements to the multiline container element in the workflow container.

In the step definition, enter the multiline workflow container element on the tab page *Other*. The number of parallel work items depends on the multiline element entered on the tab page. One work item will be created for each value in the container element. If the table is empty this step is skipped.

> **Caution** The multiline container element may have a maximum of 99 values.

The data passed to each work item depends on the workflow-to-task binding definition. The multiline container element values do not need to be passed to the task at all. Usually you process the list via one of the following mutually exclusive techniques:

▶ You use a list of objects with the same object type as the task definition in the *Other* tab page, binding the relevant current object to the task, thus processing each object exactly once.

▶ You use a list of values (or objects of a different type to the task definition) in the *Other* tab page, binding the same object and the relevant current value to the task in the workflow/task binding, thus processing the same object multiple times, once for each value.

If you want to pass the relevant current value of the container element to the work item, in the *Control* tab page define a binding from the multiline container element in the workflow container to a single value container element in the task container. The single value container element in the task container must have the same data type reference as the multiline container element.

You can use the F4 Input Help for the binding definition, choosing the entry *<source_element> with index*. The binding definition will then have the following syntax:

▶ `TargetElement <== &MultilineElement()&`

> **Tip** You will sometimes need a table-driven dynamic loop where different agents process the different work items. For example, you may want different agents to enter the data for different views of a master record. If this is the case, you should start a subworkflow rather than a task in the dynamic loop. Use the dynamic loop binding to pass the subworkflow both the object and the agent involved in the processing so that the agent can be specified in the subworkflow's step via an expression.
>
> For example, `TargetAgent <== &MultilineElement().agent&`

How Do You Implement a Fork?

A fork is used in a workflow definition when several different sub processes can be executed in parallel. You can configure the fork definition to decide whether all branches have to be completed before the workflow can continue.

In the workflow definition, the start of a fork is shown with the symbol ⇥ and the end with ⇥.

You can create any number of branches in a fork. All branches of the fork end in a **Join operator** (⇥). As each branch of a fork reaches this *join operator* at runtime, the end conditions are checked.

To define a fork, specify the number of parallel branches required and the step name. The fork, consisting of the *start operator*, the branches (initially each with an undefined step) and the *join operator*, is inserted into the workflow definition. To define the termination of the fork, you enter the number of branches required (*n*-of-*m*-logic) or an end condition.

> **Tip** You can transfer an existing modeled block into a fork as a new branch by copying or cutting the block, then choosing ⇥ and choosing **Paste block** in the context menu.

If *n*-of-*m* logic has been specified in the fork definition, the system checks whether the number of branches processed agrees with the number of branches required, as specified in the definition. If an end condition has been specified in the fork definition, the system then checks whether the end condition is true.

Once the *n*-of-*m*-logic or end condition has been satisfied, any uncompleted work items of the fork are set to the status LOGICALLY DELETED, and the workflow is continued after the *join operator*.

> **Tip** The individual branches of a fork should be functionally independent.

The *n*-of-*m* branch is particularly useful for prematurely ending part of a process and moving on to the next stage when further processing is unnecessary. For example, if a decision is final when either two out of three users have approved or when one has rejected, you can model the process using a fork. This will speed up the process because you will not have to wait for the third decision before analyzing the result.

If you do not enter an end condition or restrict the number of branches required, the system assumes all branches are required before the workflow can continue.

7.5.4 Linking Workflows Within or Between Systems

The ideal way to link workflows within a mySAP.com component is by using events (see chapter 10, *Business Interfaces*). An event within a workflow is triggered by an *event creator* step to which another workflow responds, for example via triggering events or *wait for event* steps.

If you want to link workflows across system boundaries, you can use the Internet messaging functions. These include:

▶ Sending XML documents to other systems from a workflow

▶ Starting a workflow on another system

▶ Reacting to the results of a workflow executed in another system

▶ Starting a workflow when an appropriate message is received from another system.

Use the *Web activity* () step type to enable your workflow to send Wf-XML messages to other systems. To learn more about this technique read chapter 11, *E-Process Interfaces*.

7.5.5 How to Influence a Currently Executing Workflow

Review workflows[3] are useful when expert opinions are needed (such as in a workflow controlling the transport of dangerous goods), or when several users have a vested interest in the outcome of a workflow and want to be able to follow and influence its progress. Normally, only recipients of workflows and system administrators can influence the flow of the workflow. Other users can only view the workflow log—with a review workflow this is different. The review workflow should include a task based on object type REVIEW and method EXECUTE (passing the workflow ID in the binding). This review workflow's ID is entered in the basic data of the workflow to be monitored. As a result, the graphical workflow log of the workflow to be monitored receives an additional column. From here, the authorized user can start the review workflow. When the review workflow is started, data from the workflow to be monitored is automatically transferred to the review workflow. As well as receiving notification of the workflow to be reviewed, the reviewer can add attachments that can be seen in the workflow being monitored.

---

3 Available from Release 6.10.

7.5.6 Ad-Hoc Features to Change Workflows on the Fly

Usually a workflow is designed in the development system, and changes to the design are not possible during execution. However, the following special features make limited design changes possible even during execution. These are called ad hoc features:

▶ Modeled ad hoc agent assignment

You can insert a dialog step in your workflow through which you determine responsible agents for a subsequent step. The recipient of the work item has the opportunity to select the responsible agent from the possible agents of the subsequent step. The chosen agent then receives the work item. The Workflow Wizard *Include "Choose agent"* can help you model this step.

▶ General ad hoc agent assignment[4]

When starting the workflow, the workflow system determines the responsible agents for the steps using ad hoc agent objects. To use general ad hoc agent assignment, first remove the responsible agent assignment from the relevant steps. Ad hoc agent assignment is then activated for all steps without responsible agents by choosing **Extras · Ad hoc functions · Enable ad hoc agent assignment**, and replacing the default ad hoc agent object AAGENT with your desired ad hoc agent objects in the generated container elements.

The responsible agents of work items that have not yet been completed (or started) can be specified (for example by the workflow administrator) during execution of the workflow.

▶ Ad hoc extension of a workflow

At runtime, you can extend a workflow at predefined places using an *Ad hoc anchor* (⚓) step.[5] This step can be replaced by a subworkflow at runtime. The container definition of the subworkflow must be identical to that of the ad hoc anchor. This subworkflow can itself contain ad hoc anchors. At definition time, you specify which workflows can be chosen to replace the ad hoc anchor.

At runtime, an authorized user viewing the graphical log (fig. 6.4) can replace the ad hoc anchor with one of the designated workflows. The workflow being executed is then extended, i.e. by incorporating the steps of the selected workflow. This is immediately visible in the log. If the anchor is not replaced, the ad-hoc anchor is ignored when the workflow is executed.

---

4 Available from Release 6.10.
5 Available from Release 6.10.

7.5.7 Documenting Workflow Definitions

A workflow definition can be documented in several parts. First of all, you can describe the purpose of the workflow, how it is started and which subworkflows it calls in the description (long text) of the workflow definition. You can document at the task level all steps that refer to a task. Objects can be documented at the object level.

> **Caution**—Note that the task description for dialog steps is displayed in the work item preview, so for dialog steps only instructions to the user should be entered here. Only add technical documentation to the task description if the step is to be executed in the background.

Choose 🖨 to print the graphical representation of a workflow definition. You can specify the size and arrangement of the printed workflow definition in a dialog box.

> **Tip** If you choose 🖨 in the *alphanumeric view* of the Workflow Builder, the textual structure of the workflow definition is printed. This prints what is displayed in the navigation frame.

Choose **Workflow · Print · Details** to print a list of all the steps involved in the workflow definition with their most important properties, including containers and bindings. A dialog box is displayed, in which you define the scope of the list.

Obviously, there is a lot more needed to document a workflow project than simply the workflow definition. The checklists in the appendix help you with this.

7.5.8 Translating a Workflow into Other Languages

You can translate all language-dependent texts that appear in the workflow definition. This applies to:

▶ The names of steps and outcomes
▶ Decision texts and titles
▶ Container element names

A user can use their personal settings to specify whether work item texts and the work item preview are to be displayed in the original language of the workflow or in the logon language (if the text is available in this language).

To get a complete translation, you have to translate the steps in the Workflow Builder and also translate all the tasks used in the workflow in the translation transaction (SE63). Finally use the compare translation function in the Workflow Builder to import the changes into the current workflow version; otherwise the changes will only be visible when the workflow is imported into the next system downstream.

7.5.9 Transporting New Versions of a Workflow

A new workflow always has one version with the number 0000. This version is overwritten by default every time you save your workflow. If you do not want the system to do this, you can generate a new version. Choose **Workflow · Generate version**. The workflow definition is set to status *new, saved*. To avoid increasing the disk space requirements for workflow definitions excessively, only generate a new version under the following circumstances:

▶ If you have made incompatible changes

▶ If there are production workflows running that refer to the current version

> **Tip** As long as you are still in the test and development phase, you do not usually have to create new versions. Every time you transport to a production system, generate a new version in your development system after the transport has taken place (important for older releases).

The system manages several versions of a workflow definition. Only one of the versions of a workflow is the *active version*. Select the active version by activating the appropriate version.

> **Tip** The import and export parameters of the workflow container are not subject to any versioning.

The information tray displays the version you are processing and whether an active version is involved. To display an overview of all versions, choose 🗗 in the Workflow Builder. The version number is displayed on the tab page *Version overview* in the version-independent basic data. An overview of all versions of the workflow definition can be found on the tab page *Versions* in the version-dependent basic data.

A running workflow always refers to the version of the workflow *active at the time it started*.

> **Tip** Even if subsequently a new version of the workflow becomes the active version, workflows still running continue to refer to the version active when they were started. If you overwrite this version while there are still active workflows, for example by making changes directly in the production system, unexpected errors can occur.

If a workflow definition is transported into another system, only the active version is transported. If the workflow definition exists in the target system with the same version number, it is overwritten by the transported version if it has no workflows running. Otherwise, the transported workflow definition is saved with a new, free version number. The transported workflow definition becomes the active workflow definition in the target system.[6]

> **Tip** Use the *output options* flag in transaction SWI1 to view the version number of workflow work items.

7.5.10 How Do You Share Workflow Development Within a Team?

The Workflow Builder offers team-working functions that support workflow development by a team of developers.

It also offers the option to assign a self-defined grouping characteristic to each step. In the optionally displayable *Teamworking* tray, you can search for steps that have a particular grouping characteristic and/or particular change data. The Workflow Builder options can also graphically highlight the steps according to the grouping characteristics or according to the last user to make a change. The last user can be seen on the *Change data* tab page of the step definition. You define the grouping characteristic of each step on the *Change data* tab page in the step definition.

A grouping name can be assigned to every step. Using this grouping name, you can structure the graphical representation of the workflow. The selection field displays all the group descriptions previously defined. One of the group descriptions just entered is automatically entered in the selection field and is also available as a selection for all other steps. You can use this to mark steps that need rework or that are to be transferred to a sub-workflow, or you can use this to demarcate the different logical parts of a large workflow.

---

6 In early Releases new versions were not created during import. Check the SAP Library Help to confirm that you do not need to explicitly create new versions in the Release that you are working in.

8   Business Objects

Business objects integrate the data and functions of business applications into your workflows. They enable SAP's WebFlow Engine to communicate with business applications with all the flexibility and robustness required for a production environment. Whether you are extending existing SAP objects or creating your own, you will quickly come to appreciate the power that business objects give you.

The purpose of most workflows is to bring together related business applications into a cohesive business process. Given the vast number of existing business applications in SAP components, SAP's WebFlow Engine needs to readily communicate with business applications to minimize development and maximize return on the investment you have already made in implementing your SAP component.

Business objects are the main interface between SAP's WebFlow Engine and the business applications in SAP components. This chapter describes the interface and how workflows use it to influence business applications. In chapter 10, *Business Interfaces* you will see the complementary side, namely, how business applications in SAP components use business objects to influence workflows.

This chapter will describe the main features of business objects, giving you a good foundation to use them in your workflows or even to develop your own objects. However, in the interests of space we have had to leave out many features. If you find you need more information, the SAP Library help describes all the business object features, fields, and buttons.

The section on business object basics will help you understand basic business object terminology and concepts that are referenced throughout the rest of the chapter. It will also help you to find, view, and understand existing business objects that you want to use in your workflows, and to identify whether you need to extend them or even create new objects.

To give you a better idea of how the business objects are defined, this and the following sections will guide you through the most important transactions and features of business objects. If you have access to a system where you can follow the examples, you will find it even easier to understand the underlying concepts. If you are the functional analyst or workflow developer responsible for extending or creating business objects, the sections on creating your own business object types and creating object type components are particularly helpful for you. If you are a workflow developer the section on business object type programming is invaluable.

Finally, the section on useful predefined business objects lists some of the more useful utility functions that will save you precious implementation time and provide examples when creating your own business objects.

8.1 Business Object Basics

Business objects give the WebFlow Engine access to the data and functions in business applications.

> **Tip** SAP delivers many standard business object types—over 1100 in SAP R/3. Some contain considerable quantities of data and functions; others only a few. Most are based on business entities, for example `Customer`, `SalesOrder`, `ParkedDocument`, `Material` and `Invoice`. However there are also some utility objects, including `WF_TASK` (representing the workflow or task) and `SELF-ITEM` (representing the work item).

Business data can be used:

▶ In control steps (including conditions, loops, container operations)
▶ In bindings (including event to workflow, workflow to task, task to method, workflow to rule)
▶ In texts (including work item texts and user instructions)
▶ In start conditions used to determine which workflow will be started and whether a workflow will be started (more on these in chapter 10, *Business Interfaces*)

Business functions can be used:

▶ In methods, within tasks, within workflows
▶ In agent determination rules (within programmed rules, refer to chapter 9, *Agent-Determination Rules*) and XML rules (refer to appendix A, *E-Process Interfaces*)
▶ In event linkages within start conditions, check function modules or receiver type function modules (refer to chapter 13, *Custom Programs*)
▶ In secondary, before and after methods (refer to appendix A, *Tips and Tricks*) within the workflow step definition

Business objects provide you with an *object-oriented* view of business applications. That is, they organize the business data and business functions into reusable components that can be accessed throughout the WebFlow Engine.

From a workflow perspective, the main advantages of object-orientation are:

▶ **Re-usability**

Each piece of business data and each business function defined is potentially available to all workflows. More importantly each piece of data is available in the same way, using an *attribute* of an object, regardless of whether data is from the database or is calculated, a single value or a list of multiple values. Equally each business function is available in the same way, using a *method* of an object, regardless of whether the function is based on transactions, reports, programs, function modules, BAPIs, BDC (batch input), CATT, RFC calls to external system routines, etc.

▶ **Encapsulation**

Each piece of business data and each business function is defined once and only once for the most relevant business object. For example, the name of the customer is defined for the `Customer` object. Any workflow wanting to know the customer name accesses the `Name` attribute of the `Customer` object. If how the customer name is formatted or derived needs to be changed, it can be changed once for the `Customer` object and is then immediately and automatically available in the new format to all workflows.

▶ **Inheritance**

SAP provides many business objects with data and functions already made accessible to the WebFlow Engine. If you need to extend these objects (e.g. to add data and functions to them) instead of starting from scratch, you can inherit the SAP-provided business objects to your own business objects. That way your objects can immediately use all the existing data and functions, supplement the business object with more data and functions, and even replace provided data and functions with your own. When your object inherits from an SAP business object, it does not lose the existing SAP objects, so upgrades are not affected, and any new data or functions added by an upgrade are automatically inherited by your objects as well.

▶ **Polymorphism**

Business objects allow generic programming. This is not necessarily important for your own workflows, but it is vitally important for the tools provided to help you monitor and control them. For instance, from the workflow log, you can execute the `Display`[1] method of any object related to the log in the same way, regardless of which business object is involved.

---

1 In fact the method executed is the default method of the object. In practice, this should always be a display method. If your object supports several display views, you should choose the most appropriate as the default method.

Tip For object-oriented buffs, it is worth noting that, for historical reasons, business objects only approximate true object-oriented functionality. Notably they do not have any true constructor/deconstructor methods, and they use an object key to uniquely identify each object instance. However, the general object-oriented concepts of re-usability, inheritance, encapsulation, and poly-morphism still hold true, and so do their benefits.

8.1.1 Business Objects: Some Basic terminology

When discussing business objects, you may be referring to either the *object type* or the *object instance* (depending on the context).

The *object type* is the design and implementation of the access to data and func-tions, i.e. the object type contains the program that reads or calculates data and calls business functions. For example, the Customer object defines the access to all customer-related data, including customer ID and name, and all customer related functions, including "Change customer master".

Each *object instance* is a single runtime copy of its object type that holds the data or accesses the functions relevant to that particular instance of the object. For example the Customer object instance for customer ID "ACMYC" is used at run-time to access the customer name "Acme Incorporated" and the customer func-tion to change customer master "ACMYC".

An *object reference* holds the technical ID of the object type, the object key, and other technical information needed by the system to access an object instance.

Here's a quick overview of a business object type. Each object has the following components:

▶ Key
The key defines each object instance uniquely. For example, for the Customer object type the key is the customer ID.

▶ Attributes
Attributes provide access to business data. This may be data extracted from the database or calculated values. Attributes may reference a single value or multi-ple values. Attributes can in themselves be references to other business objects, letting you set up relationships between objects.

▶ Methods
Method provide access to business functions. The underlying code can be based on any business functions including but not limited to, transactions,

reports, programs, function modules, CATTs, BAPIs, and BDC (batch input). You can even include your own code (e.g. to update custom tables).

▶ **Events**
Events transmit the status change of an object (e.g. `Created`, `Changed`). They provide the hooks for business applications to influence the workflow. The event names are simply defined against the object type; the implementation is found in the relevant business application (refer to chapter 10, *Business Interfaces*).

Object types have an additional component, called *Interfaces*, that are only relevant to design and implementation, and are not used at runtime. These are not interfaces to other systems or applications; instead they refer to the object-oriented concept of interfaces. Essentially, interfaces allow generic programming, partly by helping you to standardize the names used for attributes, methods, and events.

8.1.2 Relationships Between Business Objects

A business object type can have various relationships to other business object types. Relationships between attributes are extremely useful throughout workflow. For instance in a "Fulfill Sales Order" workflow you might want to send some work item instructions that include the name and contact details of the sales person responsible for the customer. If the `SalesOrder` object has an attribute `Customer`, referring to the `Customer` object, and the `Customer` object has an attribute `PersonResponsible`, referring to the `User` object, and the `User` object has attributes `Name` and `PhoneNumber`, you can then refer to `SalesOrder.Customer.PersonResponsible.Name` and `SalesOrder.Customer.PersonResponsible.PhoneNumber` in your work item instructions.

It helps to have a basic understanding of what relationships are possible and how they are implemented in the business object type so that you can make the most of them in your workflows. This is especially true if you need to create or extend business object types.

This section describes the major relationships between business object types including:

▶ Inheritance
▶ Composition
▶ Association
▶ Interfaces

None of these relationships is mandatory (apart from the relationship to interface IFSAP), but using them will greatly improve the consistency, flexibility, and reusability of your business object types, and minimize development effort.

Inheritance

Inheritance is the most important and general relationship between two objects. The object type from which attributes and methods are inherited is called the *supertype*. The *subtype* inherits components from the supertype. The subtype has the same key fields as its supertype, but extended functionality.

For instance, using inheritance you can take a generic object type, for example Material, and create from it a more specific subtype, for example StockMaterial. The subtype StockMaterial inherits all of the components of the supertype Material, but you can add new components and redefine existing components to tailor them for the more specific object. This maximizes the use of existing access to business data and functions, and minimizes development and upgrade issues, since when using any inherited components the supertype program is referenced and no coding is needed for these components in your subtype. The chance of errors occurring is reduced, since common data and functions only need to be defined once, in the supertype.

Inheritance is implemented by creating a subtype of an existing business object type. Usually the supertype/subtype relationship is defined when the subtype is created; however, it is possible to change it later. When creating an object you need to carefully choose its supertype to avoid reworking your object later. If there is no appropriate supertype, you can create a business object without any supertype, i.e. you can create a new business object type from scratch.

You can also use inheritance to extend existing SAP objects to your own subtype. You can then effectively replace the standard SAP object with your own by *delegation*, i.e. by telling the system to use your subtype whenever the standard SAP supertype is referenced.

Composition

Composition is the "is part of" relationship between object types. For instance, the object type OrderItem "is part of" the object type Order. The object type Order is called the *aggregate* type of the object type OrderItem.

In composition, the "is part of" object type usually has an extended key when compared to the aggregate type (for example, object type Order has order number, whereas object type OrderItem has order number + item number) and a completely different functionality.

Composition relationships are implemented by creating an attribute that links one object to another. For instance the object `Order` has an attribute `OrderItems` that links the order objects to a list of related order item objects. Conversely the `OrderItem` object has an attribute `Order` that links the order item object back to the order to which it belongs.

Association

Association is a relationship between object types in which an attribute references another object type via an object reference. The object type Customer is referenced in the attribute `OrderingParty` of the object type `SalesOrder`. An object may have many of these relationships via its attributes. In many ways composition is just a special case of the association relationship.

Interfaces

Interfaces are used to ensure consistency and to enable generic programming. For instance, many objects have a method for changing the object. The interface `IFEDIT` ensures that all change methods are called `Edit` regardless of whether the object being changed is `Customer`, `SalesOrder`, `User`, `Invoice`, `Contract`, `Material` or `Service`. You can then create programs that execute the method `Edit` for any object, and choose the object dynamically at runtime from all objects that have implemented the `IFEDIT` interface. This is clearly much better than ending up with every object using a different method name for the same action, for example, `Change`, `Update`, `Alter`, `Modify` and `Adjust`.

Interfaces are combinations of attributes, methods, and events either without an implementation, or with only a default implementation. SAP provides approximately 50 of these interfaces in SAP components.

You implement an interface in a business object type by including the interface as a component of your business object type. To make generic programming possible, it is important that you create an implementation (i.e. underlying code) for all attributes and methods included in the interface if you do not want to use the interface's default implementation. This is usually easy to do, since interfaces usually contain only one or two components at most.

Every business object supports the `IFSAP` interface.

8.1.3   Business Object Tools

There are two main tools that you can use to work with business objects: the Business Object Builder and the Business Object Repository Browser.

Business Object Builder

Transaction SW01 or **Definition Tools · Business object builder**.

Use the Business Object Builder (see figure 8.1) to display, test, create, generate, change, delete, delegate, and change the status of business objects. You can see all relationships between object types using **Utilities · Relationships** on the initial screen. You can also run a where-used list on the object type to find where it has been used in tasks and workflows.

To access a business object type in the Business Object Builder, you use its technical ID. SAP provides search helps to help you find the technical ID from the object name or description, or you can use the Business Object Repository Browser.

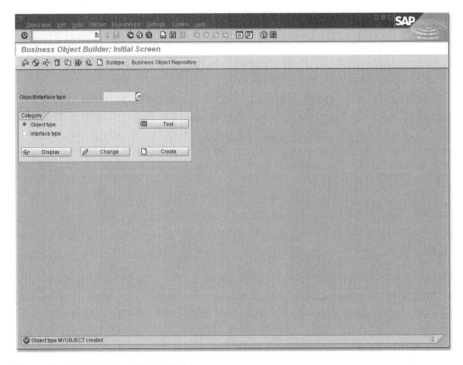

Figure 8.1 Initial Business Object Builder

Business Object Repository Browser

Transaction SW03 or **Definition Tools · Business object repository**.

The *Business Object Repository Browser* (see figure 8.2) presents a hierarchical view of all the business objects available, by SAP application module. Each object type is assigned to an SAP application module indirectly via its package.

You can inspect the definition of existing object types, but you cannot create new object types here.

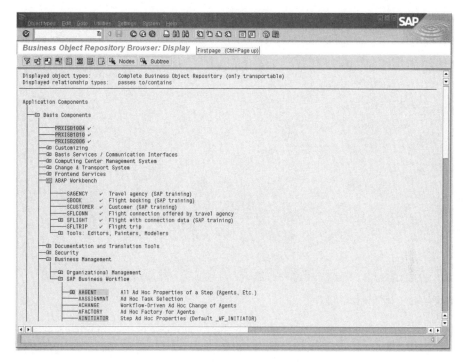

Figure 8.2 Business Object Repository with Business Object Hierarchy

8.1.4 Viewing Existing Business Object Types

To use a particular business object type in your workflow, or just understand what it does, it helps to start by having a quick look at it via the Business Object Builder. To give you some idea of what you will see, we will use a business object type that already exists in the Business Object Repository throughout this section. This object type is called SBOOK and represents an airline booking reference.[2]

If you go to the Business Object Builder (**Definition Tools** · **Business object builder** or transaction SW01), enter object/interface type SBOOK and choose *Display*, you will see a screen similar to figure 8.3.

---

2 This is a training object type that exists in all SAP components. It contains some good examples for you if you are creating or extending object types, but we simply use it here to demonstrate how to view object types, as this object type exists in all SAP components.

Figure 8.3 Object Type SBOOK

Here you can view all the components of the object type including interfaces, key, attributes, methods, and events. You can expand each node to see the individual components. The individual components are color-coded. Red components are inherited from a supertype or interface[3]; white components are local to this object type.

The *Basic Data* ( ) shows you the immediate supertype. You can see there is no supertype for SBOOK in figure 8.4.

You can see the details of each individual component by choosing (double-clicking) the component name. Individual components can be local to this object type, or come from higher supertypes (including but not limited to "parent", "grandparent", and "great-grandparent" object types) or interfaces.[4] You can see which object type or interface the component is inherited from in the details of the component (field Object Type).[5]

If you look at the details of a key field, you can see its data type definition via the Reference table and Reference field settings. By choosing (double-clicking) the field you can inspect the ABAP Dictionary data type definition of the field.

---

3 Bright red is used for interface components that have no default implementation and have not yet been implemented locally.
4 If you are using the default implementation of an interface.
5 For local components, the Object Type field will show the current object type.

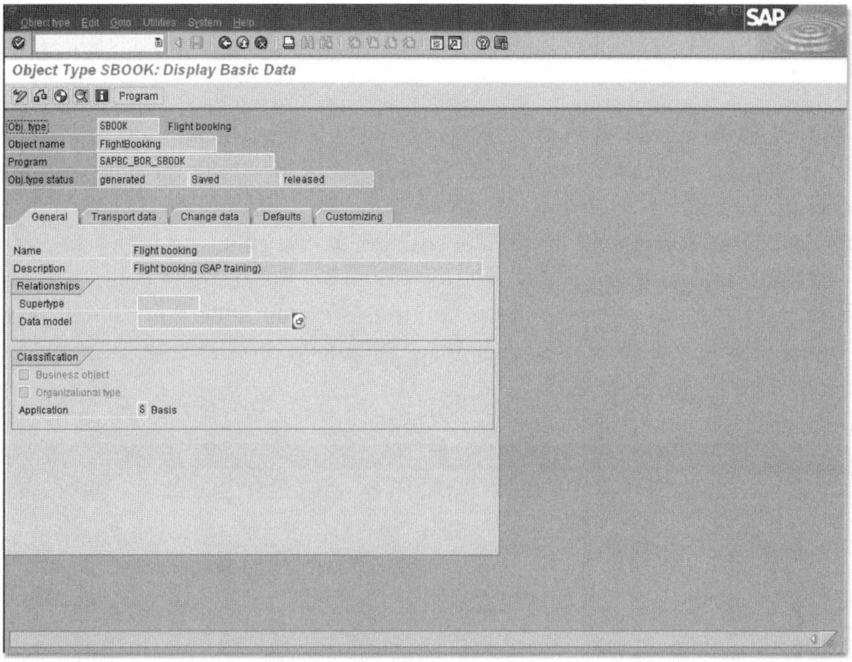

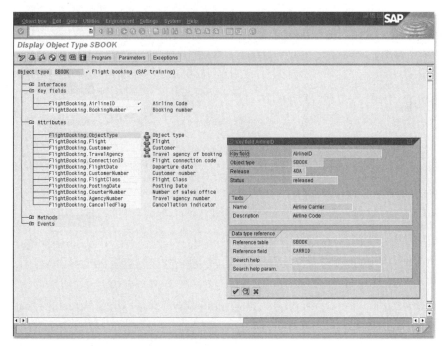

Figure 8.4 Object Type SBOOK—Basic Data

Figure 8.5 Object Type SBOOK—Details of Key Field AirlineID

In figure 8.5 you can see that the key field `AirlineID` of business object `SBOOK` has a reference to table `SBOOK` field `CARRID` (which defines it as a 3-character field).

If you look at the details of an attribute you can see if it is sourced from a *Database field* or if it is a *Virtual* attribute (i.e. calculated). Workflow does not need to know where the data comes from, but, of course, the object type needs to know this so that it can determine the attribute value. If the *Multiline* checkbox is switched off, the attribute holds one value only; if it is switched on, the attribute holds multiple values. The *Data type reference* shows you the definition of each attribute value, which may be based on a ABAP Dictionary table/field or refer to another object type.

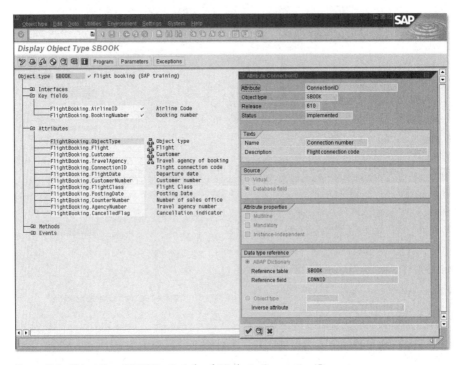

Figure 8.6 Object Type SBOOK—Details of Attribute ConnectionID

In figure 8.6 you can see that the attribute `ConnectionID` of business object `SBOOK` is sourced from the database and is a single value of data type `SBOOK-CONNID` (a 4 byte numeric text field).

In figure 8.7, looking at attribute `TravelAgency` will show you a virtual, i.e. calculated, single-value attribute based on object type `SAGENCY`. If you have access to a system, you can choose (double-click) `SAGENCY` to see the `SAGENCY` object type.

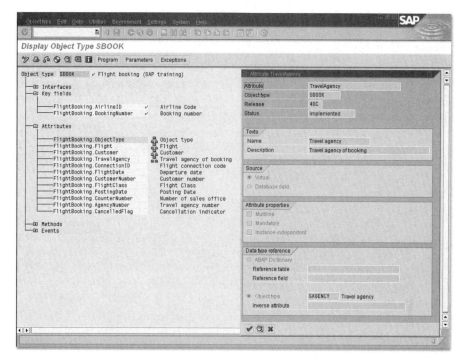

Figure 8.7 Object Type SBOOK—Details of Attribute TravelAgency

Now look at the details of a method. If the *Dialog* checkbox is switched on, the method requires user interaction. If it is switched off, the method can be executed in the background. If the *Synchronous* checkbox is switched off, the method is asynchronous.[6] If the *Result parameter* checkbox is switched on, you will see that a result type has been specified in the *Result type* tab page.

If you choose (single-click) the method name and then choose *Parameters*, you can see the parameters used by the method. You can see that parameters can be *import* or *export*. Import parameters are input criteria used to execute the method; export parameters are additional results that can be returned from the method. If you choose (single-click) the method name and choose *Exceptions*, you can see the possible exceptions (errors) that the method may return. The error type determines how the WebFlow Engine will respond to the error.

In figure 8.8 you can see that the method Edit of business object SBOOK requires user involvement, is executed synchronously, and has no result. If you have access to a system you will see it has no parameters and one exception.

---

6 Asynchronous does *not* mean that the method is launched and the workflow continues without waiting for it to finish. It simply specifies what mechanism is used for confirming that the method has finished, so that the workflow can continue. This is described in detail in section 8.3.3.

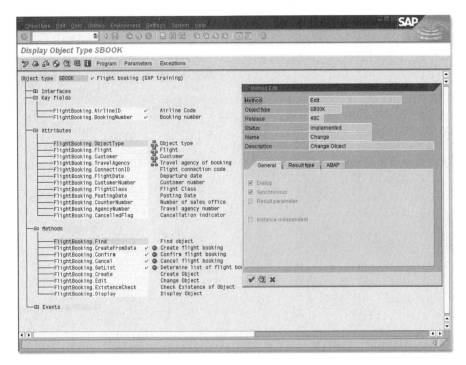

Figure 8.8 Object Type SBOOK — Details of Method $EDIT$

If you look at the details of an event definition, you can see its name. Business applications that want to communicate with the WebFlow Engine can use this name, for example, to trigger the execution of a workflow.

In figure 8.9 you can see the event `Created` of object type `SBOOK`.

To see the documentation of any component, choose (single-click) the component and choose ![i]. It is up to the object type programmer to complete the documentation. Not surprisingly, some programmers are more diligent than others. You do not need to read the object type program to work out what each attribute or method does. The name, the documentation, and a little testing (in some cases) are sufficient.

To see the program code related to each individual component, choose (single-click) the component and choose *Program*. This will take you to the object type program, positioned on the line where the code for that component starts. If you do not choose an individual component before choosing *Program*, the top of the object type program will be displayed.

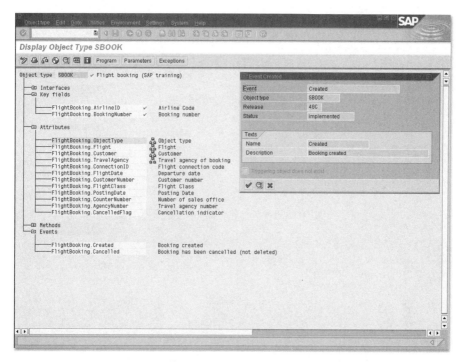

Figure 8.9 Object Type SBOOK — Details of Event Created

Key fields and events do not have any program code associated with them. Key fields are simply declared within the object and are filled when an object is instantiated. The event implementation is coded in the business application, and not the business object definition (refer to chapter 10, *Business Interfaces*).

You can use the *Test/execute* (⬛) option to test the business object type. Here you can create an object instance by entering an appropriate key. All attributes will be extracted from the database or calculated once so that you can check their contents. You can use the refresh option to recalculate virtual attributes. You can execute methods to verify that they behave the way you expect.

If you have access to a system and want to try this with object type SBOOK, go to the *Test/execute* option of business object SBOOK (see figure 8.10). Use the *Create Instance* (⬛ **Instance**) option to choose an existing flight booking.[7] When you create an instance you can either enter the key if you know it, or you can use the input help or the *Find* option to retrieve the appropriate key.

---

7 If you do not have any existing flight bookings, use transaction BC_DATA_GEN to add the training data. Make sure you read the documentation first.

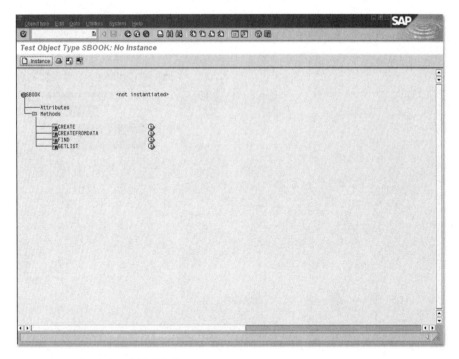

Figure 8.10 Object Type SBOOK—Test

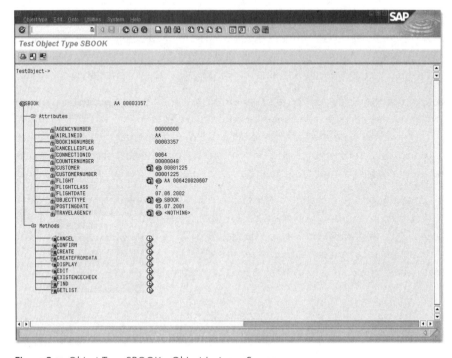

Figure 8.11 Object Type SBOOK—Object Instance Screen

Now all the attributes are displayed (see figure 8.11). Database attributes, for example AGENCYNUMBER, are simply displayed. Virtual attributes, for example TRAVELAGENCY, have a refresh option (⟳) so you can recalculate them. Multi-line attributes show you the number of values held. You can expand the list (⬇) to see the individual values. For any object references shown, ◉ shows the related object instance.

> **Tip** You can do the same thing when viewing the contents of a work item container. By expanding the objects in the container you can view the objects' attributes. This can come in handy when diagnosing workflow problems.

Try choosing ◉ to see the details of TRAVELAGENCY. This displays attributes of the travel agency (for example the multiline attribute CustomerList) and test methods of the TRAVELAGENCY object (for example method Display to show the name and address of the travel agency).

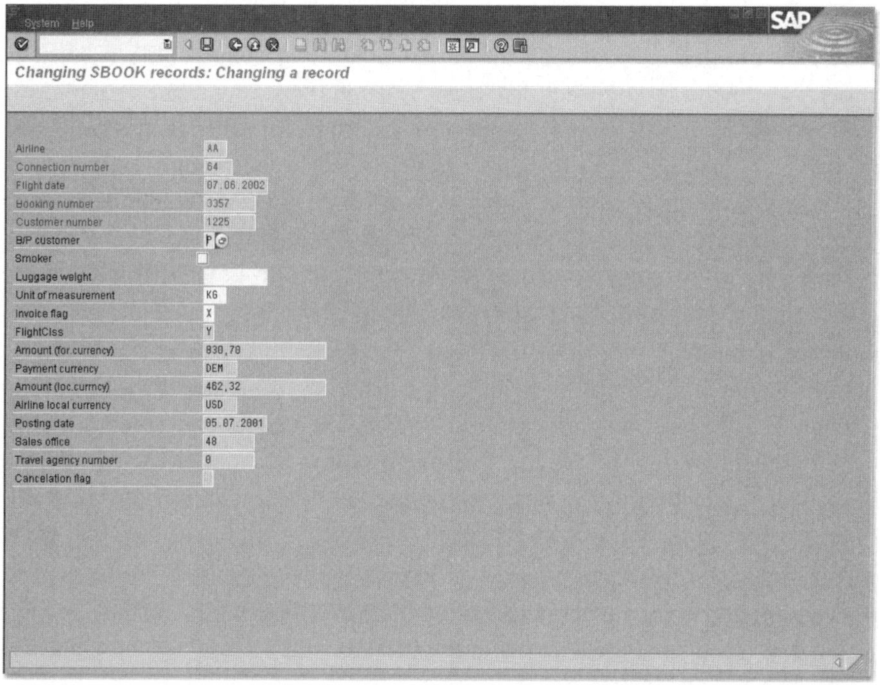

Figure 8.12 Object Type SBOOK — Execute Method Screen

Each method has an *Execute method* (⚡) option that you can use to start the method. Try executing the `Display` method of your `SBOOK` object instance (see figure 8.12). When you execute the method you will see your flight booking displayed.

8.2 Creating your own Business Object Types

Before you create your own business object type, use the Business Object Builder and the Business Object Repository to try and find an appropriate existing object type that is close to what you want. Remember that you are trying to minimize development and maximize return on investment, so it is better if you can use or extend an existing object type rather than creating your own from scratch. At the very least, looking at similar object types will give you ideas and examples for creating your own object type.

Think carefully about:

▶ What object types do you need for your workflow? For example, `SalesOrder`, `Customer`, `ParkedDocument`?

▶ What attributes do you need for your workflow? To which object will they belong? It helps to know a little object-oriented theory here, but a simple way is to think about what is the strongest relationship. For instance, the name of a customer clearly belongs to the customer object. What about a sales order? We might want to know the customer name on the sales order. Simple! Create a customer attribute on the sales order object that links to the customer object. Then you can not only access customer name but also other attributes of the customer object, including address and credit limit.

▶ What methods do you need for your workflow? To which object will they belong? Remember that each method usually performs one activity, so you might need several methods within your workflow. Rather than creating a huge comprehensive method specific to your workflow, it is better to separate the individual activities, so that they can be used in different combinations by different workflows. It also makes it easier if you later want to change your workflow to add additional activities or adjust the sequence of activities.

▶ What events do you need for your workflow? To which object will they belong? When will you need the business application to let the workflow know that the object has changed its state?

▶ Are there any relevant interfaces? For example, if you want to include a change method, use interface `IFEDIT`. If you want to include a print method use `IFPRINT`.

There are two ways of creating a new object type:

▶ To create your own object type from scratch, you can create a completely new object type, using the *Create* option on the initial screen of the Business Object Builder. A newly created object type only has the object type components that it inherits from the standard interface IFSAP, which is supported by every object type.

▶ To extend an existing object type, you create an object type as a subtype of the existing object type, by entering the existing object type and using the *Create subtype* option on the initial screen of the Business Object Builder. The key, attributes, methods, and events of the supertype are immediately inherited by the subtype. All inherited components are marked in red.

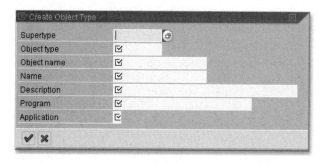

Figure 8.13 Create New Object Type

When you create a new object type (see figure 8.13) you specify:

▶ **Supertype**
If any. This field is optional.

▶ **Object type**
This is the technical ID of the object. Like most technical IDs it must not have any spaces, and must start with an alphabetic character. You do not have to start it with a Z, but it is a good idea to use the usual SAP naming conventions so that you can quickly identify your own object types from SAP object types.

▶ **Object Name**
This describes the object type. Make it meaningful since the name is displayed in monitoring tools throughout workflow.

▶ **Name**
A short description of the object type useful for finding the object type.

▶ **Description**
A longer description of the object type useful for finding the object type.

▶ **Program**

Each object type has its own program. Like any other program in SAP it, too, must be activated before it can be used at all, and activated again after changes have been made. Activating the object type activates the object type program and vice versa.

▶ **Application**

Component, for example S for Basis, M for Logistics.

The name, description and application can be changed later in the *Basic Data* of the object type. If you forget to enter the supertype or want to change it later on, you can change it using menu option **Object type · Inheritance · Change supertype** on the initial screen of the Business Object Builder.

The initial status of your object type is MODELED. A modeled object type is designed but not implemented, i.e. you cannot use it yet. When an object type has the status MODELED you can change the status to IMPLEMENTED. Once you *Generate* (⚙) the object, you can then use and test the object type. If the tests are successful, you can then change the status to RELEASED.

> **Tip** Any new components you add or any existing components you change will revert to status MODELED, even though the object type itself is released. There are similar restrictions on using individual components in statuses other than RELEASED.
>
> **Tip** There are restrictions on using object types in statuses other than RELEASED. For instance, you cannot use an object type that has merely the status MODELED in tasks or workflows.

Example:

You want to create a new object type representing a "widget" which is a particular type of material.

In R/3, SAP delivers a business object type BUS1001 representing a material that has many delivered attributes and methods. By using it in this and the following examples you will see why it is usually best to use or extend existing object types instead of creating your own from scratch.

Caution We have chosen object type BUS1001 for use in the following examples. Using an object type that represents a real business entity gives you a better idea of the benefits of extending SAP delivered object types. However you should be aware of the following:

▶ Most SAP delivered object types representing real business entities have been created and updated over many releases, and their implementation reflects changes in best practice. When you create or extend object types, *current best practice* for your SAP component release level is shown in training object types such as SBOOK, SAGENCY or SCUSTOMER.

▶ Any business object type that you prefer can be used in these examples. For instance, you might want to use LFA1 (Vendor). Make sure that if the object type has a multi-part key, you declare all key fields in the example on creating key fields.

▶ If you are in a SAP component that does not include object type BUS1001 or has no material masters, you will need to choose an existing object type from your SAP component instead. For instance, in an EBP or CRM system you could use object type BUS1178 representing a Product or BUS1006 representing a Business Partner.

▶ You can also execute these examples using the training object type SBOOK in any SAP component if you prefer.

▶ Make sure that whatever object type you use, you have first tested it so that you understand its key, attributes, and methods.

▶ Make sure you have suitable test data available. For example for BUS1001, you need a valid material ID, for LFA1 you need a valid vendor ID, for BUS1178 you need a valid product GUID, for BUS1006 you need a business partner ID, for SBOOK you need a valid booking number.

Finally, SAP delivers tutorials in the SAP Library Help, using the delivered training object types that you can execute in any SAP component. We strongly recommend that you use these tutorials to improve your understanding of the WebFlow Engine.

1. Create a new object type ZWIDGET1 without a supertype.

2. Create a new object type ZWIDGET2 with supertype BUS1001 (material).

3. Compare the two object types. Notice that you have a lot more functionality and much less to develop with ZWIDGET2. On the other hand you have a lot more freedom, although much more work ahead of you with ZWIDGET1.

4. Have a look at the object type programs your two objects by choosing *Program*. Compare them.

5. Change the status of your object type to IMPLEMENTED using menu option **Edit · Change release status · Object type · To implemented**. Look at the *Basic Data* of your objects to confirm that the status is now IMPLEMENTED.

6. *Generate* your objects.

7. Use the *Test* option to test your new objects. This is where you really start to understand the benefits of inheritance, since you will be able to access a lot of data and functions via ZWIDGET2, but not much at all with ZWIDGET1.

8.2.1 Extending Existing Object Types Via Delegation

If you create a subtype of an object type, you can choose to *delegate* the super-type to the subtype. Delegation means that wherever the supertype is referenced throughout workflow, the subtype will actually be used instead. This is particularly useful when you have found an SAP object type that has most of the attributes, methods and events that you need, and is already used in SAP tasks and workflows. By creating a subtype you can extend the SAP object type with any additional attributes, methods or events that you need.

Delegation lets you use all the existing tasks and workflows based on the SAP object type as if they were using your own subtype. That is, delegation effectively lets you replace parts of the original object type with your own, but retain all other parts of the original object type so that you can still profit from any enhancements that SAP delivers when you upgrade to future releases.

For instance, you might delegate the standard SAP object for a customer, KNA1, to a subtype ZCUSTOMER. You have added a new method IncreaseCreditLimit to ZCUSTOMER. This method does not exist in object type KNA1. Delegation lets you create a standard task that refers to method KNA1.IncreaseCreditLimit. As another example, suppose you want to extend the work item description of a standard SAP task. Here you can use a delegated object type to provide additional information (via attributes). If you use the redefine text option (mentioned in chapter 7, *Creating a Workflow*) in the task to add the new attributes, no modification in the Business Object, task or workflow is necessary.

You can only delegate to an immediate subtype. Each object type can only be delegated to one subtype.

To delegate a supertype to a subtype, from the initial screen of the Business Object Builder choose menu option **Settings · Delegate**. Enter the original object type as the *Object Type* and the subtype to which it is delegated as the *Delegation Type*.

8.3 Creating Business Object Type Components

Before creating any object type components, first check to see if there is a suitable interface that you can use to determine the component name. Using interfaces helps standardize the definition of the object type components and allow generic object type programming. Since many of the monitoring tools use generic programming, using interfaces helps makes the most of the monitoring tools.

You can use the Business Object Builder to look at suitable interfaces in the same way that you look at object types. All SAP-provided interfaces start with IF. You can create your own interfaces; however, there is no particular need to do so. When you use an interface you publish to the system that the object type fully supports the methods (with all parameters and all exceptions), attributes and events defined in the interface. Most interfaces contain only a very few attributes, methods or events. For instance, the IFEDIT interface contains only one method Edit.

To add an interface to your object type, choose the component title Interfaces and choose [ ]. You can then choose the interface you want to add to your object type, using the search help to find the interface if necessary.

Example:

1. Add the interface IFDISPLAY to your object ZWIDGET1. Notice how the method Display has now been added to your object.

2. Choose the method and choose *Program* to see the default implementation of the method from the interface.

If you want to create a new object type component from scratch, choose the component title, for example Attributes, then choose *Create*. The technical name of a component follows the usual rules of SAP technical names, i.e. it must start with an alphabetic character and must not contain any spaces.

If you have an existing component that you have inherited, and you want to redefine it, for example to change the underlying code, choose the component name and then choose *redefine* ( ). The component will then change from red (inherited) to white (local) and you can make your changes. There are some restrictions on what you can change on a redefined component. For example, you can add new parameters but not delete or change the inherited parameters of a redefined method..

What happens next depends on the type of component being created.

8.3.1 Creating Key fields

The key of an object type is not calculated or sourced from the database. Instead, it is provided (usually via an object reference) by the calling workflow, task, method, attribute or event whenever the object is used. The object instance, instantiated from the object type and key (i.e. as a runtime copy of the object type created), gives you access to all the attributes and methods of that object.

The key fields of an object type uniquely identify a single object instance of that object type. For instance, the key of the customer object is customer ID.

However, keys can also be multi-part. For instance, the key of the parked document object is company, document number and fiscal year.[8] Never include the Client (SY-MANDT) within the object key. The assumption is that you are always working in the current SAP client.

Each key field must have a reference to a ABAP Dictionary table/field. This is used to define the data type and length of the key field.

Each key field must be based on a single value, not a structure or complex data type. There is an arbitrary limit of 70 characters on the sum of the length of all key fields of an object type.

If you are creating a subtype of an existing object type, you cannot change the key of the object. If you find that you need to change the key of a subtype, then there is probably an error in your design, and you should create a separate business object instead. For instance, SalesOrder might be a subtype of the generic object type Order, since both share the same key, namely, order number. However, OrderItem, which has the multi-part key order number and order item number, is not a subtype of Order, since it has a different key.

Example:

In this example, you will add the Material ID as a key field of your ZWIDGET1 object. If you are not using BUS1001 as your example object type, create the same key fields with the same data type references as your example object type.

1. Change your object ZWIDGET1 to add a key field by choosing the component title "Key" and choosing *Create*.
2. Base the key field on the dictionary table MARA field MATNR.
3. Once the key field has been created, go back to the object type program and see that the object declaration has changed.

8　Normally you should avoid time and date fields in the object's key.

4. Regenerate and test your new changed object.

5. Attempt to add a new key field to ZWIDGET2. You will not be able to do this because ZWIDGET2 is a subtype. Compare the key and object declaration of ZWIDGET1 to ZWIDGET2.

8.3.2 Creating Attributes

An *attribute* lets you access business data based on the object instance. If you want to use business data in a workflow, for example in a work item text or a binding, it must first be defined as an attribute of an object. An attribute is something that is known or can be derived from simply knowing the key of the object, or using other attributes of the same object. For example, the customer Name is an attribute of the Customer object. Customer ID is the key of the customer object. By knowing the customer ID, the name of the customer can be read from the database. Similarly, the DaysSinceLastOrderPlaced is an attribute of customer that can be derived by reading the creation date of the last sales order linked to the customer ID.

Attributes can also be instance-independent. Such attributes do not even need an object key. For instance, the total value of all orders placed by customers can be calculated without referring to any particular customer.

Attributes do not have parameters and do not return results other than their own value.

The name of an attribute is a noun, for example TotalValue, Name, DateCreated, CreatedBy, Currency.

When you create an attribute (see figure 8.14), you must set the appropriate options to indicate whether the attribute is:

▶ Sourced from a database table/field (default) or virtual, i.e. calculated, or an object status.

Database and object status attributes are calculated when the object is instantiated. Virtual attributes are calculated only when and if they are used and are recalculated each time they are used.

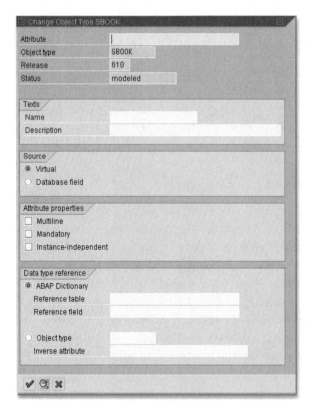

Figure 8.14 Create New Attribute

> **Tip** You will only be able to choose object status if you have implemented the interface `IFSTATUS` in your object type. An object status attribute is a flag indicating whether or not the object is in that status (according to SAP's central status management).

▶ Single (default) or multiline (multiple value). Multiple value attributes are nearly always virtual attributes.

▶ Instance-dependent (default) or instance-independent.

You also specify whether the attribute is based on a data-type definition (based on an ABAP Dictionary table/field) or an object-type reference.

Usually this is an either/or decision; however, there is one special case where you enter both. If the database field also happens to be the key of another object type, then you can define an object reference using a database attribute. You enter both the data-type table/field and the object-type reference, choosing the *object type reference* option. When the database is read, and the field value returned, the system automatically instantiates an object based on the object-type reference using the field value as the key. This avoids having to code the conversion from field value to object instance. However, this only works when the object-type reference refers to an object type with one and only one key field. Apart from this special case, attributes based on an object-type reference are nearly always virtual attributes.

Since database attributes are the most popular, when you create an attribute from scratch the system prompts you to see if you are creating a database attribute. If you answer *Yes* to the question *Create with ABAP Dictionary field proposals?*, the system provides some help in finding the appropriate table/field, then suggests defaults for the name, description, and data-type reference checkbox.

If you want to create an object status attribute or virtual attribute or you already know the appropriate table/field, it is best to answer *No* to the question *Create with ABAP Dictionary field proposals?*, go straight to the attribute details screen and fill in all the details manually.

Object status attributes are always based on the table SWCEDITOR field OBJSTATUS. At runtime, the status attribute returns X if the status is set, and blank if not.

Each local attribute has a matching implementation in the object type program. Attributes inherited from a supertype have a matching implementation in the supertype program. Within the implementation, the attribute can be buffered to prevent unnecessary recalculations.

> **Tip** Always fill in the definition's attribute details *before* creating the implementation, since the system can then propose an implementation for you.

Database attributes which refer to different fields of the same table share an implementation, so that the table is only read once. If you create a local database attribute based on a field from the same table as an inherited database attribute, the supertype implementation is shared. You can declare one attribute as the default attribute in the *Basic Data* of the object type. This is then used to describe the object in all workflow monitoring reports.

Example

In this example you will add a new attribute for "Material Type" to your ZWIDGET1 object. If you are not using BUS1001 as your example object type, choose a single value ABAP Dictionary-based attribute from your example object type, and create the same attribute in your ZWIDGET1 object.

1. Change your object ZWIDGET1 to add a new attribute by choosing the component title "Attributes" and choosing *Create*.

2. Answer "Yes" to the question "Create with ABAP Dictionary field proposals?". Base your new component on dictionary table MARA field MTART (material type). Accept the system's proposal for names and descriptions of the attribute. (If you are in an SAP component that does not include field MARA-MTART, use any other field that is relevant to your object.)

3. Notice what checkboxes and values have been set for you in the attribute details screen. You will see that the attribute ID, name, description, database flag, and data-type reference have all been set for you. Notice that the attribute is only in modeled status.

4. Save your object and regenerate it. Try testing your object. Can you use the new attribute in modeled status? No.

5. Go back to your object, choose your new attribute and choose Program. The system will ask you if you want it to create an implementation for your attribute. Answer *Yes*.

6. Do not change the code generated at this stage, just inspect it. Note that the status of your attribute has automatically changed to IMPLEMENTED.

7. Regenerate your object and test it again with a valid material number. Your new attribute will show the material type of the material chosen.

8.3.3 Creating Methods

A method is an activity that can be performed on an object, i.e. it lets you access business functions relevant to an object instance. If you want to use a function in a workflow, for example in a task, it must first be defined as a method of an object. A method is usually a single activity that can be performed on an object instance. The method may include parameters to pass additional criteria from and results to workflow, and also exceptions to report any errors to workflow.

> **Tip** All BAPIs[9] are defined as methods of business object types delivered by SAP. These can be be used without changes in workflow, although in practice you may want to create your own method as a wrapper around a BAPI to limit its comprehensive functionality.

---

9 BAPIs are standard encapsulated routines provided by SAP, which are accessible from inside or outside SAP components. They are stable, efficient business functions.

A method can be based on any business function or program code you wish, including but not limited to transactions, BAPIs, function modules, RFC calls to external system routines, BDC (batch input) or CATTs. A method may involve a combination of business functions or even call other methods within its program code.

A method name is a verb, for example `Display`, `Change`, `Create`, `Delete`, or `Post`.

When you create a method the system prompts you to use a function module as the basis of your method. If you are not using a function module, it is best to answer "No" to the question "Create with function module as template?" and go straight to the method details. If you say "Yes", the system creates parameters for the method based on the parameters of the function module, and places a call to the function module in the method implementation. As for any generated code, make sure you check it and adjust it (if necessary).

Figure 8.15 Create New Method

When you create a method (see figure 8.15), you must specify, via checkboxes, whether the method is:

▶ **Dialog or non-dialog**
Dialog (checkbox is on) indicates that the method requires user involvement. Non-dialog (checkbox is off) indicates that the method can be executed in background. The WebFlow Engine uses this to check if an agent determination is required and whether background processing is possible.

▶ **Synchronous or asynchronous**

Synchronous (checkbox is on) indicates that the activity is complete when the method execution is finished. Asynchronous (checkbox is off) indicates that the activity is not complete until a terminating event is received (e.g. from a business application).

▶ **Returning a result in the standard** `Result` **parameter**

If the *Result* checkbox is on, the *Result type* tab must be used to enter the data type definition or object reference for the result. The result can be single or multiline. Results are only relevant for synchronous methods. If the result is a single value based on a ABAP Dictionary data type that has fixed values, then the workflow will automatically make each fixed value a possible outcome of the relevant step. This is in addition to passing back the result value itself.

▶ **Instance-dependent or instance-independent**

Most methods are instance-dependent (checkbox is off), i.e. they need an object instance before they can be executed. For example, before a `Display` method of a `Customer` object can be executed, the method needs to know which customer to display. Instance-independent (checkbox is on) methods can be called without an object instance, and may be used to create an object instance. For example, a `Create` method doesn't need an object instance before it is executed, but can return the newly created object instance to the workflow.

You can also use the *ABAP* tab to enter the main transaction, BAPI, function module, or report to be used in the method. This setting is used to help the system propose an implementation for you, but merely provides information after the initial implementation has been proposed.

You can declare one object type method as the default method in the *Basic Data* of the object. The default method is usually `Display`. It is used when viewing objects from workflow logs and monitoring reports.

Example:

In this example you will add a new method "Display" to your `ZWIDGET1` object. If you are not using `BUS1001` as your example object type, choose a dialog, synchronous method from your example object type, and create the same method in your `ZWIDGET1` object. Try to choose a method without parameters based on a simple transaction call. If there is none available you may need to copy the program code and parameters from your example object type.

1. Change your object ZWIDGET1 to add a new method, by choosing the component title *Methods* and choosing *Create*.

2. Answer *No* to the question "Create with function module as template?".

3. Give your method an ID, name and description. Make it a dialog, synchronous method.

4. In the ABAP tab, choose the *Transaction* radio button and enter the transaction ID MM03 in the field Name.

5. Notice that your method is only in MODELED status.

6. Generate your object and test it again. Can you use a method in MODELED status? No.

7. Go back to your object, choose the method and choose *Program*. The system will ask you if you want it to create an implementation for your method. Answer *Yes*.

8. Do not change the code generated at this stage, just look at it. Note that the status of your method has automatically changed to IMPLEMENTED.

9. Regenerate your object and test it again with a valid material number. Execute your new method to display the material master of the material you have chosen.

When Do You Define Synchronous Methods?

Synchronous methods are called, execute, complete and return results as an uninterrupted sequence from workflow to task to method and back again. This means the activity performed by the method must be complete when the method execution ends, including any database updates.

The following are possible reasons for defining a synchronous method:

▶ The function within the method updates the data in dialog mode, i.e. it does not use an update task.

▶ The method is simply to be executed and/or does not affect the database, as in for example, the method Display for displaying an object.

▶ The user may need to call the method several times while the work item is being processed, and the user will manually confirm when the activity is complete.

▶ There is no event that can be used to determine when the activity is complete. In this case you may need to add completion conditions or subsequent steps to your workflow to check that the activity has been completed, and re-execute the method if not.

When Do You Define Asynchronous Methods?

When asynchronous methods are executed, the workflow does not continue to the next step until it receives an acknowledgement that the method has finished. This acknowledgement is returned using a terminating event, which is usually raised by the business application being called from the method.

For example, if you have an asynchonous method `IncreaseCreditLimit` for an object `Customer`, the workflow will not continue until the event `Customer.CreditLimitIncreased` is received. If the agent executing the method (via a work item) only looks at the credit limit, or decreases the credit limit, the event will not be raised and the work item will remain in the agent's inbox. This also helps agents to confirm they have completed the work correctly.

> **Tip** If you want to spawn another process to run independently of the current process, instead of creating an asynchronous method in your workflow, simply use an *event creator* workflow step to trigger another workflow.

Results are not passed from method to task to workflow, but from the terminating event to the task to the workflow. By waiting for a terminating event you ensure that the system is in a consistent state before continuing the workflow, in particular, that any database changes have been committed to the database.

The following are possible reasons for defining an asynchronous method:

▶ The business functions in the method uses the update task to change the database.

> **Tip** Although updates to the database are delayed only slightly by the update task, they can have catastrophic consequences if the workflow continues to the next step before waiting for the updates to be committed. For example, when an object is created in the database in update mode, the next step will terminate with an error if it attempts to query the database reference to the object before the database entry has been written. An asynchronous method ensures that the next step is not started until the database has been committed.

▶ The business function in the method can also be called outside the workflow. You need to know that the activity has been completed regardless of whether it was executed via the work item or directly via a business application.

- The business function called in the method has lots of navigation possibilites, in addition to allowing the task in hand to be performed. The only way you can tell that the specific activity has been completed is by receiving the specific terminating event. For example, the `RemoveBillingBlock` method calls a transaction to change a sales order, where many changes can be made. You can only be sure that the billing block was removed when the `BillingBlockDeleted` event is received.

Parameters and Exceptions

You can also define parameters and exceptions for each method. Synchronous methods can accept import parameters and return a result, export parameters, and exceptions. Asynchronous methods can only accept import parameters; they cannot return any results to the workflow directly. However, results can be returned indirectly via terminating events.

Most methods do not need any parameters—knowing the object instance is enough.

Figure 8.16 Create New Parameter for Method

Parameters (see figure 8.16) can be single or multiline, based on a ABAP Dictionary data type definition or an object reference. They can even be untyped. For example, the method `GenericInstantiate` of object type `SYSTEM` returns an export parameter `ObjectInstance`, which is an object instance. However, the object referenced is not known until runtime (in this case, based on the value of import parameter `ObjectType`).

You define method parameters for a method under the following circumstances:

▶ *Import* parameters to pass runtime data, apart from the object instance itself, to the method. These are then used in the method to perform the activity.

▶ *Result* parameter to pass results from the method. This is used for the main result of a method (e.g. the `Result` of an approve method might be the approved/rejected status).

▶ *Export* parameters to pass results, other than the `Result` parameter, from the method (e.g. the rejection reason from an approve method).

Exceptions (see figure 8.17) are used to report errors. These are useful both so that the workflow can react to error situations, for example by steps that help correct the error, and so that the workflow knows if the method has failed to complete the activity successfully. If errors are reported as exceptions, the task and workflow calling the method can take appropriate action, for example by going into ERROR status.

Caution If the errors are not reported, the method, work item and workflow will appear to complete successfully even when the activity fails! This can cause very serious problems in a production environment (refer to chapter 6, *Workflow Administration*).

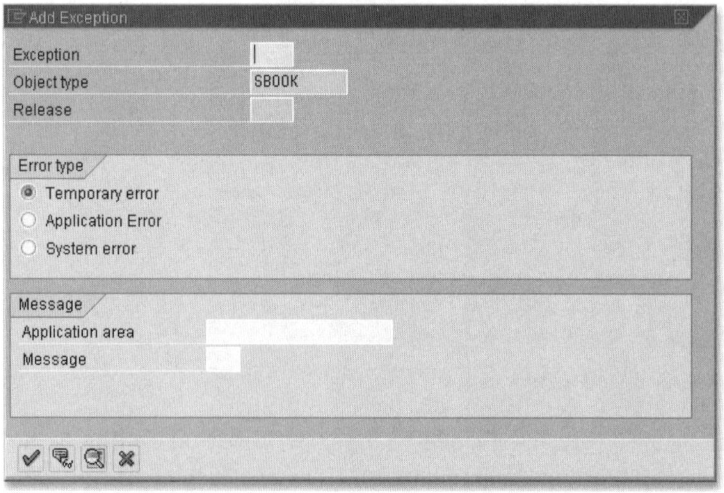

Figure 8.17 Create New Exception for Method

Each exception has a 4-digit ID. Your own exceptions can be created in the number range 9000-9999. SAP also provides many standard exceptions including:

▶ 0001-1000
Exceptions defined for interfaces

▶ 1001-7999
Application-specific exceptions, reserved for SAP development

▶ 8000-8999
Exceptions triggered by the object manager

▶ 9000-9999
Customer-defined exceptions, reserved for customers

Tip The exceptions are not visible in the task definition, but you will see them again when you inspect the workflow step's outcomes.

For each exception you specify the class and number of the message to be displayed if the exception occurs. Exceptions are further classified according to error types. The error type determines the default workflow response to be used if the exception is *not* modeled in the workflow. Here are the error types that you can declare:

▶ **Temporary error**
An error where retries can be made to rectify the problem. Suppose, for example, another user has locked the object or cancelled execution of the work item. The default workflow response is to leave a dialog work item in the inbox so it can be retried later. If a background error fails with a temporary error, the WebFlow Engine retries the method several times, waiting for several minutes between each attempt (the number of retries and the interval between them is configurable).

▶ **Application error**
An error reported by a business application, when for example, insufficient data is passed to the business function. The default workflow response is to put the work item and workflow into ERROR status.

▶ **System error**
This error type shows incorrect configuration of the WebFlow Engine or an inconsistency between object type definition and method call. Missing mandatory method parameters in a call to calling a method are an example of a system error. The default workflow response is to put the work item and workflow into ERROR status.

Each local method has a matching implementation in the object type program. Methods inherited from a supertype have a matching implementation in the supertype program. If you redefine an inherited method, you cannot change or delete the inherited parameters and exceptions that define the interface of the method. You can, however, add further parameters and exceptions.

> **Tip** Always fill in the method details and parameters *before* creating the implementation, so that the system can propose an implementation for you.

Background Method Versus Virtual Attributes

If you have a method that

▸ can be run in background

▸ returns a result

▸ has no other parameters

▸ has no exceptions

▸ does not perform write operations (e.g. update the database),

it is best to convert the method to a virtual attribute. This is better for overall system performance, since an attribute uses fewer resources than a method, and it also minimizes development. To execute a method you usually require an activity step in your workflow, but a virtual attribute can be accessed directly, for example in a container operation. Like methods, virtual attributes are only executed when they are used in your workflow.

8.3.4 Creating Events

Events announce a change of state of a business object. Business applications change the state of business objects; so the appropriate business application must include the event-raising implementation, not the object type itself. The object type merely defines the event name so that if several business applications change the state of an object, they will all use the same events consistently and notify the WebFlow Engine of the changes in state.

An event name is typically a verb, usually in the past tense. For example, the customer object may have the events Created indicating a customer object instance has just been created, and Changed indicating a customer object instance has just been changed.

Example:

1. Change your object ZWIDGET1 to add an event by choosing the component title *Events* and choosing *Create*.

2. Give your event a name.

3. Regenerate your object.

All events automatically include certain parameters within the event implementation, including the object instance and the event initiator (the user executing the business application when the event was triggered).

Events can have additional parameters, which are defined similarly to parameters of a method. When you define additional parameters for an event, you must make sure that the event implementation can fill those parameters. This usually means coding your own event implementation, rather than using generic SAP event implementations (refer to chapters 10, *Business Interfaces,* and 13, *Custom Programs*). Since the implementation is not part of the object type, it is worthwhile ensuring that the event documentation (choose ▮) explains how the event is triggered for the benefit of other workflow developers.

> **Tip** Make sure that you document exactly which mechanism raises the event. If it is raised by a program or transaction directly, include the name of the program in your documentation. If your event is raised from outside the SAP component, this documentation is all the more important.

8.4 Business Object Type Programming

The access to business data and the calls to business functions are implemented in ABAP code in the business object type program. You have seen in the previous sections that the system can help generate some code for your object type program, but usually you will need to adjust or add your own code to what has been generated. It is important that you only edit the object type program via the object type in the Business Object Builder, since the relationship between the object type and its program is very tight. Avoid using the standard program editor transactions SE38 (*ABAP Editor*) and SE80 (*Object Navigator*), to minimize the risk of synchronization problems between the object type and its program.

> **Caution** The ABAP editor in the Business Object Builder is more restrictive than some of the other ABAP editors, so you will need to take a little more care when creating object type program code.

When you generate a business object type, the system performs a syntax check before generating the object type program. The object type cannot be generated until all syntax errors have been corrected.

If you have examined the code generated by the attribute and method examples, you will have noticed that the object type programs use *macros* extensively. Macros are fragments of code encapsulated in pseudo-ABAP commands. They are used to short-cut development. It is important that you use the macros provided for workflow, particularly when working within the object type program, to ensure consistency and to avoid problems on upgrade.

All macros used within the object type program are included in the Include Program ⟨OBJECT⟩. This program is automatically included in your object type program when the object type is first created at the very top of the program using the statement:

```
INCLUDE <OBJECT>.
```

Workflow macros that can be used outside of the object type program, for example by business applications sending events to workflow, or by programmed agent determination rules, are included in the Include Program ⟨CNTN01⟩. Program ⟨OBJECT⟩ always includes program ⟨CNTN01⟩.

8.4.1   Key fields and the Object Declaration

At the top of each object type program is the object declaration bounded by the macros BEGIN_DATA and END_DATA. The object declaration is a complex structure that includes the key fields and the attribute buffer. There is also a private attribute data area where you can buffer intermediate calculation fields that are used by more than one attribute.

Listing 8.1 shows the object declaration that we will use in many of the examples in the rest of this chapter. The table ZWIDGETS is an imaginary ABAP Dictionary table that contains a number of fields including MANDT (client), ID, Widget_Type, Price and Quantity. This is presented as an model example of object type programming, showing current best practice at time of printing. However, if you want to recreate this programming in your SAP component, training object types such as SBOOK, SAGENCY, SCUSTOMER, etc. can be used as a guide instead.

```
BEGIN_DATA OBJECT. " Do not change.. DATA is generated.
* only private members may be inserted into structure private
DATA:
   begin of private,
"    to declare private attributes remove comments and
"    insert private attributes here ...
     accountlist type standard table of zwidget_account,
   end of private,
    BEGIN OF KEY,
        ID LIKE ZWIDGETS-ID,
    END OF KEY,
        TOTAL LIKE ZWIDGETS-PRICE,
        COSTCENTERLIST LIKE ZWIDGET_ACCOUNT-COST_CENTER OCCURS
0,
        OWNER TYPE SWC_OBJECT,
        _ZWIDGETS LIKE ZWIDGETS.
END_DATA OBJECT. " Do not change.. DATA is generated
```

Listing 8.1 Object Declaration in Implementation Program

Provided the object has been instantiated, the key fields will always be filled. You can refer to the key fields in any attribute or method of the object type directly. For example, in Listing 8.1, you can refer to the key field ID as `object-key-id`.

The attribute buffer is used to minimize recalculations. When the implementation of each attribute is executed, it fills the attribute buffer. When the attribute is called again, instead of re-executing all of the code in the attribute implementation, it can retrieve the previously calculated value from the attribute buffer.

Since you do not have full control over when attribute implementations are executed, never retrieve the attribute buffer value of an attribute directly anywhere other than in that particular attribute. If you want to retrieve an attribute value from another attribute implementation or from a method implementation, always use the appropriate macros.

▶ For a single-value attribute use the macro `SWC_GET_PROPERTY`.

   `SWC_GET_PROPERTY <Object> <Attribute> <AttributeValue>`.

   For example, to retrieve the value of attribute Name of the same object use:

   `SWC_GET_PROPERTY self 'Name' namevalue`.

   Make sure that the variable `namevalue` has the same data type definition as the Name attribute. `Self` is a special object reference back to the same object instance.

▶ For a multiple value attribute use the macro SWC_GET_TABLE_PROPERTY.

SWC_GET_TABLE_PROPERTY <Object> <Attribute> <AttributeValue>.

For example, to retrieve the value of attribute SalesOrderList (i.e. all sales orders placed by a customer) from a reference to object Customer use:

SWC_GET_TABLE_PROPERTY Customer 'SalesOrderList' salesordertab.

Make sure that the variable salesordertab is an internal table with each row having the same data type definition as the SalesOrderList attribute. Customer is an object reference pointing to the customer object instance.

▶ All object references, regardless of object type, have the data type definition SWC_OBJECT. In the above example, Customer would have previously been declared using the statement:

DATA: Customer TYPE SWC_OBJECT.

▶ To fill the object reference you can instantiate the object using macro SWC_CREATE_OBJECT.

SWC_CREATE_OBJECT <Object> <ObjectType> <ObjectKey>.

To do this you need to know the technical ID of the order object, in this case KNA1 (standard object for a customer), and the key of the object instance. In this case the customer ID is held in the field customer_number, which has the same data type definition as the key field of object KNA1.

SWC_CREATE_OBJECT Customer 'KNA1' customer_number.

8.4.2 Programming Attributes

Virtual attributes are implemented with program code. The start of a virtual attribute is the BEGIN_PROPERTY macro, and the end is an END_PROPERTY macro. The begin/end property macros effectively create a subroutine in which the value of the attribute can be calculated. You can use code and workflow macros to help calculate the value. The usual rules of subroutines apply to your code. Virtual attribute implementations are executed only if and when they are used in workflow.

The final statement of a single-value virtual attribute implementation will be a SWC_SET_ELEMENT macro to put the calculated value into the object container under the attribute ID. The WebFlow Engine reads the attribute value from the object container.

> **Tip** The container of an object holds all data accessible to workflow for that object, and is *always* called CONTAINER. The object container's contents includes all attributes requested by the workflow, and all parameters passed to and from methods.

The basic code of a single-value virtual attribute looks like this:

```
GET_PROPERTY <AttributeID> CHANGING CONTAINER.
  SWC_SET_ELEMENT CONTAINER <AttributeID> <Value>.
END_PROPERTY.
```

Between the GET_PROPERTY and the SWC_SET_ELEMENT macros you do whatever you need to do to calculate the attribute value. For example, Listing 8.2 shows the coding of a single-value data-type attribute Total, that calculates and returns the price multiplied by the quantity. Price and Quantity are database attributes of the same object; you will see how they are implemented a little later in this section.

```
GET_PROPERTY Total CHANGING CONTAINER.
DATA: price type zwidgets-price,
      quantity type zwidgets-quantity.
  If object-total is initial.
     SWC_GET_PROPERTY self 'Price' price.
     SWC_GET_PROPERTY self 'Quantity' quantity.
     Object-total = price * quantity.
  Endif.
     SWC_SET_ELEMENT CONTAINER 'Total' object-total.
```

Listing 8.2 END_PROPERTY. Example of a Single-Value Virtual Attribute

Notice how the attribute buffer field OBJECT-TOTAL is used. You do not declare it in this code fragment. That is because it has automatically been declared in the object declaration when the attribute details were created. This is evident in the object declaration above. Also, notice that before you calculate the value, you check to see if it has been previously calculated by checking whether the attribute buffer field is empty. That way you only calculate it the minimum number of times and save system resources.

Notice that you only work with the attribute buffer of the current attribute—any other attribute is retrieved using the SWC_GET_PROPERTY macro. You cannot retrieve any other attribute directly from the buffer because you cannot guarantee that the implementation for the other attribute has been executed yet. Using SWC_GET_PROPERTY ensures that the implementation of the other attribute is executed at least once before you use it.

Multiline attributes are nearly always virtual attributes. The implementation of a multiline attribute is similar to a single-value attribute. The main difference is that the attribute buffer field will be an internal table with each row having the data-type reference you specified in the attribute details. Any workflow you create can access the list of values. To write the table to the container, use the macro SWC_SET_TABLE.

The basic code of a multiline virtual attribute looks like this:

```
GET_PROPERTY <AttributeID> CHANGING CONTAINER.
 SWC_SET_TABLE CONTAINER <AttributeID> <InternalTable>.
END_PROPERTY.
```

Between the GET_PROPERTY and the SWC_SET_TABLE macros you do whatever you need to do to calculate the list of attribute values. For example, Listing 8.3 shows the coding of a multiline data-type attribute CostCenterList that calculates and returns a list of cost centers retrieved from table ZWIDGET_ACCOUNT.

For the sake of the example, the key of ZWIDGET_ACCOUNT is ZWIDGET-ID and ZWIDGET-ACCOUNT_LINE. One ZWIDGET-ID may have multiple ZWIDGET_ACCOUNT entries containing the account assignment split for the ZWIDGET-ID. Not every account assignment line contains a cost center, but the purpose of the CostCenterList attribute is to return all cost centers relevant to the particular ZWIDGET-ID. ZWIDGET-ID is the key of the current object.

```
GET_PROPERTY CostCenterList CHANGING CONTAINER.
DATA: account_tab TYPE STANDARD TABLE OF zwidget_account,
      w_account_line TYPE zwidget_account.
  If object-costcenterlist[] is initial.
     SELECT id, account_line, cost_center FROM ZWIDGET_ACCOUNT
     INTO CORRESPONDING FIELDS OF TABLE w_account_tab
     WHERE ID = object-key-id.
     LOOP AT account_tab INTO w_account_line
     WHERE NOT cost_center IS INITIAL.
        Append w_account_line-cost_center to object-costcenter-
list.
     ENDLOOP.
  Endif.
  SWC_SET_TABLE CONTAINER 'CostCenterList' object-costcenter-
list.
END_PROPERTY.
```

Listing 8.3 Example of a Multiline Virtual Attribute

Notice the reference to the object key using OBJECT-KEY-ID. Unlike the attribute buffer fields, the key fields of an object are always available, provided the object has been instantiated, since the key fields are filled during instantiation. Notice also that you can use any ABAP code in your attribute implementation including SELECT, CALL FUNCTION, etc. You just do whatever you need to do to calculate the list of values.

Of course if you had several virtual attributes that needed to read data from the ZWIDGET_ACCOUNT table and they were all used within the same workflow, you could end up calling the database many times to get the same data. There are a few ways you can improve resource usage:

▶ In the ABAP Dictionary, buffer ZWIDGET_ACCOUNT to minimize the direct reads from the database.

▶ Use database attributes instead of virtual attributes, since database attributes share the implementation (a SELECT from the database). Of course this is usually useful only when the attributes are single-value and are taken directly from fields on the table.

▶ Use a subroutine to read the data once and store it in the private object buffer. This way, every subsequent read of the data retrieves the data from the private object buffer.

You will read more on database attribute implementations shortly, so in Listing 8.4 the CostCenterList example is recoded so that other attributes can also use the same ZWIDGET_ACCOUNT data from the private object buffer.

```
GET_PROPERTY CostCenterList CHANGING CONTAINER.
DATA: account_tab TYPE STANDARD TABLE OF zwidget_account,
      w_account_line TYPE zwidget_account.
  If object-costcenterlist[] is initial.
     Perform get_zwidget_account using account_tab.
     LOOP AT account_tab INTO w_account_line
      WHERE NOT cost_center IS INITIAL.
       Append w_account_line-cost_center to object-costcenter-
list.
     ENDLOOP.
```

```
  Endif.
  SWC_SET_TABLE CONTAINER 'CostCenterList' object-costcenter-
list.
END_PROPERTY.
FORM GET_ZWIDGET_ACCOUNT USING P_ACCOUNT_TAB.
  If object-private-accountlist[] is initial.
    SELECT * FROM ZWIDGET_ACCOUNT
     INTO TABLE object-private-accountlist
     WHERE ID = object-key-id.
  Endif.
  P_account_tab = object-private-accountlist.
ENDFORM.
```

Listing 8.4 Example of Using the Private Object Buffer

The single and multiline examples so far have shown how to implement attributes with ABAP Dictionary data-type references, but of course you can also have an attribute that contains an object reference. The code used to implement an attribute based on an object reference is essentially the same, except that the data type of the object reference is always SWC_OBJECT (you can see the automatically generated declaration of owner in the object declaration above) and the object reference is filled with a reference to an object instance instead of a value. The object instance can be created using macro SWC_CREATE_OBJECT.

The example in Listing 8.5 shows how to implement an attribute Owner holding a single object reference to the object type User. The owner is the user responsible for widgets of a particular type and price. The key of User is a user ID with data type USR01-BNAME.

```
GET_PROPERTY Owner CHANGING CONTAINER.
DATA: widget_type type zwidgets-widget_type,
      price type zwidgets-price,
      owner type usr01-bname.
  If object-owner is initial.
    SWC_GET_PROPERTY self 'Price' price.
    SWC_GET_PROPERTY self 'Widget_Type' widget_type.
    CALL FUNCTION 'Z_FIND_OWNER'
      EXPORTING
       'Price = price
        Type  = widget_type
      IMPORTING
        Owner = owner
```

```
      EXCEPTIONS
          Others = 1.
      If sy-subrc eq 0.
          SWC_CREATE_OBJECT object-owner 'User' owner.
      Endif.
   Endif.
   SWC_SET_ELEMENT CONTAINER 'Owner' object-owner.
END_PROPERTY.
```

Listing 8.5 Example of an Object Reference Virtual Attribute

Notice that the main difference between this and the `Total` attribute implementation is simply the creation of the object reference. In a multiline attribute based on an object reference, each row of the attribute's internal table is an object reference and the object reference is created in the same way. Notice also that you call a function module from an attribute in exactly the same way as you would in any other ABAP program.

Database attributes whose data-type reference shows they belong to the same table share an implementation, i.e. there is one implementation per table rather than one implementation per field. This is to minimize resource usage so that each of these tables is read only once when an object is instantiated. The start of the shared database attribute implementation is the `GET_TABLE_PROPERTY` macro, and the end is the `END_PROPERTY` macro.

```
GET_TABLE_PROPERTY <Tablename>.
END_PROPERTY.
```

The begin/end table property macros effectively create a subroutine in which the value of all database attributes using the same table can be calculated. When you create the database attribute details and choose Program, something like the following implementation is generated (or will be displayed if it has already been generated). In Listing 8.6 is the implementation that you would create to implement the Type, Price, and Quantity database attributes that come from table ZWIDGETS.

```
TABLES: zwidgets.
*
GET_TABLE_PROPERTY ZWIDGETS.
DATA subrc LIKE sy-subrc.
PERFORM select_table_zwidgets USING subrc.
IF sy-subrc ne 0.
  Exit_object_not_found.
```

```
Endif.
END_PROPERTY.
*

FORM select_table_zwidgets USING subrc LIKE sy-subrc.
  If object-_zwidgets-mandt is initial
  And object-_zwidgets-id is initial.
      SELECT SINGLE * FROM ZWIDGETS CLIENT SPECIFIED
        WHERE mandt = sy-mandt
          AND id = object-key-id.
      Subrc = sy-subrc.
      If subrc ne 0. exit. Endif.
      Object-_zwidgets = zwidgets.
  Else.
      Subrc = 0.
      Zwidgets = object-_zwidgets.
  Endif.
ENDFORM.
```

Listing 8.6 Example implementation of Database Attributes

The macro EXIT_OBJECT_NOT_FOUND sends an exception, i.e. an error message, "Object does not exist" to workflow. This tells workflow that the ID of the widget is invalid, or that something is seriously wrong or inconsistent in the database.

Notice the special use of the TABLES statement (remember the TABLES statement is mostly deprecated throughout other ABAP code). Instead of putting the attributes into the container, you fill the TABLES work area ZWIDGETS with the data, and the WebFlow Engine retrieves it from here. This is unique to database attributes. Otherwise the use of the attribute buffer and the calculation of the values is much the same as any other attribute.

> **Tip** You can replace the generated code with your own, but you must make sure when implementing database attributes that all table fields used in the data-type reference of all of the database attributes in this object *and* its subtypes are filled. You saw when creating attribute details that a database attribute created in a subtype shares the database attribute implementation in the supertype if the supertype already has a database attribute implementation for the relevant table.

8.4.3 Programming Methods

Methods have one implementation per method. The start of a method implementation is the macro BEGIN_METHOD and the end is macro END_METHOD. The begin/end method macros create, in effect, a subroutine in which the appropriate business functions can be called. The basic implementation of a method looks like this:

```
BEGIN_METHOD <MethodID> CHANGING CONTAINER.
END_METHOD.
```

Between the begin/end method macros you do whatever you need to do to call the desired business functions.

> **Tip** Make sure you define the method details and any parameters and exceptions before you create the method implementation. This enables the Business Object Builder to generate not just the start and end of the method but also the macro code to read import parameters from the container at the start of the method. In addition it copies the result/export parameters into the container at the end of the method.

Listing 8.7 shows an example of a dialog-type (i.e. requiring user involvement), synchronous method called Display that calls a transaction ZWIDGET_DIS. The method is synchronous because it does not involve any database changes. This method does not use any parameters or exceptions.

```
BEGIN_METHOD display CHANGING CONTAINER.
  SET PARAMETER ID 'ZWIDGET' FIELD object-key-id.
  CALL TRANSACTION 'ZWIDGET_DIS' AND SKIP FIRST SCREEN.
END_METHOD.
```

Listing 8.7 Dialog Synchronous Method Calling a Transaction

Notice in Listing 8.7 that methods access attributes in the same way that attributes access other attributes, either using the attribute buffer for the key fields, for example OBJECT-KEY-ID, or using the SWC_GET_PROPERTY macro for any other attribute.

The call to the transaction is made with a CALL TRANSACTION statement exactly the same way you would call a transaction from any other program.

Listing 8.8 shows an example of a dialog-type, asynchronous method called `Edit` that calls a transaction `ZWIDGET_CHG`. The method is asynchronous because `ZWIDGET_CHG`, like most SAP transactions, uses `UPDATE TASK` to update the database. This method does not use any parameters or exceptions.

```
BEGIN_METHOD edit CHANGING CONTAINER.
  SET PARAMETER ID 'ZWIDGET' FIELD object-key-id.
  CALL TRANSACTION 'ZWIDGET_CHG' AND SKIP FIRST SCREEN.
END_METHOD.
```

Listing 8.8 Dialog Asynchronous Method Calling a Transaction

Notice in Listing 8.8 that marking a method as synchronous or asynchronous does not necessarily affect the code you use to implement a method; it simply affects how the work item that calls the method will be completed. In the above example, transaction `ZWIDGET_CHG` would be responsible for sending a terminating event `ZWIDGET.Changed` to the task calling this method when the database update was complete, for instance by using change document event creation. You will see how business applications send events in chapter 10, *Business Interfaces*. The work item will not complete until the terminating event is received. Calling transactions is usually reserved for dialog methods, where essentially all workflow needs to do is to take the agent to the transaction where the user can complete the business activity.

Background methods usually call function modules or BAPIs where the business activity is performed automatically without any user involvement. Usually function modules require some sort of parameter input to complete the activity. You use macro `SWC_GET_ELEMENT` to retrieve single-value parameters from the container, and macro `SWC_GET_TABLE` for multiline parameters.

```
SWC_GET_ELEMENT <Container> <ParameterID> <Value>.
SWC_GET_TABLE CONTAINER <ParameterID> <InternalTable>.
```

Listing 8.9 shows an example of a background, synchronous `Delete` method that uses a BAPI to perform the deletion. The BAPI requires an import parameter `AuthorisedBy` to receive (via bindings from workflow to task and task to method) the name of the person who authorized the deletion, as well as the `ZWIDGET-ID` to be deleted.

Workflow will pass the user ID of the person who authorized the deletion in the import parameter `AuthAgent`, a single-value parameter with data-type reference `USR01-BNAME`. The method will find the name of the authorizing agent from the attribute `Name` of object type `User`, instantiated using the user ID passed in the `AuthAgent` parameter.

```
BEGIN_METHOD delete CHANGING CONTAINER.
Data: authagent type usr01-bname,
      authoriser type swc_object,
      authname type addr3_val-name_text.
  SWC_GET_ELEMEMT CONTAINER 'AuthAgent' authagent.
  SWC_CREATE_OBJECT authoriser 'User' authagent.
  SWC_GET_PROPERTY authoriser 'Name' authname.
  CALL FUNCTION 'BAPI_ZWIDGET_DELETE'
  EXPORTING
    ID = object-key-id
    AuthorisedBy = authname
  EXCEPTIONS
    Others = 1.
```

Listing 8.9 END_METHOD. Background Synchronous Method Using a BAPI

Notice that methods create object references and retrieve attribute values just as you saw in the attribute implementations, and they call function modules in the same way that they are called in any other ABAP program.

There is one major problem with the above method. If anything goes wrong with the activity, the WebFlow Engine will not be notified. It will complete normally, since everything was apparently successful. Methods that do not return errors can be a very serious problem from a business perspective. Not only do they let a business process abort in midstream—they also make it extremely difficult to find out what went wrong when everything in the workflow log states that the method has been successful. Thus, it is important to have some way of detecting these errors within your method, for example using the exceptions returned by function modules or the MESSAGES option of a CALL TRANSACTION USING statement. Alternatively, you could make the method asynchronous and use a terminating event to confirm that the business function called was successful.

You could improve this method by reporting any errors. Two major errors could occur. Firstly, the AuthAgent might not be a valid user. Secondly, the deletion itself may have failed, for example due to someone locking the ZWIDGETS table entry. The exceptions would need to be defined within the method details, in the *Exceptions* section of the method, before they can be used.

Each exception has a 4-digit number, for example 9001, that is linked to the message class and message number to be displayed, and also an error type (Temporary, Application, or System error) that helps the workflow to decide on how to handle the error. To send an exception to workflow, you use the macro EXIT_ RETURN, specifying the exception number and the parameters for the message.

Messages have a maximum of 4 parameters (SY-MSGV1 to SY-MSGV4) and the macro requires that you always send 4 parameters, so for any unused parameter you simply use the reserved word SPACE.

EXIT_RETURN <Exception> <Var1> <Var2> <Var3> <Var4>.

In the example in Listing 8.10 below you are reporting system exception 9001 (AuthAgent &1 does not exist) and temporary exception 9002 (Widget &1 could not be deleted).

```
BEGIN_METHOD delete CHANGING CONTAINER.
Data: authagent type usr01-bname,
      authoriser type swc_object,
      authname type addr3_val-name_text.
  SWC_GET_ELEMEMT CONTAINER 'AuthAgent' authagent.
  SWC_CREATE_OBJECT authoriser 'User' authagent.
  If sy-subrc ne 0.
    EXIT_RETURN 9001 authagent SPACE SPACE SPACE.
  Endif.
  SWC_GET_PROPERTY authoriser 'Name' authname.
  CALL FUNCTION 'BAPI_ZWIDGET_DELETE'
  EXPORTING
    ID = object-key-id
    AuthorisedBy = authname
  EXCEPTIONS
    Others = 1.
  If sy-subrc ne 0.
    EXIT_RETURN 9002 object-key-id SPACE SPACE SPACE.
  Endif.
END_METHOD.
```

Listing 8.10 Implementation of Exceptions

Notice that the error type of the exception does not affect the implementation.

As with function module exceptions, when you send a method exception no result or export parameters are sent, so use exceptions only for error or abort situations. Workflow can respond to the error by either retrying the work item at a later time, putting the work item into ERROR status, or performing alternative steps in the workflow, depending on the error type and whether the exception has been modeled in the workflow.

Methods can also return results in export parameters or in the special `Result` parameter. The result parameter and any export parameters must be defined in the method details before using them in the method. To return results to the container you use macro `SWC_SET_ELEMENT` for single values and `SWC_SET_TABLE` for multiline parameters.

```
SWC_SET_ELEMENT <Container> <ParameterID> <Value>.
SWC_SET_TABLE CONTAINER <ParameterID> <InternalTable>.
```

Listing 8.11 shows an example of a dialog, synchronous `ApproveDeletion` method that returns a result of 0 'approved' or 1 'rejected', and if rejected also returns an export parameter `RejectionReason`.

```
BEGIN_METHOD approvedeletion CHANGING CONTAINER.
Data: approvalstate type syst-index,
      rejreason type zwidget-text.
  Clear rejreason.
  CALL FUNCTION 'BAPI_ZWIDGET_APPROVEDELETE'
  EXPORTING
    ID = object-key-id
  IMPORTING
    Approvalstate = approvalstate
    Rejection_text = rejreason
  EXCEPTIONS
    Cancelled = 1
    Others = 2.
  Case sy-subrc.
    When 0.
      SWC_SET_ELEMENT CONTAINER RESULT approvalstate.
      SWC_SET_ELEMEMT CONTAINER 'RejectionReason' rejreason.
    When 1.
      EXIT_CANCELLED.
    Others.
* Send exception "approval failed"
      EXIT_RETURN 9003 object-key-id SPACE SPACE SPACE.
  Endcase.
END_METHOD.
```

Listing 8.11 Dialog Synchronous Method with Result

The special variable RESULT ensures that the result is returned with the special predefined parameter name _RESULT.

Notice the special exception EXIT_CANCELLED, which is used to tell workflow that the user has opted not to complete the activity at this time. By default the workflow will keep the work item in the agent's inbox in IN PROCESS status so that the agent can complete the activity later. Like any other exception, you can also model alternative steps to be taken if this exception is received.

If you are implementing an instance-independent method that returns an object reference to an instance of the current object type instead of a parameter you use macro SWC_SET_OBJECTKEY.

SWC_SET_OBJECTKEY <ObjectKey>.

Sometimes you might want to call a method to help calculate an attribute or within another method. To do this you use the macro SWC_CALL_METHOD.

SWC_CALL_METHOD <Object> <Method> <Container>.

You can use the macros SWC_SET_ELEMENT and SWC_SET_TABLE to fill the import parameters of the method to be called in the container, and the macros SWC_GET_ELEMENT and SWC_GET_TABLE to read export parameters and results after the method is executed. If you want to create a separate temporary container just for calling the method to avoid putting stray data in the current object container, you can use macro SWC_CONTAINER to declare it and SWC_CREATE_CONTAINER to initialize it.

You will find a list of common workflow macros in the appendix.

8.5 Some useful predefined Object Types

8.5.1 Object Type SELFITEM

The object type SELFITEM provides methods that operate on a work item that represents its own task. When you execute the work item, the object on which the method operates is this work item itself. This is chiefly useful when you want to send an e-mail using the method SendTaskDescription, or for manipulating attachments. All attachments must be objects of the type SOFM. Useful methods of SELFITEM include:

▶ SendTaskDescription
The task description is sent as a mail in background. If the mail cannot be sent the method will report this with an exception.

▶ PrintTaskDescrBatch
Printing a task description in the background to a nominated printer.

▶ PrintTaskDescrDialog
Printing a task description in dialog. The agent is asked to supply the print parameters, including the printer to be used.

▶ Note_Create
A document is created and then added to the work item as an attachment. The agent is prompted either to create the document or to import it from a document on their local file system or from an SAP Office folder.

▶ Note_Display
Displaying an attachment. Most inboxes allow you to optionally display attachments. You can use this method to force the display of an attachment to an agent.

▶ Note_Change
Changing an attachment.

> **Tip** The SELFITEM object cannot be delegated. This is the only object type in the system that is prevented by the system from being delegated. However, you may delegate derivitives lower down the hierarchy.

8.5.2 Object Type WF_TASK

The object type WF_TASK provides methods for finding and assigning agents for steps in the workflow. An object of the type WF_TASK is a task specified with type (for example TS for standard task) and number (eight digits).

The most useful attribute of WF_TASK is AllAgentsOfTask. This returns a list of all possible agents assigned to a task.

The most useful method of WF_TASK is AllAgentsOfTaskGetAndDispatch. This lets an agent dynamically decide who will be the agent for a subsequent step, from a list of all possible agents of the task underlying the subsequent step. The Workflow Builder wizard *Choose Agent* uses this method.

8.5.3 Object type SYSTEM

Object type SYSTEM holds a few useful utility methods including GenericInstantiate. Creates an object reference from an object type and its matching key. The parameters are untyped, so you can use this to create any object reference.

8.5.4   Object Type FORMABSENC

This object type provides an absence notification example of a business applica-tion object. It is also used in the many SAP-supplied demonstration workflows and in the SAP Library workflow tutorials (**Reference Documentation · Tutorials**).

8.5.5   Object type USR01

Object type USR01 represents a user. It includes a very useful method FindUser-FromAgentStructure. This an agent and converts it to a user object (object type USR01). You can then access attributes of the user including name and contact details.

> **Tip**   This object type is often included as an attribute in other object types, for example DialogItem. So by delegating to extend it, you automatically make your extensions (for example you might add the e-mail address of the user) available to all other object types and workflows within the system without even editing them. Even the SAP-supplied workflows will have access to your extension.

9 Agent-Determination Rules

Determining the responsible agents for a work item is one of the most important and interesting parts of workflow development. Agent determination rules can use a number of different techniques. Some have dedicated maintenance transactions while others require programming. This chapter explains the different techniques that you can use.

You have seen in chapter 5, *Agents*, that selected agents are a subset of the possible agents assigned to a task. Possible agents provide security over tasks and are in essence a relatively static list of everyone who is allowed to execute work items belonging to a particular task. The set of selected agents determines who will receive the work item initially. That is, selected agents are your company's chosen decision-makers for a particular work item. Since the selected agents will vary for each work item, depending on the data relevant to the particular work item or workflow instance, a static list is not enough. Instead, agent-determination rules are needed to assess who should receive the work item according to the criteria you specify.

For example, all strategic account managers are possible agents of the task *"Respond to customer complaint"*. Suppose, for example, that strategic account manager Sue Kendel has to process the work item *"Respond to customer complaint from Igloos Incorporated"*, since the agent-determination rules specify that the strategic account manager for all customers in the Far North region are assigned to Sue Kendel. It is vital that the work item be sent to the correct strategic account manager, i.e. the person who understands the current relationship with the customer, and who can make good decisions when executing the work item, so that the best possible result is achieved. Making these decisions is not always easy. This chapter deals with the different techniques you can use for agent-determination rules. The techniques that you choose will affect the development, performance, and maintenance of the rules you create.

9.1 Determining Agents Through Rule Resolution

Determining the responsible agents is one of the most important parts of any workflow. It is also the one area of a workflow that is most likely to fail in practice, so it is worthwhile making sure that your rule resolution is as robust as possible. Where there are many possible agents, rule resolution enables work to be distributed among the possible agents according to the business rules you define in the rule. That is, rule resolution enables you to push work to the agents who are supposed to do the work. Rule resolution enables you to calculate who is the responsible agent for a particular work item, usually based on runtime criteria. For instance, you might have a rule that calculates the manager of an employee. At runtime, if you pass the rule an employee ID, the rule will resolve who is that particular employee's manager.

Within workflow, there are a number of different options for creating standard rules, i.e. rules that may be linked directly to a workflow step. You can use:

▶ Responsibility rules

▶ Evaluation paths

▶ Function modules

▶ SAP Organizational Objects

You can also use techniques such as ad hoc agent assignment or custom defined methods if you want to resolve a rule prior to the workflow step in which it is used. This can be helpful if, for example, you want to use the same rule resolution result for multiple steps in your workflow.

A number of rules are provided in each SAP component. These can be used without adjustment or as examples for creating your own rules. All rules have some common features and functions that you need to understand before you create your own rules.

9.2   Rule Basics

You create or edit agent-determination rules with transaction PFAC.

When saved, the system assigns each rule an eight-digit number created by the system preceded by "AC", which is used for identification purposes.

All standard rules contain the following basic parts.

▶ ID
The technical ID for the rule assigned automatically by the system.

▶ Abbreviation
A short free-format text primarily used when searching for rules.

▶ Description
A free-format text describing the rule.

▶ Long Description
A longer text area where rule documentation can be placed. It is a good idea to use this to explain how the rule works for the benefit of other workflow developers or for those maintaining the rule data.

▶ **Type**

Whether the rule is a responsibility rule, based on a function module, or based on SAP organizational objects. Some systems contain additional options. For instance, CRM systems also allow agent assignment based on organizational attributes.

▶ 🔢 **Container**

This is where the criteria on which the rule is based are defined. Any data you need the workflow to pass to the rule to let the rule determine responsible agents must be defined here. Like any other container in the workflow environment, the elements can be simple values (e.g. Employee Ids) or object references (e.g. Employee object reference). They can be single or multiple values. Defining an object reference as a container element enables easy access to any attribute of that object. However, usually only simple values are used, since it is easier to see what are the true criteria of the rule.

▶ **"Terminate on rule resolution failure" flag**

This specifies whether the workflow should terminate (i.e. go into ERROR status) if no agents can be found via the rule at runtime. If this flag is set, the default agent determination rule which is defined in the task will be ignored.

Rules can be tested and simulated either by using the built-in test facility provided in transaction PFAC (Release 4.6 and higher), or by calling RH_GET_ACTORS[1] from a custom-defined test program. The standard test facility enables you to enter values against the container elements in the rule. You can also opt to see whether the agents found have related user IDs. This is important: if the agents do not have matching user IDs, no work item can be sent to them. Sometimes it is more convenient to write your own custom-defined program to check rules, for example, to run the rule through a predefined series of tests, or to test whether the responsible agents found are also possible agents.

Listing 9.1 is an example program showing a rule based on a single criterion 'Plant'. This rule finds the plant manager. You don't need to know how the plant manager is found by the rule to test it. It could be found by a rule function module or by responsibility rules: the testing process would be the same whatever rule type is used.

```
PROGRAM ZTESTRULE.
Include <CNTN01>.
```

---

1 This function is widely known but not an official API so it is liable to change in future releases. Make sure that you document its usage.

```
* Here we have a parameter so that we can test our rule against
* different plants.

Parameters: p_plant type t001w-werks.

data: ev_holders    type standard table of swhactor,
      actor_tab     type standard table of swhactor,
      ac_agents     type standard table of swhactor,
      wa_ac_agents  type swhactor,
      num_lines     type i.



* Here we define our rule container
swc_container ac_container.
swc_clear_container ac_container.

* Here we fill the container with the plant value entered via
the
* parameter
swc_set_element ac_container 'Plant' p_plant.

* Call the rule to find the plant manager
* Note our rule id is number 90000001—so the technical id of
* the rule is AC90000001
* The list of agents will be returned in table ac_agents
  CALL FUNCTION 'RH_GET_ACTORS'
    EXPORTING
      ACT_OBJECT                   = 'AC90000001'
    TABLES
      ACTOR_CONTAINER              = ac_container
      ACTOR_TAB                    = ac_agents
    EXCEPTIONS
      NO_ACTIVE_PLVAR              = 1
      NO_ACTOR_FOUND               = 2
      EXCEPTION_OF_ROLE_RAISED     = 3
      NO_VALID_AGENT_DETERMINED    = 4
      OTHERS                       = 5.
  IF SY-SUBRC <> 0.
* Message ...
  ENDIF.
```

```
* Here's an extra step to resolve the agents found to user IDs
* using an evaluation path SAP_TAGT
* This isn't necessary here—WebFlow will resolve the agents to
* user IDs at runtime—but it helps us check that valid agents
* were found
 loop at ac_agents into wa_ac_agents.
   if wa_ac_agents-otype = 'US'.
     append wa_ac_agents to actor_tab.
   else.
     clear ev_holders[].
     swc_clear_container ac_container.
     swc_set_element ac_container 'OTYPE' wa_ac_agents-otype.
     swc_set_element ac_container 'OBJID' wa_ac_agents-objid.

     CALL FUNCTION 'RH_GET_STRUCTURE'
       EXPORTING
         ACT_WEGID            = 'SAP_TAGT'
       TABLES
         ACTOR_TAB            = ev_holders
         AC_CONTAINER         = ac_container
       EXCEPTIONS
         NOBODY_FOUND         = 1
         NO_ACTIVE_PLVAR      = 2
         OTHERS               = 3.
     IF SY-SUBRC <> 0.
* Message ...
     ENDIF.
     APPEND LINES OF ev_holders TO actor_tab.
   endif.
endloop.

* Reduce the list of agents to user IDs only
delete actor_tab where otype ne 'US'.

* Check for no-one found
describe table actor_tab lines num_lines.
if num_lines is initial.
  Write: 'No agents found'.
endif.
```

```
Write: / 'The following agents were found:'.
Loop at actor_tab into wa_ac_agents.
  Write: / wa_ac_agents-otype, wa_ac_agents-objid.
Endloop.
```

Listing 9.1 Rule Based on Single Criterion

As you can see from the test program, the principles of rule resolution are the same regardless of the rule type:

▶ The contents of the rule container are read.

▶ The rule is evaluated, based on the data in the rule container and the rule type.

▶ The list of agents found is returned in an internal table. This table contains the agents as organizational objects (user, person, position, job, organizational unit).

9.3   Agent Determination Rule Resolution in the Workflow Step

To include a rule directly in a workflow step in the Workflow Builder (or as a default rule in a standard task), enter the rule number, press the Enter button so that the workflow-to-rule binding button appears, and enter the binding. Check that the binding is correct. For some rules (e.g. AC00000168–*manager of a user*) the system will generate bindings automatically when they are first entered against the workflow step. Always examine the generated binding, as this usually only compares simple container elements in the workflow to the rule container elements. If, for example, you want to pass an attribute of an object reference you will need to do this manually.

Caution The binding is executed between the workflow container (not the task container) and the rule container. That is, the rule is evaluated *before* the work item is created. If the rule resolution fails, and the terminate-rule-resolution flag is set, this will mean the workflow stops *before* the work item is created. When you restart the workflow, it restarts at the rule evaluation. However, prior to Release 4.6C, if the first work item in the workflow fails, no workflow item is created and so restart is not possible. This can even lead to the event-linkage being disabled. To avoid this, avoid setting the terminate-rule-resolution flag for the rule used in the first step of the workflow or preceed the step with an empty background step to ensure that the workflow starts.

When a work item is created, you can see the result of the rule resolution as the recipients (i.e. *selected agents*) listed in the work item display or workflow. However, remember the recipients are only those agents determined by the rule who are also possible agents. Agents found by the rule (i.e. *responsible agents*), who are not possible agents will not appear. From Release 6.10 on, you can also preserve the result of the rule resolution in the standard _RULE_RESULT rule container element, if you define a binding from the rule to an appropriate workflow container element.

Once a work item has completed, you will normally only be able to see the actual agent. If you need to see the recipients after the work item has been completed, calculate the recipients in a prior step and store them in a multiline workflow container element of data type SWHACTOR or use the _RULE_RESULT container element.

To calculate the agents in a prior step you would usually use either the ad hoc agent assignment technique or create an object attribute or object method and accompanying task to call the relevant rule using function module RH_GET_ACTORS. Another option is to use the *Choose Agent* wizard that allows an agent to dynamically select the agent of a future step from a list of possible agents. In older releases, before the wizard was available, you can use the WF_TASK business object type to achieve the same effect, as described in appendix A, *Tips and Tricks*.

Determining the recipients in advance is a useful technique if you want to:

▶ Use the same list of agents for several steps in the workflow.

▶ Report all agents responsible for the work item who have failed to act when the work item is not completed within deadlines.

▶ Further test the agent list by getting an administrator or business process owner to choose an appropriate agent, rather than letting the workflow fail with a rule resolution error. For example, check that at least one of the agents is a possible agent and if not, use the workflow to fix this.

▶ Send an e-mail to all agents identified by a rule resolution.

9.4　What Happens If Rule Resolution Has No Result

Every rule has an indicator that determines how the system reacts if rule resolution fails to produce a result, the *Terminate if rule resolution has no result* flag. Rule resolution failure is defined as when:

▶ A function module based rule resolution returns the exception NOBODY_FOUND.

▶ An empty agent list is returned.

The advantage of setting the *Terminate if rule resolution has no result* flag is that if no agents are found by the rule, the workflow stops, goes into error status, and the administrator is notified of the error by e-mail. The administrator is then able to correct the rule data or agent assignment (depending on what caused the failure) and restart the workflow from the point of failure, i.e. from the rule evaluation. However, the termination only occurs if the rule itself finds no agent. If the rule finds agents but the agents are not possible agents for the workflow step, no termination occurs. Similarly, if the rule finds agents but none of the agents resolve to user Ids, the termination will not be raised.

> **Tip** You can prevent this to a certain extent by configuration in table T77S0. By setting the entry WFLOW.ROLE to "X", the workflow will evaluate both the rule assigned to the workflow step and the possible agents of the underlying task, and terminate if there are no responsible agents who are also valid agents.

If the responsible agents in the workflow step are based on an expression or an organizational object (job, position, etc.), and the agents are not possible agents, no termination occurs either.

Normally, if no valid responsible agents are found for a workflow step and the terminate-on-failure flag is not set, then either:

▶ The work item is either assigned to the workflow administrator or orphaned (Release 4.6C and above)—i.e. it stays in ready status with no agents assigned (refer to SAP Note 491804 for details).

> **Tip** If the administrator receives a failed work item they can forward it to the correct agent. The Work Item Without Agents report (transaction SWI2_ADM1) lets you view and correct orphaned work items. From release 6.10 on, once you have fixed the rule resolution problem, you can re-execute the rule resolution using this report, too.

▶ The work item is sent to all possible agents that are not excluded agents (prior to Release 4.6C). This can be somewhat disconcerting, particularly if the underlying task is a general task—i.e. all agents in the system are sent the work item!

Agent-determination problems are usually a result of lagging data maintenance, due, for example, to manual paper-based forms being used to trigger update of personnel data after the personnel change has actually occurred. Usually it is enough to let the administrator fix these problems as described in chapter 6, *Workflow Administration*. If you have a particularly critical workflow, where rapid personnel changes and delays in data maintenance cause frequent agent-determination problems, you may want to use default agents instead.

In general, for critical workflows, it is usually best to create rules with default agents rather than let the rule terminate. Relying on the workflow administrator to act on the rule resolution error, fix the problem, and restart the workflow takes time. During that time, the business process is stopped for that workflow instance. A better way is to set up default agents who are also possible agents of the workflow. This is easy to do if you are using responsibility rules (using secondary priorities) or programmed rules.

This not only stops the workflow going into error, but the default agent can forward the work item to the appropriate agent, or even act on their behalf, keeping the business process moving. The cause of the rule resolution error can be corrected afterwards, rather than have to rush the correction just to keep the workflow working. Making sure the work item text includes some indication of why the agent was chosen can help default agents decide what action to take. For instance, you might end your work item text with: *"You have been sent this work item because you have been identified as the manager of employee John Doe."*

9.5   Responsibility Rules

Responsibility rules are usually the easiest and simplest rules to create and maintain. You can easily see both the rule criteria and how the rule will be evaluated. By using secondary priorities you can also define default agents as part of your responsibility rule, reducing the likelihood of rule resolution failure. With a responsibility rule, as with any other rule, you create container elements for each of the criteria you want to evaluate. It is worthwhile keeping the number of container elements small—too many criteria become confusing and increase the cost of maintenance of your rule.

If you have a large number of criteria, consider whether you should have more than one rule, rather than create one very confusing rule. For instance, suppose you want to find a manager based on account assignment and value. Possible account assignments are cost center, internal order, and work breakdown structure (WBS) element. So you could create one rule with criteria:

▶ Cost center
▶ Internal order
▶ WBS element used in production planning
▶ Value

However, in practice, if the assignment is to a cost center, then only the cost center and value are relevant; if the assignment is to an internal order, then only the internal order and value are relevant, and so on. So it would be less confusing to create three rules:

- **Rule 1**
  Cost Center, Value
- **Rule 2**
  Internal Order, Value
- **Rule 3**
  WBS element, Value

If you still wanted to evaluate all three rules against the same workflow step, you could create a function module based rule that determines which of the three rules applies and calls it.

Don't confuse this, however, with using supporting criteria, for instance:

- Controlling area
- Cost Center
- Value
- Currency

In this case, controlling area helps to further define the cost center, and currency helps to further define the value. So the rule is still based on cost center and value—you are just using controlling area and currency to make sure the cost center and value are accurately depicted.

Once you have created your container elements, you create "responsibilities" which are combinations of container element values. Single, multiple, and ranges of values can be specified in the one responsibility. The rule definition is a client-independent development object, but the responsibility definitions are client-dependent customizing.

For instance, for a rule based on *Cost Center* and *Value*, you could create the following responsibilities in table 9.1:

Responsibility	Cost Center	Value
a	1000	$0.00
b	1000	$0.01 to $500.00
c	2000, 3000, 4000	$0.00 to $500.00
d	1000, 2000 to 4000	$500.01 to $1000.00

Table 9.1 Responsibilities Defined in a Responsibility Rule

You then assign agents to these responsibilities. You can assign any of the organizational objects including organizational units, jobs, positions, user IDs, etc. By default, agents are assigned from the current date until 31.12.9999, but you can restrict the agent assignment to end on an earlier date, for example when an agent leaves the company.

It is very easy to see who will be chosen as agents by using a few test examples.

If you test the rule with Cost Center = 1000 and value = $450, the agents assigned to responsibility "b" would be chosen.

If you test the rule with Cost Center = 3000 and value = $550, the agents assigned to responsibility "d" would be chosen.

Figure 9.1 shows how this rule is configured in practice.

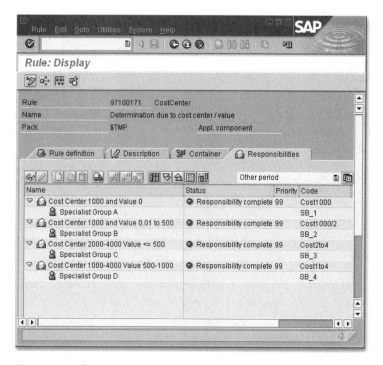

Figure 9.1 Configuring a Responsibility Rule

By using secondary priorities you can create default agents for your rule. You must specify in your rule that secondary priorities are to be taken into consideration by setting the flag *take secondary priorities into account*. Priorities take a value of 01 to 99. Higher priorities are evaluated before lower priorities, i.e. responsibilities with priority 99 are evaluated before responsibilities with priority 98.

When priorities are used, at runtime the highest priority responsibilities are evaluated first. If a matching responsibility and agents are found the rule evaluation stops. However, if no matching responsibility is found, then the next highest priority responsibilities are evaluated, and so on until agents are found or there are no more responsibilities left to evaluate.

Responsibility	Cost Center	Value	Priority
e	*	$0.00 to $9999.99	01

Table 9.2 An Example of a Responsibility Assignment

To demonstrate how priorities are used we will add a new responsibility 'e' with priority 01 as shown in table 9.2. Contrast this with the responsibilities 'a' to 'd' shown in table 9.1, which have been given priority 99, i.e. the highest priority. You can see the asterisk '*' acting as a wildcard. So this responsibility will match any cost center combined with value up to $9999.99. If you then tested the role with Cost Center = 6000 and value = $600, first the highest priority responsibilities 'a' to 'd' would be checked to see if any included this combination. Having failed to find a match, the system would then look at the priority '01' responsibilities, and match the combination to responsibility 'e'. So the agents assigned to responsibility 'e' would be the responsible agents in this case. That is, as there are no specific agents for cost center 6000 and value $600 the system will go to the default agents for all cost centers combined with a value up to $9999.99. However, if you tested the rule with Cost Center = 1000 and value = $450, the agents assigned to responsibility 'b' would still be chosen. Even though responsibility 'e' matches with all cost centers combined with a value under $9999.99, responsibility 'e' would not be evaluated, because a match was found with responsibility 'b', which has a higher priority.

So you can use a high priority to choose agents responsible for particular cost center/value combinations. If, for instance, you have a cost center used to capture expenditure on hardware/software you might want a specific manager to be responsible for that cost center. Lower priorities can be used to send other cost center/value combinations to default agents. For instance, cost centers used for office equipment and stationery might be managed by a group of default agents, rather than a specific manager.

Although you can have up to 99 levels of priority, generally two or three priorities are sufficient for most business situations.

Given the flexibility of the responsibility rules, you will now understand why it is worth explaining the criteria used in the rule documentation for the benefit of other workflow developers as well as for the people maintaining the rule data. Since responsibility rules involve agent assignment, be careful to watch for buffering problems if you assign agents and then use the rule straight away. It is worthwhile using transaction SWU_OBUF to refresh the buffers after the agents have been assigned and prior to the rule being used.

9.6   Evaluation paths as rules

Evaluation paths describe how to find one or more organizational objects based on an initial organizational object. For instance, common evaluation paths include:

Evaluation Path	Meaning
WF_ORGUN	Find the organizational unit of a user ID or person
WF_ORGUS	All users of an organizational unit, job, position, etc.
US_CHEF	Superior of a user
SAP_HOLD	Holder of a position

Table 9.3 Useful Standard Evaluation Paths

Evaluation paths exist in all SAP components. Evaluation paths work by using the relationships specified in the organizational plan to move from one organizational object to another. You can create your own evaluation paths. Evaluation paths can be displayed and maintained via transaction OOAW.

The evaluation path is described as a sequence of relationships to be tested. For example, using evaluation path WF_ORGUN to find the organizational unit of a user or person the following happens:

1. An initial user ID or person ID is supplied as the starting organizational object.
2. If a user ID is supplied, the evaluation path checks whether there is an equivalent person ID (in case we are in a system with the HR module implemented).
3. The evaluation path then looks for any positions held by the user ID and/or person ID.
4. From the positions found, the evaluation path looks for any organizational units to which the positions belong.
5. The organizational units found are returned.

You can use report RHWEGID00 to find suitable evaluation paths based on the initial and result organizational objects desired.

To create a rule based on an evaluation path:

1. Determine the evaluation path you want to use.
2. Create a rule as normal, setting the type to "Function to be executed", i.e. this is a function module based rule.
3. Enter the function module RH_GET_STRUCTURE.
4. Automatically (or on pressing the Enter button), an additional field *Evaluation path* appears. Enter your evaluation path ID in this field.
5. Create the following rule container elements:

Name	Data Type Reference	Description
OTYPE	OBJEC-OTYPE	Type of the Organizational Management object
OBJID	OBJEC-REALO	ID of the Organizational Management object
ORG_AGENT	WFSYST-AGENT	Organizational Management object

Table 9.4 Agent Determination Rule Container for an Evaluation Path

These container elements are used to hold the initial organizational object at runtime. You can pass the initial organizational object to the rule by filling in

▶ Either ORG_AGENT with the complete organizational object ID (e.g. USSMITH for user ID SMITH)

▶ Or OTYPE with the organization object type (e.g. US) and OBJID with the organization object ID (e.g. SMITH).

As evaluation paths evaluate organizational plan relationships, be careful to watch for buffering problems if you change the organizational plan and then use the rule straight away. It is worthwhile using transaction SWU_OBUF to refresh the buffers after the changes have been made and prior to the rule being used.

9.7 Function Modules as Rules

Using a function module as a rule gives maximum flexibility but minimum visibility. You can look up data from just about anywhere within the current system and even in external systems to help determine your agents. You can even combine several other rules into one function module. For example, you can try one rule first, and if no agents were found, default to an alternative rule. However, it is very difficult for the agent or process owner or even other workflow developers to understand how the rule finds the agent, so it is important to make sure that the rule is well documented.

Function-module based rules are most useful where complex criteria need to be evaluated. If the rule is simple, it is usually better to use one of the other rule types such as responsibility rules or evaluation paths that don't require explicit programming.

The basic process for creating a rule based on a function module is as follows:

1. Create the function module. At this stage, it is enough to create the interface of the function module, assign it to an appropriate function group, and activate it. For the function module to be used in the rule, the following interface must be defined. If you do not use this interface you will not be able to enter your function module against the rule.

Parameter Type	Name	Data Type Reference	Meaning
Table	AC_CONTAINER	SWCONT	This is the incoming rule container
Table	ACTOR_TAB	SWHACTOR	This is the outgoing list of agents in agent format
Exception	NOBODY_FOUND		Raising this exception indicates no agents were found

Table 9.5 Agent Determination Rule Container for a Function Module

2. Create a rule as normal, setting the type *Function to be executed*.
3. Enter the function module name. The system will check that the function module interface is correct and return an error if the interface is invalid.
4. Create the container elements for your rule criteria.
5. Enter the code in your function module using the following algorithm:

   ▶ All of the workflow macros must be made available to the function module by putting an INCLUDE <CNTN01>. statement in the global data area of the function group.

   ▶ Workflow macros must be used to read the incoming data from the rule container AC_CONTAINER. Use macro SWC_GET_ELEMENT to read single values and object references from the container, and macro SWC_GET_TABLE to read multiline values and multiline object references.

- Find the agents. This is where you put your complex criteria. You might be finding agents by reading tables, master data, calling other rules, calling another system, etc. Do whatever is necessary to find the responsible agents.
- Convert the agents to agent format. In other words, all user IDs must be preceded by US.
- Fill the outgoing ACTOR_TAB with the list of agents.
- Check whether ACTOR_TAB is empty and if it is raise the NOBODY_FOUND exception.

> **Tip** Note that raising any exception other than NOBODY_FOUND is not helpful. The various parts of workflow that use rules will only be looking for the NOBODY_FOUND exception or an empty ACTOR_TAB to determine if the rule has failed. Any other exceptions are ignored.

In the example below you can see a realistic example of a rule function module. In this scenario the rule function module calls another rule in another SAP component to find the relevant agents. This is quite useful if you are running several SAP components, for example an R/3 system and an EBP system, and you wish to share the rules so the data is only set up in one place. In this case, the rule and the data exists in the other SAP component. From the current SAP component we want to:

1. Get the criteria values from the current system.
2. Fill the rule container with the criteria names from the rule in the other SAP component, matched to the criteria values from the current system.
3. Call the rule in the other system with the prepared rule container.
4. Read the agents returned by the rule in the other system. At this point, the agent list may contain organizational objects, such as positions, that only exist in the other SAP component. A function module is called in the other SAP component to find the holders of those positions in the other SAP component as user IDs.

For this scenario we have assumed that an agent will have the same user ID in all systems. So we could improve this example by checking that the user IDs found in the other SAP component exist in the current system, i.e. that the agent exists in the current system.

In the example in listing 9.2, the <CNTN01> include has already been included in the global data of the function group. The rule container has single value container elements CostCtr, Value, and Destination.

```
FUNCTION Z_FIND_COSTCTR_MGR.
*"----------------------------------------------------------------
--
*"*"Local interface:
*"  TABLES
*"      ACTOR_TAB STRUCTURE  SWHACTOR
*"      AC_CONTAINER STRUCTURE  SWCONT
*"  EXCEPTIONS
*"      NOBODY_FOUND
*"----------------------------------------------------------------
--

data: Costctr         type reqacct-cost_ctr,
      TotalValue      type reqhead-total_VALUE,
      Destn           type rfcdes-rfcdest.

data: lt_holders      type standard table of swhactor,
      lt_agents       type standard table of swhactor,
      wa_lt_agents    type swhactor,
      num_lines       type i.

*Read values assigned to the rule criteria in the current sys-
tem
swc_get_element ac_container 'CostCtr'        costctr.
swc_get_element ac_container 'Value'          totalvalue.
swc_Get_element ac_container 'Destination'    destn.

* Call backend rule to determine responsible agents
* Fill container for backend rule—a separate container
* "lt_container" is used to keep the containers for the two
* rules separate

  swc_container lt_container.
  swc_clear_container lt_container.
  swc_set_element lt_container 'CostCenter'     costctr.
  swc_set_element lt_container 'Amount'         totalvalue.
```

```
* Call the rule in the other system
  CALL FUNCTION 'RH_GET_ACTORS'
    DESTINATION destn
    EXPORTING
      ACT_OBJECT                      = 'AC90000001'
    TABLES
      ACTOR_CONTAINER                 = lt_container
      ACTOR_TAB                       = lt_agents
    EXCEPTIONS
      NO_ACTIVE_PLVAR                 = 1
      NO_ACTOR_FOUND                  = 2
      EXCEPTION_OF_ROLE_RAISED        = 3
      NO_VALID_AGENT_DETERMINED       = 4
      OTHERS                          = 5.
  IF SY-SUBRC <> 0.
  ENDIF.

* Return the list of agents in agent format
* As the agents belong to another system, we will need to use
* that other system to convert them to user IDs—if we did
* everything in the current system this step would not be
* necessary.
* Here we have assumed that both systems use the same user Ids

loop at lt_agents into wa_lt_agents.
  if wa_lt_agents-otype = 'US'.
    append wa_lt_agents to actor_tab.
  else.

* Here we call an evaluation path in the other system to find
* the holders of positions/jobs/etc. assigned as agents
    clear lt_holders[].
    swc_clear_container lt_container.
    swc_set_element lt_container 'OTYPE' wa_lt_agents-otype.
    swc_set_element lt_container 'OBJID' wa_lt_agents-objid.

    CALL FUNCTION 'RH_GET_STRUCTURE'
    destination destn
      EXPORTING
        ACT_WEGID               = 'SAP_TAGT'
```

```
       TABLES
          ACTOR_TAB            = lt_holders
          AC_CONTAINER         = lt_container
       EXCEPTIONS
          NOBODY_FOUND         = 1
          NO_ACTIVE_PLVAR      = 2
          OTHERS               = 3.
     IF SY-SUBRC <> 0.
     ENDIF.
     APPEND LINES OF lt_holders TO actor_tab.
   endif.
endloop.


* Return list of agents as user IDs only
* Remove all non-user ID agents as the org plans in the two
* systems are different so any jobs/positions/etc. will be
* meaningless in the current system

delete actor_tab where otype ne 'US'.


* Check that at least one agent was found
describe table actor_tab lines num_lines.
if num_lines is initial.
   raise nobody_found.
endif.


ENDFUNCTION.
```

Listing 9.2 Rule Function Module That Calls Another Rule in Another SAP Component

You can test your rule using the rule testing option in transaction PFAC as normal, or by using the function module testing option in transaction SE37.

9.8   SAP Organizational Objects as Rules

SAP Organizational Objects as a rule type refers to a very specific technique. This technique allows you to match codes entered in Customizing tables against organizational objects in the organizational plan. For example, if you have a code representing a particular laboratory, you can relate this to an organizational unit representing all the people in the laboratory. Or if you have a code representing an MRP controller, you can relate this to a particular job or position in the organizational plan.

There is a little more visibility in using this technique rather than using a pro-grammed rule; however, it requires the use of special transactions to see the assignments to the organizational plan.

The basic technique is as follows:

1. Select or create a business object representing the Customizing table. This busi-ness object must have a key representing the code in the Customizing table to be assigned, at least one attribute Description, and one method Existence Check. A special flag *Organizational type* in the business object header must also be switched on.

2. Create a rule with type *Organizational data* and enter your business object ID.

3. In table T7791, you can define which organizational objects (organizational unit, job, position, etc.) can be assigned to instances of your business object.

4. Use the special transactions PFOM (Create assignments to SAP Organizational objects) and PFOS (Display assignments to SAP Organizational objects) to assign the values from the Customizing table, i.e. instances of your business object, to the relevant organizational units, jobs, positions, etc. These transac-tions use the HR infotype 1208 to define relationships between the business object instances and the organizational plan. If you want to create your own program to update the assignments, then function module RH_SAP_ORG_OBJEC_RELATE can be used for this purpose.

5. When you use the rule in your workflow step, you will need to bind an instance of your business object from the workflow container to the rule. You can either create this instance explicitly, for example by using a SYSTEM.GENERICIN-STANTIATE task to create an instance from your code value, or implicitly by creating an attribute referring to the Customizing table business object in one of the other business objects used in your workflow. For instance, if your work-flow is based mainly on business object Material, you might create an attribute Laboratory against the object that links to the organizational type business object for laboratory codes.

A newer variation on this technique is to implement the interface IFSTROBJCT in the business object. This interface includes an attribute Agents, which finds all agents assigned to an instance of the business object, i.e. it finds all infotype 1208 relationships to that instance. That way you don't need to create a rule at all; you can just assign your agents as an expression. For example if you have created an attribute Laboratory of your workflow's main business object Material, you could define the responsible agents as the expression &Material.Labora-tory.Agents&. In other words, the agents are assigned to the laboratory that relates to the material used at runtime in the workflow.

More information on this technique is detailed in the SAP Library documentation, and it is worth reading this if you decide you want to use this technique.

9.9 Other Options for Responsible Agent Assignment

There are a number of rules provided as-is that are worth examining rather than creating your own rules. For example:

▶ AC30000012 returns all agents assigned to an SAP office distribution list. This is perfect when you want a subscription-based agent determination. Agents subscribe and unsubscribe themselves (self-service), so there is zero administration.

▶ AC00000168 returns the chief position of an organizational unit to which a user has been assigned.

There are also a number of rules delivered by SAP that are specifically tailored for SAP workflows. For example, rule AC00000148 *Person responsible for requisition release*, which reads some Customizing tables to determine the responsible agents, specifically for SAP-provided workflow WS00000038 *Workflow for requisition release*. If you want to use the SAP-provided workflow as-is, you will need to use the accompanying rule. However, you can also use these same rules in your own workflows if you wish.

Instead of using a rule, you can assign an expression to a workflow step as the responsible agent. For instance, it is quite common to see the expression &_Workflow_Initiator& (the workflow initiator) used as the responsible agent of a workflow step. An expression refers to a workflow container element or some reference based on a workflow container element, so it is up to you to ensure that the container element is filled correctly prior to the workflow step in which it is used. For instance, &_Workflow_Initiator& is usually filled with the 'event creator' as part of the event linkage between the workflow and the triggering event at the start of the workflow.

If you want to make sure the same agent performs a number of steps in your workflow, you can store the actual agent from one step in a workflow container element, and pass it to another step. The actual agent of a work item can be found in the task container element _Work_item. The _Work_item container element will contain an instance of business object WorkingWI, which has an attribute ExecutedByUser. So if you want to pick out the agent of the step, in the binding from the task to the workflow (i.e. after the work item has been completed), you could assign the value of &_Work_item.ExecutedByUser.Name-WithLeadingUS& to your workflow container element to provide the actual agent in agent format.

Always remember that however your agents are chosen, agents must be passed to the workflow step in agent format (type SWHACTOR), i.e. the 2 character agent type (US for user ID, S for position, C for job, etc.), followed by the 12 character agent ID (for example. the user ID, position ID, job ID, etc.).

10   Business Interfaces

Business Interfaces enable business applications in the SAP component to proactively communicate with workflow, so that your workflow can react to changes outside of its immediate control. Events handle the background interaction, and the generic object services handle the dialog connections.

10.1   Introduction

Since workflows represent business processes, it is vital that business application programs are able to communicate with workflows. For instance, a business application may need to tell the WebFlow Engine:

▶ When to start a business process

▶ When a business process or activity is finished

▶ When a business process or activity that has started is no longer required

▶ Or simply when changing circumstances dictate a change in the behavior of the business process.

Chapter 8, *Business Objects*, showed how workflow uses business objects to access business data and routines once the workflow has started. Now you will see how business application programs can interact with workflow to start workflows, stop workflows and notify workflows when a business application program has changed the status of an object. The primary business interface between business application programs and workflows is the *Event*.

At the end of this chapter, you will find additional ways of interfacing business application programs with workflows, such as *Generic Object Services*.

10.2   Understanding Events

Simply put, an *Event* is the change in state of a business object instance. An event from a business application program notifies the WebFlow Engine of that change in status. For example, if a business application program changes customer master data, then to communicate to the WebFlow Engine that the customer master has been changed, the application must raise an event Changed for business object Customer, passing the customer ID with the event to indicate which customer was changed. The WebFlow Engine can then react to this event, for example by starting a workflow to confirm the changes, which notifies the sales and support personnel who regularly work with that customer.

To use an event as the interface between a business application program and workflow, you need the following:

▶ **Event Definition**

This is a technical name formally defined as part of the business object type. Any special event parameters must also be defined here. By default, events pass the object type, event name, object instance, and the event initiator (i. e. the user ID of the person running the business application program at the time the event was created). Event parameters have to be filled explicitly by the mechanism generating the event. Not all event-raising mechanisms support this. Similarly, event parameters that can be filled by an event generation mechanism can only be used in the workflow if they are explicitly defined in the event definition. The event definition does not contain information about how the event is triggered; instead, it describes the interface of the event (name and parameters) so that it can be used by both the *event creator* and the *event receiver*.

▶ **Event Creator**

This is usually a business application program, but it may be a workflow itself using the step type *Event Creator*. The event creator is sometimes referred to as the *event producer, event raiser,* or *event publisher*. The event can be created via a code routine (usually the case in SAP transactions) or as a generic mechanism (useful for triggering your own events from SAP transactions). Run-time execution of the event-creation mechanism is called *raising the event*.

▶ **Event Receiver**

This is the generic term for whatever reacts to the event. This is sometimes referred to as the *event consumer* or *event subscriber*.[1] Usually the receiver is a workflow, but it may be a task, or a *Wait for Event* step within a workflow. Non-workflow receivers are also allowed, such as a routine that simply creates a mail notifying someone that an event has occurred (refer to section 10.6.3, and chapter 14, *Advanced Diagnostics,* for some techniques that do this).

▶ **Event Linkage**

This specifies the relationship between the event and the event receiver. You must also specify the rules governing the relationship. Rules can be used to determine whether or not the receiver should be notified, and what event data should be passed to the receiver and how. Rules can even dynamically determine the event receiver at runtime. Event linkages may be *active* or *inactive*. Only active linkages are evaluated at runtime. Linkages may be inactive because they are incomplete, in error, or because you just don't want to use the interface at the moment.

---

[1] You can think of the term *event receivers* as equivalent to event consumers (as in *producer and consumer*) or event subscribers (as in *publish and subscribe*). We simply refer to them as receivers to keep things straightforward.

It is worth noting that each event may have none, one or many receivers. For each receiver a linkage between the event and the receiver must be created.

> **Tip** The *Event Creator* does not need to know whether there are any receivers. It is simply telling the WebFlow Engine that the event has occurred. If there are no active event linkages—when for example there are no workflows currently interested in the event—nothing happens.

10.3 Defining Events

You can find existing events in the Business Object Repository, for example, by examining the relevant business object type in the Business Object Builder (transaction SW01, or menu path **Definition Tools · Business Object Builder**). If no suitable event exists, you can create a new event using the Business Object Builder as described in chapter 8, *Business Objects.*

> **Tip** This may mean first delegating a standard SAP business object to your own subtype or even creating a new business object type altogether. Refer to chapter 8, *Business Objects,* for more details.

There is never any coding behind an event definition, since the coding to create the event is in the business application program itself. Most events do not have special parameters, since the standard event container elements suffice. The standard event container elements include:

▶ Object type
▶ Event name
▶ Object instance
▶ Object key
▶ Event initiator (i.e. the person under whose user ID the event was created)
▶ Event creation date/time

You can pass any of the container elements from the event to the event receiver.

10.4 Raising Events from Business Applications

Before a business application can raise an event, the event creation needs to be coded into the business application program. Fortunately, you will often find that SAP has already done this for you. Usually the event is coded in such a way that you only need to configure what status changes should create events and which events you want to use. For instance, the parked document application programs check a configuration table to see whether the parked document is relevant for workflow before raising events for that document.

Often it is possible to enter new events in the configuration, and the provided event creation coding will raise the event for you. Read the configuration documentation to check what needs to be configured, and whether you can add your own events. Some of the configuration possibilities are described later in this chapter. However, to add event creation to your own programs, you can implement the event creation code yourself (the APIs are described in chapter 13, *Custom Programs*). User-exits and Business Add-Ins can provide an appropriate place to add event creation code to existing SAP programs without modifying them, as do the generic mechanisms listed below:

▶ **Change documents** (i.e. audit trail)
Wherever a change document is written, for example on change of master data, you can configure pre-defined events or add your own.

▶ **General status management**
Events can be configured to be raised through status changes monitored by status management. Both your own customer-defined statuses and those provided by SAP can be used to raise standard events or your own events.

▶ **Message control**
Events can be raised when a document is created via message control, e.g. via output of a sales order. You can configure pre-defined events or add your own.

▶ **Logistics Information System (LIS)**
Events can be raised when an exception situation occurs (LIS exception). You can configure pre-defined events or add your own.

▶ **Human Resources (HR) master data**
Events can be raised by HR *infotype* operations. You can configure pre-defined events or add your own.

▶ **Business Transaction Events**
Events can be raised by Business Transaction Events in financial application programs. You can only use the existing events.

▶ **Application-specific Configuration** (e.g. Parked documents, Requisition Release Strategy)
Events can be based on the application-specific configuration. Since the configuration is different for each application, you need to read the configuration documentation to see if you can also create your own events. If a business application has special workflow configuration, it will appear in the application's configuration, not in the workflow menus.

Wizards can help you set up the event creation configuration. Wizards are available for the following:

▶ Change documents

▶ Logistics Information System

▶ Business Transaction Events

The following sections describe the principle mechanisms in detail.

10.4.1 Raising Events Via Change Documents

If the business application program writes a *Change Document*, the creation of the change document can raise an event. Many business objects are changed frequently. It is often useful and necessary (for audit purposes) to be able to trace the changes made. Many business applications log changes using change documents. This is particularly true of master data maintenance applications. Usually change documents are written when objects are created, changed or deleted.

To log changes in a change document, an appropriate change document object must be defined in the system. In its definition, a change document object has tables, which represent a business object in the system, and some generated code, which is incorporated into the relevant business application program. You can incorporate change documents into your own programs if you wish.

A change document is written only if a table field designated as *change document-relevant* (in the ABAP Dictionary) has been changed. For example, changes made to the R/3 cost center data in the field BUS0012-PersonInCharge (*Cost center owner*) are automatically logged in a change document for the change document object KOSTL.

> **Tip** Before configuring events to be raised by changed documents, check that a change document will be written for the table field you want to track. The easiest way to do this is to make the appropriate change via the business application and check that a change document was created via the relevant change document report.

To create an event from a change document configure the event via transaction SWEC, menu path **Definition Tools · Events · Event Creation · Change Documents · Linkage**. You specify at a minimum: the change document object, the business object type, the event name, and whether the event is to be created for inserted, updated, or deleted data. The event can be restricted further by specifying the old and new values of table fields or a condition (i.e. a logical expression) that must be satisfied before the event is raised. For instance, you might specify that the field MARA-WRKST (*basic material*) must be non-blank before the event is created.

The system will raise the event whenever a change document is written that satisfies your configuration entries. Change documents are usually written after the change itself has been updated in the database. Using change documents to create the event, thus ensures that the event is only raised when the relevant change has actually been made.

The system fills the event container with information about the change document. You can force the system to write the old and new values of a changed field into the event container by defining the field as a database field attribute for the object type in the Business Object Builder, making sure that the ABAP Data Dictionary reference of the attribute is identical to that of the field in the change document. To transfer these values from the event container to the workflow, you must define event parameters with the same name as the attribute but as multiline parameters. At runtime, the system will write the old and new values of the attribute as two lines (new value with index 0001, old value with index 0002) in the matching event container element.

> **Tip** The system also writes the elements CD_OBJECTCLAS (Change object class), CD_OBJECTID (Change object ID) and CD_CHANGENR (Change number) to the event container. You can use these to access the change document from within the workflow. This is particularly useful when the change document object contains line items which you need to analyze. To use these elements in the workflow, you must define them as event parameters so that you can specify them in the event-workflow binding.

10.4.2 Raising Events Via Status Changes

If a business application uses *General Status Management*, you can configure event creation according to changes in system statuses. Business applications for internal orders, funds management, projects, production orders, quality inspection and engineering change requests are among those that use status management. Status management makes it possible to document the current processing state of an application object using statuses. For instance, you could use status management to track whether all quality inspections have been completed for an object going through the quality inspection process.

A *status object type* identifies the application object being status managed. *Status profiles* are used to link statuses to status object types. If you want to create your own statuses, you need to create an appropriate status profile. For system-set statuses, the relationships are predefined.

Each status is an indicator that is either active or inactive. For instance, the status "inspection close completed" (indicating that all inspections have been completed) is either true (active) or false (inactive). Statuses can be set by the system or by the user, depending on the status-type. Both system-set and user-set statuses can be used to create events.

You can configure an event to be raised when a status is changed using transaction BSVW menu path **Definition Tools · Events · Event Creation · Status Management**. You need to specify the status object type, the business object type and the event name. You then specify which status changes raise the event by restricting the event creation to a particular status and whether that status is active or inactive.

To learn more about this you can refer to the tutorial about raising events upon status changes in the SAP library help documentation.

10.4.3 Raising Events Via Message Control

If a business application uses *Message Control* to exchange information between business partners, you can configure event raising as part of message control. Business applications for sales orders and purchase orders are among those that use message control. When message control is executed, any configured events will be raised. For instance, when a sales order is created, message control is executed to output the order to the customer (e.g. by print, e-mail, fax, XML, etc.). You can configure a workflow event (e.g. SALESORDER.CREATED) to be created simultaneously with the order being output to the customer.

An event can be raised whenever message control is executed using transaction NACE menu path **Definition Tools · Events · Event Creation · Message Control**. For the appropriate business application, create a separate output type (e.g. EVEN "Trigger event for workflow") and designate transmission medium 9 "Events (Workflow)".

> **Tip** You can alternatively designate transmission medium T "Task (Workflow)" if you merely want to start one and only one workflow without exception. However, using events will give you more flexibility in defining how, which and whether workflows are affected.

Your new output type requires a processing routine. SAP provides program RVNSWE01, form routine CREATE_EVENT for this purpose. This routine holds the event creation code. It can be replaced with your own program or routine, for example, to assign values to your own event parameters before the event is raised.

Assign your new output type to an appropriate *access sequence*. The access sequence specifies what *conditions* can be used to define the output. In the case of events, the conditions are used to define which event will be created. For instance, you might have a condition based on document type. Then for each document type, you could create a *condition record* for that document type and for the event to be raised. When the message control is executed, the correct event will be raised in accordance with the document type.

The access sequence requires appropriate condition records. In the *communication* section of the condition record, you enter the business object type and event name. Your new output type appears in the *control* section of the appropriate message control procedure. The procedure lets you specify what will happen when message control is executed, for instance, that it outputs the order by fax and raises a workflow event at the same time.

The business application configuration determines which message control procedure will be used at runtime.

10.4.4 Events Raised by Changes to HR Master Data

Changes to HR (Human Resources) master data can raise events. Configure an event to be raised when HR data is changed using transactions SWEHR1, SWEHR2 and SWEHR3 or menu path **Definition Tools · Events · Event Creation · Change to HR Master Data**. HR *infotypes* and their *subtypes* determine the type of master data being changed.

The HR infotype must be linked to a business object type, which can be restricted to a particular subtype, if appropriate. For example, you might link the infotype 4000, which represents job applicants, to the business object APPLICANT. SAP provides a number of predefined links and you can add to these.

An infotype operation determines the type of change being made. It must be linked to a business object type and event name. For example, to create an event when a new job applicant is entered into HR, you might want to link the operation 'insert' for infotype 4000 to business object type APPLICANT event CREATED.

SAP provides a number of predefined links between infotype operations and events. You can use these links as-is, replace them with your own links, or add completely new links to your own events or those provided by SAP. Instead of linking the infotype operation to one particular event, you can specify a function module, where the event to be raised can be determined dynamically, based on the old and new values of the infotype. SAP provides numerous working examples of these function modules, such as HR_EVENT_RULES_PB4000, which specifies which events are to be created for job applicants.

10.4.5 Events Raised Via Business Transaction Events

Events can be raised when a *Business Transaction Event* occurs. *Business Transaction Events* are not related to Business Object events. They are triggered from financial applications, such as *G/L accounting* and *accounts receivable/payable accounting* in R/3, and are used to notify other parts of the system of operations being performed in financial accounting, such as a document being created. You can link a Business Transaction Event to a business object event using transaction SWU_EWBTE or menu path **Definition Tools · Events · Event Creation · Set up with wizard · Business Transaction Event**.

If a Business Transaction Event is linked to a business object event, when a Business Transaction Event occurs, the system calls a function module containing the event creation code. The function module converts the data from the Business Transaction Event into workflow event container-elements and creates the business object event.

When you link the Business Transaction Event to a business object event, SAP generates a function module with the appropriate interface and implementation. You have to specify the new function module name and its function group. You can see the existing function modules you have created via the wizard using transaction BF34. Now assign a new *business product*, which identifies your extensions to the Business Transaction Event functions, as opposed to system-provided functions. Existing business products can be inspected via transaction BF24. Only the predefined Business Transaction Events and business object events are allowed here. Transaction BF01 displays all Business Transaction Events. Table 10.1 lists the predefined event relationships.

Business Transaction Event	Event	
00001030 POST DOCUMENT (on update of standard data)	BKPF *Accounting document*	CREATED *Document created*
00001040 REVERSE CLEARING (after standard update)	BKPF *Accounting document*	CLEARINGREVERSED *Clearing reversed*
00001050 POST DOCUMENT: FI/CO interface	BKPF *Accounting document*	CREATED *Document created*
00001110 CHANGE DOCUMENT (on Save of standard data)	BKPF *Accounting document*	CHANGED *Document changed*
00001320 CUSTOMER MASTER DATA (on Save)	BUS3007 *Customer account*	CREATED *Account opened*
00001420 VENDOR MASTER DATA (on Save)	BUS3008 *Vendor account*	CREATED *Account opened*
00001520 CREDIT MANAGEMENT (on Save)	BUS1010 *Customer credit account*	CREATED *Account opened*

Table 10.1 Relationships Between Business Transaction Events and Events

10.4.6 Raising Events by Calling a Workflow API

If none of the event configuration options are suitable, or you want to include events in your own programs, you can code the event creation yourself using SAP-provided function modules. For details on how you can do this, read chapter 13, *Custom Programs*.

10.5 Using Events in Workflows

Having the business application raise an event is the first step. Your workflow will need to listen for each event, in the context of the business process, and carry out a response to it.

10.5.1 How to Use Events in Workflows

Workflows, *wait for event* workflow steps, and tasks can react to events; in other words, the workflows, steps and tasks can be event receivers. Any number of receivers can react to the event. This means that any number of workflow definitions, steps, or tasks can be triggered or terminated by the same event, if they have an active link to that event.

You can use events to:

▶ Start a workflow or task (i.e. a *triggering event*).

▶ Stop a workflow or task, or complete a *wait for event* step (i.e. as a *terminating event*).

▶ Force the workflow to perform an action on itself such as refresh the assignment of agents to work items or restart the workflow without jettisoning the data acquired by the workflow so far. From the point of view of the event linkage, these are identical to terminating events because the event reacts with a workflow instance that is already running.

In addition to this, the workflow itself can raise events via step type *event creator*. For instance, if an "implement hiring freeze" workflow is started, you may want the workflow to create an event ALLHIRINGFROZEN, which is then used to cancel all currently active "process job application" workflows.

10.5.2 Triggering events

An event that is used to start a workflow or task is called a *triggering event*. Remember that the same event may also be used as a terminating event in the same or another workflow—it is simply the context in which it is used (or *consumed*) that makes it a triggering event.

When a properly defined triggering event is raised, some other process begins. Putting it more scientifically, for every event raised, a new workflow instance of the workflow definition is launched, providing that this definition is linked to the event, the linkage is active and the start conditions are satisfied.

For instance, when in a business application called "create purchasing request", a new request is saved, a "purchasing request created" event is created. The system should then start the "Approve purchasing request" workflow automatically. Of course, a workflow (or task) can have several triggering events. If any one of the triggering events is raised, the workflow (or task) is started.

> **Tip** Linking a triggering event to a task effectively uses the task as a single-step workflow. However, even if you only have a single step in your business process, it is usually better to embed it in a workflow rather than use the task directly, since the workflow gives you more control. For instance, you can specify deadlines in the workflow step linked to the task.

Linking Workflows to Triggering Events

If you want a workflow (or task) to be started automatically when an event is created, you need to create an event linkage between the event and the workflow (or task). In the technical documentation this linkage is known as an event type linkage. That is, the link is the same for all object instances of the business object type of the event.

> **Tip** The same event can be used as a triggering event (e.g. for one or more workflows) and as a terminating event (e.g. for one or more tasks and wait for event steps), but a separate event linkage is needed for each receiver, and the event linkages will be significantly different.

You can define triggering events for a workflow in the Workflow Builder using the *Basic Data*, *Version-Independent* tab, and within that, the *Start Events* tab. A triggering event for a task is defined in the *Triggering Events* tab of the task definition. (Prior to Release 4.6, triggering events for workflows were defined in the same way as triggering events for tasks.)

To assign the triggering event to your workflow you must also define a binding between the event container and the workflow container to pass event information to the workflow. event container elements can be bound only to workflow container elements marked with the *import* flag. Usually you want to transfer the event object instance (event container element name _EVT_OBJECT) and the event initiator (event container element name _EVT_CREATOR) as a minimum. The event initiator is usually the user ID of the user indirectly raising the event, preceded by the two characters US to show that this refers to a user ID. If you define *import* elements in your workflow container with the same ABAP Data Dictionary type or object type reference as the elements in the event container before assigning the triggering event to the workflow, the Workflow Builder will try to match up the event and workflow container elements for you.

Once the event to be used is designated as a triggering event and the binding is defined, the system automatically creates a type linkage consisting of:

▶ The business object type and event name

▶ The current workflow (or task) as the event receiver

Other linkage settings, such as the receiver function, are created automatically. These are described in detail in chapter 13, *Custom Programs*.

> **Tip** You can change most fields in the event linkage, but be careful not to change the given receiver function module.

Initially the event linkage is created inactive. Remember to activate the event linkage if you want the system to use it at runtime. Otherwise, it will be ignored. If you are still developing your workflow, you can leave the linkage inactive until you are ready.

Event linkages can be transported from one system to another (e.g. from a development system to a production system) using standard SAP transport management. After transport, check that the event linkage is active, since some releases automatically deactivate the event linkage in the new system. You will need to reactivate them manually, e.g. using transaction SWU0.

You can see all triggering event linkages via transaction SWE2 or menu path **Definition Tools · Events · Event Linkages · Type Linkages**. To check the event linkage has been defined correctly, simulate the event linkage via transaction SWU0 or menu path **Utilities · Events · Simulate Event**.

Start Conditions for Workflows

Start conditions specify for a particular event whether or not a workflow should be started. Start conditions are only used for triggering events.

The start condition itself is a logical expression that can be based on constants, attributes of the event objects, and system fields. Only if the logical expression is true will the workflow be started. Since start conditions are configuration entries, business analysts, administrators and super-users can view or change the start condition (i.e. the logical expression) without any programming knowledge. Start conditions may include complex logical expressions, which contain logical AND/OR/NOT operators, existence checks, pattern comparisons, and multi-level parentheses.

> **Tip** Start conditions are not available in releases prior to Release 4.6C. Instead you can use check function modules and/or receiver type function modules as described in chapter 13, *Custom Programs*.

Starting a workflow always consumes system resources and processor time, so if you can find an appropriate start condition (or a check function module), you can prevent unnecessary workflows from starting at all, and avoid situations that start a workflow only to have the first step of the workflow cancel it because it is not needed.

Start conditions (or receiver type function modules) are also useful for sending an event to one of a choice of workflows. They are also likely to be more efficient than a monster workflow that simply triggers other workflows. For instance, three alternative approval scenarios for a purchase request (no approval required, one approver required, two approvers required) could be linked to three mutually exclusive start conditions to trigger the appropriate workflow for each purchase request based on, e.g. the costs involved in the request and the spending limit of the user who created the request.

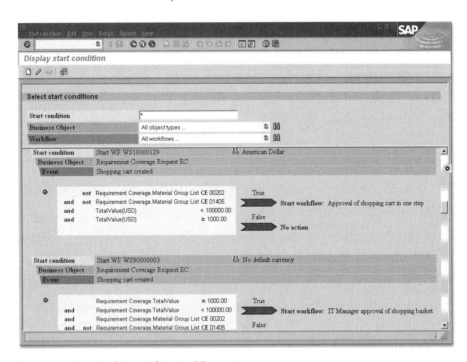

Figure 10.1 Start Condition with Logical Expression

Define start conditions via **Events · Event linkages · Start conditions** (transaction SWB_COND) or usually anywhere that you can link a workflow or task to a triggering event. An example of a start condition is shown in figure 10.1.

If you create a start condition for an event, the system automatically adds a predefined check function module to the event linkage, such as SWB_CHECK_FB_START_COND_EVAL. If you change the event linkage later make sure to keep this check function module, or the start condition will not work.

10.5.3 Terminating Events

When an event is used to stop a workflow or task, or change the behavior of an already started workflow, it is called a *terminating event*. Remember that the same event may also be used as a triggering event of the same or another workflow—it is simply the context in which it is used that makes it a terminating event.

When the event is created, if the event linkage is active and the linkage rules are satisfied, the status of the work item is set to COMPLETED and the next step is started.

> **Tip** Prior to Release 6.10, you could not define a terminating event for a workflow; instead, you had to use a *wait for event* step and ensure the subsequent processing ended the workflow.

Linking Workflows to Terminating Events

Whenever a workflow, task, or *wait for event* step is to be completed when an event is created, an event linkage is created automatically between the event and the appropriate event receiver. However, whereas a triggering event only needs to know the workflow definition for which a new workflow instance should be started, a terminating event needs to know exactly which workflow instances, work items, or wait for event step instance should be terminated.

For example, when an event terminates (completes) the workflow step "release engineering change request 103", all the other engineering change requests that are waiting for release must remain unaffected. For this reason, the linkage for terminating events always consists of two parts:

1. An *event type linkage* to specify the rules that are the same for all object instances of the event

2. An *event instance linkage*, which identifies the particular receivers (i.e. work item IDs) per object instance

When you specify the terminating event in your workflow, task or *wait for event* step, the system creates the event type linkage automatically. The event instance linkage is only created at runtime. It is always created automatically and is always active. Once the system has processed the terminating event, the instance linkage is automatically deleted.

Define terminating events for a task in the *Terminating Events* tab of the task definition.

Define the terminating event for a *wait for event* step in the step definition itself.

Define terminating events for a workflow in the Workflow Builder, using *Basic Data*, *Version-Dependent* tab, and within that, the *Events* tab in the Workflow Builder.[2] Here you specify whether the event should:

▶ Terminate (cancel) the workflow

▶ Restart the workflow (preserving the data already collected)

▶ Recalculate the conditions in the workflow (particularly the work item start/end conditions)

▶ Re-evaluate the agent determination rules for all active work items linked to the workflow instance (for example when the cost center owner changes)

To assign the terminating event to your workflow, task or *wait for event* step, as well as specifying the business object type and event name, you must also specify a container element that holds a reference to the object instance. This object instance is used to automatically create the event instance linkage at runtime. That is, a workflow, task, or *wait for event* step is always waiting for a terminating event for the business object type, event name, and object instance combination. For instance, an "Update customer master data" work item based on object instance "Customer: ABC Pty Ltd" with a terminating event "Customer updated", should only be completed if the event is raised for that particular customer and no other.

If more than one work item is waiting on the same terminating event (e.g. two work items waiting for event "*Customer updated*" for "Customer: ABC Pty Ltd"), then at runtime both receivers will finish when the event is raised.

A binding definition is optional for terminating events. Usually it is enough to know that the event has occurred for the specified object instance. However, you can define a binding between the event container and the workflow container to pass event information to the workflow if you wish. In fact, this is the only way of passing information back from an asynchronous method to the task that started it.

---

2 This is available from Release 6.10.

> **Caution** You can only bind terminating event container elements to the workflow/task container elements marked with the *import* flag.

Once you have designated the event to be used as a terminating event and designated the container element that will hold the object instance at runtime, the system will create an event type linkage consisting of:

▶ The business object type and event name

▶ A generic name for the event receiver. E.g. WORKITEM for terminating events linked to tasks and workflows or EVENTITEM for terminating events linked to *wait for event* steps

▶ A flag indicating that the instance linkage needs to be examined at runtime

The event is automatically activated. Do not deactivate it.

An appropriate receiver function module and the default settings for the other event linkage fields are automatically included in the event linkage. You can change most fields in the event linkage, but be careful not to change the given receiver function module. The type linkage of a terminating event usually does not need to be changed at all.

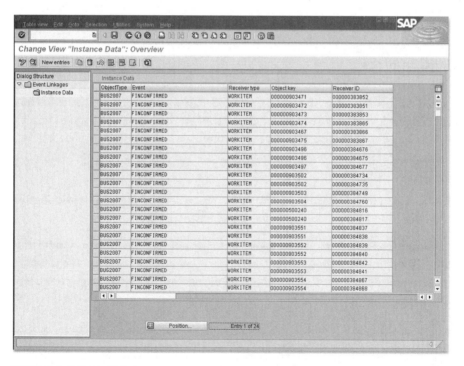

Figure 10.2 Instance Linkages

All terminating event linkages can be inspected via transaction SWE3[3] or menu path **Utilities · Events · Instance Linkages**.

The *Instance linkage*[4] section of transaction SWE3 shows the event type linkage for the terminating event.

The *Object Data*[5] section of transaction SWE3 (see figure 10.2) shows the instance linkages (i.e. the event receivers currently waiting for the terminating event). Here you can see the particular object instance to be checked and the event receiver (i.e. the work item ID).

10.5.4 Event Queues

In Release 4.6C or above, *Event Queues* can be used to improve overall system performance and manage events in error. Event queues store the results of the event linkage temporarily in a database table after the start conditions and check functions have been evaluated. This means there is a slight delay before the workflows are started, which helps to spread out the system load caused by the creation of workflows. To use the event queue to spread system load, you need to set the flag *Enable Event Queue* in the event linkage.

The event queue can also store erroneous event linkages, so that they can be restarted later, once the error has been corrected. To send events in error to the event queue, set the *Behavior Upon Error Feedback* flag in the event linkage to either *Mark linkage as having errors* or *Do not change linkage*.

> **Tip** It is a good idea to set the Basic Data of transaction SWEQADM so that by default (i.e. via the default setting of the *Behavior Upon Error Feedback* flag to *System Presetting* in the event linkage) all event linkages in error are sent to the event queue. That way you can redeliver them once the problem has been corrected.

The background job SWEQSRV periodically processes the queued items. Starting with Release 6.10 this is set up in workflow customizing.

Administer the event queue via transaction SWEQADM or menu path **Administration · Workflow Runtime · Event Manager · Event Queue**. The *Basic Data* tab specifies the default error handling for all events. In the *Background Job* tab you

---

3 In releases prior to Release 4.6C, the type linkage is viewed via transaction SWE2 and only the instance linkage is viewed via transaction SWE3.

4 Before Release 6.10 this was referred to as *event linkage* in the transaction.

5 Before Release 6.10 this was referred to as *instance linkage* in the transaction.

can schedule and view the background job, SWEQSRV, that periodically processes the event queue. The *Linkages with Errors* tab shows all events that are currently in ERROR status.

Examine the event queue via transaction SWEQBROWSER or menu path **Utilities · Events · Event Queue Browser**. This tab shows those events waiting in the event queue that have already been processed along with their status. If processing failed the first time, the event will be automatically retried in the next run. If an event has not yet been delivered, or is in error, you can opt to redeliver it.

Do not confuse the *event queue* with the *event trace*. This is used for problem solving and is described in detail in chapter 14, *Advanced Diagnostics*.

10.6   Generic Object Services

Generic Object Services are a set of business object based services you can include in business application programs. In many cases SAP has already built this into the appropriate SAP transactions. Usually Generic Object Services are included in the business applications that display or change the business object instance. For instance, while displaying an engineering change request or a marketing lead (shown in figure 10.3), you can access the generic object services for the lead. The available services are visible via the menu (**System · Services for Object**), as a button on the screen or as a floating toolbar, depending on the SAP release and GUI used.

Although the list of services varies from release to release, it includes:

▶ Starting new workflows ad-hoc based on the object instance via the *Start Workflow* service

▶ Viewing all current and completed workflows involving the object instance via the *Workflow Overview* service

▶ Subscribing (or canceling subscriptions) to events based on the object instance via the *Subscribe to/Cancel Object* service, a service that simply notifies when an event occurs for that object instance

▶ Sending a mail with this object instance as an attachment via the *Send Object with Note* service.

So, for example, you could use generic object services to view all current workflows based on the marketing lead selected and track their progress (fig. 10.3).

Note that you can only reach these services if the transaction has first implemented generic object services. To add generic object services to your own transactions consult chapter 13, *Custom Programs*.

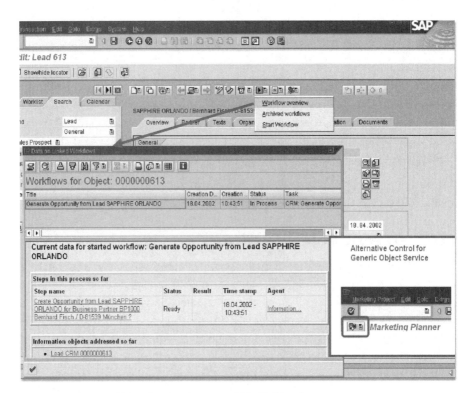

Figure 10.3 Generic Object Services from a mySAP CRM Lead

10.6.1 Starting Workflows Manually

Sometimes it makes sense for business personnel to start workflows manually on an ad hoc basis. For example, while viewing material master data someone might notice a value that needs to be updated, but they may not have the privileges to change it themselves, so instead they want to start a workflow to contact the person responsible for that material.

By starting a workflow manually, rather than by sending a mail, they can make sure the correct material is passed (no chance of typing errors), let the workflow find the current person responsible for that material, follow the workflow's progress, and be notified by the workflow automatically when this person has made the changes.

If a user needs to start the workflow manually, they should do it via custom forms (see chapter 12, *Forms*) or via *Generic Object Services.*

When you start a workflow manually, the workflow begins immediately, and may even take you directly into the first step (see synchronous dialog chains in chapter 4, *Work Item Delivery*). If you have defined a start form for the workflow, then this form is displayed.

To be able to start a workflow manually, you need to be a possible agent of the workflow.

> **Tip** In an emergency, all workflows can be started manually by a system administrator, via **Runtime Tools · Test Workflow** (transaction SWUS), unless the administrator is assigned to the workflow as a possible agent, in which case they can use transaction SWUI (via **Runtime Tools · Start Workflow**).

As you can see in figure 10.4, the standard screen for starting workflows has two sections. On the left-hand side, all the workflows are listed for which you are a possible agent. When you select a workflow, the description of the workflow is displayed on the right.

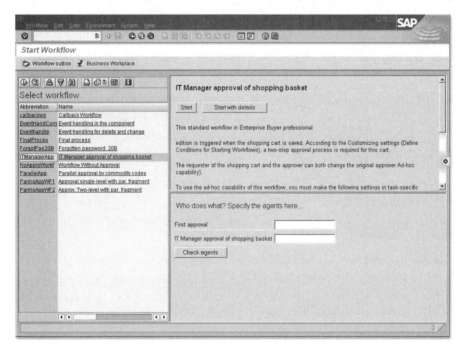

Figure 10.4 Starting a Workflow Manually

The function *Start with details* is used to add information such as attachments, notes or deadlines to the workflow via three tab pages. These attachments and notes are made available to all agents of the workflow.

10.6.2 Viewing the Logs of Related Workflows

The generic object services menu lets you browse the status of all workflows that are processing the displayed business object. A list of workflows that reference this business object instance is shown and you can navigate to the different logs of each workflow. Even ad hoc workflows, and workflows where the object was added as an attachment rather than part of the workflow definition, are displayed in this list.

10.6.3 Subscribe to an Object Instance

If you do not need to start a workflow, but just want to be notified of particular events related to a particular object instance, then you can subscribe to an object instance, using the Generic Object Service SUBSCRIBE. This function is useful for users who want to know when events occur that are related to a particular object instance, e.g. whenever a particular cost center master is changed. To make yourself a receiver of the event occurrence mail, in the application that supports generic object services for this object, use generic object services to subscribe to (or cancel subscription, if you are already subscribed) events for this object.

So that users can subscribe to your own events, create an event linkage (transaction SWE2) for your event, listing SUBSCRIBE as the receiver type, SGOSSUB_REC_FB_SEND_MAIL as the receiver function module, and SGOSSUB_CHECK_FB as the check function module.

The texts of the mail and the specific check function module to be used can be customized in configuration table SGOSSUB.

10.6.4 Sending a Mail

Use this option to send a mail to someone else with this business object instance as an attachment. The object can only be viewed if the receiver receives the mail in the Business Workplace. Microsoft Outlook and Lotus Notes may support this feature depending on whether the groupware interface has been installed.

A reference to this mail is attached to the object so that anyone who calls up the transaction used to display the object will see that the mail has been sent. If you intend to use this feature, make sure that all users are aware of how to use it and for what purposes it should be used. Make sure that they realize that they cannot send the mail to a user outside the system because the attachment will not be usable.

10.7   Starting Workflows from Messages

Whenever a message (e.g. error message or warning message) is sent to a screen, a user can view the long text of the message. If you create a workflow to be started from the error message, an extra *Start workflow* button is added to the error message long text screen that users can optionally push to start the workflow.

> **Caution**   Workflows cannot be started automatically when an error message is created.

For instance, if the error message indicates some master data is missing, you might set up a workflow that the user can start in order to contact the person responsible for the master data. To create a workflow linked to an error message use the wizard via transaction SWUY or menu path **Definition Tools · Workflow Wizard "Create Workflow-Message Linkage"**. This creates an entry in table T100W and generates the stub of a workflow definition with all the relevant container elements so that the details (including message type, message class, message number, message text, message parameters) of the error message can be evaluated in the workflow.

11 E-Process Interfaces

A business process has to remain flexible. At short notice you may need to adapt a few steps of the process to communicate over the Internet instead of internally within the SAP component. The technology is available in the heart of the SAP's WebFlow Engine to help you.

11.1 Internet and Beyond

It is very rare that a business process stops at your software system's boundaries. To remove this artificial boundary, SAP's WebFlow Engine supports different protocols for quick and robust integration with other components. Some of these may be SAP components but others will be completely independent of SAP.

There are two principle interface types you can use (see figure 11.1). On the one hand, there are interfaces to access other systems, allowing business methods to be called or attributes queried in systems outside SAP. These are the *inside-out* interfaces because they are called from inside the SAP component to communicate with the outside world. On the other hand, there are *outside-in* interfaces to SAP's WebFlow Engine allowing external systems to communicate with the process within the SAP component. An outside-in interface can be used to trigger the process, query the data in the process or reset the status of the process, thereby freezing, restarting or canceling the SAP workflow.

The inside-out type of interface extends the range of your workflow, often reaching out over the Internet to systems belonging to business partners. These are called collaborative scenarios and are best integrated with an open interface. Wf-XML is just such an interface, and in this chapter you will see how it works. It can also be used for integrating SAP components with each other. For example, the processes running in a backend R/3 system can be synchronized with those running in mySAP CRM using Wf-XML. Whether or not you connect two SAP components using Wf-XML or use a propriety SAP function instead is determined by your company's policy on interfaces. The proprietary interface may appear to be quicker to implement, but it is not XML-based, not as transparent and not as robust.

The outside-in type of interface is useful if you want your workflows to be triggered and controlled from another system.

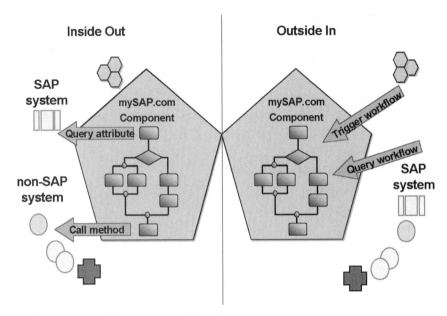

Figure 11.1 Diagram of the Two Types of Interface

11.2 Wf-XML

Wf-XML is an open interface, originally intended for use in collaborative processes with other workflow systems from other vendors. However, because Wf-XML is so tightly integrated into the Workflow Builder and the WebFlow Engine, it is also a convenient way of creating cross-system workflows within an SAP environment.

As the name of the interface implies, it is an interface based on XML messaging between the different workflows. These messages are sent as HTTP-POST requests because this is a widely accepted way of exchanging messages over the Internet. The HTTP-POSTs can also use the Secure Socket Layer (HTTPS) to prevent eavesdropping. There are also widely accepted methods of authenticating HTTP-POSTs, which means that the transport mechanism will be accepted anywhere by any of your partners.

The WebFlow Engine goes one step further by using the existing infrastructure of the SAP Web Application Server to handle the HTTP-POSTs so that when you are creating such a workflow you are freed from the maintenance of the transport layer. Indeed, the first test we performed with a non-SAP component (Staffware 2000, a major independent workflow and e-process management system) proved to be extremely easy to set up. A simple e-mail describing the data to be used in the workflows, together with the URLs of the respective services, was all that was needed to configure the workflows in the respective systems. Minutes later the workflows were up and running, triggering each other and transferring data over the Internet between the two systems.

11.2.1   A Collaborative Scenario Example

Imagine a car manufacturer who sets out to modify the design of one of the cars that they produce. Let us say they are unhappy with the brake lights and need a new design. The engineering change process is complex, and will probably use many workflows to streamline the critical parts of the process and document the way decisions were reached. However, after establishing the business case and the technical case for the change they have reached the point where they can ask their suppliers whether they are willing to supply the new brake lights in the volume required, how much they will cost, and how quickly they can deliver.

This is a *request for quotation* (RFQ), and traditionally the request will be made via e-mails or a B2B exchange (which may also lead to further e-mails being sent). Of course, the partner will usually not be able to provide a detailed response on the spot. Costing as well as checking that the technical specifications are met and that production and logistics can deliver the goods as promised will involve many highly skilled personnel, and to coordinate this the partner company will also use a workflow. Traditionally this workflow would be started by hand, but there will be far fewer errors and the process will deliver a result more quickly and reliably if it is triggered automatically and returns the results automatically as soon as it has finished.

This is where the strengths of Wf-XML come into play. The car manufacturer's workflow sends a Wf-XML message over the Internet to trigger the partner's workflow. When the partner's workflow finishes, it immediately returns the results. These Wf-XML messages are used to synchronize the processes with each other.

If you stop to look at this process in more detail, you will notice certain characteristics of the Wf-XML mechanism.

1. The car manufacturer does not dictate the internal details of the partner's workflow. This enables the supplier to set up their process however they like. One supplier might have many different experts coordinating their activities while using their ERP system to determine the tightest margins they can offer. Another supplier might have a very simple process, but a lot of experience. The best partner will win in the long term, and the secret of how their internal process runs will remain hidden within their company firewall. This is the private part of the process.

2. The details about what information the manufacturer will supply and what results they require have been arranged in advance. These details are passed within the Wf-XML message (the context data) but they are not determined by the Wf-XML interface. Wf-XML is a generic interface which gives precise rules about how the processes can synchronize with each other, but offers no suggestions as to which data is used and the format in which the data should be stored. So it is very different from EDI or RosettaNet, which offer precise data and process definitions. But, being generic, Wf-XML can be used for any process without restraints.

3. The complete process now has a structure and is transparent. There are private details but the workflow in the manufacturing system is able to show a graphical log of the process and offer deadline handling of the supplier's process spawned by the Wf-XML message. The process is no longer a series of isolated clicks in the Web; it now has a transparent structure (as you can see in figure 11.2).

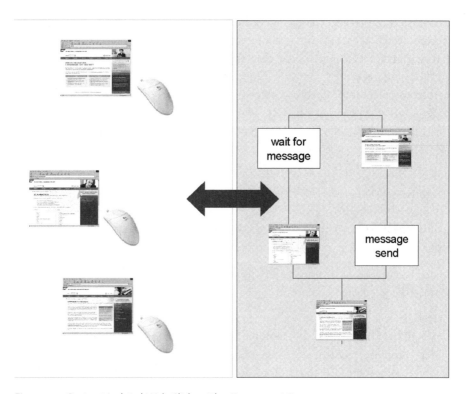

Figure 11.2 Contrast Isolated Web Clicks with a Transparent Process.

11.2.2   The History of Wf-XML

Wf-XML was the brainchild of Keith Swenson, at that time with Netscape, who envisaged a simple protocol for allowing different workflow systems to communicate with each other over the Internet. This was called the SWAP initiative. The underlying motivation was that the various workflow vendors would accept only a simple protocol, but a simple protocol is all that is needed to get the different systems synchronized with each other. As the project matured it was moved to the Workflow Management Coalition (http://www.wfmc.org) for the final touches. The Workflow Management Coalition is a body of workflow customers, eager to leverage their investment in workflow technologies, and workflow vendors eager to be part of the big picture. SAP is one such vendor.

Wf-XML 1.0 was ratified in May 2000 and is supported by SAP Release 4.6C. Wf-XML 1.1 is supported in Release 6.20. Within the workflow step definition, you can specify which standard and version is to be used to generate the XML messages.

11.2.3   What You Can Do with Wf-XML

In Wf-XML Release 1.0 you can:

▶ Trigger a workflow in another system (send a Wf-XML request: `CreateProcessInstance`) and wait until it returns results to your workflow. At this point your workflow continues just as if an internal subworkflow had been called and completed.

▶ Trigger a workflow in another system (send a Wf-XML request: `CreateProcessInstance`) and continue immediately, ignoring any results that are returned. This is the equivalent of a notification step.

▶ Allow your workflow to be triggered by another system without the need to reply (your system receives a Wf-XML request `CreateProcessInstance`).

▶ Allow your workflow to be triggered by another system, supplying the master workflow with results (send a Wf-XML request: `ProcessInstanceStateChanged`) when your workflow finishes.

In addition, the workflow can be cancelled by the remote system when that system dispatches a `ChangeProcessInstanceState` message. How these messages are used in the RFQ process to synchronize the supplier's workflow with the main manufacture workflow (on the left) is shown in figure 11.3.

Now that Wf-XML 1.1 has been released, there is even more flexibility, relating to the way that workflows interact with each other over the Internet. Analogous to the way workflows within a system can influence each other with events as they run, Release 1.1 allows the same type of control over the Internet. Release 1.1 of Wf-XML is beyond the scope of this book, but you can refer to the SAP Library Help to learn more.

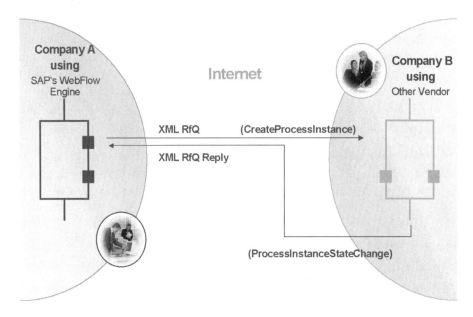

Figure 11.3 Diagram of the RFQ Process Showing Message Types

11.2.4 Configuring the System

From Release 6.10 onwards the HTTP-POST handling in both directions is performed via the SAP Web Application Server.[1] To create a Wf-XML (Web activity) step in your workflow you will need to know which parameters are required by the partner's workflow. If the parameters are simple data structures, rather than nested hierarchical structures, it only takes a few minutes to get the workflows talking to each other across the Internet, as follows:

1. Create a reference workflow with the correct container definition.

2. Add a Web activity step in your main workflow.

3. Create the binding within the step definition between your workflow and the reference workflow.

4. Add the URL of the partner's workflow to your step.

---

1 In Release 4.6C an Internet Transaction Server (ITS) was required to handle the incoming messages.

Creating the Reference Workflow

First create a reference workflow in your own system to represent the workflow in the partner's system. This workflow will simply be used to create a binding between your workflow and your partner's so it does not need to contain any steps. In fact it does not even need to be activated.

Define the container elements needed by the partner workflow, making sure that they are defined as export or import (or both) according to what your partner expects. Bear in mind that if your partner is not using an SAP component you will have to be careful about the data definition of the container. Your partner may not have ISO support for the different data types.

> **Tip** You can use an alternative binding to construct elements that have a different format from the standard data types.

Creating the Web Activity Step

The Web activity step type has its own step type, *Web activity*, because it needs parameters additional to the standard activity step, and because it has its own logic for supporting future interfaces from different standards bodies.

After selecting this step type, you should select which version of Wf-XML to use. This determines the format of the XML messages that are sent from your system, so it is critical that you get this right. If the wrong protocol is selected, the partner system may not be able to parse your messages. New workflows should be created using WF-XML 1.0 or higher. Protocol XML without envelope simply packs an object of type XML_DOC into the message, without any accompanying Wf-XML tags.

As newer versions of Wf-XML bring more features, you may have to decide, on a case-to-case basis, which is the lowest common denominator of workflow version that can be used between the different collaborating systems.

Add the URL of the partner's workflow (they will supply this). Do not use the wizard to create the URL unless your partner is using an SAP component or unless you want to generate your own workflow's URL to send to a partner.

Example

A URL to an SAP component: based on release 6.10

```
HTTPS://www.sapcompany.biz:80/SAP/BC/WORKFLOW_XML/?~proto-
col=03&~localkey=WS99999999
```

Now decide whether your workflow requires a reply from the partner's workflow after it has completed. If so, as is usually the case, set the *wait for reply* flag to be true. If you do not set this flag you will trigger their workflow and continue down through your workflow without waiting for a reply. Not waiting for a reply is appropriate when you simply want to notify the partner and a primitive e-mail notification is not sufficient.

The last step is to create a binding between the Web activity step and the partner's workflow. Do this using the binding editor just as if you were starting a sub-workflow. If you have checked the box declaring the step to be a *wait for reply* step then you can create a binding in both directions. In other words the partner's workflow may return a result. You will see now why it was necessary to define the reference workflow. This reference workflow is used to determine the container elements offered in Wf-XML binding. Wf-XML is so tightly integrated into SAP's WebFlow Engine that it is child's play to use it.

Binding Business Objects or Complex Structures

Often the world is a little more complicated than the simple case illustrated above. You may need to pass an object or complex structure in the context data of the Wf-XML message. Obviously, it makes no sense to transfer the key of a business object because the partner system will not be able to reference this object in your system.

To pass a complex structure to the XML message, simply define a binding with the complex container element as an importing parameter. Structures, multi-line elements and combinations of the two are supported in Release 6.10. The complex structure is simply packed in the Wf-XML context data as a nested structure.

To pass a business object you need to write code that converts the data to the XML format agreed with your partner. This XML code should be passed to the container in the form of a business object of type XML_DOC. For example, you could create a method[2] for a purchase order, which creates a business object XML_DOC. The code of the method renders the XML document using the data extracted from the purchase order. In the binding you pass the XML document to the partner's workflow. The WebFlow Engine will wrap this context data with more XML so that it conforms to Wf-XML and it will then transmit the Wf-XML message to the partner system. The partner parses the XML context data (after first interpreting the Wf-XML header data) and uses it within their process.

---

2 The reason an attribute is not used, is that the xml_doc is created in the database. Using an attribute would cause a new xml_doc to be created in the database every time the object is tested or inspected in the workflow container.

If you have to support a very complex XML representation of the context data, you can use the exit in the Web activity step to calculate the context data. If in doubt, take a look at the business object FORMABSENC, which includes an XML method TO_XMLdocument. This method returns a result of object type XML_DOC that you can add to the workflow.

The XML toolkit is particularly useful for rendering the XML code. Bear in mind that the 6.10 Release supports complex data types, including nested data types as well as multiline elements. For this reason it is often not necessary to write your own code to do the conversion. The WebFlow Engine automatically converts the structures and tables into XML context data.

11.2.5   SOAP (Simple Object Access Protocol)

SOAP, which is supported by Microsoft, SAP, IBM and others, is a commonly supported way of making remote procedure calls. In Release 6.20, the Web activity steps can pack the workflow container elements into a SOAP message, and send this message to a remote system. Although SOAP does not define the content of the message as exactly as Wf-XML does, it is a widely accepted message format, which is very useful when making a Remote Procedure Call (RPC) to other systems. Although this does not give you the plug-and-play comfort of Wf-XML with its predefined requests and responses, SOAP allows you a great deal of flexibility and certainly makes it a lot easier to integrate SAP's WebFlow Engine with other software that supports SOAP.

If you do use SOAP or the XML without envelope protocol for the Web activity step, then you will not be able to use the *wait for reply* flag because the message transmission and acknowledgement are handled synchronously.

Wf-XML 2.0 will incorporate SOAP into the interface.

11.2.6   Allowing Your Workflow to Be Started by a Wf-XML Message

If you have a slave workflow that will be started by your partner, then all you have to do is ensure that the workflow user configured in the Wf-XML service is assigned to the workflow as a possible agent for starting the workflow or define an authentification rule in the workflow header. If you do not do this, the partner's attempts to start the workflow will fail.

Make sure that your workflow container elements, which will be filled by the partner when starting the workflow, are configured to be *import* parameters. By the same token make sure that any container elements that are to be returned to the calling workflow are configured as *export* parameters.

The WebFlow Engine takes care of parsing the incoming messages, triggering the correct workflow, passing the data into the workflow, and returning the data to the calling workflow in a Wf-XML message.

> **Tip** When the partner asks for the URL of your workflow, create a Web activity step in your workflow (but do not save it) and use your own workflow id as the reference workflow. The URL generated by the URL wizard is what you send to the partner so that they can configure their system.

11.2.7 Viewing the Wf-XML Documents as the Workflow Proceeds

While you are setting up a workflow you will often want to inspect the XML messages that are transferred to check that responses are being received and that these responses are correct. You will quickly see that debugging a collaborative workflow is a simple matter because all the messages are logged.

A workflow step that triggers a workflow in a different system should have four (4) different XML messages associated with it (as you can see in figure 12.4):

▶ A `CreateProcessInstance` request (transmitted by your workflow)

▶ A `CreateProcessInstance` response (received by your workflow)

▶ A `ProcessInstanceStateChanged` request (received by your workflow)

▶ A `ProcessInstanceStateChanged` response (transmitted by your workflow)

If the *wait for reply* flag is switched off the two `ProcessInstanceStateChanged` messages are not received.

To view these messages you can navigate in the workflow log to the Web activity step and look at the objects attached to the work item.

If you want to view the messages used to start a workflow in your system you should navigate to the workflow log and display the workflow work item (type F). Once again, viewing the attached objects will show you the Wf-XML messages transmitted and received in conjunction with this particular workflow.

Alternatively, you can use the transaction SWXML to view all the XML messages within a certain period. You should be able to locate the Wf-XML messages sent from the partner and see the correlation with the work item ID of the workflow spawned by the message. If worst comes to worst, you can even compare the time stamp of the Wf-XML message that is received with the work items that were started around this time.

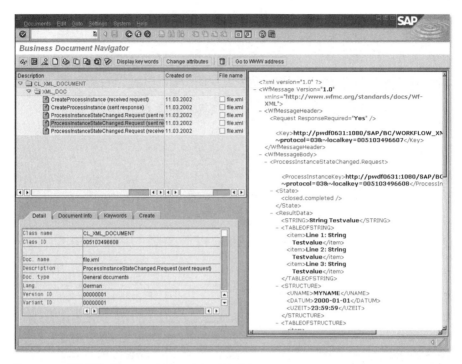

Figure 11.4 Wf-XML Messages Assigned to a Work Item

11.3 Inside-Out: Web Services

The World Wide Web contains a plethora of services, which can be called via a URL. Many of these services allow parameters to be passed, such as a query string that is passed to a search engine. Even more significant are the number of services provided within a company's intranet. These are easy to develop using, for example, Java servlets, Perl, Server Side Includes or SAP's *Business Server Pages,* so it is easy to see why the number of intranet services in particular is multiplying so quickly.

Examples of Web Services are search engines, who-is-who directories, B2B order catalogues and Fax/SMS[3]/pager messaging services.

In addition to Web Services that support a formal open interface, a typical company will have developed its own Web transactions independent of any standard, e.g. the company's who's-who or news about the company's product offering. These intranet services will play an important role in the workflows, and so Web-Flow supports these non-standardized Services too, even when they are dialog services.

---

3 SMS (Short Message Service) is a protocol, commonly used in Europe, for sending messages to mobile phones. It is similar to pager services commonly used in the USA.

Figure 11.5 A Workflow Calling a Dialog Web Service

In Releases 4.0 to 6.10, SAP's WebFlow Engine supports non-standardized services, which can be called via HTTP-GET calls over the Web.[4] From release 6.20 there is support for the open standard WSDL (Web Service Definition Language) for importing Web Service definitions. Additional support is planned for future releases. The WSDL support makes it even easier to integrate external services into a workflow. However, because the majority of Web Services have been created independently of any open standard, particularly on the intranet where a company usually has developed its own Web Services, this non-formalized mechanism is what we will concentrate on here.

The syntax for a simple service that does not return information to the workflow is a HTTP-GET to a URL of the form:

```
Domain + Directory + "?" + parameter1 + "+" value1 "&"
parameter2 + "+" + value2…
```

---

4 The only prerequisite is that the R/3 plugin is installed and that a Release 6.10 system is available in the system landscape to use as a launch handler.

The following example (see figure 11.6) shows how a Web Service can be used to send a text message to a mobile phone. The text message is a short string.

The URL, which includes the text as a parameter, is:

```
HTTPS://www.unimobile.com/services/sms?partner_
phone=0049123432123&msginv=How_are_you&partner_id=1234
```

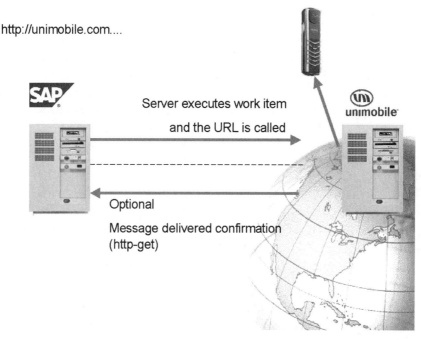

Figure 11.6 Example of a Web Service to Send SMS Messages

This example is particularly interesting because although most people think of the Web as a browser medium there is nothing to prevent such services from being called without a user interface. In other words many of the Web Services can be called as background tasks in the workflow. In fact, this possibility may turn out to be more important than dialog services in the end.

It is worth pointing out that the scenario depicted in figure 11.6 was enabled after a single phone call to the service provider explaining the requirements. The parameters and URL were sent back by the company within one working day. Half an hour later the service had been incorporated into a workflow. This is the beauty of Web Services. They exist, the interface is simple, and they can be added very quickly and easily to existing workflows definitions. Although Unimobile also supports WSDL and other standardized interfaces, this implementation uses a proprietary interface that is nevertheless very quick and simple to install. As increasingly support for Web Services is added to SAP's WebFlow Engine, the implementation will be made easier and allow for flexibility. For example, the UDDI.org interface supports a discovery mechanism so that Web Services can be located automatically using a standardized Web yellow pages rather than manually searching.

11.3.1 Parameter Transfer

As you have probably guessed, SAP's WebFlow Engine is capable of transferring the container elements from the workflow instance to the URL. In the example shown in figure 11.6 the partner phone number and the message text will come from the workflow because the text and phone number will probably vary in each flow. The customer ID, which is the billing ID for this service, can be either a constant in the workflow definition or a default in the service definition, as you will see later.

11.3.2 Callback Services

In the SMS example in shown in figure 11.6, the workflow calls the URL in the background and expects the message to be sent. If the service is unavailable, an error code will be returned immediately to the workflow, which can take corrective action. It is important to understand that this is a synchronous call because the reply is immediate.

Technically, what happens behind the scenes is that the workflow generates the URL from the workflow data and makes an HTTP-GET call which receives an immediate acknowledgement or error code back from the service. In this example a success code does not say whether or not the text message has been received, it simply reports that the URL has been understood, parsed correctly and that a text message has been generated and placed in a queue for sending.

If it was important to your workflow to receive feedback when the mobile device has received the text message then you will have to use a callback service. The service is called, and as in the above case it sends back an acknowledgment that the message has been understood, but it also sends back a reply much later (maybe hours) to say that the text message has been delivered to the mobile phone. Because this delay is unpredictably long, this call is handled asynchronously via a callback.

Callback services are also used for most dialog activities in the Web. As an example consider the URL that is called for a room reservation in the intranet, with parameters from the workflow specifying the date and size of room that is required. When the work item is executed a Web browser is launched, displaying the room reservation service with the date and room size pre-filled. However, at this point the user will probably specify additional features directly in the Web browser (such as whether a projector or sandwiches are required) and may even take various detours in the Web (such as online help) before finally making a selection and pressing the "Reserve" button. At this point, the Web Service must reply to the workflow with the reservation details as a parameter.

A callback URL is used to allow the service to reply to the workflow when it has finished. When the workflow calls the service, it passes the service a unique URL as an extra parameter. This URL is generated by the workflow and it is different every time a work item is executed. When the service dialog has finished (for example the "Reserve" button is pressed) the service calls this callback URL together with the list of parameters that the workflow is expecting back.

In the example shown in figure 11.5 these parameters would be the reservation number together with the maximum number of seats in the room and maybe even whether or not the room contains a projector. The URL (see figure 11.7) is generated uniquely every time a work item is executed, so that the system can map this service result to the work item that was called and the person who executed it. It also makes it impossible to fraudulently send service results to work items assigned to someone else.

To support the callback scenarios the Service must be able to handle the callback URL parameter. Because this involves programming support within the service, you must have access to the IT department providing this service. This will typically be the case for intranet services or services provided by close partners. This limitation does not apply to synchronous services. These can be called without the service having any knowledge of the SAP component calling it.

The name of the parameter that specifies the callback URL is `SAPWFCBURL`. This is automatically generated by the workflow when the service is specified as an callback service in the service cache.

11.3.3   SOAP

The current implementation supports the parameterized URL method of calling services, rather than SOAP, to provide the maximum coverage. However future Releases of SAP's WebFlow Engine will provide SOAP support.

http://intranet/hotels?Detroit

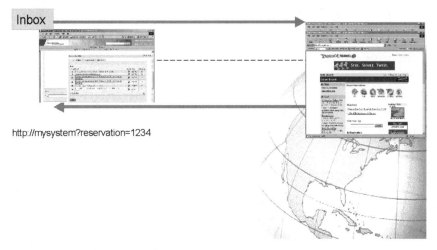

Figure 11.7 The URLs Exchanged in the Room Reservation Example

11.3.4 WSDL (Web Services Description Language)

WSDL provides a formal language for defining Web Services so that they can be interpreted automatically. This is useful because it allows a WSDL file to be imported directly into SAP's WebFlow Engine Web Service cache. There are some limitations in the 6.20 implementation, such as the fact that only the HTTP binding is supported and that complex data types are not supported. However, this is a significant step in making Web Services easier to deploy in SAP's WebFlow Engine.

It is the WSDL 1.1 release that is supported in 6.20.

11.3.5 Defining a Service

Once you have located the service you need, you should identify the URL and the parameters used. The steps required to use this service in a workflow are shown below:

1. Maintain a service definition in the central WebFlow service cache

2. Generate a task in the SAP component where the workflow runs

3. Add the task to the workflow definition defining the binding for the parameters

Adding the Service to the Service Cache

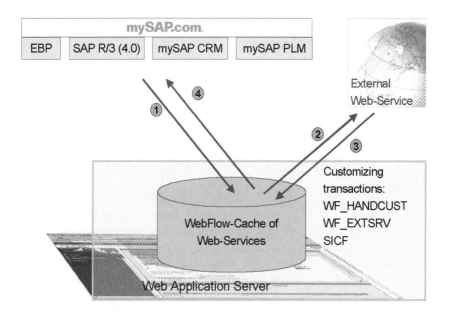

Figure 11.8 Architecture of Web Services Customizing

As you can see in figure 11.8, the services you define are stored in one central service cache rather than being replicated in each system where they are used. This makes good business sense because most services will be used by several different SAP components. For example, the mobile text messaging described above could be used in mySAP CRM to notify agents on the road about changes to a customer's status, and it could also used in mySAP PLM to notify service engineers about breakdowns and by a Release 4.0[5] R/3 workflow for urgent notifications.

Use transaction WF_EXTSRV to add the new service description. Decide whether you will be using HTTP or HTTPS (secure) protocol. The URL is divided into the domain and the directory. The next part of the service definition specifies how it will be called, i.e., whether it is dialog or background and whether it returns results for processing in the workflow. If you use a simple dialog task such as a Yahoo search, then you will also need to specify whether the "Cancel" button is displayed in a separate browser window (like an advertising pop-up) or in a separate frame above the main search results frame.

---

5 The prerequisite for using these services in an R/3 4.0 workflow is that this system has the Workplace plug-in installed and that there is an SAP Web Application Server (Release 6.10 minimum) in the system landsacpe.

The full list of service types is shown in table 11.1. Note that you can distinguish between *simple* services and *callback* services.

User Interface	Service type	Results	Example
Dialog	*Simple*, no callback. Instead a "Complete" button is displayed in a new browser pop-up.	No	Yahoo search
Dialog	*Simple*, no callback. Instead, a "Complete" button is displayed in the main browser frame	No	Yahoo search
Dialog	The service uses a *callback* to return the results.	Yes	Room reservation
Background	*Simple*, without a callback.	No	Send a preformatted pager message
Background	The service uses a *callback* to returns the results.	Yes	Send a preformatted pager message and return an acknowledgment after the message has been received on the mobile phone.

Table 11.1 Different Types of Web Services

Example

The example shown in figure 11.9 shows a service configuration.

```
HTTP://intranet.mycompany.biz/whoiswho?name=Einstein&dept=sup-
port&sapwfcburl
```

```
Protocol = HTTP
Domain = intranet.mycompany.biz
Directory = whoiswho
Parameter 1 = name , import parameter of type string.
Parameter 2 = dept, import parameter of type string
Parameter 3 = userid, export parameter of type string
```

The service is a dialog service with callback. Note that the SAPWFCBURL parameter does not need to be defined in the service cache, but the result parameter does.

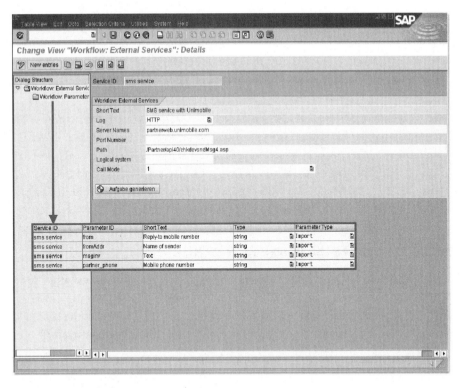

Figure 11.9 Example for a Service Cache Entry

Generating the Task

Unlike normal workflow tasks the service tasks are generated outside the system where they are to be used. A business server page (`WF_SRV_TASK_GENERATE`) is used to generate the task. For example,

`HTTP://intranet/sap/bc/bsp/sap/wf_srv_task_generate/cre-atetask.html`

You will need to specify a name and abbreviation for the task and then pick the Service that you require from the pick list.

> **Tip** If the service is not listed you should verify that it has been defined in transaction `WF_EXTSRV` in the central cache.

Next pick the RFC destination of the system into which you want the task to be generated.

Finally you will need to pick a transport request and package from this system and choose the *generate* button.

After a few seconds you will see that the generation has been performed correctly. Make a note of the task ID that has been generated.

> **Tip** If you prefer to generate the tasks from within your system then you should create a workflow to do this within your system. Because task generation is itself a Web Service (based on a Business Server Page) there is nothing to prevent you from creating a workflow with a single step assigned to the workflow initiator. This single step calls the task-generate service with the RFC destination pre-filled with that of the current system.

Adding the Task to the Workflow Definition

Adding the task to the workflow definition is as easy as adding any other task. Navigate to the spot in the workflow definition where you require the new step and add an activity step. Specify the name of the task to be added in the task field (or search for it if you did not make a note of it after it had been generated).

The binding is straightforward. You should create a binding to fill the parameters used by the task but do *not* pass data to the _OBJECT_ID parameter. This is unconventional but necessary because of the way the WebFlow Engine handles it.

If the service is a callback service you will be able to define a binding to fill the return parameters in the workflow. The return binding is either directly between the task and the workflow or between the terminating event and the task, depending on whether a synchronous or an asynchronous task is generated by the system. This is release-dependent. You will find that you cannot define a return binding for the simple services, which is what you would expect.

The rest of step definition is straightforward. If it is a dialog service you must assign agents to the generated task and define agents for the step.

> **Caution** A common mistake is forgetting to assign agents to the generated dialog task so be especially careful about this.

Activate the workflow and test it as usual.

11.3.6 How the User Calls the Web Service

When a user receives a Web service work item, it will look identical to his normal work items. In other words, the display of the work item text, attachments, and deadline information is identical to all the other work items in the agent's inbox. However, when the agent executes the work item, the default browser will appear with the service displayed within it.

If the service is a simple dialog service without callback, the user will cancel it using the "Complete" button in the frame or popup (depending on which is configured in the service definition). The browser will close and the work item will disappear from the agent's inbox.

If it is a dialog task with callback, the user must perform the action required (e.g. make the reservation) to complete the work item.

This behavior is the same, independent of which type of inbox (Web, iView, R/3, Outlook integration…) is used.

11.4 Inside-Out: SAP Business Connector

Describing how to use the SAP Business Connector in detail is beyond the scope of this book. Excellent documentation can be downloaded from the SAP service portal (http://sap.service.com/connectors). However it is worth mentioning in this section that the SAP Business Connector is a very robust middleware product, which can be downloaded from the SAP service portal. In addition, there are further connectors available from WebMethods, which can be used to create and parse XML messages, which conform to most XML schemas. In addition the EDI-FACT standard is also supported, making a good medium for collaborative communication with legacy systems.

There are two ways of using the SAP Business Connector within a workflow.

1. SAP Business Connector methods
2. XML content generation for Wf-XML content.

11.4.1 Business Connector Methods

You can write business object methods that call the SAP Business Connector to render XML messages and dispatch them. For example, an EDIFACT message in XML form can be generated from an SAP business object and dispatched to a partner company if your installation does not have an EDI engine installed. On the other hand, a method can be written to call the SAP Business Connector directly to render XML and dispatch it to partners.

11.4.2 XML Generation for Wf-XML Content

Using the content generation exit in a Wf-XML step, you can call the SAP Business Connector to generate the content part of the message for complex data types. By doing this you have the benefit of both worlds. The process handshaking is controlled by the Wf-XML but the content of the message can be mapped using a separate XML schema, which is rendered by the SAP Business Connector. The SAP Business Connector can be called synchronously with the key of the business object and will return the XML code, which is then included within the Wf-XML message.

11.5 Inside-out: Integration With Other Systems

The Actional Control Broker is a partner product from Actional Technologies (www.actional.com) but it is worth mentioning here because it maps directly into the WebFlow Engine. This is a middleware product, which generates SAP proxy objects from other systems such as Tuxedo or CORBA. The product makes the different systems transparent. This enables developers with different skills to collaborate easily on large-scale integration projects where many different systems need to be integrated quickly.

11.6 Outside-in: Calling APIs to the WebFlow Engine

11.6.1 SAP_WAPI Calls

You can make calls to the SAP component using the WAPI calls described in chapter 13, *Custom Programs*. The WAPI calls are all RFC-enabled, which also allows them to be packed in XML and transferred over the Internet in SOAP format. If you are simply connecting systems within your own landscape you can use a RFC destination to make the calls.

The most important rule when using these APIs is that you must document their use centrally so that the team doing upgrades knows at a glance whether upgrade issues are likely to arise. This also makes it much easier to test before the upgrade is applied.

11.7 Outside-in: Wf-XML

Wf-XML is described extensively above. What is relevant to this section is that Wf-XML is a very good medium for starting workflows from a Java environment or from a workflow system from a different vendor who supports Wf-XML. The only data you need supplied is the container data and the workflow ID to be started. By specifying `Request ResponseRequired="No"` no callback will be made to your Java application.

Listing 11.1 shows just such an XML message. Note that the protocol is 03 and the localkey is the ID of the workflow to be started. Element1 to element4 are the container elements expected by the workflow in this example.

```
<?xml version="1.0" ?>
<WfMessage Version="1.0"
        xmlns="HTTP://www.wfmc.org/standards/docs/Wf-XML">
  <WfMessageHeader>
    <Request ResponseRequired="No" />
    <Key>HTTP://intranet/ /scripts/wgate/wf_handler/!?
            ~protocol=03&amp;~localkey=WS90000012</Key>
  </WfMessageHeader>
  <WfMessageBody>
    <CreateProcessInstance.Request StartImmediately="true">
      <ObserverKey>HTTP://intranet/myapp</ObserverKey>
      <ContextData>
        <ELEMENT1>123</ELEMENT1>
        <ELEMENT2>more data</ELEMENT2>
        <ELEMENT3>4</ELEMENT3>
        <ELEMENT4>20011225</ELEMENT4>
      </ContextData>
    </CreateProcessInstance.Request>
  </WfMessageBody>
</WfMessage>
```

Listing 11.1 Wf-XML (1.0) message used to trigger a workflow

Any workflow or task can be started in this way. The only prerequisite is that the system has been customized to allow Wf-XML messages to be received.

11.8   E-Process Security Issues

The primary issue in e-process management, after agreeing on the technical communication protocols, is that of security, both from the user perspective and the system perspective. The issue of user security for the extranet users has been dealt with elsewhere, so we will concentrate here on the system security.

Achieving system security for e-process scenarios means finding the right balance between openness to all partner systems across the Internet and impenetrability to all possible attackers. Transmitting messages is not an issue because you can choose to whom you transmit, but receiving messages is another matter, as you want to restrict who you receive from and also remove the chance of data being stolen from your system or malicious message tampering with data in your system.

A complete treatment of Internet security is beyond the scope of this book but a short rule-of-thumb view will help you to understand how to tackle the issue. Comprehensive information including whitepapers and guidelines is available on the SAP security portal at http://service.sap.com/security.

The most important rule is to talk to the security experts in your company and establish what they will allow you to do. You must accept the company's security policy and work with this to find a solution.

Normally, the SAP component should be within your firewall to prevent direct access from the outside world. To enable limited communication with the outside world you will need a communication gateway outside the firewall that accepts certain messages and passes data to and from the internal system in an organized fashion. This ensures the safety of the business system but allows it to communicate indirectly with the outside world via the communication server. If the worst comes to the worst and the communication server is attacked then the internal system will continue to operate properly without losing any data but there will be a temporary stop on outside communication until the source of the trouble is located and blocked. Even if a computer worm damages the server the internal SAP component will survive unscathed.

Authentication is the technique used to verify that the business partner really is your business partner and not someone else. For example, you may have a particular workflow that your partner starts via a Wf-XML message. You must ensure that only messages from your partner are acted on while fraudulent messages are discarded.

SAP supports two types of authorization:

▶ Basic authorization
▶ Certificates

Basic authorization checks that the user ID and password that are transmitted in the HTTP header correspond to the user ID/password combination used in the system. If you are dealing with several partners in a Wf-XML scenario, each of whom triggers the same workflow in your system, you must create one user ID for each partner and assign these user IDs to the workflow task so that they are authorized to start the task. Your partners may use certificates (e.g. X.509 or X500) to authenticate themselves.

Similarly, your partners will require you to authenticate yourself when starting a workflow in their system using a Web activity. In Release 6.20 you can use the server certificate to authenticate your system. If they want to you be more specific you can specify a user for the basic authentication at the step level by defining a rule that returns the user ID/password combination.

Authentication plays an important role for Web Services because these external services will usually want to authenticate that you are who you say you are. For example if you call an external service to handle your company's car fleet then the car fleet management company will want to verify that you are a paying customer before executing the service. The SAP Web Application Server 6.20 supports certificate authentication via client certificates. Similarly, the callback can be authenticated in your system by specifying the use of certificates in the callback handler configuration in transaction SICF.

11.9 Other Options for Communicating with External Systems

Apart from using Wf-XML to communicate with external workflow systems, there are a few other options available for communicating with other systems.

▶ **Raising an event in an external system**
If you want to raise an event in an external system, use a task based on object SELFITEM and method TriggerRemoteEvent. You will need to pass the object type, object key, event, and destination to the method.

▶ **Triggering a receiver in an external system**
If you want to use a workflow event in the current system to trigger a receiver in an external system, in the event linkage, enter a receiver destination. You will need to code your own receiver function module to pass the event data and call the receiver.

▶ **Calling a method in an external system**
If you want to call a method or routine in another system, create your own business object method, and within it use an RFC call to call the external routine.

12   Forms

Electronic forms are the simplest way of displaying or maintaining data used in the workflow process for occasional users. Many types of form are supported, but choose your form-management with care to get the most out of your SAP component.

12.1   Introduction

Electronic forms are a great way of integrating occasional users into a workflow process. They are little more than the electronic equivalent of paper forms, displaying existing data and providing simple data entry fields, with no sophisticated controls or navigation to confuse or unsettle the occasional user.

Forms are easy to create, and easy to use. However you must make sure from the outset that using electronic forms really is the direction you want to take. There is a danger that what starts off as a form will gradually turn into a complex transaction, since the requirements from the stakeholders change and grow as they start to realize what can be achieved with workflow. Avoid this trap as best you can, because forms that evolve into transactions are difficult to develop and maintain. Often you are better off creating a Web transaction in the first place.

The types of forms supported by SAP's WebFlow Engine are:

▶ Simple forms (*forms* step)
▶ WebForms (SAPForms for HTML, using the ITS)
▶ E-Mail
▶ Web services including Java and Business Server Pages
▶ PC document forms
▶ SAPforms for Lotus Notes
▶ SAPforms for Microsoft Outlook
▶ SAPforms using Microsoft Visual Basic

The last three types of forms in this list require client installations of the SAP GUI, including the SAPforms runtime library. They also require the forms to be published to the client or to a server agent, that in turn publishes to the client, and this makes them difficult to deploy without a good distribution strategy. Because server-based forms as opposed to client-based forms are far more popular, and because development of client-based forms has been discontinued, we are not covering them in this book. The online documentation describes the client-based form generation in detail if you want to follow up on this yourself. PC document forms also require the SAP GUI for Windows as well as the relevant PC program, but because it is so easy to implement it is described at the end of this chapter.

Bear in mind when designing a process that although forms can be used in a process, there are probably other steps involving power users who access the data through their standard transactions with all the navigation and data verification that this supports. So your process should still use business objects where possible rather than collecting the data in flat container structures. You will usually want to transfer from one to another, which can be done via the binding between the steps and the workflow or via your own business methods. A typical example of this type of hybrid forms/transaction process arises when data is initially collected in forms before being written to the database using a BAPI and then processed as a business object in the following steps.

12.2 Simple Forms

The simplest way of generating forms is to use the *forms* step. These forms are generated Dynpros, which can either be used without modification in the GUI for HTML (as well as the equivalent GUIs for Microsoft Windows and Java) or can be used as the basis for generating IAC Web transactions. The advantage of these forms is in the simplicity of generation together with the degree of integration with the WebFlow Engine.

Simple forms have been available since Release 4.6D. The form requires a container element based on a structure to pass the data into the form and accept the modified data when the form is saved. When the form is generated, a screen is generated containing all the fields and their descriptions. The information about the data types and descriptions of the fields is taken directly from the ABAP Dictionary to simplify the generation process. It is now a simple matter of deleting the fields that you do not want, dragging the remaining fields to their correct positions and tidying up and beautifying the layout with the Screen Painter.

When the work item is executed, the agent will see three tabs as shown in figure 12.1.

▶ The primary tab displays the screen that you have generated.
▶ A second tab shows a summary of information relating to the work item, such as deadline information and its current status.
▶ A third tab shows the workflow toolbox, displaying the task description, attachments and allowing ad hoc activities such as forwarding the work item. Chapter 13, *Custom Programs*, provides further details on the workflow toolbox including how to use it in your own programs.

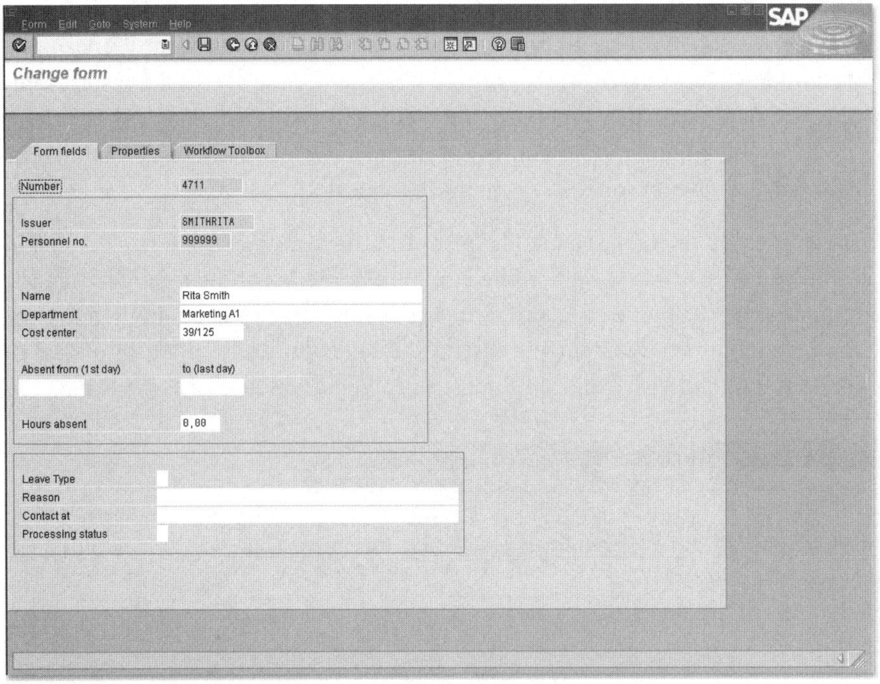

Figure 12.1 Form with Tab Pages

Using the *forms* step is a very powerful technique because the primary tab displaying the form preserves simplicity. But by switching to the other tabs you can easily access all the other workflow features, such as the workflow log or attachment handling.

In the step definition (🗐) you can decide on which type of form handling to use. Your choice determines the buttons that are displayed in the generated form (e.g. approved/rejected) as well as the possible outcomes of the step. The combinations are shown in table 12.1.

Form Type	Buttons Available
Display	Cancel
Edit	Save, Cancel
Approve	Approve, Reject, Cancel
Approve with query	Approve, Query, Reject, Cancel

Table 12.1 Simple-Form Types and Their Buttons

Bear in mind that the form is generated with all the fields open for input (unless you generate your form as a display type). This is deliberate so that you can add your own PBO Screen logic to the form to determine which fields are display-only and which fields are open for input. For example an edit-form may contain fields that cannot be edited and an approval-form may well contain fields that can be edited (such as the reason for rejecting the request).

You can even use extra hidden fields to control the display of the form. For example you could reserve one field in the structure to represent the role of a user and another field for the type of record that is being displayed. You could then use the PBO logic to control whether the rest of the fields in the form are displayed or open for input according to both the user's role and the type of record.

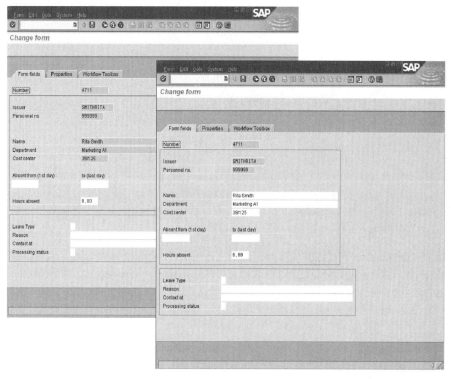

Figure 12.2 Two Views of the Same Form

The display logic is fully under your control, and the Screen Painter allows you the full flexibility of normal screen development. You can even allow the ABAP Dictionary definition of the relationships between the fields to control the error handling in the form and the input help.

Different forms (see figure 12.2) can be generated for the different steps in the workflow, but if you do consolidate them and use the PBO logic to enable or disable the individual fields, you will be spared a lot of maintenance work and make life easier for your users since they will be presented with the same basic form throughout the process. The beauty of this method is that you do not have to program any workflow logic into the forms, but at the same time all the workflow features are available through standard tabs in all the different views of the form.

You can use these forms in the SAP GUI for Windows, the SAP GUI for Java or the SAP GUI for HTML without any further development. If you find your form is becoming more sophisticated and you need a more powerful environment to extend it you can generate an Internet Application Component (IAC) from it—but beware of the maintenance issues involved.

Forms can also be generated to trigger a workflow. To generate a triggering form, navigate to the *Basic Data* of the workflow definition (*Version-independent*) and generate the form from the *Start-Forms* tab. From here you can generate the accompanying transaction and add it to a favorites list to make life easier for the workflow participants.

One final note on the technical side: You may be surprised to see that in the workflow definition there is no binding between the form and the workflow. This is correct. Data is transferred directly from the workflow container to the form. When *save* is chosen, the data is written directly back to the workflow container. Because *Display forms* do not have a "Save" button, they cannot change the contents of the workflow container.

12.3   WebForms

WebForms allow you to generate HTML forms from the workflow definition for viewing in a Web Browser. Because the forms are generated, they automatically include SAP features such the F4 input help. The fact that they are generated in HTML ensures that you have complete freedom of design, letting the form merge into your Intranet seamlessly. The main limitation is that the forms should contain no navigation or business logic otherwise, maintenance will not be simple

WebForms can be used to start a workflow or to execute a work item. WebForms use SAP's *Internet Transaction Server* (ITS) as the middleware between the SAP component and the Web Browser.

This section describes how to generate HTML forms, which you can rework to match your company's style guide. For example, you could add cascading stylesheets and your company's logo and standard images to merge seamlessly into an

Intranet or Extranet Web site. The forms will display in any modern Web Browser when the work item is executed from the IAC Inbox (ITS service BWSP), the Workplace MiniApp (ITS service BCBMTWFM0001) or the Enterprise Portal universal task list iView (see fig. 4.4).

The form is generated according to the import/export container elements declared in the workflow (if it is a triggering form) or the import/export task container elements (if it is a workflow step). Structures and complex data types may *not* be used directly; they are ignored when the form is generated.

If you do use WebForms, make sure that your stakeholder swears that there is going to be no navigation or intelligence in the form; otherwise, you will find yourself with excessive maintenance tasks. You cannot regenerate the form without destroying the HTML templates. You can change the underlying generated program, but this requires an in-depth understanding of the generated program and its limitations.

If the form needs to be intelligent, you are better off generating a WebForm stub and using this to spawn your own IAC, which you can create with complete freedom. The next section describes how you can trigger the IAC.

Prerequisite: Configure a namespace for the form using the workflow settings in transaction SPRO. The namespace should not exceed two characters.

1. Create a task, paying special attention to the container elements that it uses and whether these are import or export parameters. Use method FORM.HTML-PROCESS (in pre 4.6C releases, also select the *Internet enabled* checkbox) and generate the WebTransaction from the menu. This will also generate the Screens that are used to control the application logic within the form.

   ▶ Screen 50 is the entry screen, which is suppressed when the form is executed on the Web.

   ▶ Screen 100 is the form to execute work items based on the task.

   ▶ Screen 150 is the form to trigger a new workflow or task.

   ▶ Screen 200 is used for displaying success/error messages.It is displayed after the form has been executed and completed.

2. Enhance the HTML template so that it meets your requirements. From release 4.6C on, you should use transaction SE80 to do this, since this keeps the change management synchronized with the matching transaction. In earlier releases use *SAP@Web Studio* or your own HTML editor and check the templates into SAP change management using transaction SMWO.

3. Publish the service. From release 4.6C, use the ITS `IACOR` service to publish the Internet service and templates to your web server and ITS from transaction `SE80`. For pre 4.6C releases, *SAP@Web Studio* can be used to publish the Internet service and templates to the web server and ITS.

The Web Form will be started automatically when the work item is executed from the Easy Web inbox or the Enterprise Portal iView. The form is called via a URL to an ITS service as follows:

```
http://<webserver>:<port>/scripts/wgate/
<WebTransaction>/!?WEB_FLAG=X&~OkCode=CONT&WI_ID=<wi_id>
```

12.4   WebForms That Call an Internet Application Component

Using WebForms to launch IACs gives the form flexibility and power. Both SAP and Web development skills are required to implement this solution, but maintenance is simpler than using WebForms on its own. Navigation within the form is restricted to whatever has been defined in the IAC.

Combining WebForms with IACs is a useful technique because it provides the workflow agent with a natural Web Interface while at the same time making sure that the maintenance of the form is easy to control. As stated in the previous section, simple WebForms have a tendency to mutate into complex Web transactions once the testing begins and the workflow participants start providing their input. They will want more stringent checks, more computed data and complex navigation to other related objects or views. A form that starts off as a simple form but is developed into a transaction is difficult to maintain. It is far better to start with an IAC. The simplest way of doing this is to generate a WebForm without a user interface, which spawns the IAC. This is described here.

The prerequisite for using an IAC as a task is that the IAC exists, and that it can complete the work item. To complete the work item you can either use the workflow API as described in chapter 13, *Custom Programs*, or have the transaction trigger an event when processing has finished. If you trigger an event this must be used as the terminating event of the task, in other words the task must be asynchronous.

As in standard WebForms, before starting development you must first define a namespace as described in the previous section.

Now follow these steps:

1. Create a dialog method (asynchronous or synchronous) in your business object which calls the IAC as if it were a normal transaction. The parameters can be passed in whatever way you think fit, for example using GET/SET parameters or shared memory. For example,

```
SWC_GET_ELEMENT CONTAINER 'INPUT' INPUT_DATA.
SET PARAMETER ID 'INP' field INPUT_DATA
CALL TRANSACTION 'ZIAC'
```

2. Create a task based on this method (in pre 4.6C releases make sure you also select the *Internet enabled* checkbox). Generate the WebForm from within the task definition.

3. Include the HTML templates of the IAC in your newly generated service by using the ~SOURCES parameter of the WebForm services file. This should include both the IAC service name, as well as the WebForms service name. The names should be separated by a comma and no blank. The service file should not contain a user ID or password because it is the inbox user's ID which will be used. There is no need to edit the HTML template for Screen 50 because it will not be displayed.

4. Publish this new service to your web server and ITS.

5. If your method is asynchronous, you must make sure that the IAC triggers an event when processing is finished. For example the event Object Changed should be triggered whenever the *Save* button is pressed.

When your work item is excuted in the iView or Easy Web inbox, your IAC form will be displayed in the Web Browser.

12.5 Native WebForms

Developing your forms in a native Web language, such as Java Servlets or Perl (and of course SAP Business Server Pages) allows complete freedom of the design of the form and the navigation that is involved. Although this method involves calling BAPIs from the form, it is the most flexible when it comes to appearance and navigation. This is the only type of Web form that executes in both the Web inboxes and the Business Workplace.

If you have written your own Java servlet-based forms then you can use the Web services feature of SAP's WebFlow Engine to execute them from any inbox, not just the Web inboxes. In fact they are so well integrated that they even run in place in the IAC Web inbox as shown in figure 12.3. The same applies to other forms that are based on Web scripting such as Perl, SAP Business Server Pages, or Microsoft Active Server Pages (ASP). These forms are essentially dialog services with callback (refer back to chapter 11, *E-Process Interfaces,* for exact details). When launched from the inbox, they spawn a Web Browser displaying the form. When the *save* button is selected, a callback is made to the WebFlow Engine. The callback HTTP-GET includes results, as well as confirmation that this step in the workflow has completed.

Business Workplace

In the Business Workplace, the form launches a browser.

IAC Web Inbox

In the IAC Web Inbox, the form executes within a frame in the lower part of the window without launching a new browser session.

Figure 12.3 Native Web Forms Executed from the Business Workplace (SAP GUI for Windows or Java) and the Web Inbox (Browser)

To integrate the forms you should create an entry in the WebFlow service cache and generate a task as described in chapter 11, *E-Process Interfaces.* However, you should limit the amount of data passed initially between the WebFlow Engine and the form so that the HTTP-GET is not overloaded. The best technique for passing large amounts of data to the form is to execute this data transfer after the form has been called, using internal routines within the form's own code. For example, the form can query the SAP component for data using BAPI calls made with the SAP Java connector (JCo). Use the initial HTTP-GET (defined in the service cache) to pass the keys of the objects being handled in the form but not the complete data. The same applies to data that is returned to the workflow. Small amounts can be returned in the callback HTTP-GET but large quantities should be written directly to the workflow container or system via JCo RFC calls. The callback is also used to signal that the work item has completed.

This technique works in Releases as far back as R/3 Release 4.0, provided the Workplace plugin is installed and a SAP Web Application Server is available somewhere in the system landscape. You will be surprised how easy this is, particularly if you have access to Java or Web scripting skills, and may well end up deciding to do all forms management based on internal Web Services.

12.6   PC Document Forms (Including Microsoft Word)

A simple and powerful way of presenting information to the users. This can also be used for creating complex documents, but cannot be used for simple forms that input data.

Strictly speaking these are not forms but they can be used very effectively in many situations where forms are required. These forms can be created using any PC program that supports the Microsoft COM[1] interface (previously known as OLE), Microsoft Word being the most widely used. The limitation is that you can only display data from the workflow, or have agents edit the complete document directly. You cannot use these forms to return new or changed data to the workflow (other than the complete document) and these forms will not run in a Web Browser.

Nevertheless, the use of PC documents for forms is very effective, because they are so easy to read and the templates are so easy to create and maintain. The user who creates the document template does not need a technical background, so the users that will be actively involved in the workflow can design the form themselves. The documents are stored centrally in the SAP Knowledge Provider (Kpro) so they are available to everyone with access to the system. Because Kpro is used, different versions of the forms can be deployed. For example, the same form in can appear in several languages, or the form can give different views of the same data according to role of the workflow agent. The Business Object that is used to represent the PC document is WF_DOC, but there is no need to call this as an activity because it has been integrated directly into the PC document step type ().

When the work item is executed in the SAP GUI for Windows (such as from the Business Workplace), the work item is displayed with the PC document embedded within it. The user can cancel processing to keep it in the inbox or save the form to enable the workflow to continue to the next step.

---

1 Component Object Model

To create a form, use the *document templates* tray of the Workflow Builder to create a new template. You will be presented with a list of document types that have been configured in your system. Select the appropriate document type and enter the content that you require, including graphics or whatever else you choose to do to make it easier for your users to digest the data. Add the variables from the workflow by double-clicking on the container elements you want to add.

Having designed your template you can now create a *document from template* step, specifying the template that you have just designed.

The PC documents are not suitable for mass printing although mass e-mailing is supported. To send the document by e-mail you must convert it to an office document first. This is done by calling up the background WF_DOC CREATE_SOFM[2] method, which creates a PC document in the SAP office tables. This office document can be processed further with the methods based on the SOFM object type, such as the SEND method.

When the agents execute the work item they will display the form that you have created, with the variables replaced by data in the workflow.

The primary use described here is for the simple display of data, which has been collected during a workflow process. However, the same technique can be used for creating complex documents such as contracts, presentations, marketing collateral, or spreadsheets. By using workflow to support the document creation process you are ensuring that the process follows a predefined path, and that all the attachments and comments are preserved with the process and visible to everyone in the process. All the standard workflow functions can be integrated into the document step, including deadline management and notifications.

---

2 Available from Release 6.10 of the SAP Web Application Server.

13 Custom Programs

When your stakeholders require you to enhance the process with your own reports or control mechanisms, then in the interests of robust, stable, future-proofed programs you are best off keeping to the well-trodden path of public interfaces. These include the workflow open APIs, advanced business interface options, and e-mail (office document) interfaces. This section is also useful to the system administrator who wants to understand the WebFlow Engine in more depth.

13.1 The Engine

The WebFlow Engine provides a number of ways to add your own functionality. Before you create your own custom programs, it helps to understand very crudely how the WebFlow Engine works. This chapter presents a snapshot of the current implementation—there is no guarantee that the exact workings will be preserved in future.

> **Caution** This detailed description here is meant to help you understand how the system works. It is not meant to encourage you to extract information from the system or modify its behavior. As you can well imagine, a badly conceived periodic query of a table containing many millions of work items can seriously dampen the performance of any system.
>
> You should also be aware that by writing to the database tables directly or via internal SAP function modules, you can cause inconsistencies which can have a fatal effect on the workflows currently executing. In addition, you will have to check your programs carefully at every Release upgrade, because the tables and internal function modules could well change from Release to Release.
>
> Play safe, stick to the public interfaces, and use these carefully.

13.1.1 Work Items

When a workflow runs it generates an anchor, the workflow instance, which references all the relevant data of this particular instance. This is called the workflow work item and is stored in table `SWWWIHEAD` as a work item of type F. The workflow ID is unique in the system and is allocated using a number range that can be customized but uses a default if no customizing is performed.

The major steps in the workflow are given their own anchor, the work item ID. This can be of type W, B or F, depending on whether or not the step is a dialog task (appearing in a user's inbox), a background task (performed automatically without user intervention) or a subworkflow (a workflow called as a step of a parent workflow) respectively. There are other work item types, which you will see later.

Some technical steps, such as the container operation, are not represented as work items in any form. However, all dialog tasks and background tasks are represented by work items. Even though you can customize a workflow step based on a task so that it does not appear in the chronological and graphical logs (fig. 6.4), a work item is still created and this does appear in the technical log (fig. 6.5).

The detailed history of what has happened in each step is stored in a separate table (SWWLOGHIST[1]), referencing the original work item.

The agents assigned to a work item are also stored in separate tables. However this varies from release to release. Some tables are simply transient buffers which are deleted after the work item has been executed so only use the public interfaces to query the agents assigned to a work item.

Every work item references the task on which it is based and its parent workflow work item (if any) as shown in figure 13.1. This allows the WebFlow Engine to climb from a work item through the tree of parent work items until reaches the root workflow instance. Workflow work items reference the workflow task (e.g. WS0000001) with the version number. This is important because when you change the workflow definition you will have old work items that need to follow the old workflow definition, and new work items that need to follow the path of the newly activated workflow definition. In some systems where the process duration is long, you will find more than two versions of a workflow definition being followed at any one time, depending on when the workflow was started.

The complete list of work item types is shown below in table 13.1. If you look into a system that has been productive for many releases you may well find some of the obsolete work item types shown in the list. Bear in mind that a workflow instance can live longer than a release cycle; so be very careful before deleting them (see the section on archiving).

---

1 This is true up to Release 6.10, but changes are planned.

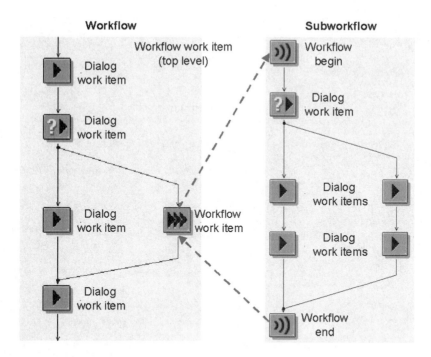

Figure 13.1 Work Item Hierarchy

Work Item Type		Purpose
A	Work queue work item	Used for work queues. These are many work items bundled together so that they can be processed simultaneously and split up after processing has finished.
		This is used in the asset management workflow.
B	Background work item	Background work items are executed by the user WF-BATCH in the background. A background task will have no agents assigned to it and will not appear in any inbox. You can think of them as automatically processed steps.
C	Container anchor	Obsolete. Container anchor work items are strictly speaking not workflow items because they are not associated with any workflow. They were used to link IDOCs to the business object that is created from the incoming IDOC. From Release 4.6B onwards the link is maintained without the container anchor work items.
		To delete these work items use report RSWWCIDE as described in SAP Note 153205.
		These work items are not deleted with SARA, the archiving transaction.

Table 13.1 Different Work Item Types

Work Item Type		Purpose
D	Missed dead-line work item	Missed deadline work items are created when a deadline is missed. They are dispatched to the deadline agents.
E	Wait step work item	Event work items are created when you have wait-for-event steps in your workflow. When the event arrives, and matches the conditions set in the wait step, the event item is set to completed.
F	Workflow work item	The workflow item represents a single workflow or subworkflow. Assigned to it will be work items representing the different steps in the workflow. Double clicking on a work item in the transaction SWI1 will display the workflow log.
N	Notification work item	Obsolete. Notification work items were used in early releases to represent a notification sent to an agent whenever a notification was configured in a workflow step. This has been replaced with mails.
R	Web work item	This work item is created for each web activity step. It is used in a web activity to represent the workflow that has been triggered in a remote system via the Wf-XML message.
W	Dialog work item	This is the commonest and simplest work item. It represents a task executed in the foreground by an agent. Dialog work items appear in the agent's inbox.

Table 13.1 Different Work Item Types (cont.)

While you should only access SWWWIHEAD via the public interfaces, it is helpful to know some of the principal fields available as shown in table 13.2 since most public interfaces return these.

Technical Field Name	Meaning
Wi_id	The work item ID
Wi_type	An abbreviation to show the type of work item. See table 13.1.
Wi_stat	The status that the work item is in. See table 13.3.
Wi_chckwi	The parent work item. If this field is blank then this work item is a top level work item.

Table 13.2 Prinicipal Fields of the Work Item Table SWWWIHEAD

13.1.2   Container

The data needed by the workflow is stored in containers. These can be standard tables, your own table (from Release 4.6D) or XML container tables (from Release 6.10). Every work item has its own container. This includes the workflow work item and every subworkflow, dialog or background work item beneath it. Although the workflow container is used to fill other work item containers (as shown in figure 13.2), having their own container allows the tasks to work independently of one another. This is especially important when they are executed in parallel. When the tasks finish, the contents of the work item container are passed back to the workflow container according to the binding rules as described in chapter 7, *Creating a Workflow*. To make maintenance easier, you can define which of the container elements are public (e.g. can be filled using events or by the application) and which are simply internal within the workflow definition.

The container contents are stored in table `swxml_cont` if the workflow containers are stored in XML format (the default for workflows created in Release 6.10 upwards). Older workflows, or workflows where the definition has been configured not to use XML will use the tables `sww_cont` and `sww_contob`. `Sww_contob` contains elements based on object references, whereas `sww_cont` contains structures and simple elements. If you want to write a report which accesses the containers you do not have to worry which table is used; simply use the APIs described later in this chapter.

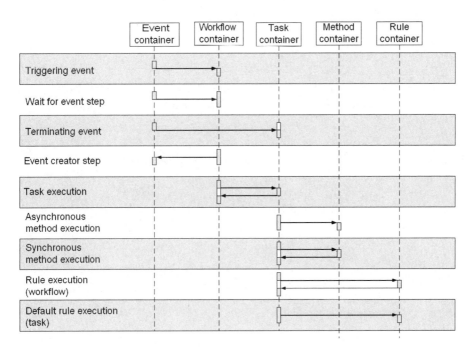

Figure 13.2 Possible Binding Definitions Within a Workflow

The flow of data from one container to another is defined by the binding between them. Figure 13.2 shows the different bindings possible.

13.1.3 Events

Events are transient. You can capture snapshots of them if you like using the event trace, workflow trace or event queue, but bear in mind that when the event has finished its job (such as triggering a workflow) it will disappear (almost) without trace. This is also true of the event's container.

13.1.4 Work Item States

You can see at a glance if a workflow is in progress or has completed by examining the state of the workflow work item. There is no need to access the workflow's history unless it is the detailed information (e.g. Who added which attachment when?) that you are interested in.

The parent work item is not completed until all of the steps in the workflow are completed or logically deleted. Each work item may pass through a number of states depending on the steps and techniques used. Table 13.3, Work Item State, gives a summary of all work item states and their causes.

Work item status	Short text and Description
CHECKED	*In preparation* The work item can be created, but the *Create Work Item condition* for the step is not yet fulfilled.
WAITING	*Waiting* The work item has been scheduled for its *requested start*. A work item has this status ▶ If it already exists but the *requested start* specified in the workflow definition has not yet been reached. ▶ If it has been set to resubmission Work items in the WAITING status are not displayed in the workflow inbox.
READY	*Ready* The work item has been released for execution and appears in the workflow inbox of all recipients. The *Replace* option in the inbox also sets a work item to READY status.

Table 13.3 Work Item State

Work item status	Short text and Description
SELECTED	*Reserved* The work item has been reserved (e.g. via the "Reserve" option in the inbox) by one of its recipients with the result that its status has changed from READY to SELECTED. A work item in the SELECTED status is then displayed to this recipient only. It is no longer displayed in the workflow inboxes of the other recipients.
STARTED	*In process* The work item is currently being processed by an agent or it is in the middle of being executed in the background. A work item also has this status ▶ If the work item is waiting for a terminating event ▶ If the user cancelled out of the method ▶ If the method was terminated with a temporary exception for which no subsequent steps have been modeled
COMMITTED	*Executed* The work item has been executed but is awaiting explicit confirmation of its completion. The work item only has this status if it is necessary to confirm that it has been completed. A work item with COMMITTED status can be repeatedly executed or forwarded until it is set to the status COMPLETED.
COMPLETED	*Completed* The execution of the work item is completed. The result of the task represented by the work item is correct, i.e. the result modeled in the workflow definition. Work items in the COMPLETED status are not displayed in the inbox but they are displayed in the outbox.
CANCELLED	*Logically deleted* Execution of the work item is no longer meaningful or required by the workflow logic. A work item is changed to the CANCELLED status when: ▶ The required number of processing paths has been executed in a fork, and the work items in the other paths that have not yet reached the COMPLETED status are automatically set to the CANCELLED status. ▶ A process control step sets the status, for example as part of modeled deadline monitoring. ▶ An administrator intervenes—the administrator can only set a work item to the CANCELLED status if it has not yet reached the COMPLETED status and is not part of a higher-level workflow. Work items in the CANCELLED status are not displayed in the inbox. A work item with the CANCELLED status may have caused database changes or other actions (raise event, send e-mail). These changes are not rolled back automatically.

Table 13.3 Work Item State (cont.)

Work item status	Short text and Description
![Error icon] ERROR	*Error* Execution of the work item was terminated with an application or system error. When a step in a workflow terminates with an error, the parent workflow itself is assigned the status ERROR. These items appear in the administrator's report displaying erroneous items, and a notification is sent to the administrator's inbox.

Table 13.3 Work Item State (cont.)

Although not all types of work items can be found in all of these states, it is nonetheless a very useful guide as to what is possible. The status changes of dialog work items are shown in figure 13.3.

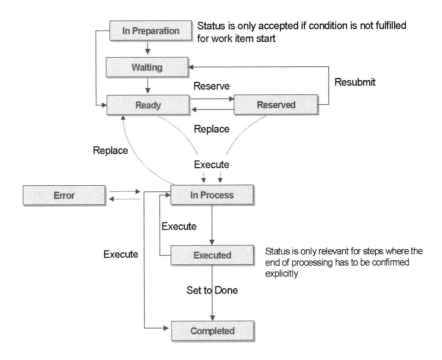

Figure 13.3 Status and Status Transitions of a Dialog Work Item

13.2 The Workflow APIs

The workflow APIs allow you to develop your own custom user interfaces instead of using the more generic interfaces provided by SAP as standard. You might use an API if you wanted to create your own work list for service engineers with additional features which are only relevant to service engineers and contain only the work items relevant to service management. Or maybe a supervisor wants a process monitor where it is easy to see at a glance which workflows are at a particular status.

Of course, one way of finding an interface to the system is to dive into the development workbench and search for suitable function modules and reports. You might even be tempted to debug your way to the primary SQL tables used by the engine. The disadvantage of this approach is that these modules are liable to change from release to release, making maintenance expensive and release upgrades difficult to perform. Even if you have checked the database indexes for performance and tested your routine to perfection, there is no guarantee that the database table's properties will not change in the next release. By sticking to the workflow interfaces, you will not only be spared this gratuitous maintenance but you will also automatically gain from performance improvements made by SAP to the interfaces in new releases. You can be sure that there will be performance improvements, because performance is one of the most significant focuses of the development team for every new release.

Your calling program may be either an ABAP program within the SAP component or an external program programmed in another language such as C or Java. In a typical installation you may also need to call the API from one mySAP.com component to access another component in the same installation via an RFC destination. This next section shows the APIs available.

13.2.1 WAPI (Workflow Application Programming Interfaces)

The WAPI calls are delivered as part of the SAP Web Application Server, so they are available in all the mySAP.com components.

The parameter interface to the calls has been designed so that it is easy to call the WAPIs from outside the workflow environment. All SAP_WAPI function modules may be called via an RFC connection or via SOAP.

The Simple WAPI Container

The simple WAPI container is used by several WAPI calls and differs in structure from the container used within the Business Objects (also used internally in the WebFlow Engine). The WAPI container is made up of simple name value pairs. In other words, the container structure has two fields—name and value, each of type string, making them easy to fill. The time format used is hhmmss and the date format is yyyymmdd (the internal SAP format). The SWC container macros may not be used to fill the WAPI container.

SAP_WAPI_CREATE_EVENT

As the name suggests, this call generates an event, which can be used to start a workflow or some other event receiver.

This call will normally be used in preference to SAP_WAPI_START_WORKFLOW, but to find out which is most appropriate consult section 13.3.1 first.

In common with all other WAPI calls, this call uses the WAPI container to pass data to the event container, which is in turn transported to the workflow.

SAP_WAPI_START_WORKFLOW

This, together with SAP_WAPI_CREATE_EVENT, is the simplest and most useful WAPI call. Simply fill the container with value pairs and specify a workflow definition to start. If the return code is zero the workflow has started properly. For an analysis of whether to start a workflow with an event or whether to start it directly, refer to section 13.3.1 first.

When this API is used to start a workflow, make sure that the user running the program that starts the workflow is assigned to the workflow as a possible agent, otherwise they will not have the authority to start it. This is true even if it is a background job that calls the WAPI.

SAP_WAPI_WORKITEMS_TO_OBJECT

This function call is useful when you are creating your own status reports about the lifecycle of an object. For example you may want to create a report to show who created which view for a material master record creation. By collecting all the work items related to this material master record and by sorting them chronologically, you can create a simple status report showing who did what when and who is currently working on the record.

The amount of data collected depends on the input parameters used. You can speed up the call by leaving the *TEXT* flag blank so that the work item text is not returned with the list of work items. If you simply want to know whether or not running work items exist use the SAP_WAPI_COUNT_WORKITEMS with the appropriate filter. This can be executed very quickly because very little data is extracted from the database. Coupled with a filter this can be used to check whether or not a particular workflow process is already running for a particular business object. If necessary the process can be cancelled and restarted if only one running instance is required.

The SELECTION_STATUS_VARIANT variable can have the value 0001 or 0002. 0001 will only select work items that are still in progress (READY, IN PROCESS, EXE-

CUTED, RESERVED) whereas Status 0002 will only select work items that have finished or not yet started (Status CANCELLED, WAITING, COMPLETED, ERROR). You must specify one variant or the other. If necessary your transaction will have to perform the query twice, combining the results from each status variant.

SAP_WAPI_READ_CONTAINER

Use this call to read a workflow's container. This can be very useful when writing your own custom reports to show details of a workflow's progress using your own custom report rather than the generic log.

For example, if your process consists of three phases, data collection, data validation and transfer to production, you might want to produce a simple report showing which of the phases the workflows are currently in. Assuming that the binding in your workflow definition is used to fill a status element with values representing the three phases, your report can then read the container to determine the workflow's status, in business terms.

Because each phase may consist of several steps, it is not enough to look at which step the workflow is on. This would be dangerous anyway because the steps are likely to be deleted or added when the process definition is improved from time to time. Instead of using the steps, add a new container element "phase" and fill it using the binding after each phase has finished. You can fill the element with a meaningful text, but in the long run you are better off having the display portion of the report interpret numeric or text constants to describe the status. This information can be complemented by standard attributes, such as those showing when the workflow was started and who triggered the process.

You can use the same technique to highlight processes where a deadline has been missed or to specify selection criteria for the report. For example, you can show all workflows in the data verification stage. If you use flags in the container to show that a deadline has been missed, make sure the flag is reset after the step has finished because that missed deadline is then simply history.

It is very simple to program fancy display features into the report using the SAP List Viewer (ALV). ALV handles formatting, filters, alerts, and sorting automatically without you having to do any development work yourself.

SAP_WAPI_WRITE_CONTAINER

Writing directly to the workflow container is dangerous because it can compromise the integrity of the process. However, if done carefully you can provide a number of useful administrative functions using a simple homegrown user interface. For example in your own transaction which overwrites flags used by the workflow to evaluate branching, you can allow the administrator to override the normal flow logic skipping steps or adding in new steps elsewhere.

The sky is the limit to what you can do by combining your own custom report with flags and conditions in the workflow definition, but be careful that you do not waste time duplicating existing ad hoc features of SAP's WebFlow Engine. For example you can use events (combined with wait steps), instead of container modifications to force the workflow to restart. You can define anchor steps in the workflow to allow an administrator to override the normal flow path.

When changing container elements, make sure you take into account the time/date data conversions as described at the beginning of the WAPI section.

SAP_WAPI_COUNT_WORKITEMS

This is used to count how many work items have been generated for an agent. If no agent is specified the results are the total for all agents, in other words for all work items in the system that match the filter criteria passed to the WAPI call. You can pass it a task filter, a status filter or a work item type filter. The results are returned in a table. If the `detail_level` parameter is two or more a breakdown of the work items is returned. A detail level of zero is much faster but simply returns the total number of work items in the agent's inbox.

13.2.2   Function Modules

SWE_EVENT_CREATE

This function module can be used to raise an event, which in turn can trigger a workflow. It is described in detail in section 13.3. The difference between this and `SAP_WAPI_CREATE_EVENT` is that `SWE_EVENT_CREATE` uses the same container structure as the Business Objects. This makes it more convenient to use for programs executing within the SAP component.

13.3   Advanced Business Interface Techniques

13.3.1   When Should I Start a Workflow with an Event?

Whenever you want to automatically start a workflow, it is usually best to use an event. It is possible to automatically start a workflow directly from a business application program, for example by using function module `SAP_WAPI_START_WORKFLOW` in the code. However, events are much more flexible because:

- You can start none, one, or many workflows without changing the business application.
- You can change the conditions under which the workflow starts and which workflows start without changing the business application.
- You can activate/deactivate them whenever you want. For example, you can deactivate an existing workflow and activate a new workflow in its place without changing the business application.
- You can use the same event not just to start workflows but also to complete work items, complete workflows, restart workflows, or change the direction of existing workflows.
- You can use event queues to spread peak loads for improved system performance.

The disadvantages of triggering a workflow via an event are:

- Events use additional resources and therefore cost a little additional performance (minimal in recent releases).
- Events could overrun the RFC queue if triggered thousands of times in a short time interval, typically in overnight background reports.
- There is no handle (work item ID) returned to the calling program.
- Prior to Release 4.6C the event linkage is disabled automatically if there are problems with it. This can cause administration problems in the production environement.
- If you want the first step of the work item to popup immediately without the user visiting their inbox (synchronous dialog chain), you cannot start the workflow with an event.

Unless you need to cover one of the exceptional circumstances described above, it nearly always makes sense to start the workflow by raising an event. Only if you are using a release prior to 4.6C or if you have serious performance problems that cannot be resolved by using the event queue, or if you are triggering large volumes of workflows in background jobs, should you consider starting the workflow directly from your own programs.

> **Tip** If you are using a Release 4.6C system or above, and are dealing with workflows creating a high volume of work items, you should use the event queue to distribute event creation at peak times. This gives better results than starting the workflow directly. The event queue is described in detail in chapter 10, *Business Interfaces*.

13.3.2 Raising Events by Calling a Function Module

If none of the event configuration options described in chapter 10, *Business Interfaces,* are suitable, or you want to include events in your own programs, you can code the event-raising yourself using SAP-provided function modules.

It is up to you to make sure that the event is raised at the right time. For instance, if you are creating an event to tell the WebFlow Engine you have just created a new application object, you must make sure that the event is only raised if the application object is created (i.e. you don't want to raise the event if the user cancels out of the program or the object creation fails). Otherwise the workflow could start out in error (if the object doesn't yet exist) or look at old instead of new data (if changes have not yet reached the database).

Events notify workflow about object status changes that have already occurred. So make sure the event is not raised until the relevant status change has actually taken place, i.e. has updated the database. For this reason, the function module for raising an event should be called in the same *logical unit of work* (LUW) as the one in which the status change is made.

> **Caution** The event will not be raised until the ABAP command COMMIT WORK is called. The commonest mistake in custom programs which raise events is that no explicit COMMIT WORK is made following the function module call. If you forget this, the data changes made in the program will still be committed to the database (via an implicit commit when the program finishes) but no event is raised. If you are using this call in an SAP user-exit or Business Add-In (BAdI), rely on the SAP programs to make the COMMIT WORK call so that the SAP commit logic (the logical unit of work) is not interfered with and the data remains consistent. SAP_WAPI_CREATE_EVENT has a parameter which determines whether or not a commit work should be performed by the WAPI call itself.

It is usually sufficient to raise events by calling one of the relevant function modules such as SAP_WAPI_CREATE_EVENT or SWE_EVENT_CREATE. At a minimum you need to specify the event to be raised, including the object type and object key. The event container is optional but very useful, since it allows you to transfer additional information to the workflow.

If you use SWE_EVENT_CREATE, use the workflow macros in include <CNTN01> to fill the container (you will find a list of the workflow macros in the appendix). Immediately after filling the container call the swc_container_to_persistent macro.

Below is some sample code that raises an event Cancelled for business object SBOOK when a matching application table is updated. Note that the event is raised only after the database has been successfully updated.

```
PROGRAM ZCREATE_EVENT.

* Change your application object ...
  UPDATE sbook ...
* Check that the change has worked before raising the event
  IF sy-subrc EQ 0.

* If the new data needs to be committed to the database
* for the receiver type function module, check function
* module or start condition to work, you can add another
* COMMIT WORK statement at this point

* Fill the container with any event parameters ...
    EVENT_CONT-ELEMENT = 'Element1Name'.
    EVENT_CONT-VALUE   = value1.
    APPEND EVENT_CONT.

* Cast the reservation number to the object key.
    OBJ_KEY = reservation_no.

* Raise the event
    CALL FUNCTION 'SAP_WAPI_CREATE_EVENT'
      EXPORTING
          OBJECT_TYPE                = 'SBOOK'
          OBJECT_KEY                 = OBJ_KEY
          EVENT                      = 'Cancelled'
          COMMIT_WORK                = ' '
      IMPORTING
          RETURN_CODE                = rc
      TABLES
          INPUT_CONTAINER            = EVENT_CONT.

      IF rc is not initial.
```

```
        MESSAGE….
    ENDIF.
  ENDIF.
* Perform additional database access
…
* Save all the work in the one logical unit of work
  COMMIT WORK.
```

Listing 13.1 Event-Rasing for a Business Object Type

For more complicated situations you must use alternative function modules to ensure the event is raised at the right time. These function modules have the same interface as SWE_EVENT_CREATE.

SWE_EVENT_CREATE_IN_UPD_TASK

This function module makes it possible to raise events in an update task, where the logical unit of work is split between dialog and update processes. In contrast to the function module SWE_EVENT_CREATE, it can be called with the addition of IN UPDATE TASK, so that it is synchronized with the database changes.

Use this function module if your program updates the application object using the update task. Most SAP-provided programs use the update task for making database changes. Make sure the event is created after the application object update in the update sequence, but before COMMIT WORK.

Typical situations are when the event is raised within a user-exit or BAdI or within your own transactions. Make sure that the user ID of the person triggering the workflow is added to the event container so that it makes its way through the update task and the RFC queue to the workflow. This ensures that the workflow initiator is set correctly despite the triggering from within the update task. The same applies to the next function module, SWE_EVENT_CREATE_FOR_UPD_TASK.

SWE_EVENT_CREATE_FOR_UPD_TASK

This function module is for a very specific situation, namely that you have an asynchronous task based on a "Create" method. In other words you want the task to be completed when the object is physically created in the database. Normally terminating events need to know the object key when the work item is created, but if you are creating an object you often will not know the new object key until after the method has completed.

Your own program code that creates a new object should include this function module, which picks up the last work item as the work item requestor before raising the event, so that the terminating event can be correctly matched to the waiting work item. Make sure the call to this function module is made after the application object update in the update sequence, but before `COMMIT WORK`.

> **Caution** The commonest cause of synchronization problems in a workflow arise when a terminating event precedes the database changes. Choose your triggering function module correctly to avoid such problems.

Incidentally, the SAP programs that control the General Status Management or the Change Document event-raising use these function calls. That is why you must specify explicitly whether or not you are triggering a creation event in these transactions. Remember that regardless of which function module you use, the event creator never knows whether there are none, one or many receivers, so the function call cannot tell you if any workflows were affected by the event.

Check Function Module

A check function module dynamically determines whether a receiver should be notified of an event being raised, e.g. whether the workflow is triggered. From Release 4.6C onwards you should use start conditions wherever possible to determine whether or not to trigger a workflow (as described in chapter 10, *Business Interfaces*). Only revert to check function modules for very complex rules.

The result of a check function module is either:

▶ Successful execution—in which case the receiver will be called. In other words, the workflow is triggered or the step is terminated properly.

▶ An exception—in which case the receiver will not be called. In other words, the event is ignored.

In practice, you usually only create a check function module when you want to determine whether a workflow should be started. Check function modules are rarely used for terminating events.

You can use any of the information in the event container to determine the outcome in the check function module. The interface of the check function module is described in the documentation for the function module `SWE_TEMPLATE_ CHECK_FB`. You must use this interface exactly as specified. There is no naming convention restriction on the name of the function module, and of course the code inside the function module is completely up to you.

Here is an example of a check function module for a `SBOOK.CREATED` event. Notice that all parameters are information you can use to determine whether the receiver should be notified. The only result is either an exception or successful

execution. So that the appropriate workflow macros can be used (such as SWC_
GET_ELEMENT), the statement INCLUDE <CNTN01> should be included in the global data area of the matching function group.

```
FUNCTION Z_CHECK_CHANGED_BY_VALID_USER.
*"----------------------------------------------------------------
*"*"Local interface:
*"  IMPORTING
*"    VALUE(OBJTYPE) LIKE  SWETYPECOU-OBJTYPE
*"    VALUE(OBJKEY) LIKE   SWEINSTCOU-OBJKEY
*"    VALUE(EVENT) LIKE   SWETYPECOU-EVENT
*"    VALUE(RECTYPE) LIKE  SWETYPECOU-RECTYPE
*"  TABLES
*"    EVENT_CONTAINER STRUCTURE  SWCONT
*"  EXCEPTIONS
*"    INVALID_USER
*"----------------------------------------------------------------
* This check function module checks if the user who created
* the flight booking is one of a pilot group of workflow users.
* The pilot group of workflow users is held in a custom
* table.
* For the pilot, the workflow will only be started if the
* user is in the custom table.
* Once the pilot phase is over, and the workflow can be rolled
out
* to the rest of the company, this check function module
* will be removed from the event linkage

  DATA: pilot_users LIKE pilot_user_line,
        initiator   LIKE swhactor,
        user        LIKE sy-uname.

* Read the event initiator from the event container
* The standard container element for the event initiator
* is called _EVT_CREATOR and is in agent format
  SWC_GET_ELEMENT event_container '_EVT_CREATOR' initiator.

* Check if the user is a pilot user
  SELECT user FROM ZPILOT_USER
   WHERE user = intiator-objid.
   IF sy-subrc NE 0.
```

```
* Stop the workflow being notified if the user is not a
* pilot user
    RAISE invalid_user.
  ENDIF.
ENDFUNCTION.
```

Listing 13.2 Check Function Module for Event

To use the check function module, insert it into the appropriate event linkage entry (transaction SWE2) after first activating the event linkage in the Workflow Builder. Before diving in to create your own check function module, remember that if you want to determine whether or not to start the workflow based on event parameters or attributes linked to the event object, then it is easier, quicker, and far more transparent to create a start condition.

13.3.3 Advanced Event Linkage

The event linkages (transaction SWE2) are normally created for you automatically from the Workflow Builder.

The only exceptions to this are when you want to:

1. Raise an event in a remote SAP component, in which case you will have to define the event linkage manually

2. Use a check function module

3. Create your own receiver type function module to determine which workflow to start dynamically.

Before discussing how to create your own receiver function module, it is worth looking in to the processing of the event linkage table in a little more detail.

At runtime, when an event is raised the *event manager*:

1. **Creates the event container**
   This includes creating and adding the object instance (based on the object key used when raising the event) and the event initiator (based on the current user). Any special event parameters passed during the event creation are also added.

2. **Checks to see if a specific work item requestor has been saved**
   (Via function module SWE_EVENT_CREATE_FOR_UPD_TASK)

3. **Finds all active event linkages for the event**
   This involves finding all active linkages, not just for this object and event, but also any supertype objects linked to the same event. For instance, if you create

an event `RetailCustomer.Created` and `RetailCustomer` is a subtype of business object type `Customer`, the `Customer.Created` event-linkage will also be evaluated.

If the work item requestor has been passed, the work item requestor is used to find the appropriate event linkage.

4. **Determines the receiver for each event linkage**
If a single receiver is specified in the event linkage then that receiver is used. If a receiver type function module is specified in the event linkage, then it is called to dynamically determine the receiver.

5. **Checks whether the receiver should be notified for each event linkage**
If a check function module is specified in the event linkage this is run to determine whether the receiver should be notified. If the function module is successful, the receiver should be notified. If the function module raises an exception, the receiver should not be notified.

Remember that if you have specified a start condition, the check function module (automatically added by the system when you defined the start condition) will check the start condition. If the start condition is true, the receiver will be notified. If the start condition is false, the receiver will be ignored.

6. **Starts the receiver for each event linkage**
Provided that both the receiver type function module and the check function module calls were successful, the receiver is started by calling the receiver function module or receiver method. Unless you have turned on event debugging, the receiver is started in a separate logical unit of work.

7. **Writes an entry to the event trace for each event linkage if the trace is active**
The event trace entry will show if any errors occurred, such as if the check function module raised an exception. If no active event linkages were found, a single entry is written to the event trace, so that you can confirm that the event was raised correctly. (Refer to chapter 14, *Advanced Diagnostics*.) The same is true of the workflow trace.

Receiver Type Function Module

A *receiver type function module* dynamically determines the receiver at runtime. Only one receiver can be returned, and this is usually the ID of the workflow or task that is to be started. SAP's Document Management System uses this to determine which process to follow (i. e. which workflow to start), according to the document type. You can use any of the information in the event container to decide which workflow should be started.

The interface of the receiver type function module is described in the documentation for the function module SWE_TEMPLATE_RECTYPE_FB. You must use this interface exactly as specified. There is no naming convention restriction on the name of the function module, and of course the code inside the function module is completely up to you.

Here is an example of a receiver type function module for a SBOOK.CREATED event. Notice that the result is returned in parameter RECTYPE; all other parameters are information you can use to determine the receiver. So that the appropriate workflow macros can be used (such as SWC_GET_PROPERTY) the statement INCLUDE <CNTN01> should be included in the global data area of the matching function group.

```
FUNCTION Z_RECTYPE_BY_FLIGHT_CLASS.
*"----------------------------------------------------------------
*"*"Local interface:
*"  IMPORTING
*"    VALUE(OBJTYPE) LIKE  SWETYPECOU-OBJTYPE
*"    VALUE(OBJKEY) LIKE  SWEINSTCOU-OBJKEY
*"    VALUE(EVENT) LIKE  SWETYPECOU-EVENT
*"    VALUE(GENERIC_RECTYPE) LIKE  SWETYPECOU-RECTYPE
*"  EXPORTING
*"    VALUE(RECTYPE) LIKE  SWEINSTCOU-RECTYPE
*"  TABLES
*"    EVENT_CONTAINER STRUCTURE  SWCONT
*"  EXCEPTIONS
*"    OBJECT_NOT_FOUND
*"----------------------------------------------------------------
* This receiver type fm determines the process to be started
* by flight class of the reservation specified in the
* object key

  DATA: OBJECT  TYPE SWC_OBJECT.
  DATA: FCLASS  LIKE SBOOK-CLASS.

* To find the flight class, first instantiate the
* reservation object from the object type and key.
  SWC_CREATE_OBJECT OBJECT OBJTYPE OBJKEY.
  IF SY-SUBRC NE 0.
    RAISE OBJECT_NOT_FOUND.
  ENDIF.
```

```
* Then get the flightclass attribute of the reservation
* object
  SWC_GET_PROPERTY OBJECT 'FLIGHTCLASS' FCLASS.

* Finally we set the appropriate receiver based on
* the class value.
  IF FCLASS EQ 'F' AND …
    RECTYPE = 'WS96000011'.
  ELSE.
    RECTYPE = 'WS96000012'.
  ENDIF.
ENDFUNCTION.
```

Listing 13.3 Receiver Type Function Module for Event

A receiver type function module lets you pick one of a number of possible receivers using a single event linkage entry. You can achieve the same result by having separate event linkage entries for each of the receivers and using mutually exclusive start conditions to determine which receiver should be started. Whether to use start conditions or whether to develop a function module depends on the number of possible workflows and how the event-linkage configuring is to be performed.[2]

13.3.4 Adding Generic Object Services to Your Own Transactions

Generic Object Services are described in detail in chapter 10, *Business Interfaces*, but here is nutshell description to refresh your memory. The Generic Object Services are a sort of Swiss Army Knife of useful functions, two of which are related to workflow. They include:

1. A mechanism linking the application transactions to the workflow logs related to the object being displayed. In other words you can navigate directly from the record to the logs of the workflows that have processed the record (or are in the middle of processing it).

2. A list of workflows that you can start directly, based on the record being displayed. This is very useful when a user notices an irregularity (such as incomplete customizing or an erroneous record) and wants to manually start a corrective workflow.

---

2 Never use receiver type function modules in Enterprise Buyer Professional (EBP).

If you want to add the Generic Object Services to your own transaction you should publish the object instance just before it is displayed. In the following examples you see how to publish an object instance with key 4500000138 and type BUS2105.

► In Releases prior to 4.6C, call function module SWU_OBJECT_PUBLISH passing the object type and object key

```
    CALL FUNCTION 'SWU_OBJECT_PUBLISH'
EXPORTING        objkey  = 'BUS2105'
                 objtype = '4500000138'
    EXCEPTIONS      OTHERS  = 1.
```

► In Releases 4.6C and above, instantiate an instance of class CL_GOS_MANAGER, passing your business object instance.

```
  DATA:
  borident    TYPE borident,
  gos_manager TYPE REF TO cl_gos_manager.
borident-objtype = 'BUS2105'.
borident-objkey  = '4500000138'.

CREATE OBJECT gos_manager
  EXPORTING    is_object = borident
     EXCEPTIONS    OTHERS    = 1.
```

Listing 13.4 Publish of an Object Instance

The result of this simple call is that when your transaction is executed (e.g. display custom record) the generic object service toolbar is displayed and these services are also activated in the system menu. When you consider how many useful features this gives your users, compared with the five minutes spent adding this code to your transaction, there is little excuse for *not* implementing this interface. In terms of ROI, the Generic Object Services are unbeatable value.

Tip Avoid publishing parts of a business object, such as the line items in a posting. Instead, publish the header object only.

13.3.5 Implementing the Workflow Toolbox in Your Own Transactions

The workflow toolbox is a set of work-item based services you can use from any appropriate screen in an SAP component while executing a work item. For instance, you may have a task that asks you to update a material master by calling the material master update transaction. If you execute a work item based on that task, while you are in the material master update transaction, the workflow toolbox appears, allowing you to check the work item description, add attachments to the work item, view the workflow log, etc. without returning to the inbox. If the material master update transaction is executed normally in the SAP component without workflow, the workflow toolbox will not appear, since it is not relevant. This is described in more detail in chapter 10, *Business Interfaces*.

To include the workflow toolbox in your own transactions and screens, you need to instantiate a toolbox object based on class CL_WAPI_WF_TOOLBOX before the appropriate screen is displayed. The mode parameter controls how the toolbox is displayed, i.e. modally or modeless, as buttons or menus, or as a floating toolbar. The following example shows how to include the workflow toolbox on your own screen 0900 of your own program called ZMYPROGRAM, passing the relevant work item ID. The variable CC_TOOLBOX refers to an instance of class CL_GUI_CUSTOM_ CONTAINER, i.e. a custom container specifying where the toolbox will appear on the screen.

```
data: c_toolbox  TYPE REF TO CL_WAPI_WF_TOOLBOX.

CREATE OBJECT c_toolbox
  EXPORTING
    i_container = cc_toolbox
    i_mode     = cl_wapi_wf_toolbox=>c_mode_inplace_with_info
    i_repid    = "ZMYPROGRAM"
    i_dynnr    = "0900"
    i_wi_id    = workitemid
  EXCEPTIONS
    OTHERS     = 1.
```

Listing 13.5 Including the Workflow Toolbox

You can also control which functions are available and react to events such as USER_TOOK_WORKITEM_AWAY (i.e. user has forwarded or resubmitted work item). You can find more detailed documentation in the SAP Library help and on the http://service.sap.com/webflow web site.

13.4 Office Document Interfaces

SAP offers many communications interfaces including telephone integration, calendar management, document management, and mail integration. Most of these are beyond the scope of this book but are fully documented online. However, because the question of how best to send e-mails often comes up, here is a brief summary of the interfaces available.

- **Send mail step**

  Available from Release 4.6C. A wizard generates a task that sends a text, including variables (container elements and attributes) to an external or internal recipient.

- `SendTaskDescription` **method of the object type** `SELFITEM`

  This is equivalent to the send mail step but does not include the wizard. It is decribed in detail in appendix A, Tips and Tricks.

- **Business Communications Interface**

  Available from Release 4.6C on. Online documentation is available. Based on an ABAP OO class, this interface offers very flexible generation of e-mails and attachments.

- `SO_*_API1` **function modules**

  These modules are the forerunner of the Business Communications Interface. The function modules themselves are documented.

Using the `SO_*_API1` function modules as an example[3], we will show how e-mails can be generated from the data in the workflow and transmitted as notifications or reminders to the workflow agents. The calls support different types of recipients, including SAP office users and Internet mail addresses.

- `SO_OLD_DOCUMENT_SEND_API1`

  Sends an existing mail to one or more addressees. This is good for standard replies where the text does not change. The main import parameter is the key of the message that will be sent.

- `SO_NEW_DOCUMENT_SEND_API1`

  Creates a new message (the text is passed as a parameter) and sends the message to one or more addressees.

- `SO_NEW_DOCUMENT_ATT_SEND_API1`

  Creates a new message together with attachments. The text of the mail and of the attachments is passed as a parameter. The mail is sent in MIME format if it is sent over the Internet so that any e-mail client can read the attachments.

- `SO_DOCUMENT_READ_API1`

  Requires the key of an existing mail as an import parameter. The function exports the text of the mail. This is useful if you want to parse incoming messages.

Sending existing mails to different users is slightly different to other mail systems because SAP office does not copy the mail but sends a reference instead (to allow tracking and to cut down disk space). If `WF-BATCH` forwards a reference to a mail

---

3 A detailed description of each call and the other interfaces mentioned at the start of this section can be found in the function module documentation or the SAP Library Help

that is in its inbox to another user, the recipient will not be able to view it because WF-BATCH's inbox is confidential. All mail in the inbox is protected from being read by other users. To make it accessible you must either move the mail to a public folder or move the mail to WF-BATCH's "DARK" folder. The "DARK" folder is a private folder, which is completely accessible to all other users. The function used to transfer a message into this folder is SO_DOCUMENT_MOVE_API1. The function used to find the handle for the dark folder is SO_USER_READ_API1 for the user WF-BATCH. The handle does not change, so this call is only made once.

You will find more information about using e-mails in appendix A, *Tips and Tricks.*

13.5 Configuring RFC Destinations

Finally, we will consider how to configure the RFC destinations that are used to communicate into and out of the SAP component. This is a very short overview. More detailed information is available in the SAP Library Help.

In order to make calls into a component from outside the system you will need to create an RFC destination for this task. You will want to ensure that access via this RFC destination is secure but comfortable.

The following options are available to you. Which you select depends on the type of application that is calling the workflow.

▶ RFC destination with single sign-on access to the component system. This is secure and comfortable because the user logs on only once to the calling system and has access to the target system with the authorization configured there. This can be used from an SAP component without any additional customizing. However, if it is used from a foreign environment (such as JAVA outside the system) then additional programming is needed to enable the single sign-on for that system.

▶ RFC destination with a pre-configured user ID password combination. Make sure that this user ID is configured as a non-dialog user but do not use the system user WF-BATCH. This allows you to configure a separate authorization profile. It is important that the RFC destination authorization is invoked so that access through this RFC destination is limited to the function group for workflow APIs and nothing else. This type of configuration is most suitable for server-to-server communication (background) rather than direct user access to the system.

▶ RFC destination without any user id pre-configured in the destination definition. This will cause a login screen to be called up the first time a call is made to the target system. This is secure but not as comfortable as the other options.

14   Advanced Diagnostics

Troubleshooting workflows is not the simplest of activities, but the army of tools provided will help you quickly diagnose and correct derailed workflows. This chapter is particularly useful for anyone creating or extending workflows. Although you rarely have to troubleshoot workflows in a production environment, this chapter is also useful as preparation for the workflow administrator.

14.1   The Tools of the Trade

This chapter is a companion to chapter 6, *Workflow Administration*, in which recovery procedures for run-of-the-mill production problems are described. Luckily the WebFlow Engine has proved to be exceptionally stable, so the problem diagnosis in this chapter will primarily be of use in the development environment where anything, from programming errors to inconsistent customizing or authorization problems, is possible.

Since workflows implement whole business processes and not just individual activities, workflows involve more dimensions than simple transactions that start, execute and terminate in one logical unit of work. A workflow involves different users. It is spread over time and it may involve synchronization with other workflows or business transactions as it progresses. All these factors prevent you from simply stepping through the workflow in the way you can step through a simple program. However, WebFlow provides a set of diagnostic tools that will make your troubleshooting work much easier, even though you will have to rethink your analysis techniques if you are simply used to debugging programs.

> **Tip**   The better you document your workflows, the easier it will be for you and for anyone else maintaining them to understand and troubleshoot your workflows once you have moved on to your next project. Remember that the business process owners and administrators will inevitably want to change the process later themselves, without having to call you back for every minor adjustment. You will not be their favorite consultant if they are forced to spend hours troubleshooting, simply because you have not left enough documentation for them to make even minor modifications to the process, such as changing texts or the way agents are assigned.

Tip Be especially careful to document any part of the workflow that is liable to fail due to neglected or inaccurate data maintenance in the production environment.

To give you an idea of how troubleshooting workflows differs from debugging transactions, here are some examples of the sort of symptons that can occur:

▶ The wrong agent receives the work item.

▶ The workflow disappears (meaning that the expected agent has not received the work item).

▶ Too many agents receive a work item.

▶ No one receives the work item.

▶ The workflow does not trigger automatically.

▶ Duplicate instances of the workflows are triggered.

▶ The workflow stalls (it suspends operation).

▶ A background step starts but occasionally does not finish.

▶ The workflow stops and goes into ERROR status.

As you can see, there are plenty of uncomfortable situations that can occur, although most can be resolved very quickly and most are very unlikely to appear in the production environment. Some will probably be due to an incorrectly modeled workflow; some result from neglected administration or data maintenance. You should be very aware that there is only a thin line between the symptoms of a badly modeled workflow definition and the sort of problems that can occur in a typical production environment when duties have been neglected. So avoid the 'holier than thou' attitude and make sure that your administrators are also trained in elementary troubleshooting so that they can confidently master the situation when the developer leaves.

14.2 The Diagnosis Logs

The diagnosis logs are your best allies when it comes to pinpointing problems, so it is worth taking a moment to learn about each of them in a bit more detail, before going through the list of symptoms and solutions.

14.2.1 The Workflow Log

The *Workflow Log* charts the progress of the workflow. A new log is written for every workflow started. Everything that takes place while the workflow is running, from system interactions (such as work item created) to user interactions (such as work item forwarded), is logged. There are different views of this log; the most important one for troubleshooting is the technical log (*List with technical details*).

> **Tip** In the development environment you can set the technical view as your default view in your personal workflow settings. You can even customize your own view as described in chapter 6, *Workflow Administration*.

The technical log (figure 6.5) shows all the steps in the workflow, including those that have been masked out of the standard logs either because they are too technical in nature or because they have been explicitly excluded in the workflow step definition (refer to chapter 7, *Creating a Workflow*).

The technical log shows the steps that are executed and the messages that are generated as it progresses. Some of these are warnings (yellow traffic lights) that can be ignored but the errors (highlighted with red traffic lights) will yield the most significant information when troubleshooting the workflow. When a fatal error is generated it will be logged under the workflow step where it occurred, and it will also trigger a new fatal error message at the top level of the workflow, i.e. in the work item representing the workflow instance. The workflow step error message is the more significant of the two.

Symptoms worth investigating with the workflow log:

▶ Workflow goes into ERROR status
▶ User does not receive a work item in their inbox
▶ Workflow appears to take the wrong branch

Starting points for investigation:

▶ In which step does the error occur?
▶ Who is a possible agent for this step?
▶ What were the container values just before branching?

14.2.2 The Event Trace

The *Event Trace* writes a trace for all events raised (as shown in Fehler! Verweisquelle konnte nicht gefunden werden.). Do not confuse this with *Event Queues*, described in chapter 10, *Business Interfaces*, which smooth the workload of high volume events at peak times and put failed events in a separate queue for reprocessing later.

The trace writes an entry for every event raised in the system, even when no workflow has been assigned to this event. Switching the trace on in your development environment enables you to track down errors related to workflows (and their steps) that do not trigger or terminate as expected.

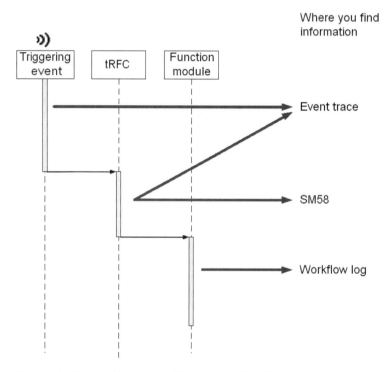

Figure 14.1 Diagram of Sequence of Events (Log, RFC, WI Log)

Bear in mind that as the next step after writing the trace entry, the "start workflow" command is placed in the RFC queue, as shown in figure 14.1. So an event trace that shows success does not really tell you that the workflow has started. The event still has to work its way through the RFC[1] queue, so this RFC queue is worth checking next via transaction SM58 or SWUD.

---

1 RFC = Remote Function Call. This is SAP's remote procedure call. Workflow uses it to separate event creator and receiver, so that any problems in starting the workflow will not affect the business application that created the event.

Symptoms worth investigating with the event trace:

▶ Workflows not triggering
▶ Duplicate workflows triggering
▶ Terminating events failing to stop a workflow step

Starting points for investigation:

▶ Is an event logged at all?
▶ Are start conditions used? Note that if any object attributes used in the start condition return an exception, such as "object does not exist", this will cause the start condition to abort unexpectedly.
▶ Is a check function module called, and what is the result?
▶ Is the event duplicated?
▶ Do two different events trigger one workflow definition?
▶ Is the object key correct, including any leading zeros?

14.2.3   The Workflow Trace

The workflow trace used to be known as the "technical trace" and to put it mildly, it *is* technical. Although originally intended for use by developers for all manner of problem analysis (locking, synchronization problems, etc.), its primary use has turned out to be for investigating binding issues. It will show you in detail every single binding operation that takes place for one workflow instance. You can see the containers before the operation and the values that are appended or modified in the target container after the operation.

This trace can be switched on for one particular event or workflow instance and will continue to be written during the complete lifecycle of the workflow, however long it takes and however many users are involved. There is no danger of switching it on globally in the productive environment for workflow.

The main ways of starting the workflow trace are:

▶ **Setting the workflow trace flag in the diagnosis test environment (transaction SWUD — event start or workflow start options)**
This is the simplest method because the trace is automatically switched off once the workflow has started, and the correct log will be presented to you straight away.

▶ **Switching on the workflow trace for the session (transaction SWU8) and then executing the application without switching to another session window**
Switch the trace off (transaction SWU8 again) or close the session window after

executing the transaction, so that no new workflows are traced in the same log file. Even after you switch the session trace off your workflows started in that session will continue to be traced. You will need to call transaction SWU9 to view the trace.

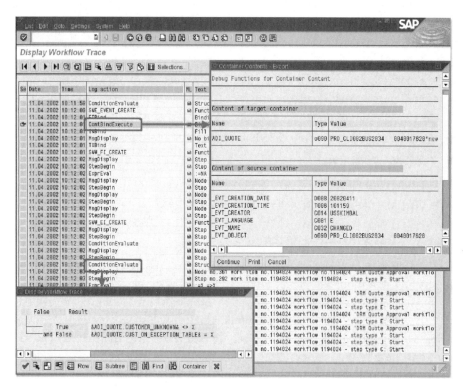

Figure 14.2 The workflow trace showing the results of a binding

Tip You rarely need to switch a workflow's trace off because only the workflow that is started while the trace is switched on is traced. When the workflow finishes, the trace finishes too. However, the workflow trace makes the execution of the workflow very slow, so you might occasionally want to abort it manually. To do this, use the work item list viewer (transaction SWI1). Choose the workflow work item and switch the trace off using the menu.

The same technique can be used to start a workflow trace for a workflow that has already been triggered. If you only want to trace one section of the workflow, switch the trace on for the workflow work item just before the work item that you are interested in is created.

To analyze bindings, look for the `ContBindExecute` entries (or choose the binding filter from the menu) and double click on the entries. As you can see in figure 14.2 this will show you the binding in detail. The log entry preceding the `ContBindExecute` entries shows the type of binding that is being performed (workflow to task, workflow to rule, method to task, etc.).

You see the source container and the target container. New entries in the target container are marked `*new*` and modified entries are shown with their previous value and the value after the binding has executed. Table entries are shown with their index value. Structures are shown one field at a time.

Caution Complex data types stored in XML format cannot be displayed in the workflow trace.

You can also use the workflow trace to analyze condition evaluation in steps that use logical expressions as part of their step definition (e.g. loop until, loop while, condition, multiple condition, conditional work item start or completion and start conditions in the event linkage configuration). Double-clicking on `CondEval` entries will not only show the result of the condition but also give detailed information about how this final result was reached. You will see the container used for the condition, together with the final results, partial results of the different expressions in the condition, and any warnings and errors (e.g. "object does not exist") that occurred during the evaluation.

Symptoms worth investigating with the workflow trace:

▶ An event fails to trigger a workflow
▶ Inconsistent data in the workflow
▶ A workflow step does not execute

Starting points for investigation:

▶ Is the binding performed correctly?
▶ Is the target container being filled as you expected? Watch out for truncation problems if the elements being bound do not use matching data types.
▶ Are warnings recorded when the condition is evaluated?

Workflow trace files are deleted automatically two weeks after the last trace entry is written. The same trace mechanism is used in other parts of the system, such as for communications; so do not be alarmed to see other trace files created that are not related to workflow.

14.2.4   The RFC Log

The workflow engine makes internal RFC calls for background steps and event-raising. If a workflow stalls without reason or an event fails to trigger a workflow, then there is a chance that the RFC call is still stuck in the RFC queue or has aborted while it was being processed. Two queues are used; the WORKFLOW_LOCAL_xxx destination and the destination NONE (the queue must be searched according to the user logged in at the time the WebFlow Engine made the call). The diagnosis transaction SWUD will display the relevant queue for you.

Symptoms worth investigating with the RFC Log:

▶ Sporadic load-based problems leading to the RFC queue choking (workflow stalls—corrected via customizing)

▶ Incorrectly programmed background methods, which abort or hang in the middle (workflow stalls—corrected by improving the BOR object)

▶ Event to workflow bindings that are erroneous (workflow does not start—correct the workflow definition).

Starting points for investigation:

▶ Is the queue empty? Entries are automatically deleted from the log as they are succesfully completed.

▶ Is a background method stuck due to an unexpected need for dialog input? This problem is particularly likely if the method is based on BDC—batch input—or CATTs, especially after an upgrade if the underlying transactions being called have changed.

▶ What error messages are showing for stalled entries?

14.2.5   The XML log

The transaction SWXML displays all XML messages received and transmitted by the system relating to the workflow handling. This is ideal for troubleshooting e-processes where the communication between the two systems is flawed.

14.3   Debugging with the ABAP Debugger

Occasionally you may want to debug a section of the ABAP code, such as a business object method or the code that precedes an event being raised. When you do this you should bear in mind that some calls are made via an internal RFC call, so you will lose control if you do not set a break point where the RFC call is made. Other calls, especially those related to event-raising, are made in the update task, so you will need to switch on update task debugging in the ABAP debugger in order to keep control. Set the debugger switch on in the workflow test transaction (SWUS).

The WebFlow Engine uses RFC calls and dynamic function calls extensively, so you will find it hard work trying to debug through the WebFlow Engine. Intelligent use of the different workflow logs and traces, together with unit testing of the individual components (such as methods and tasks) is much more rewarding.

14.4 The Diagnosis Transaction

The diagnosis transaction (SWUD) is your primary diagnostic tool. When it is called it will analyze your workflow definition and present a list of checks to perform based on this analysis, so it is worth getting to know the transaction in a bit more detail. The order in which the tests are listed is based on a pragmatic approach. The tests that determine the most common errors are displayed first. So it is worth following the tests in the order they are suggested.

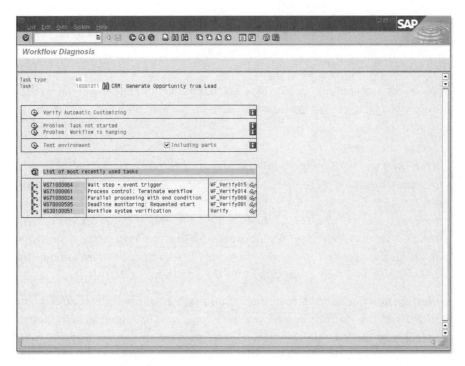

Figure 14.3 Diagram of Initial SWUD Screen

The first screen (see figure 14.3) is divided into three sections.

1. The current workflow definition to be analysed

2. The list of test options

3. A list of the last ten workflow definitions that you have worked on.

To diagnose a new workflow definition, simply type in the ID of the workflow or use the search function to find it based on the standard search criteria.

The four test options are your main testing paths:

1. **Verify workflow customizing**
   A customizing check is the first in the list simply because incomplete customizing is the most frequent source of problems in an unfamiliar system (and the rarest check performed in practice). Always call this when you suddenly discover that the workflow you created and tested last week no longer works today! There is a chance that someone else has changed the customizing settings without your knowledge.

2. **Problem: Task does not start**
   When the workflow does not start or cannot be found, then you should call this option to track down why this is happening.

3. **Problem: Workflow is hanging**
   When the workflow starts but stops before completion, either with an error or simply by failing to start the next step in the workflow, then this is the path you should follow.

4. **Test environment**
   When you are developing a workflow and want to access the complete suite of test tools from one place then this is the option for you. Not only will you see a list of all the checks available, tailored to the components used in your workflow, but you will also see a list of all the components (subworkflows, tasks, business objects, delegated business objects) that are used in the main workflow. You can also see at a glance if possible agents have been assigned to the tasks used, so this is a useful option for the administrator too.

The last section of the first screen shows you a history of previous workflows you have worked on. To pick one of your previous workflows for analysis, simply choose 🔳 to the left. The workflow ID that you have chosen will pop into place at the top of the screen, ready for more detailed analysis. After you have investigated it you will see that this ID has jumped to the top of the history list and the workflow that you were working on before has slipped down one place.

If you simply want to display one of the workflows that you had been working on previously, just choose 👓 on the right of the definition.

14.5   An Apple a Day

The best way of ensuring a smooth and trouble-free introduction of your new or changed workflow into your production environment is to vigorously test and comprehensively document the development work in advance. This is particularly true of workflow where troubleshooting is more complicated than traditional programs, as we saw at the beginning of this chapter. This last section reminds you of some of the duties you need to perform before going live.

14.5.1   Testing New or Changed Workflows

There are many test utilities in the WebFlow Engine and you should take advantage of them where you can. This section will show you which tools to use in different types of tests. You can use the following sequence as a general guide for testing a typical, brand new workflow from scratch:

▶ **Test the business objects**
Use the business object test option (accessible from the Business Object Builder or from the diagnosis tool test environment by choosing the relevant business object) to check that all new and changed attributes are working correctly.

▶ **Test the methods**
Use the business object test option to test any new or changed object methods. This includes testing that exceptions are raised by methods in the appropriate circumstances. Unless you are testing an instance-independent method (such as "Create" or "Find") you will need to create an object instance first. This is simpler than it sounds. You simply create the business object equivalent of the application object you want to test by choosing *Create instance* and specifying the key of the object. This reads the tables in the SAP database for this object key to build a virtual business object equivalent that you can then test. Bear in mind that the methods tested are not simulated—they will really do what they are meant to do. For example, the method `PurchaseOrder.Delete` really deletes the purchase order.

> **Tip** If you need to debug a method, it is easiest to put a break-point statement into the method itself, prior to running the test. Do not forget to remove the break-point afterwards. Make sure that you turn on the debugging switch (in the "settings" menu) before you start to debug the method.

▶ **Test task/workflow consistency**

Perform a consistency test (think of this as similar to a syntax check on a program) on the workflow and all related tasks and events using transaction SWUD (results shown in figure 14.4).

▶ **Test the tasks**

Use the *Start Task* tool to test each new or changed task. Make sure you have assigned yourself as a possible agent of the task first, or you will not be able to execute the task. It is good practice to test even background tasks in this way, but you will need to remove the *Background processing* flag from the task first, so that you can test it in dialog mode. Once you are satisfied the task is working you can replace the background flag, and test it again in background mode to ensure it still behaves correctly. If the task is asynchronous, make sure you also check that the terminating event (e.g. using the *Create Event* tool) completes the work item as expected.

▶ **Test the agent determination rules**

Simulate the agent determination rules used in the workflow by using the rule simulation in the rule editor (transaction PFAC). From Release 6.10 on, you can also check the results in the _RULE_RESULT container element if you have defined a return binding for the agent determination rule. It can be useful to define this binding just so that you can easily track any problems in the productive environment.

▶ **Test the conditions**

The complex conditions used in the workflow are evaluated according to the mathematical priority of the operators, and if this is difficult for you to resolve simply use a liberal supply of parentheses to explicitly define the order of evaluation. The rule is parsed when it is saved so the parentheses have no effect on performance. Simulate any conditions used in the workflow. The condition editor includes a powerful simulation tool that is very useful when the conditions are complex.

▶ **Test the workflow and subworkflows**

Use *Start Task* tool to test each subworkflow and then the workflow as a whole. If you are having binding problems, turning on the container monitor and/or the workflow trace can be useful. Do not forget to turn them off when you are finished.

▶ **Test the event linkages**

Use *Simulate Event* to check that the event linkages for triggering and terminating events you are using (see figure 14.5) are defined correctly and activated.

▶ **Test the triggering event manually**

Use *Create Event* to trigger the events manually and the *Event Trace* to check that they affect your workflow in the way you expect. Simulate any start conditions (or check function modules or receiver type function modules) used to trigger the workflow.

▶ **Test the triggering event from the business application**
Test the workflow by raising the events from the application. Make sure you do this for all triggering and terminating events.

▶ **Test the authorizations**
Most developers in the development and QA systems have more authorization than the users in the production environment. It is essential that before going live, you test the workflow with the authorization profiles that the operational users will have.

▶ **Test error scenarios**
Once everything is working correctly, do not forget to test all possible workflow paths, including simulating error situations (e.g. by forcing the object method to send an exception) to make sure they behave as expected. You do not need to model a response to every possible error in your workflow but it is vital that serious errors throw an exception so that if one does occur the default WebFlow Engine error handling and the administrator can catch the error and resolve it. Be particularly careful to simulate any error situation that might be caused by neglected or incorrect data maintenance.

Figure 14.4 The Results of a Consistency Check

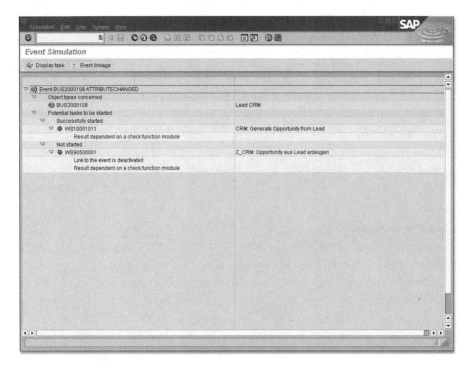

Figure 14.5 Diagram of the Event Simulation Check Menu

If you need to test deadlines in your workflow, avoid putting short test deadlines in your workflow step, which you may forget to remove later. Iit is better to put the real deadline times in your workflow steps. You can then check that the correct deadline time is calculated, and change the deadlines (from the work item display, choose **Work item · More functions. · Change Deadlines**) to verify that the escalation process is working. Do not forget to check that the deadline background job has been activated (refer to chapter 3, *Configuring the System*).

You will find an extensive step-by-step guide to diagnosing the typical symptoms in the Appendix.

Part 3
Examples of the Use of
WebFlow in mySAP.com

15 WebFlow in Enterprise Buyer Professional

SAP's Enterprise Buyer Professional (EBP) uses SAP's WebFlow Engine as the central process controller of the system. Most business processes initiated by an EBP user (who may be an employee, business partner, service provider, etc.), or by receipt of an XML document (e.g. confirmation of goods/service delivery, invoice), are screened by at least one workflow before affecting financial and logistics backend systems.

15.1 Workflow in EBP

EBP is SAP's Web-based eProcurement solution, and is part of SAP Markets' SRM (Supplier Relationship Management) solution. EBP covers a full range of Web-based procurement related activities such as:

▶ Self-service indirect procurement by requestors

▶ Procurement for plant maintenance and projects

▶ Direct procurement to inventory

▶ Procurement approvals

▶ Confirmation of goods/service delivery

▶ Invoice creation/status

▶ Sourcing cockpits for professional purchasers

▶ Vendor self-service functions

▶ Bidding and tendering

▶ Procurement card reconciliation

Web-based catalogues (whether intranet, extranet or Internet-based) can be used to find potential procurement items. Communication between EBP, the backend ERP systems (there may be multiple SAP and non-SAP backends for the one EBP system), and the vendor systems can be automated, for example by transferring predefined XML documents over the Web.

Like many e-Commerce solutions, being able to enter or view information via the Web is only a small part of the picture. Real e-Commerce success depends on ensuring that the backend ERP processes that support the solution run as smoothly and quickly as possible. That is why EBP contains so much workflow as standard, and uses some of the most interesting and exciting workflow techniques available.

One of the most striking features of EBP's use of workflow is that it is the first of a new breed of applications that have added their own user interface on top of the WebFlow Engine. In this case it is a Web interface (including a graphical log), offering intuitive access to the EBP and workflow functions in a consistent way. New features were added to the WebFlow Engine to support the style of processing required in an EBP environment. Highlights include: the reviewer function, replacing approvers, adding steps on the fly at predefined places in the process and start conditions. These features have since made their way into the standard WebFlow Engine on the Web Application Server.

A list of SAP-provided workflows with their exact workflow IDs for the appropriate EBP release is included in the EBP installation guides.

In this section you will discover the most important WebFlow Engine features used in EBP, how they affect procurement workflows you may already be using in your SAP R/3 component (if you have one and are using it as a backend system to EBP), how to configure the WebFlow Engine for EBP so that you can start assessing the EBP workflows, and some of the special workflow techniques used throughout EBP.

In following sections, you will find techniques for changing the most important workflows in EBP. Towards the end of the chapter you will find sections on monitoring and troubleshooting workflows in EBP. Finally, if you want to understand EBP at a deeper technical level, you will find an overview of the underlying architecture used to support EBP.

> **Tip** Note that EBP functionality has changed significantly from release to release. Although this chapter is based on the current version at time of printing (i.e. EBP version 3.0) most statements apply to prior releases too.

15.1.1 Standard EBP WebFlow Features

The WebFlow features offered by EBP are extensive, so you will only find the most important features described here. It is worth noting that all EBP provided workflows will work as-is. That is, there is no immediate functional or technical need for you to change, copy or modify them.

When the EBP system is first installed and configured, it is worthwhile to first run the provided workflows without changes. This gives both functional and technical personnel an opportunity to understand how EBP and its workflows operate, in particular, how EBP users interact with the workflow, how they can benefit from the many WebFlow features, and what impact the workflow has on each business process. Once EBP and its workflows are understood, you can make an informed decision about whether there is a need to adjust the workflows to suit your company's business processes.

WebFlow Features Applicable to All EBP Users

You can enter user data (including your manager's name) from the login screen even before you have access to the EBP system. Depending on configuration, this then starts a workflow that asks your manager to approve the *creation of your user ID* and suggest the appropriate authorization profile for you. If you later change managers, you can similarly enter your new manager in your EBP personal data, and a workflow will be started to have your new manager approve the change.

When a new user ID is approved, an automatically generated initial password is returned via e-mail to the new user. Note that the user ID does *not* appear on this e-mail—for the obvious reason that if the user ID were sent with the password, anyone able to read the e-mail could then access the EBP system.

As an EBP user, you immediately see on your EBP home page how many work items you have outstanding. The count of outstanding work items is also a hyperlink that takes you straight to your inbox.

The special EBP inbox allows rapid decision-making. For example if a procurement request has already been discussed with the approver, the approver can choose to approve or reject from the work item list based on the subject text alone.

Whenever an object under approval (such as a procurement request, confirmation of goods/services delivery or invoices) is rejected, the initiator and all previous approvers (if a multi-step approval process was used) are notified by e-mail directly to their e-mail address. This is especially useful when vendors have used self-service functions, for example to enter confirmations of goods/services delivery, since the vendors are automatically notified of any problems via their own e-mail system. All e-mails are sent as text mails that can be viewed from any inbox, no matter what groupware is used.

As an EBP user you can maintain your own e-mail address and decide whether or not you want e-mail notifications of outstanding work items.

WebFlow Features Applicable to Procurement Requestors

While creating procurement requests ("shopping carts") you can preview the approval (see figure 15.1) requirements in the form of a web-friendly graphical log. This approval preview is dynamically updated as items are added, changed, or deleted from the request.

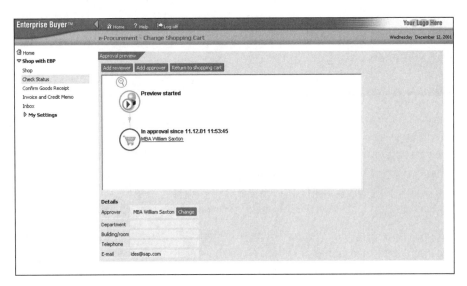

Figure 15.1 Approval Preview in EBP

You can also view the same graphical log when monitoring the status of procurement requests. It shows at a glance how many approvals are required, who are the nominated approvers for each approval required, contact details for each approver (such as phone number and e-mail address), which approvals have been granted, and which approvals are outstanding. The number of approvals required and all of the approvers involved can be seen even before the workflow has started. Any changes to the approvers (e.g. due to a subsitute acting for an approver) are immediately visible in the graphical log (fig. 6.4).

If so authorized, you can even change the approvers, for example, to proactively substitute an alternate approver when the usual approver is unavailable. Only valid approvers can be chosen as alternates.

From the graphical log you can nominate a reviewer (see figure 15.2), thereby starting a review workflow. The review workflow allows the reviewer to monitor what is happening in the procurement request approval workflow, add attachments to the procurement request approval workflow, and use the graphical log to escalate the approval process by contacting the approvers.

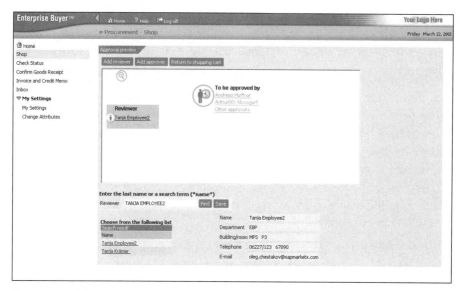

Figure 15.2 Add Reviewer Dynamically in EBP

When creating or changing a procurement request, from the graphical log you can add extra approval levels on the fly, as shown in figure 15.3 (e.g. to request a second opinion on the items to be purchased) or to have someone else add additional items to the shopping cart. Extra approval levels can be added before,[1] between, or after the predetermined business approvals. Regardless of what approvals have been added, the predetermined business approvals will still take place.

Partially rejected procurement requests are automatically returned to your inbox. You can then opt to accept the rejected items (i.e. automatically delete the disputed items from the request) and continue the approval process, or change the procurement request thereby restarting the approval process. This depends solely on the security level.[2]

WebFlow Features Applicable to Approvers

When approving procurement requests you can see the entire shopping cart exactly as the requestor created it. You can see all details of the request including financial account assignment and sourcing information, such as whether or not the item was purchased from an approved catalogue.

---

1 Obviously, you can only insert new approval levels in front of Steps that have not yet been started.
2 From Release 3.0.

You can be authorized to change procurement requests during approval, up to and including replacing rejected items with new items. These new items can be sourced from the catalogue, or added directly, exactly as if the requestor had added them.

Included in the authorization to change shopping carts during approval is an assessment of whether or not the approval process needs to be restarted after changes have been made. For instance, your authorization may specify that any change requires the approval process to restart from scratch, or that all changes are to be accepted automatically. The EBP configurers can even freely specify business rules to decide whether or not the approval process should be restarted, depending, for example, on which data was changed or whether the shopping cart value has changed.

When approving a procurement request, from the graphical log you can add extra approval levels on the fly (e.g. to have a specialist department review the items to be purchased) or have a professional buyer replace free text items with the equivalent approved items from a catalogue. Extra approval levels can be added before, between, or after the predetermined business approvals. Regardless of what approvals have been added, the predetermined business approvals will still take place.

You can receive e-mail notification of work items. The EBP e-mail notification of work items sends not just a textual reminder of work items to be completed, but also a summary of the object to be approved, a hyperlink to open a web browser and enter EBP at the work item involved, and pre-generated responses to approve/reject the relevant work item via offline e-mail. You will find more details on this in section 15.8) and in appendix A, *Tips and Tricks*.

WebFlow Features Applicable to EBP Administrators

Common problems with the approval process are reported to you via the web-accessible application monitor, a 'traffic light' overview of what has failed, used to monitor many parts of the EBP component.

All workflow monitoring transactions are available via a Web Browser (using the SAP GUI for HTML rendering of the SAP GUI screens).

15.1.2 EBP Shopping Cart Approval Versus R/3 Backend Requisition Release Strategy

Even given all the EBP WebFlow features available, the pros and cons of using the standard EBP shopping cart approval workflow versus the R/3 requisition release strategy approval workflow are often hotly debated in EBP projects in which EBP is connected to a single backend SAP R/3 component. Particularly where firms are already using the requisition release strategy workflow successfully, they can be a reluctant to replace this workflow with the shopping cart approval for EBP sourced items. However there are some very good reasons for doing so.

The primarily reason has to do with visibility. In EBP the requestor can see the approver via approval preview during shopping cart creation, and via shopping cart status throughout the approval process. The R/3 requisition release strategy only shows how many more approvals are needed, in a rather user-unfriendly fashion (you can only see somewhat cryptic "release codes"), and it does not show who are the actual approvers.

Visibility of the approval process is a major benefit for requestors. This, along with the ease of navigation, access to Web catalogues, etc. provides a strong incentive for requestors to use the EBP system for procurement, rather than to indulge in maverick buying. In general, the more personnel use your EBP system, the more likely your company will realize the expected benefits of the system.

This visibility goes beyond seeing the approver's name. The requestor is also able to see their contact details, such as phone number and e-mail address, enabling the requestor to discuss or escalate the approval process with the approver.

While viewing the approver's details, the requestor can proactively substitute a different approver via the change approver option, if the original approver is unavailable (and provided they have sufficient authority to change the approver). They can also add a reviewer to help monitor and escalate the approval process, when, for instance, they are attending on an off-site training course and will not be able to monitor or escalate the process themselves. All of this functionality increases the benefit of the EBP system to the requestor.

The requestor and approvers also have the option to add new approval steps. This gives real flexibility to the approval process. For instance, the majority of purchases may only require manager approval, but sometimes the manager would like another party to also review the purchase. Being able to add an approver allows the manager to dynamically call for a second opinion.

A further good reason for using EBP shopping cart approval instead of requisition release strategy approval is its increased speed of purchase order creation. As soon as the shopping cart has been approved in EBP, all fully sourced items (e.g. items from Web-based catalogues) can be immediately transferred to backend purchase orders and sent to the supplier electronically. By contrast with the requisition release strategy, once all releases have been made, the purchasing officer still needs to run a program to convert the requisition to a purchase order.

What about cost of order? Should you not have EBP create only requisitions, then consolidate them into the fewest number of purchase orders possible? Actually, consolidation should rarely bring significant benefits. Cost of order is the cost of processing a single order regardless of how many items it contains. For paper-based orders, the cost of processing an order is high. But e-Procurement, maximizes the electronic processing (e.g. by sending orders to the supplier over the Internet using an XML format) thereby greatly reducing the cost of order.

What about training costs where managers need to approve both EBP shopping carts and backend requisitions? Managers will indeed need to be able to execute both EBP and backend approvals. However, the greater cost is in training managers in executing requisition release work items. The EBP approval work item is far more self-explanatory, and gives more control. For instance, starting with EBP Release 3.0, approvers can be given the authority to add additional or replacement items from pre-approved Web-based catalogues during approval. Whether the shopping cart then needs to be re-approved can also be controlled depending on the approver's authorization and your business rules.

In fact, to reduce training costs it is worth considering making some changes to the requisition release strategy workflow to make the approval work item simpler and closer to the EBP approval work item. One possibility is to implement the EBP offline e-mail approval technique in R/3 to make the look and feel of the two systems similar.

Note that it is possible to combine EBP shopping cart approval workflow and backend requisition release strategy workflows if you wish. For example, if you only allow the shopping cart to be changed via the requestor, you might do the initial approval in EBP. All fully sourced items can then immediately create a purchase order. Items that require source of supply to be determined by a purchasing officer may then create requisitions.

In the backend, you might set up a release strategy to detect changes to requisition items. If a purchasing officer needs to change certain values such as price, you can use the requisition release strategy workflow to send it for re-approval back to the manager, by using a shared rule to identify the same approver in EBP and the backend. This way, requestors can always see who is the approver, and the history display in the shopping cart status transaction will show whether the item has been converted from a requisition to a purchase order yet.

If you allow approvers to change shopping carts during approval, subject to business rules and approver's authorization, and adjust your EBP workflow to make the buyer another "approver" where un-sourced items exist, then of course even this scenario can be fully implemented using EBP workflow without any need for the requisition release strategy at all.

15.1.3   Configuring the WebFlow Engine for EBP

Configuration of the WebFlow Engine, activating of workflows, and assignment of agents (and substitutes) is done using the normal WebFlow Engine functions. For example, configuring the WebFlow Engine for EBP is much the same as configuring the workflow environment for any other SAP Web Application Server system (as described in chapter 3, *Configuring the System*).

Start conditions (i.e. logical expressions) can be configured, via the start condition maintenance (transaction SWB_COND), to determine which approval scenario should be started according to the contents of the object being approved and your company's business rules. For instance, you may want shopping carts under $500 to be processed via the auto-approval workflow and carts over $500 to be processed via the one-step approval workflow.

The most important point to remember when creating or changing start conditions in EBP is that the criteria being used must exist when the event is raised. For example, shopping cart approval workflows are started when the shopping cart is saved. At this time, we know a lot about the shopping cart such as its total value, whether any free text items exist, the material groups and the account assignment used. However, we do not know if the shopping cart items will be converted to local or backend purchase orders, backend purchase requisitions or backend reservations, since this decision is not made until after approval. So we can create a start condition for a shopping cart approval workflow based on total value and material group, but not on the total value together with the backend object type.

You can find more details on start conditions in chapter 10, *Business Interfaces*.

If you always want to use just one approval workflow, assign it to a start condition that is always true.

> **Caution** In the most recent releases of EBP (2.0 and above), the shopping cart saved (BUS2121.SAVED) event is not actually raised. However the activated event linkages for this event are still evaluated at runtime to determine which workflow should start when the shopping cart is saved. Do not use the receiver type function modules; use start conditions instead.

Possible agents are usually assigned via activity groups to minimize the maintenance burden on the organizational plan. Within certain EBP workflows, such as shopping cart (i.e. procurement request) approval, possible agent assignments not only control who is able to execute work items, but also:

▶ Determine whether an employee is allowed to dynamically change the approver.

▶ Determine which approvers can be selected via the add/change approver options.

Delivered approval scenarios include auto-approval, one-step approval, two-step approval, and spending limit approval of procurement requests. A limited choice of approval scenarios is also available for approving confirmations, invoices, etc. All approval scenarios can be used as-is or as patterns for creating your own approval scenarios.

When using the spending limit approval scenario (i.e. approval is only required if the request exceeds the requestor's spending limit), the spending limit can be configured to a default based on the user's activity group or role and overridden on an organizational object basis or even on a per user basis if necessary.

When authorizing approvers to change procurement requests during approval, the decision as to whether changes require approval can be configured to a default, based on the approver's activity group or role, and they can be overridden on a per user basis, and/or according to business rules specified in the relevant BAdI (Business Add-In, i.e. the new and more flexible form of user-exits).

All texts in work items and e-mails sent by SAP's WebFlow Engine can be redefined without modification to suit your company's needs.

15.1.4 Special Patterns and Techniques in EBP Workflows

All workflows delivered with EBP are designed to work as-is, once agents have been assigned and the appropriate event linkages activated.

The majority of the EBP workflows delivered by SAP are approval workflows. To ensure a consistent process, even if no explicit user approval is required, the workflow must still be run to auto-approve the relevant object.

Most approval workflows consist of:

1. An initial sub-process to determine approvers and obtain the approval/rejection decision.
2. In parallel, a sub-process to listen for change or deletion of the object being approved.
3. A final sub-process to take the appropriate actions based on the approve/reject/change/delete decision made in the first two sub-processes.

If the object requested is approved, most EBP workflows trigger the transfer of the object (procurement request, goods/services confirmation, invoice) into its final form. For example, a procurement request may be transferred to purchase requisitions, reservations, and/or purchase orders in the local or potentially multiple SAP and non-SAP backend systems.

> **Caution** It is essential that every object is transferred via one and only one approval workflow; otherwise, the application monitors will display errors. This can be controlled via start conditions.

The majority of EBP workflows make heavy use of e-mail (via send mail steps) to notify employees, business partners, etc. In some situations this includes sending a hyperlink in the e-mail sent by the workflow so that the user can click on the link to go directly to the relevant Web transaction. The hyperlink approach is also used in EBP e-mail notifications so that approvers are not just told that there is work outstanding, but are also directed to it.

> **Note** Normal deadline items cannot be viewed in the EBP inbox, so modelled deadlines should be used to send mails instead.

Ad Hoc Agent Assignment

Assigning an approver to a shopping cart is done via ad hoc agent assignment.[3] Ad hoc agent assignment enables agents to be determined at the start of the workflow via a reference to an ad hoc agent business object. The agents can then be manipulated generically throughout the workflow, regardless of how the original agents were found.

In EBP, ad hoc agent assignment is used to enable agents to be determined prior to the approval steps so that they can be displayed in approval previews and status displays. It also enables proactive substitution via the change/replace approver functions. Thus if authorized, you can dynamically change the agents selected for a particular work item. As a side benefit you can also see in the workflow log, via the workflow container, all agents that were chosen before *and* after work items have been executed.

Ad Hoc Workflows—Additional Approvers

Ad hoc workflows enable extra steps to be added to an existing workflow dynamically (see figure 15.3).

---

3 This feature is standard from Release 6.10 of the Web Application Server but heavy use of this is made in EBP. The same is true of the reviewer and anchor features described in the following sections.

Figure 15.3 Add Approver Dynamically in EBP

Add approver functionality enables additional approval steps to be included in an existing shopping cart workflow. In EBP, both requestors and approvers can be permitted to add approvers via the "add approver" option during shopping cart creation and change, and during approval of the shopping cart.

To enable this, *ad hoc anchor* steps are included in the workflow flowchart. These are essentially placeholders to indicate where it makes sense to add another approver. Several ad hoc anchor steps can exist in the one workflow.

The ad hoc anchor references a subworkflow that holds the steps to be inserted if the ad hoc functionality is activated at that point. The subworkflow container must be identical to the main workflow (i.e. have the same element names and types). The subworkflow itself can include another ad hoc anchor to itself allowing a potentially limitless number of approvers to be added (until memory or the requestor's patience runs out). In EBP, when someone elects to add an approver, the workflow is extended with the additional steps in the subworkflow.

Ad Hoc Workflows—Add Reviewers

A *reviewer* is someone who can monitor an active workflow instance (e.g. for escalation purposes) and make limited changes (e.g. add attachments). For instance, if you created a shopping cart in EBP but were about to leave for a training course, you might want to make one of your colleagues a reviewer so that they could monitor the approval process on your behalf.

Add reviewer functionality enables a reviewer workflow instance to be created. This instance runs in parallel with the original approval workflow. To do this, the review workflow is entered in the version-dependent basic data of the Workflow Builder for the relevant workflow. The workflow has the property "has a review workflow", whereas the workflow that performs the review has the property "review workflow".

When the review workflow is started, data is passed from the current workflow to the review workflow. Container details and the instance number of the main workflow are passed to the review workflow on creation. The review workflow can then use its own steps/tasks/methods to perform the review as it sees fit.

Retry Mechanism Through SPOOL Function Modules

A number of the EBP workflows including shopping cart approval, confirmation approval, and invoice approval, may end with the relevant object being transferred to the local or one or more backend systems. Given the possibility that this step of the workflow might final (e.g. because the backend system is unavailable), it is important to understand how EBP handles transfer errors and how this affects the workflows involved.

The process for handling errors and retrying failed transfers is the same for all workflows:

1. The workflow is used to trigger the initial attempt to transfer the object to the backend. Regardless of the result of the transfer, the workflow then continues to completion.

2. The transfer routine passes the object to the backend, sets the status of the object (e.g. object transferred, transfer failed), and, if necessary, starts the retry process. Possible errors at this point include communication errors (i.e. could not reach the backend), backend system errors (i.e. routine is unavailable or invalid), and application errors (i.e. the object could not be transferred due to missing/invalid data). For all of these errors, the error detection and retry process is coded within the transfer routine itself.

3. When an error is detected the transfer routine evaluates whether the transfer should be retried. If the transfer attempt has failed, the transfer routine checks how many attempts have been made. If the number of attempts within the configured number of retries, the transfer routine creates a background job to rerun itself at the next retry interval. If the number of attempts exceeds the configured number of retries, a log entry is added to the appropriate application monitor.

4. The administrator can view the application monitors. For any transfer error, the application monitors show a 'red light' icon and the error message returned. After looking at the details of the object in error, the administrator usually has the option to delete the object or resubmit it (i.e. run the transfer routine again).

From a workflow perspective, this means that the workflows are only responsible for starting the initial transfer. Once the initial transfer has been made, the retry process takes over and the workflow has no further part to play in the transfer process.

15.2 Changing Shopping Cart Approval Workflows

Before you consider changing the supplied shopping cart approval workflows, you should make sure you are making the most of standard EBP functionality. For instance:

▶ If you need to change which approval workflow is started, use *configuration* to change the start conditions.

▶ If you only need to add more approval levels in exceptional circumstances, consider using the standard *add approver* functionality to do this.

Although you can of course change the shopping cart approval workflow using any of the workflow techniques at your disposal, the two changes you are most likely to make are:

▶ Add new start condition criteria

▶ Change the shopping cart approvers.

Some more advanced options include:

▶ Finding agents for EBP workflows from rules in the backend ERP system

▶ Adding more approval levels

▶ Implementing parallel and dynamic approvals

▶ Commissioning and decommissioning workflows.

15.2.1 Creating Your Own Start Condition Criteria

Start conditions are based on attributes of the object in the event linkage. For shopping cart approval workflows, the event used is the shopping cart SAVED event, and the object is the shopping cart (i.e. BUS2121).

If you want to create additional criteria to be used as part of the logical expression of a start condition, you need to create additional attributes. To create additional attributes, first create a subtype of BUS2121 (e.g. ZBUS2121) and use system-wide delegation to delegate BUS2121 to ZBUS2121. Additional attributes can then be added to the subtype ZBUS2121, and through delegation these will be available to all start conditions, event linkages, workflows and tasks using BUS2121.

When programming your own attributes for start conditions, keep the following points in mind:

▶ Any exception raised by an attribute will cause the start condition to fail. Usually if you cannot find a value for an attribute, you want to set the attribute to its empty value (e.g. blank or zero) and return normally.

▶ Every attribute checked should have a valid value (which may be an empty value) for *all* shopping carts. This is particularly important when creating attributes that are only relevant to goods or service items. Make sure your attribute still returns a valid value if the shopping cart contains only goods items, only service items, or a mixture of goods and services items.

▶ When a shopping cart is transferred to a local or backend object, significant data changes may occur (depending on the EBP release). For this reason, when testing your new criteria, always test against parked ('held') shopping carts or unapproved shopping carts, which still contain all data in a pre-approved state, and never against carts that have already been transferred.

▶ It is recommended that you do *not* read data directly from database tables; instead use the routines in the standard business object definition (e.g. `select_table_reqhead` in BUS2121), since the relationship between the various shopping cart tables is quite complex and varies from release to release. A further complication is that data needs to be read and returned in a slightly different way when the shopping cart does not yet exist (i.e. for approval preview scenarios). The safest option is to closely examine the standard business object BUS2121 for the code behind similar attributes to make sure your new attributes use a consistent approach.

15.2.2 Creating Your Own Shopping Cart Approvers

If you want to create your own shopping cart approvers, you must use ad hoc agent assignment to retain all the functionality of the approval previews and approval displays including:

▶ Viewing of agents
▶ Viewing agent details (e.g. phone number, e-mail address)
▶ Changing the agent (i.e. proactive substitution)
▶ Adding approvers
▶ Adding reviewers
▶ As part of the workflow log, being able to see the list of agents before *and* after the shopping cart has been approved via the workflow container.

You can mix steps using the usual agent determination techniques with steps using ad hoc agent assignment in the same workflow. To use ad hoc agent assignment for your own workflow steps, you can use menu option **Extras · Ad hoc functions · Enable ad hoc agent assignment** in the Workflow Builder. This will:

▶ Mark the workflow as allowing ad hoc agent assignment (you can see this in the Workflow Builder → version-dependent basic data section).

▶ Add workflow import container elements referencing ad hoc object AAGENT, e.g. Agent_0001.

▶ Replace the responsible agent assignment on all workflow steps that do not have any responsible agent assignment with expressions linking to the Agents attribute of the ad hoc object container elements. E.g. Agent_0001.Agents

▶ Adds a call at the start of the workflow to fill any import container elements referring to ad hoc agent objects by executing the relevant Create method. This is done using a constructor for the workflow. In EBP 3.0 (SAP Web Application Server 6.10) you can see this in the *Basic Data* of the Workflow Builder, *Program Exits* tab within *Version-dependent* data.

Once your workflow is ad hoc agent-enabled, all you need to do is change the new workflow container elements to reference your ad hoc agent object instead of AAGENT.

Of course, if you are copying or modifying a workflow that is already ad hoc agent-enabled, all you need to do is change the relevant container elements to reference the desired ad hoc agent object.

All ad hoc agent objects are subtypes of business object AAGENT. The most important method in the ad hoc agent object is Create, since this is where the agents are initially determined. The Create method includes finding the criteria by which the agents are determined as well as determining the agents.

If you want to create your own ad hoc agent objects, the process is as follows:

1. Create your new ad hoc object as a subtype of AAGENT. It must be a direct subtype (not a subtype of a subtype).

2. Redefine the Create method.

3. Copy the program code from any other AAGENT subtype. This program code should include the Create method and constructor subroutines.

4. Try and copy the code from an existing ad hoc object that is similar to your desired new ad hoc object.

5. Change the code in the Create method. The code contains sections that:

   ▶ Run the constructor subroutine to initialize the object. Use the copied code.

- ▶ Find the criteria needed to determine the agents. This usually involves reading container element `ReqReq` (the shopping cart object instance) from the workflow container. Use workflow macros, as shown in chapter 8, *Business Objects*, to read the container element and derive the criteria, for example from attributes of the shopping cart object.

- ▶ Determine the agent, for example by calling a rule function module such as `SWX_GET_MANAGER` (in the case of `ASBMANAGER`), or by calling a rule using function module `RH_GET_ACTORS`.

- ▶ Fill the `Agents` attribute of the ad hoc object with the agents found. Use the copied code since this involves use of the workflow ad hoc property class `CL_WFD_ADHOC_PROPERTY_DB` to ensure ad hoc functionality is possible. Make sure the agents are also returned in the simulated agent list for the approval preview used during shopping cart creation.

> **Caution** Because all ad hoc agents are evaluated at the same time, you should not try to determine one agent on the basis of another ad hoc agent object. If you look at ad hoc object `ASBMANOFMA`, manager of shopping cart requestor's manager, you will see that it does not read the workflow container element referencing `ASBMANAGER`, since you cannot guarantee that this ad hoc object has been instantiated yet. Instead it calls function module `SWX_GET_MANAGER` twice, to find first the manager, then the manager's manager.

To support the ad hoc agent assignment, every shopping cart approval workflow should have a container element called `ReqReq`, which is a reference to the shopping cart object `BUS2121`. This enables any shopping-cart-based ad hoc agent object to be used in any shopping cart workflow.

If you need to extract additional information about the shopping cart or related objects (such as details about the requestor), you can use macro `SWC_GET_PROPERTY` to obtain the appropriate data via the object reference.

It is important to implement all shopping cart data you are using against the shopping cart object (`BUS2121`), and similarly all requestor data against the EBP user object (`BUS4101`), rather than reading shopping cart data via function modules or directly from database tables in the `Create` method. By implementing all reads as attributes, performance can be improved by allowing the object to selectively buffer data, and the attributes can easily be re-used, for example in work item texts or other ad hoc agent objects. Additionally, your agent determination mechanism is insulated against changes in how the shopping cart data is stored on the database.

If you want to read attributes of the requestor to determine who is the approver, function module `BBP_READ_ATTRIBUTES`[4] can be used.

Some easy ways of determining approvers are to use an existing rule, such as a distribution list rule or to create a responsibility rule.

Responsibility rules have already been discussed in chapter 9, *Agent-Determination Rules*. They enable you to specify criteria for your rule, create combinations of criteria (including ranges and multiple values), and assign organization units, positions, and user IDs to it. This is a quick and convenient way to create a new rule, and it is more flexible than creating a custom configuration table of criteria-to-agent relationships. In addition, you can set priorities on which combinations are evaluated first. For example, you can have the rule look at specific combinations and fall back to a default approver if no agent is found.

To call another rule from the `Create` method, use function module `RH_GET_ACTORS`.

Once you have found your agents, if they are not in user ID format you will need to convert them to user IDs (e.g. convert user ID SMITHJ to USSMITHJ). If your agents have been returned as organization units or positions, you can use function module `RH_GET_STRUCTURE` with evaluation path `SAP_TAGT` to determine the user ID.

> **Tip** Note that if the `Create` method fails to return any agents or returns only invalid agents (i.e. users who do not have access to the relevant task), the approval work item will usually be sent to an administrator. Read SAP Note 491804 for further details.

15.2.3 Finding Agents Via Backend Rules/Organizational Plans

It is possible to use a backend system rule from EBP, and vice versa. This can be very useful where you want shopping carts created in EBP and requisitions created directly in the backend system to be approved by the same person. Each system can have its own workflow with its own approval methods and processing, but share the approver determination via RFC calls.

Within the EBP system, function module `BBP_DETERMINE_LOGICAL_SYSTEM` can be used to determine the backend system, based on a variety of criteria. This function module includes a call to BAdI `BBP_DETERMINE_LOGSYS`, where further business rules can be added to control which backend system is found.

---

4 Prior to Release 3.0, use function module `BBP_GET_ATTRIBUTES`.

Function module `LOG_SYSTEM_GET_RFC_DESTINATION` can be used to read the appropriate RFC destination for the logical system.

To call a rule in the backend system you can call function module `RH_GET_ACTORS` via RFC, inputting the rule ID in its technical format (e.g. AC90000001 where 90000001 is the rule number). Often rules return organization plan references, such as positions, that only exist in the backend system. To find the matching user IDs in the backend, call function module `RH_GET_STRUCTURE` via RFC with evaluation path `SAP_TAGT` (find workflow agent). The example code in the "Function modules as rules" section in chapter 9, *Agent-Determination Rules* will assist you.

You do need some way of mapping backend users to EBP users. There are a number of ways this can be done. For instance, if your company has a naming convention for user IDs, then you can assume user IDs are the same in all systems. Or your company may use an LDAP (Lightweight Directory Access Protocol) system that maps user IDs across systems. Or you could perform a search on your user master if sufficient information is available (do not search on first name and last name only—you may have more than one "John Smith" in your company). Or you could use SAP's CUA (Central User Administration) to keep your users synchronized across multiple SAP components.

Finally, you should check that the users exist in the EBP system, using function module `BAPI_USER_EXISTENCE_CHECK`.

15.2.4   Adding More Approval Levels

More approval levels can be added to the shopping cart approval workflows by copying the SAP-provided shopping cart workflows and modifying your copy to create additional levels. Follow the pattern of steps for the approval, following the provided workflows to make sure you keep features such as the ability to dynamically add more approvers, and to keep the new workflow consistent for approval status displays.

It is important to retain the standard sub-processes for handling change/deletion events and for handling the final processing once the approve/rejection decision is made, so that your new workflow does not restrict use of, and operates consistently with, standard EBP functionality.

You will need to create your own rules for the additional approval levels; refer to section 15.2.2.

You need to check that the approval status display in the shopping cart status still shows the approval flow in an acceptable format. A Java Applet is used to represent a simplified graphic workflow log. Complex operations such as "loops" cannot be visualized. It helps to mark any steps that should **not** appear in the approval status display as *step not in workflow log* in the workflow step definition.

15.2.5 Parallel and Dynamic Approvals

Parallel and dynamic approvals are possible in EBP as in all approval workflows, although no complete example templates are delivered with EBP.

> **Caution** The behavior of the approval applet cannot be guaranteed in such complex scenarios.

The basic process for parallel approval is to create a fork with as many branches as needed to perform the approvals. Each branch should include the block of steps consisting of:

▶ The approval step itself

▶ The assessment of whether all items have been approved and, if some items have been rejected, the step where the requestor can opt to delete those items and continue on, or change the shopping cart and start the approval process again.

Once all approvals have been received, the shopping cart's approval status is evaluated. If any approvers have rejected the shopping cart, the whole cart is rejected. The final processing of the shopping cart after the approval decision has been made should be done using the same subworkflow as found in SAP-provided shopping cart approval workflows.

Alternatively, you can use the ad hoc approver functionality as a form of dynamic approval by having the workflow automatically add approvers on request.

An example: At one company, a dynamic decision about whether particular approval steps could be automated was based on which approvers were found for each approval step. In this scenario, at the start of the workflow the approvers for each approval step were determined as usual by ad hoc agent assignment. Prior to each approval step, the approvers were examined, and if the requestor was also a valid approver, approval was set automatically. If the requestor was not an approver, then the approval step was used. This particular scenario did not require any changes to the approval applet status display.

15.2.6 Commissioning/Decommissioning Workflows

If you need to decommission an old workflow, and commission a new workflow in its place, you can either change the start conditions at the crossover time, or you can include the shopping cart `CreateDate` attribute to identify which shopping carts should use the old workflow versus the new workflow. By using the `CreateDate` attribute in your logical expression, you can then set up the start condition in advance of the crossover time.

If you are using start conditions, you activate and deactivate the event linkage from the start condition configuration transactions. This is because the start condition configuration transaction needs to create the event linkage with the check function module that checks the start conditions; otherwise the start conditions will not be checked at runtime.

15.3 Changing Confirmation and Invoice Approvals

For changing confirmation and invoice approval workflows the basic process is the same as for shopping cart approval workflows. Confirmations and invoices can either be auto-approved (e.g. if the no-approval-required workflow is active or if the requestor is the confirmation/invoice creator) or go through a one-step approval process. The usual approval process is to send the confirmation/invoice back to the EBP requestor, if the confirmation/invoice is related to a shopping cart. If for some reason no requestor can be identified, approval is sent to an administrator.

15.3.1 Changing the Auto-Approval Criteria and/or the Approvers

For confirmations, the `BUS2203.APPROVERGETLIST` method calls function module `BBP_APPROVER_GET_LIST` to determine whether a requestor created the confirmation and return a list of approvers.

For invoices, similarly the `BUS2205.APPROVERGETLIST` method calls function module `BBP_APPROVER_GET_LIST` to determine whether a requestor created the invoice and return a list of approvers.

If you want to use your own method for determining the approvers, create subtypes of `BUS2203/BUS2205`, delegate `BUS2203/BUS2205` to their subtypes, and redefine the `APPROVERGETLIST` methods.

15.3.2 Changing the Administrator

The administrator who approves confirmations/invoices that require approval and for which no requestor was found, is simply assigned as a possible agent of the relevant "administrator approval" task.

If you want to change this, a simple approach is to create your own rule (e.g. a responsibility rule) to determine an alternate approver, copy the standard workflow and include your new rule against the appropriate step.

15.4 User Approval Workflows

New users are able to request a user ID to EBP via a Web-based form, as part of which they nominate their manager. Once the form has been completed, the new user request is sent to the manager for approval and assignment of appropriate authorizations.

A similar workflow exists for capturing significant changes to a user's data, for instance, change of manager. The user is sent to the new manager for approval. If the user forgets their password, they can request a new password, and the password request is sent for approval to their manager to ensure that they should still have access to EBP. Often, security administrators as well as managers may also need to approve users.

15.4.1 Adding Another Approver

To add another approver, copy the existing workflow. In your new workflow, duplicate the approval step.

Next, create a new approval task by copying the existing approval task. You will also need to link it to an Internet Service, so use one of the existing tasks and its Internet Service as a guide. It is best to create a new task for the approval so that you can change both the texts and if necessary change the underlying Web transaction to ensure that the security administrator has access to all appropriate functionality. Normally, a second approver would see permissions chosen by the first approver rather than all the rules, so you may want to change this in the program logic so that the administrator can override the permissions.

Insert your new task back into the new approval step.

Add agent assignment, for example a rule, into the new approval step.

15.5 Understanding the Procurement Card Reconciliation Workflow

The procurement card reconciliation workflows come in two parts. The first is an initial workflow for reconciliation of procurement card statement items by the first agent; the second is a workflow for reconciliation of items by the second agent.

An interesting behavior of the procurement card reconciliation workflows is that they are only started if items require reconciliation and if the agent does not already have an outstanding procurement card reconciliation work item. That is, since the procurement card reconciliation work item is designed to let the agent reconcile all outstanding procurement card statement items, there is no need to create a new work item if one already exists. The check for an existing work item is handled in the program code, rather than via the workflow.

This approach does put one restriction on the procurement card agents, namely that the first and second agents must not be the same user. Otherwise the second workflow will never be started, since the check for an existing work item is made prior to the first reconciliation work item being closed. So the check simply finds the current work item assigned to the user, assumes that work item can be used for any further reconciliation required, and therefore fails to start the second workflow.

15.6 Tracking Workflow Instances

EBP provides a shopping cart status function for requestors to track their shopping carts, as well as the progress of approval workflows.

As a workflow administrator, you can often benefit from more powerful reporting mechanisms. You can use any of the standard workflow reports; however, most of the time the most useful report is one that shows all work items for a particular object instance (i.e. transaction SWI6).

> **Tip** In releases before EBP 3.0, to use the standard workflow reports (such as transaction SWI14–*Workflows for an object*) business objects had to implement the IFFIND interface. This restriction has been removed in EBP 3.0 (i.e. SAP Web Application Server 6.10). Unfortunately, in earlier releases, the current EBP business objects did not include the IFFIND interface, so the standard workflow reports could not be used to find work items for a particular object instance. You could of course use delegated subtypes to add the IFFIND interface.

15.7 Advanced Troubleshooting and Solutions

Barring mistakes in your own custom workflow definitions, that there are only a few problems that you are likely to encounter. These are listed here. For more detailed guidelines please refer to chapter 14, *Advanced Diagnostics*.

The Workflow Did Not Start at all

This usually happens when you have defined incorrect start conditions (such as forgetting a NOT or using AND instead of OR). Track this by turning on the event log (transaction SWELS), raising the event manually (transaction SWUE), and looking at the log (transaction SWEL) to verify that the events were successful.

Check that the logical expressions in the start conditions are correct by simulating them in the condition editor, and verify that all the relevant workflows are active. The workflow trace will show you exactly how the condition is evaluated at run-time.

The Workflow Ran to Completion but the Shopping Cart is Still in Awaiting Approval Status

This actually has nothing to do with workflow. The problem is that the mechanism for transferring the shopping cart details to backend objects has failed to report an error correctly.

If errors are reported correctly, the shopping cart is put into "Contains Errors" status, and entries are added to the application monitors.

If errors are not reported, the shopping cart simply remains in "Awaiting Approval" status. The best way to determine the source of these problems is to use the function module "Test" option (in transaction SE37) to rerun and verify the behavior of the appropriate SPOOL_*_CREATE_DO function module, especially if you are using BAdIs to manipulate the data being transferred.

The Approval Work Item Was Created but Was Not Sent to Anybody, or Was Sent to the Workflow Administrator

Both these scenarios indicate an agent assignment problem. Either no one was assigned to the relevant task on which the work item is based, or the approvers found do not have access to execute the relevant work item.

Remember that agent assignment starts with all possible agents, and then is narrowed to the subset of selected agents, and then narrowed again by removing any excluded agents.

If the selected agents are not a subset of possible agents, they are ignored and the work item is—usually—sent to the workflow administrator (read SAP Note 491804).

If all possible/selected agents are also excluded agents, the work item will be in limbo without any valid agents. Your workflow administrator will then need to forward the work item to a more appropriate agent.

The Approval Display is Wrong or Empty

The approval display is a tailored representation of the graphical workflow log. Usually problems in the display are related to new steps being included in the graphical workflow log that the display program is not expecting. Usually the problem can be fixed by making sure that, if you add extra steps to a shopping cart workflow, all non-approval steps are marked as *step not in workflow log*.

15.8 Basics of EBP Architecture from a Workflow Perspective

There are a number of pieces to the architecture of EBP, but only the Web browser, Web server, ITS (Internet Transaction Server), EBP and backend ERP systems relate to SAP's WebFlow Engine, as shown in figure 15.4.

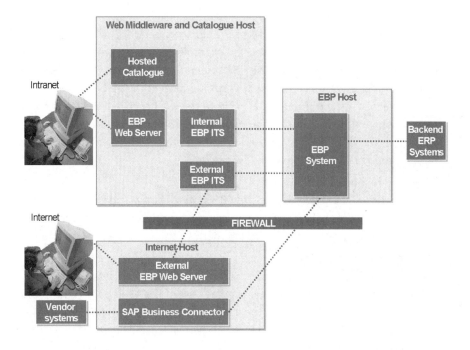

Figure 15.4 Example EBP Technical Architecture

User interaction in EBP is via a Web Browser (which browsers and browser versions are available varies from release to release). Users connect to EBP via a URL, using HTTP-POST protocol (HTTPS and Digital certificates can also be used if desired). Normally the URL is added to the company's intranet or included as part of a Portal, so that all a user has to do is click on a hyperlink.

The Web server connects to the Internet Transaction Server (ITS) (SAP's middleware between SAP components and Web servers) via the WGATE. The WGATE is a small program added to the Web server by the ITS installation to enable the Web server to connect with the ITS.

The ITS (Internet Transaction Server) connects to the EBP system. Usually the ITS is a virtual server dedicated to the EBP system. It is possible to connect to other SAP components from the same ITS, if necessary, but this is not usual since it is confusing from a maintenance and administration viewpoint.

The ITS contains a number of files:

▶ **Service files**
When a new Web transaction is started the parameters in these files are added to the data passed from the user and Web page to start the relevant transaction or routine.

▶ **HTML Template files**
When a Web transaction is linked to an EBP transaction, and the transaction needs to show a screen to a user, for example to collect further data, these templates are used to translate the EBP screen to a Dynamic HTML Web page. HTML Templates can also be used in conjunction with ITS Flow files, which allow function modules and external routines to be called directly without transactions, with the template providing the complete look and feel of the Web page. In EBP, flow files are used in some areas such as user administration, but are not usually used for workflow features.

▶ **Language resource files**
Most texts can be extracted from the EBP system, but where this is not appropriate (e.g. texts for help pages), language resource files enable additional texts to be added. Translation of texts to alternative languages is also supported.

▶ **Multimedia (MIME) files**
These include graphics files, JavaScript files, Java applet/servlet files, HTML[Business] function files, etc. that may be used as part of the Web pages. These multimedia files are actually held on the Web server. Most EBP multimedia files are held under the BBPGLOBAL service, which was specifically created to group all common multimedia files.

All end user transactions delivered in EBP are called via the Web. This includes all workflow transactions. The workflow transactions are implemented using Easy Web transactions (refer to chapter 12, *Forms* for details of this technique).

It is important to realize that the EBP installation includes the SAP Web Application Server, so the WebFlow Engine used by EBP resides in EBP itself, not in the backend ERP installation.[5]

---

5 If this is an SAP system, it will also contain the Web Application Server, opening up the opportunity of using Wf-XML to tighten up the inter-process communication between both components.

The EBP system connects to the backend ERP system, which may be SAP or non-SAP. Backend communication may be via RFC (the usual process for an SAP component) or via XML documents using the SAP Business Connector to handle the messaging between the systems (the usual approach for a non-SAP component).

Since multiple and different (SAP and non-SAP) backend systems are possible, a meta-BAPI process is used to determine which routine should be called for an appropriate system. Like BAPIs, meta-BAPI calls are always background calls, in other words they do not communicate directly with a user via screens. All dialog activity (i.e. screen-based) is controlled via programs and routines in the EBP system itself. If a dialog activity needs to call the backend system, (e.g. to check account assignment changes made during shopping cart approval) the EBP program calls the appropriate meta-BAPI in the background, and the result is presented to the user by the program in EBP.

Whenever an EBP program needs to call a backend routine, the program calls a meta-BAPI for the appropriate object/method. For example, to call a backend routine to create a purchase order you use object BUS2012 (Purchase Order) and method CreateFromData. The meta-BAPI accepts the standard parameters, evaluates which system is to be called, finds the matching system-specific routine in EBP from table BBP_FUNCTION_MAP (e.g. B46C_PO_CREATE for a backend SAP 4.6C system) and calls it. The system-specific routine then reformats the input parameters as necessary for the appropriate backend routine, calls the backend routine in the backend system (e.g. BAPI_PO_CREATE in the 4.6C system), reformats the output parameters (including error messages) as necessary, and returns the result to the meta-BAPI. The meta-BAPI then returns the result to the calling program.

Usually the meta-BAPI process is not needed in workflows, but if you decide to change or develop new workflow-accessible routines that include calls to backend routines, you should implement those calls using the meta-BAPI process.

If you are developing or enhancing EBP, it is worthwhile knowing that EBP and CRM are implemented using the same server, although usually in different clients. So if your company is using both EBP and CRM, business objects and workflows created for EBP are also available to CRM and vice versa. This is particularly useful when working with shared objects such as business partners.

EBP has its own Web inbox service BBPBWSP, an enhanced version of the standard Web inbox service BWSP. The most noticeable difference is that BBPBWSP displays work items differently and allows approvals and rejections to be made directly in the work item list, without having to execute the work item first.

EBP has its own e-mail notification program RSWUWFMLEC, based on the standard e-mail notification program RSWUWFML. The most noticeable differences are that RSWUWFMLEC:

▶ Reads the agent's e-mail address from the EBP user master

▶ Reads an auto-forward indicator from the agent's EBP attributes (instead of from the standard workflow auto-forwarding)

▶ Dynamically generates hyperlinks to the Web work item in the e-mails using the agent's EBP attributes

▶ Includes generated hyperlinks that allow offline approval/rejection via a generated reply e-mail.[6] The incoming reply e-mails are parsed and processed against the original work items using program RBBP_OFFLINE_EVAL. There are more details on this technique in appendix A, *Tips and Tricks*.

All workflow administration and monitoring tools are accessible to the workflow administrator via the Web browser using SAP GUI for HTML, which is included with EBP. Unlike the dedicated Web user interface for normal users, the administrator user interface is simply a SAP GUI for HTML rendering of the standard Web-Flow administration transactions.

15.9 Business Object Types

The main business objects used in EBP are shown in table 15.1.

BUS2121	Shopping Cart (also known as the "Requirement Coverage Request")
ASBMANAGER	Ad hoc agent: Manager of shopping cart requestor
ASBMANOFMA	Ad hoc agent: Manger of shopping cart requestor's manager
ASBMANOFSL	Ad hoc agent: Spending limit manager of shopping cart requestor
BUS1006200	EBP Business Partner
BUS1006210	Business Partner Bidder Data
BUS2200	Bid Invitation
BUS2201	EBP (local) purchase order
BUS2202	Vendor bid
BUS2203	EBP (local) confirmation
BUS2205	EBP (local) invoice

Table 15.1 Primary EBP Business Object Types

---

6 Starting with EBP Release 3.0

BUS4101	EBP user
BBP_PCARD	Procurement Card
BBP_PCSTAT	Procurement Card Statement

Table 15.1 Primary EBP Business Object Types (cont.)

In addition, standard Basis workflows are also included such as IDoc error processing and execution of Change/Transport proposals.

16 WebFlow in mySAP CRM

> *Customers expect fast responses. So it comes as no surprise that workflow plays a central role in Customer Relationship Management, ensuring that the customer gets a response that is both fast and accurate. Workflows are used so that the processes are flexible enough to cope with the inevitable changes that go hand in hand with market trends.*

16.1 mySAP CRM and Workflow

mySAP CRM (Customer Relationship Management) lets you integrate all internal and external business processes related to customer management. Using CRM, all those who have contact with customers, whether sales staff, service staff, or call center staff, access the same uniform source of information. As a result, the customer feels that the company knows him and his needs, since from his perspective it speaks "with one voice".

Clearly workflow plays a key role here, ensuring that processes are tracked and that the log of activities is viewable by the employees within the company. Part of this workflow is provided by the WebFlow Engine, particularly the more complex and sophisticated processes, which are unique to each company. In addition, mySAP CRM handles standard activities itself, offering a selection of customizable activities to accompany the relevant interaction.

16.1.1 Some Technical Observations

mySAP CRM is a stand-alone product that can be implemented with or without a mySAP R/3 backend. It essentially consists of CRM-Middleware and an SAP Web Application Server, which contains the CRM database, the workflow functions, and the SAP-provided workflows described in this chapter.

On the backend system, mySAP CRM can access

▶ An OLTP-R/3 adapter (for connecting an R/3 backend, such as an FI system)

▶ A BW adapter (for connecting the mySAP Business Warehouse)

▶ External interfaces (for connecting non-SAP Systems by using IDoc or XML)

At the frontend, it uses

▶ An adapter for mobile clients

▶ An ASCII adapter

16.1.2 mySAP CRM from a Workflow Viewpoint

In a way similar to SAP's Enterprise Buyer Professional (EBP), mySAP CRM uses workflow as the controller for specific business processes. This is possible because the CRM system includes the SAP Web Application Server. You can use workflow for process automation in all mySAP CRM areas. As usual, the *Business Object Repository* (BOR) is the basis of the business logic here. You can also create your own business objects and use them in your own workflows.

As you can see in the following list, all business objects with parent objects in the Business Process object family, BUS20001xx, share via inheritence the business transactions in the central CRM area, so that all sales actions can be handled generically. This inheritance is the technical implementation of the mySAP CRM *OneOrder* concept, i.e. the idea that the same generic business object is always involved in a sales transaction (from getting a lead to the offer and credit check). This concept is directly related to the idea of the central availability of information.

The following list shows the most important business objects that are supplied for the mySAP CRM area.

CRM Business transaction handling

Business Object	Business process
BUS2000108	Lead CRM
BUS2000109	Contract CRM
BUS2000111	Opportunity CRM
BUS2000115	Sales transaction CRM
BUS2000116	Service transactiasdasdn CRM
BUS2000117	Service confirmation CRM
BUS2000120	Complaint CRM
BUS2000125	Task CRM
BUS2000126	Business Activity CRM

Table 16.1 Derivatives of BUS20001

Business Object	Business process
BUS2200	Bid invitation
BUS2201	Purchase order EC
BUS2202	Vendor quotation EC
BUS2203	Confirmation of goods/services EC
BUS2205	Vendor invoice EC

Table 16.2 Other business transactions

Marketing

Business Object	Business process
BUS20100	Marketing project
BUS2010010	Marketing project plan
BUS2010012	Marketing project plan element
BUS2010020	Marketing project campaign
BUS2010022	Marketing project campaign element

Table 16.3 For the marketing planner's use

Master Data

Business Object	Business process
BUS1006	Business Partner
BUS1178	Product
BUS2300	Product Catalogue

Table 16.4 For general use throughout CRM

These business objects are used in the SAP-provided workflows. However, you can of course use the objects in your own workflows. Often, customers find that they prefer to use the SAP-provided workflows as a starting point, copying and adapting them to their own use. This lets them leverage the work that SAP has done, instead of starting from scratch.

Here is an overview of the main uses of workflow in CRM:

▶ Marketing

  ▷ Authorization of marketing campaigns

  ▷ Handle errors in mail sending (during e-mail campaigns)

  ▷ Generate opportunities from leads

▶ Sales transaction and credit management

  ▷ Release credit block

  ▷ Authorizing of offers

  ▷ Automatic release of offers

  ▷ Review of Internet sales orders with long texts (i.e. complex customer requirements)

▶ Customer Interaction Center

  ▷ Business routing and editing of incoming e-mail messages

  ▷ Call Center support

16.2   Customizing

Workflow Customizing

The workflow environment must be customized. As for all mySAP.com components that use the workflow as a control instrument, in mySAP CRM you only have to perform workflow customizing once. Chapter 3, *Configuring the System*, can be used as a guide.

CRM Customizing

To use the workflow scenarios supplied by mySAP CRM, you must make settings in addition to the basic workflow customizing. As always, this includes activating event linkages, integrating a valid organizational structure (agent assignment, rule integration) and maintaining workflow start conditions.

16.3   'Specials' of mySAP CRM

The SAP-provided CRM workflow scenarios cover a wide range of business areas pertinent to CRM, from marketing to sales transactions to customer service, with the help of a Customer Interaction Center or the Internet. Thus, the SAP-provided workflows already support and extend the mySAP CRM functions in all important areas.

This chapter shows some special features of CRM. You will also find some examples, where these special techniques are 'used' by workflow.

16.3.1   BUS20001 (Business transaction), OneOrder Concept

As described in section 16.1.2, one of the central building blocks of mySAP CRM is the OneOrder concept. The technical implementation of this concept is object type BUS20001.

You should define workflows on this object type, if they represent functions, that all CRM business operations have in common. This allows the main OneOrder attributes and methods to be inherited by the generic process (see Example 1). Process-specific functions should be defined on the respective sub-object type. This allows you to reuse the inherited methods and objects of the super type, or overdefine them to make them sub-object specific. In the CRM System you can use and copy an existing business operation as base for the following operation. The creation of such a subsequent operation can be automated with a workflow, as shown in the following example.

Example 1: Credit management (WS10000246)

Credit management limits financial risks for your organization by allowing you to carry out credit checks in transaction processing, and by forwarding documents, blocked for credit reasons, directly to the employees responsible for reviewing them.

This workflow supports credit management in CRM by automatically forwarding to the designated employee any transactions that have been blocked due to a credit check in the backend system.

The workflow is triggered if a credit check for a transaction leads to the status *Credit check not OK* (i.e. event BUS20001.CREDITCHECKTOBEPROCESSED). Using the CRM organizational plan, the system determines the manager of the employee who created the transaction, and sends a work item to his inbox. The manager can then display the transaction document from his inbox. He can then release or reject the entire transaction, on the *Status* tab page at the header level. He also can release or reject individual items at the item level on the *Status* tab page. If he rejects the entire transaction, he will need to enter a reason for the rejection. If he edits individual items, the workflow for the business transaction remains active until all blocked items are either released or rejected.

Being based on the OneOrder business object BUS20001 (the CRM business transaction), this workflow covers the complete field. It is thus unnecessary to create separate workflows for all the sub-objects, such as an *opportunity*, *contract* or *sales transaction*. This is a great example of useful software economy.

Example 2: Generate opportunity from lead (WS10001011)

The interesting aspect of this workflow is that it shows how the workflow process controls the extension of one business object (the *lead*) into another (the *opportunity*).

A *lead* is a business transaction that describes, retains, updates, and manages the potential business interest of a business partner and the subsequent interaction over a period of time. The aim of lead management is to make the information gained available to the sales department as a possible basis for decision-making. This in turn can call for the creation of an *opportunity*.

The *Generate opportunity from Lead* workflow takes the information gathered in the lead, optionally passes it to a responsible sales department employee for review, and generates a matching opportunity. If the lead-specific attributes *Priority* and *Lead group* meet specific criteria, the workflow automatically creates an opportunity. Otherwise, the workflow for manual creation sends a work item to the sales employee responsible. After checking the data in the lead, the sales employee can either reject this lead or create an opportunity.

The workflow is started automatically when the lead is saved.

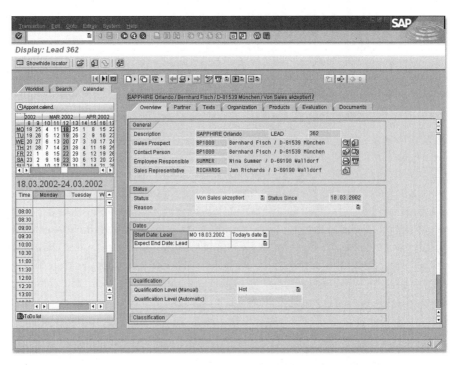

Figure 16.1 Lead Management, Showing the Workflow Generic Object Service Buttons

The workflow uses the sales representative indicated in the lead to determine who (that is, which sales employee) is to create the opportunity. If this is to be done automatically, then the workflow uses mySAP CRM's *partner determination* technology (which incorporates data about interested parties in the lead) in order to locate the correct recipient.

The *Generate opportunity from lead* workflow is started if a lead with the qualification level *Hot* is saved. Start conditions are used to check that the secondary conditions are met. The system then checks whether an opportunity can be created automatically or if a sales employee has to make the decision. The sales employee is determined according to the lead-specific attributes *Priority* and *Lead group*. If the sales employee decides that an opportunity can be created, the lead status is set to *Accepted by sales* and an opportunity is created in background.

By examining the workflow graphical log (fig. 6.4), you will see directly the process path followed in order to generate this *opportunity* with the *lead* as the starting point.

16.3.2 Starting Workflows Via Actions

Another method for handling consecutive functions and messages in CRM is offered by the *actions* component.

Actions are important for maintaining and improving business relationships. You can schedule and start predefined processes with the *Actions* component by means of user-definable conditions from transaction documents. You can tailor the type and time of actions to the requirements of your customers and the processes in your company. This component thereby offers you the possibility to automate your service and sales and distribution management while at the same time adjusting them even more closely to customer needs. The *Actions* component also provides a technique for controlling output. This is the CRM evolution of *Output Determination* as used in R/3 .

Actions in CRM use the Basis *Post Processing Framework* (PPF) component, which is embedded in the SAP Web Application Server, as the uniform interface for different processing methods. The processing of the actions is performed by methods (Business Add-ins), SAP's WebFlow Engine or Smart Forms. Although workflows can still be started using status management in CRM, triggering the workflows through actions extends workflow's availability considerably.

Example: Automatic Approval of Quotations (WS10001068)

The *Release quotation automatically* workflow is triggered indirectly through the PPF using a quotation *action*.

This quotation action raises the event BUS2000115.RELEASEAUTOMATICALLY.

This workflow automatically releases quotations without the need for approval in advance by a manager. It releases quotations that do not need to be approved by the manager. For example, if a quotation has a net value of under $50 and the *For Release* status has been set, then the release can take place automatically without the authorization of the manager.

As with the approval workflow, your own conditions can be defined to determine whether the explicit release or the automatic release workflow should be used for a particular quotation.

16.3.3 Partner Processing

The partner processing determines how the system operates with business partners in processes.

One of the most important pieces of information during partner processing is the partner's identification, hence the ability of the system to find and enter a partner automatically in a process. In most processes the user inputs manually one or more partners; the remaining partners are filled in by the system by partner identification. The partner identification is derived from various sources of information, the most important: business partner being master data and the organization data. In the workflow these partners can be selected from the corresponding document. The partner becomes an agent for a workflow step via an expression.

Example: Generate Opportunity from Lead (WS10001011)

Have a look at this workflow again. The BOR object BUS2000108 (*LeadCRM*) shows the implementation of partner-based agent determination in the attribute LeadCRM.ResponsibleUserName. You can use this attribute for your data binding. Instead of using normal OrgManagement (or roles) for agent assignment, you have the information as an attribute of your actual business object.

Alternatively, you can implement the agent identification via rules or allocation of organization objects (see chapter 9, *Agent-Determination Rules*).

16.4 Using Your Own Workflows with mySAP CRM

In the previous section, you may have noticed that nearly all mySAP CRM provided workflows are started via events. This makes it easy to replace the SAP workflows with your own workflows. All you need to do is create a new event linkage to point to your workflow.

> **Tip** Do not forget to set up start conditions for your new event linkage if appropriate.

If you need to change the agent determination, create your own rule (refer to chapter 9, *Agent-Determination Rules*) and replace the provided rule in your copy of the workflow with your own rule. Bear in mind that most CRM agent determination uses the partner relationship rules determined from the CRM order.

17 Setting Up an SAP-Provided R/3 Workflow

This chapter describes how to activate one SAP workflow. Even if you do not require this particular scenario, this section will give you an idea of the time and effort involved. SAP workflows are delivered in all mySAP.com components.

17.1 Introduction

In this chapter, you will learn how to activate workflow definitions delivered by SAP. The chapter is short because activating an SAP workflow is simple. This should, at the very least, convince you that it is worth activating an SAP workflow to demonstrate to colleagues what workflow is all about, even if you intend to create your own workflow later. Of course, you may well decide to use the SAP workflow as-is. Do not feel guilty about this. SAP application developers have spent a lot of time:

▶ Blueprinting the best business process

▶ Developing the workflow definition

▶ Adjusting the application transactions so that they leverage the workflow benefits as tightly as possible

▶ Documenting the workflow and its customizing

So the value gained when you activate a supplied workflow can be immense, which is the whole purpose of the exercise.

There are two levels of workflow activation:

1. You use the workflow without any enhancement whatsoever. All you have to do is assign agents to the different steps, activate the triggering events and performing any IMG activities related to the process.

2. You can add your own simple enhancements such as deadline handling and your own task descriptions to make it easier for your users to use the workflow. These activities are not modifications, so if you go live with the workflow, your improvements are retained, even if SAP development enhances the next release of the workflow definition.

The example that we have chosen is the *Release of a blocked vendor*. You will find detailed notes about this in the online documentation in the R/3 Logistics (MM) module or the catalogue of workflows in the workflow tool section of the online documentation. mySAP CRM has its own workflow definition for this process but we have selected the R/3 component because this is readily available to more readers.

To make things easier for you when you want to try this out in your own system, we have created an electronic tutorial, which can be downloaded from the publisher's Web site. This tutorial takes you through the process step by step, showing exactly which button should be pressed when.

17.2 What is the Business Scenario?

The workflow we are going to activate in this example deals with the following common scenario. For various reasons, a company may need to prevent orders from being placed with a particular vendor. For example, vendors can be locked as a matter of course when a new vendor record is created or when an existing vendor record is changed. This is simply a procedural action to ensure the data quality of the vendor record or to provide a chance to perform background checks, e.g. a credit check, on the vendor. Existing vendors can also be blocked when they deliver substandard goods too often. Many companies activate additional quality management workflows, which deal with quality checks on delivered goods and some companies have created custom workflows to assess vendors that supply services. These are beyond the scope of this section, but thinking about the possibilities may give you an idea of how one workflow process can easily engender others.

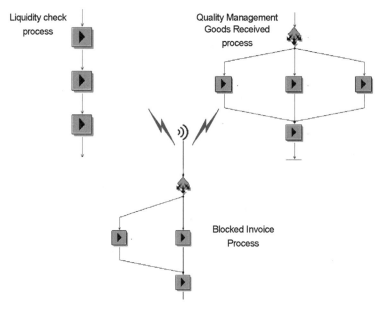

Figure 17.1 Relation Between the Blocked Vendor Process and Other Processes

A vendor that has been blocked unnecessarily or for too long is just as bad for business as a vendor block that has been released without the necessary checks. By driving the process with a workflow you are adding control to the business process. This part of the process then becomes transparent and SAP's WebFlow Engine drives it faster and reliably. You can see from figure 17.1 that the next step in improving efficiency and cutting costs is to automate other parts of this process, such as the liquidity check or the quality management of received goods.

When the vendor's record is blocked, the vendor maintenance transaction raises an event, which in turn triggers the workflow. The workflow alerts the responsible agent, who checks the vendor's record (and anything else that needs to be checked) before releasing the block.

17.3   Which SAP Workflows are Involved?

From the documentation you can see at a glance which workflows are involved. In this case it is a single workflow, WS20000001. In more complex scenarios involving several workflows the documentation may refer to a task group, which is simply a package of workflows.

In this case the documentation shows the tasks that are involved, but you can easily view this catalogue for yourself by:

▶ Inspecting the workflow in the workflow builder or
▶ Executing the IMG activity *Task specific customizing* or
▶ Viewing the main workflow in the diagnosis transaction SWUD

These are the tasks involved:

▶ Workflow WS20000001, which encompasses the complete process and can be started by three different events.
▶ Task TS00300025, which is used to decide whether or not the vendor data will be displayed.
▶ Three tasks (TS20000002, TS30000034, TS00300028), which can be used to inspect the block, depending on which type of block is set.
▶ Task TS00300034, which is used to decide whether or not to release the block.
▶ Tasks TS20000003, TS00300029, which are used to release the block, depending on what type of block has been set.

17.4   How is the Workflow Started?

The three possible triggers for this workflow are shown in table 17.1.

Technical Triggering Event	Meaning
Event BlockedForPurchasing from the business object LFA1	The vendor has been blocked completely.
Event BlockedForPurchOrg from the business object LFM1	This vendor has been blocked for a particular purchasing organization.
Event BlockedForVSROrPlan from the business object LFM1	One particular sub-range or plant belonging to this vendor has been blocked for one particular purchasing organization.

Table 17.1 Triggers for the Process

When one of these events is raised in the background, the workflow is started. The data that the workflow needs depends on the type of block that is set. This data is passed from the transaction to the event and from the event to the workflow (see Figure 17.2).

17.5   How Do I Activate This Scenario?

First check if the workflow system has been customized. To do this, call the workflow customizing transaction (SWU3). Check that the run-time system has a green check mark showing that it has been set up properly. If this is not the case press ⊕, as described in chapter 3, *Configuring the System*.

The event linkage for every workflow in the system is inactive by default until you decide to activate it. This is true of workflows that you create yourself as well as the workflows delivered by SAP. The workflows will not trigger until you activate this linkage. It is not essential that workflows are triggered by events, but this is nearly always best practice because it allows the workflows to be activated, deactivated or substituted by other workflow definitions easily. The blocked vendor workflow is no exception.

Before you activate the event linkage, you will need to assign possible agents to the tasks. When a task is created or delivered by SAP, it will have no agents assigned to it, so you must do this yourself as part of the customizing activity.

In a production environment, you will want to be restrictive about who may perform the task. You will probably want to create an organizational module using the organization management part of the SAP Web Application Server and assign a job to the task.

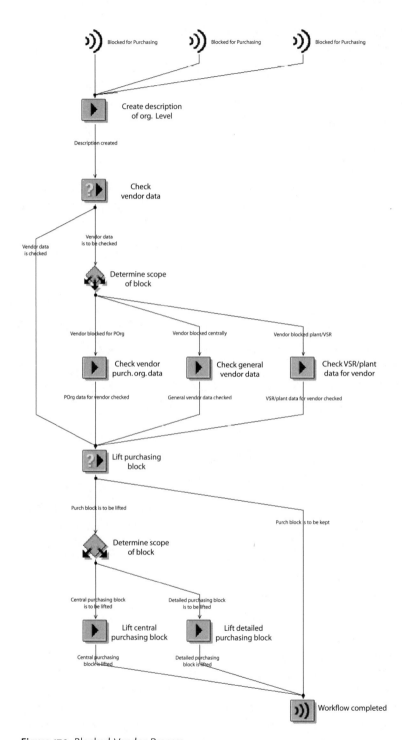

Figure 17.2 Blocked Vendor Process

By doing this you simplify authorization, organization, user and role management in addition to indirect benefits such as substitution management and reporting. This topic is covered in detail in chapter 5, *Agents*. In this example we will simply make all users in the system possible agents by declaring the tasks to be *general tasks*. In this particular workflow the agent that performs the first step is automatically assigned to the following steps of the workflow.

1. Navigate to the IMG activity task-specific customizing of SAP Business Workflow.

2. Expand the tree to the branch **Logistics—General · Logistics Basic Data · Business Partner · Vendor Master**. Here you can assign the agents to the tasks and activate the event linkage.

3. Select *Assign agents to task*. You will see the following dialog tasks (ignore the background tasks) as in table 17.2.

Task ID	Name	Possible Agents
TS20000002	Check general vendor data	General task
TS20000034	Check the vendor's purchasing organization data	General task
TS00300028	Check the vendor's sub-range or plant data	General task
TS00300034	Decision to release vendor data	General task
TS20000003	Lift central vendor purchasing block	General task
TS00300029	Lift detailed purchasing block for vendor	General task
TS00300025	Check vendor data decision	Assign yourself and anyone else in the system who wants to be involved in the scenario. Normally this would be assigned to the job responsible for vendor data maintenance.

Table 17.2 Tasks Used in the Process

Tasks that are classified as general tasks can be executed by everyone in the system. In practice the workflow makes sure that the correct user is selected. The first step in the workflow appears to all the agents assigned to the *check vendor data decision* task. The agent executing the task is assigned to all subsequent work items in the workflow. So only assign the task *Check vendor data decision* to users that are responsible for the vendor data maintaince. In a production environment you would probably do this by assigning the task to a job, but in order to demonstrate the workflow you can assign users directly.

4. Select *Activate event linkage*. When you expand the workflow WS20000001 branch you will see all three possible triggering events. Activate all of them.

This SAP-provided workflow will now be started every time a vendor is blocked. All the users that you have assigned to the first step will receive a work item in their inbox. Once an agent executes the work item, this agent must decide whether or not to display the vendor data (this depends on how familiar they are with the vendor). Finally, they can release the vendor block, which they can do themselves.

Congratulations—you have configured and activated your first workflow.

If you are feeling adventurous, you can go to the workflow configuration transaction and assign a deadline to the first step by specifying a time limit and activating the deadline as shown in figure 17.3.

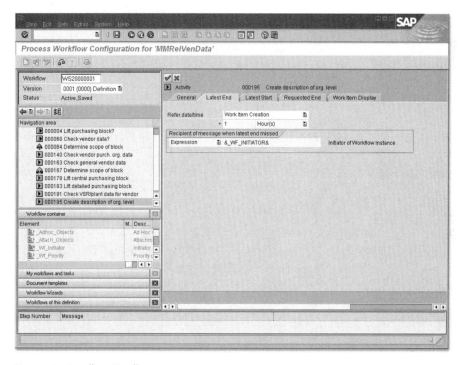

Figure 17.3 Deadline Handling

18 WebFlow and ArchiveLink

ArchiveLink provides the necessary infrastructure to make document information directly available to every authorized user. Workflow is used to coordinate the storage of digitized documents and how they are linked to the business objects in the mySAP component. From here workflow is used to accelerate the subsequent business processing.

18.1 Intelligent Organization and Distribution of Business Documents

Even in the Internet age, documents are carriers of business information. Documents are exchanged between companies, initiating business processes or providing data for processes that already in progress. The timely knowledge of business document contents and the course of their subsequent processing provide necessary information for the correct processing and evaluation of a company's procedures. Whether authorization or release procedures, procedures for purchasing, sales or requests, or decision processes, all processes require the availability, transparency, and legal certainty of business information, which can be achieved most efficiently by integrating the documents electronically.

Regardless of the original media, all business documents such as letters, faxes, or e-mails can be digitized upon arrival in the company. Then, in electronic form, they can be stored, distributed, and assigned to existing business objects or to business objects that have yet to be created. As a result, time-consuming procedures such as the duplication of these documents, the search for procedure-related information and many other core activities in paper-based research are avoided. Documents can be displayed at any time and in any place to provide business information with no delay. ArchiveLink is the technology needed to integrate business documents in electronic procedures.

18.2 What Is ArchiveLink

ArchiveLink has to be viewed from two perspectives—the functional business perspective and the technical perspective.

18.2.1 The Technical View of ArchiveLink

On the technical side, ArchiveLink can be understood by looking at its components.

ArchiveLink provides the mySAP.com application components with a bundle of interfaces, services, and scenarios, with which documents and business processes can be easily integrated. In addition, ArchiveLink has a certified interface to the storage systems (content servers) that enables features of the storage system to be called within the SAP component. To access documents stored externally, ArchiveLink includes an integrated, extendable user-interface for complex search queries (*Document Finder*) and a flexible set of routines related to displaying documents, together with its own *Document Viewer*.

A typical ArchiveLink constellation consists of SAP components in conjunction with a content server for the storage of documents that cannot be changed, and possibly an SAP Content Server for the storage of documents that are being processed (i.e. can be changed). On the client-side, you can use centralized or local work centers for scanning and storing documents (see figure 18.1). Local entry can be important for sensitive documents, such as HR documents, which you do not want left lying around. The document images can then be accessed from every client that has the necessary display components installed, when the user has the correct authorization.

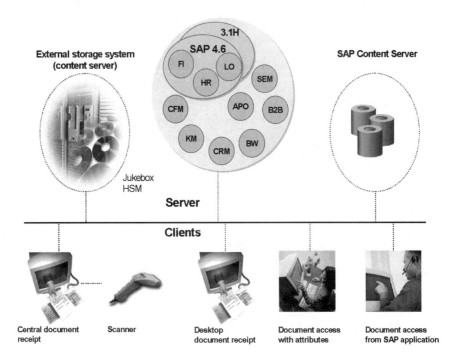

Figure 18.1 Example Configuration of an ArchiveLink System

Different display programs can be selected depending on the storage formats of the documents, the IT requirements, or the user roles. Examples of these are:

▶ An ECL (Engineering CLient viewer) display program for the display of incoming documents with the SAP GUI for Windows.

▶ An integrated Internet Browser (HTML Control) for all SAP user interfaces. This HTML Control lets plug-ins be called for mime-compatible external display programs in the Internet Explorer, but there are no restrictions for the display of different formats.

The ArchiveLink Interface is an open interface to content servers that is implemented by SAP. Every system provider of content servers that are functionally compatible with the ArchiveLink Interface can be certified by SAP. This comprises a comprehensive technical evaluation of the interface between SAP and the third-party software.

18.2.2 The Business View of ArchiveLink

The central task of ArchiveLink is the integration of documents in business processes and the linking of business objects with documents (see figure 18.2).

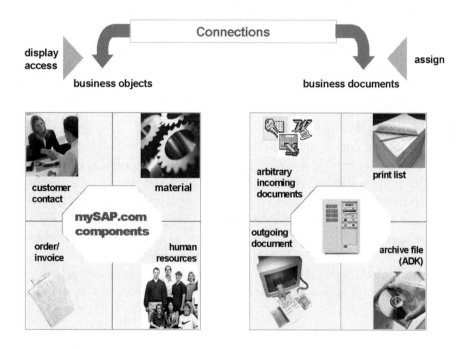

Figure 18.2 Integration of Business Objects and Business Documents

In this context, ArchiveLink supports displaying, storing, and retrieving documents and thus enables the intelligent organization and distribution of business documents. The advantages of this type of processing are:

▶ From an application record, all relevant image documents can be searched for and displayed (from any client worldwide).

▶ The authorization concept of ArchiveLink prevents unauthorized access.

▶ Documents can be integrated in processes from the start by using workflow.

18.3   ArchiveLink Standard Scenarios

ArchiveLink supports the storage of documents that arrive in your company (incoming documents), such as invoices, orders, credit memos, complaints, inquiries or contracts. These initiate processes or are assigned processors to extract the content of the document and continue the possessing. For example, suppose the contents of an incoming invoice have been extracted and posted as an electronic record of the invoice, and this has to be matched to the original purchase order. Linking the electronic image of the invoice to the invoice record is important for auditing and correcting mistakes. Similarly, the SAP component generates outgoing documents, such as order confirmations, purchase orders, invoices and dunning notices. These are also taken care of by ArchiveLink. The image of the electronic document is important when, for example, a customer calls the customer interaction center to query an invoice. That customer will have the paper invoice in front of them and the CIC agent will need to both see the image of the invoice as well as the electronic record in order to help with the enquiry.

It is also worth knowing that ArchiveLink can archive print lists (i.e. report output) such as account update journals in finance or warehouse stocks in materials management. This is either done simultaneously with the printing or as an alternative to printing. Using indices and freely definable search functions, you can also find the required list records on an ad hoc basis. Hyperlinks are used so that when a row in an archived report is selected, the original document is displayed. In special cases, content servers (external storage systems) can also include archive files that were created with the Archive Development Kit (ADK) as part of a data archiving project. In this scenario, the content server is used purely as a storage system because all access to the stored data is controlled using the component ADK.

18.3.1 How WebFlow Integrates ArchiveLink

WebFlow is used for streamlining the processing of incoming documents. There are two sub-processes (phases) involved. Phase one is the creation of the electronic document and phase two is the subsequent processing of this document, such as the release of payment for an invoice. We will only look at the first phase of processing in this chapter, because the second phase is more or less a standard WebFlow scenario with very little ArchiveLink specifics.

Consider the typical case of how an incoming paper invoice is processed. The process begins when an invoice arrives in your company. Legal considerations require the invoice to be archived, and in some countries there is a legal requirement to archive electronically, so the invoice will be scanned and archived in an electronic storage system. This invoice must also be registered in the SAP component. These two steps must be integrated together efficiently and there are two possible ways of doing this: integration using barcodes or the workflow-based procedure. Only the workflow-based procedure is described here.

Workflow-based documents scenario: Storage for later entry (previously early archiving)

The document is digitized and stored as soon as possible. This is most likely to be performed at a central scanning workplace (see figure 18.3) to reduce the total cost of the hardware as well as the cost of training and office space.

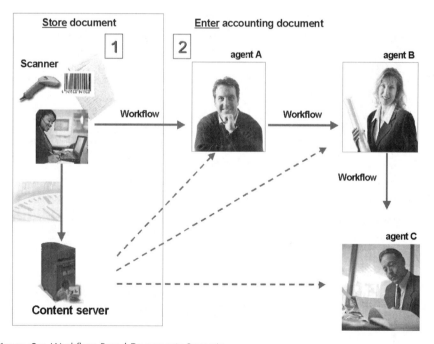

Figure 18.3 Workflow-Based Documents Scenario

After the document has been stored in the content server, a workflow is started that generates a work item for the responsible agents. When an agent executes the work item, he or she is presented with the digitized document displayed in a viewer. Simultaneously the work item starts the data-entry transaction so that the agent can enter data directly into the transaction, based on what appears in the document viewer. Some companies use Optical Character Recognition (OCR) techniques to reduce the amount of human interaction necessary. Once the data has been posted, the workflow links the electronic image to the newly created application document. This allows a user to view the posted document and to display the electronic image of the original invoice at any time and without any additional research.

If, for example, the vendor needs to follow this up with a letter (e.g. dispute the discount offered), the same workflow scenarios are available to assign the image of the letter to the existing application document. The advantage of document-based workflows is the ability to improve and accelerate the incoming document process. The following example of an incoming invoice demonstrates the advantages well:

Payment of an invoice can be made within a cash discount period, leading to a discount if the payment is made on time. To benefit from discount agreements, invoices have to be posted and released for payment as quickly as possible. In conventional financial accounting, it takes several days to process an invoice. In large enterprises, several weeks, because it has to go through various processing stages that involve offices in different geographic locations. The scenario described here considerably speeds up this procedure since the original documents were already scanned and archived when they arrived. From this point in time they are available electronically and can be processed directly.

The storage of the document described in this scenario can take place in three ways:

▶ **Control by the SAP system**
In this case, the invoice is stored under the control of an SAP transaction.

▶ **Fax inbox**
If the invoice enters the SAP component by fax (for example via SAPconnect), the fax can automatically trigger a workflow which deals with the archiving and processing of the document. The customizing is performed using transaction S028.

▶ **Upstream storage**
It is possible to completely separate the digitization process from the business processing so that digitization (and storage) is completed upstream of the SAP component. The link to the archived document, referred to as the *unique doc-*

ument identifier, is passed to the SAP component and this triggers the business process. For this purpose ArchiveLink specifies an interface for incoming documents that an external system can use to register the *unique document identifier* and document attributes to the SAP component. More sophisticated digitization mechanisms can be employed without losing the advantages of workflow. Examples of such mechanisms are *offline scanning*, *Web scanning*, *OCR*, and *classification*.

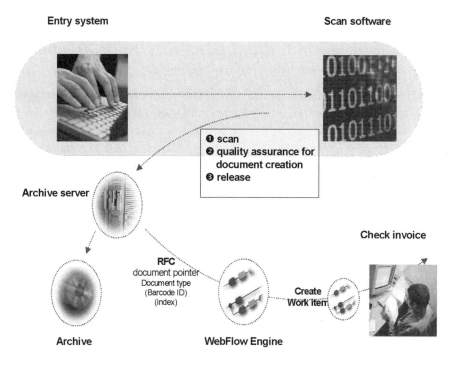

Figure 18.4 Technical View of Workflow-Based Scenarios

> **Caution** This ArchiveLink interface is not part of the ArchiveLink certification procedure, so you would have to verify with the storage system vendor that they support this interface if you intend to use it.

18.4 Business Object Types

To use ArchiveLink, the business object types concerned must support the interface IFARCH21. This interface contains the method ShowAllDocuments that displays the documents related to a business object. The interface also defines the event assigned, including the parameters passed with the event. This event is used as a terminating event to confirm that the digitized document has been assigned to the application record posted in the SAP system. In other words, the work item that a user receives to enter the data for the posting is an asynchronous task. The terminating event has two purposes:

1. It confirms that the application record has been created and committed to the database.

2. It returns the ID of the freshly created application record (i.e. the key of the new business object instance) to the workflow so that the workflow can continue processing it. This second part of the workflow is the business side of the process (not covered by this chapter), where, for example, a manager releases the invoice for payment. To do this, she has to be able to inspect both the ArchiveLink document, together with the SAP invoice.

The `assigned` event can also be used to trigger a new workflow to handle the business processing, the ArchiveLink document ID being passed as a parameter of the event. This is an example of how a single event can be both a terminating event and a triggering event. This also illustrates the power of BOR interfaces and how they contribute to software economy. This same mechanism is used for all business object types that support the `IFARCH21` interface. So the technical part of document processing is identical, irrespective of whether the document is an invoice, goods-received document or even a customer complaint.

Appendix

A   Tips and Tricks

This chapter contains a collection of our top ten useful tips and tricks. You might not use them in every workflow, but they have great value for resolving some fairly common but potentially tricky workflow situations.

A.1   Working with Wizards

Wizards exist to make your workflow development easier by helping to create workflows using tried and trusted templates. They range from generating whole workflows almost ready to use as-is to adding just a few steps to your existing workflows.

When you use a wizard, it guides you through a series of questions and answers. Be sure to read the instructions carefully.

Most wizards will help build the pattern of steps needed to perform the required procedure, but you will still need check the steps created, and adjust the agent assignment. Most wizards will assist you in searching for or creating any new tasks needed by the wizard on the fly. Even if you decide not to use the wizards, it is worthwhile running them just to get some ideas on good techniques to use in your own workflows.

Wizards can be found in the *Wizards* tray of the Workflow Builder as explained in chapter 7, *Creating a Workflow* (in releases before Release 6.10 some wizards are only found using the Workflow Wizard Explorer transaction SWF3).

The available wizards at time of going to press include:

▶ **Approval Procedure wizards**
- ▷ *Parallel Approval*
- ▷ *Hierarchical Approval*
- ▷ *Ad Hoc Dynamic Hierarchical Approval*

These wizards create complex approval procedures in minimum time. Check that the business object you want to use as the basis for approval has implemented the interface IFAPPROVE, so that approval methods and results are consistently coded.

▶ **Circular Distribution wizards**
- ▷ *Circular*
- ▷ *Parallel Circular*

- *Ad Hoc Dynamic Circular*
- *Ad Hoc Dynamic Parallel Circular*

These wizards create circular distribution procedures in minimum time.

▶ **Generic Workflow Enhancers**
Add useful processing steps to your workflow definition.

- *Simplified workflow definition*
Adds a series of steps based on one business object.

- *Creation of Customizing Workflows*
Adds a series of steps to lead the agent through related customizing transactions.

- *Choose agent*
Adds steps to your workflow to enable an agent to dynamically pick the appropriate agent for a subsequent step.

- *Call test procedure*
Adds steps to call a previously defined CATT (computer aided test tool) procedure. This can be used to batch-input data into a dialog transaction.

- *Model deadline monitoring*
Adds steps that can cancel a work item and start alternative processing if a deadline is exceeded.

- *Create object reference*
Adds a `SYSTEM.GenericInstantiate` step to instantiate an object of whatever business object you specify. In other words, a container element referencing a flat data field can be converted to a business object to give you access to attributes.

- *Execute report/job*
Adds steps to execute an ABAP report or background job or send the results to a user.

> **Tip** The very first time you use one of these wizards, it is worthwhile running it against an otherwise empty workflow first so you can see the impact the wizard will have on your workflow before using it in your own workflow.

A.2 Working with E-Mails

In most workflows, at some point you will want to send an e-mail to an interested party. The e-mail recipient does not need to be an agent of the workflow, or an employee of your company, or even a person at all, since you can e-mail to an Internet e-mail address or to a fax number (i.e. auto-faxing).

To e-mail someone, you create a document, possibly with other documents attached, and send it to recipients via your existing mail servers. All of which can be done as a background task using object `SelfItem` and method `SendTaskDescription`.

You can create your own task for `SelfItem.SendTaskDescription` and include it in your workflow in an activity step, or use the *send mail* step to generate a task for you. The result is similar; however, the advantage of using a *send mail* step is that a mail step icon appears in the flowchart, giving you greater clarity when using the flowchart to review or explain the process to business process owners and workflow users. If you have an existing task you want to reuse in a send mail step rather than generate a new task, attach your task by entering the task ID in the *Control* tab of the send mail step definition.

A.2.1 The Send Mail Step

The advantage of using the send mail task is that the task description is transmitted so it is easy to include variables in the text. The minimum you need to provide to a send mail step is:

▶ **A subject text**
You can use expressions based on container elements to provide dynamic values in your texts.

▶ **A body text**
You can use expressions based on container elements (single, multiline, or object attributes) to provide dynamic values in your texts.

▶ **A recipient type**
Note that you can only send to one type of recipient at a time. Possible types include but are not limited to: SAP user, SAPOffice distribution list, Internet e-mail address, fax number, telex number, or organizational object (e.g. send to everyone in a particular organizational unit).

▶ **A container element (single or multiline)**
Holding the recipient addresses in the format appropriate for the recipient type. For example, if the type is "SAP user" then the address strings hold user Ids; if the type is "Internet e-mail address" then the address strings hold Internet e-mail addresses; if the type is "Fax" then address strings holds fax num-

bers. You can enter as many recipients as you like but be careful that the data used matches the recipient type. Be especially careful not to confuse an organization object with a SAP userid, even if the organization object element contains a userid preceeded with US.

The send mail step details are used to generate a `SelfItem.SendTaskDescription` task and the binding from the workflow to the task. Via the *Control* tab, you can change the binding, e.g. to pass attachments to the e-mail.

Note that any recipient types you use must be permitted in your system. For instance, if you want to e-mail to HR organizational objects (jobs, positions, etc.) the relevant configuration must be done in **Business Communication · Administration · Shared office settings** (transaction SO16). If you want to send e-mails to Internet e-mail addresses, then a connection to an external mail server (e.g. via SMTP, SAPconnect, etc.) must be available.

If you want to change the binding, you may find it helpful to know that the basic components of any `SelfItem.SendTaskDescription` task include:

▶ **Work item text**
This becomes the subject line text of the e-mail to be sent.

▶ **Long description**

▶ This becomes the body of the e-mail.

▶ **Address Strings**
The address strings for the recipients in the format appropriate for the recipient type.

▶ **Receivers**
This holds recipients as instances of the ADDRESS object type. Normally you would leave this empty, since method `SendTaskDescription` will convert all the address strings into appropriate address objects based on the recipient type. However, it can be used to pass in a list of recipients of a previous e-mail.

▶ **Type ID**
Recipient type.

▶ **Express**
A flag indicating whether the e-mail is to be sent express. The actual effect of setting the express flag depends on the mail interface used. For instance, if sent to a user in an SAP component, an express pop-up box appears notifying the recipient of the incoming mail.

▶ **Language**
If you have translated your texts into several languages, this identifies which language is to be used on the e-mail. This is useful if, for example, your system language is Spanish, but you want to send the e-mail in English.

▶ **Attachments**

Multiple attachments can be passed in any format accepted by SAPOffice. This can include but is not limited to: SAPscript documents, ABAP report lists, optically archived documents, binary documents (such as multimedia files), Microsoft Office documents such as Word and Excel files, graphics files, URLs, or even another work item. Each format needs to be activated in your system and, if you wish, additional formats can be configured.

> **Tip** Remember that both the creator and the recipient of the attachment need the appropriate editors and viewers to read the attachment, and that not all attachment types are available from all inboxes. You might want to restrict the workflow participants to attachments valid from all inboxes, or at least tell them which formats they can safely use in their environment.

▶ **Line Width**

If you want to send a long unbroken text in the body of your e-mail such as a URL it can be helpful to increase the line width. Normal line width is 75 characters; maximum line width is 132 characters.

You can also add your own container elements to the task if, for example, you want to use them to add dynamic values to the e-mail texts. For instance, you might create a "Customer" container element to hold a customer object instance, passed in the binding of the workflow step, so that you can display the customer name and address in your e-mail text.

A.2.2 Working With Attachments

Since creating and viewing attachments are standard features of both work items and e-mails, it is useful to pass an attachment created for a work item to a subsequent e-mail. For instance, take the scenario where a manager receives a work item requesting approval. As part of rejecting the request, the manager creates an attachment to the work item explaining why the request was rejected. In a subsequent step you send a "Your request was rejected" e-mail to the requestor along with the manager's attachment.

Every attachment created against a work item is automatically passed to the standard workflow container element Attachments (technical ID _ATTACH_OBJECTS) via automatic binding. Each dialog work item is automatically passed attachments from all previous work items in the workflow, and automatically passes any created attachments back to the workflow.

If you want to pass all attachments created throughout the workflow to an e-mail step, you need to bind the workflow container element Attachments to the Attachments container element of the send mail task via the *Control* tab of the send mail step definition.

If you only want to pass attachments from a particular work item, change the binding of the matching workflow step to store any attachments created in your own workflow container element, which refers to object type SOFM (Office Document). You can then pass your own workflow container element to the Attachments container element of the send mail task in the same way.

A.2.3 Determining Recipients Via Rule Resolution

One of the few options you do not have available in a send mail step or Self-Item.SendTaskDescription task is the option to send to a list of recipients determined via a rule resolution.

Therefore, if you want to send an e-mail to a list of recipients based on a rule, you need to calculate the recipients in advance. There are a number of ways this can be done, but a few common options include:

▶ If you are using Release 6.10 or above and the rule has already been used in a prior step, bind the _RULE_RESULT container element from the rule back to a workflow container element. You can then use an expression to assign the Agents attribute of the rule result held in your workflow container element as the recipients of the send mail step.

▶ If the criteria for the rule are based on an object, e.g. rule "Vendor master owner" based on the city and country of the Vendor object, then create a virtual, multiline attribute against that object, based on data type SWHACTOR, that calls the rule using function module RH_GET_ACTORS and returns the list of agents. You can then use an expression to assign the object attribute, e.g. Vendor.MasterDataOwner, as the recipient(s) of the send mail step.

▶ If the criteria for the rule are based on values that will not be known until runtime, e.g. approver for authorization level (which will not be known until runtime), create a background method based on the most appropriate business object which accepts the criteria via method parameters. Then call the rule using module RH_GET_ACTORS and return a list of agents. You can then add an activity step to your workflow, prior to the send mail step, to call a task based on your new method, bind the criteria from the workflow to the task and the result from the task back to a workflow container element. You can then use an expression to assign your workflow container element as the recipient(s) of the send mail step.

A.2.4 Offline Work Item Execution Via E-Mail

Release 3.0 of EBP allows managers to make decisions through e-mails alone. This is useful for those managers who are reluctant to use any sort of software, be it Web Browser or custom-built user interfaces. E-mail on the other hand is an acceptable administrative tool for most managers because they have recognized the advantages in speed and privacy, and have become used to it for communicating with friends and relatives. So making decisions via e-mail, irrespective of the e-mail client that is used, is a useful approach.

Bear in mind that if a manager is forced to make decisions using software that she finds uncomfortable or time-consuming to operate, the chore will inevitably be done by her secretary (e.g. via delegation) or via paper printouts which the secretary enters into the system once the manager has signed the paper version. This will not speed up the process. It will also degrade the quality of the process because the error rate will increase. By now, you have recognized that the whole point of workflow is to help the agents do their job efficiently and simply, without forcing them to work in a manner against their will. So, do not be afraid to use e-mail as a low-key last resort.

There is nothing to prevent you from creating your own e-mail controlled workflows, so the approach is described here in detail. It is crude, but it is also effective. One word of caution, however; Bear in mind that e-mail security is limited, so it should only be used within a company intranet, unless additional enhancements such as digital signature are used.

In EBP the shopping cart approvals are (optionally) sent to decision makers as e-mails, while the rest of the process uses the normal workflow techniques. These e-mails contain the basic information needed to make a judgment, and each typically includes an HTML-based hyperlink for the approve path and a hyperlink for the reject path. There is nothing to prevent you from having more decision paths in your e-mail, but for simplicity's sake, we will restrict it to two here.

Both of these HTML-based hyperlinks contain a "mailto" statement that includes the addressee, the subject line and the body of the e-mail reply. The addressee is used to identify which mails are to be processed by workflow, and it should be a valid generic reply address (e.g. workflow.decision@EBP.mycompany.com) connected to a valid user ID in your system. The sender of the mail (i.e. the user ID used to send the e-mails from your system) must have a valid e-mail address in the user master, e.g. if you use user ID WF-BATCH, then make sure the e-mail address of this user, e.g. wf-batch@EBP.mycompany.com, has been maintained in the user master. The subject line is used to perform a cursory verification that this e-mail is a decision e-mail (e.g. "Re: Approve"). The body of the text is encrypted to prevent tampering. Embedded within this encryption is the decision result (e.g. "Approved") and the work item ID. The complete HTML statement will be something like:

```
<a href=mailto:workflow.decision@EBP.mycompany.com?sub-
ject="Re:workflow decision"&content="encrypted work item ID and
result-is-approve">Click here to approve</a>
```

The user will see the hyperlink *Click here to approve* in the body of the mail. All they need to do is click on the hyperlink and press the send icon to send the reply mail.

This e-mail will be sent back to the workflow system where a program is automatically called to check that the sender's e-mail address is valid (i.e. the e-mail address matches to a user who is allowed to execute the work item), decrypt and parse the e-mail, and complete the work item using their user ID. You can do this immediately or via a background program.

Transaction SO28 can be used to customize the immediate automatic processing of the incoming e-mail by the RECEIVE method of a business object. Business object WI_MAILREC, which has been available since R/3 Release 3.1, is an example of this. For instance, you might configure all replies to workflow.decision@EBP.mycompany.com to be sent to object WI_MAILREC for processing. You can create your own objects to do this by implementing the IFRECEIVE and IFFIND interfaces and a RECEIVE method to process the incoming mail. The method must create the correct termination event (reject or approve) for the decision task.

EBP uses a different approach. It periodically processes the incoming e-mails via background program RBBP_OFFLINE_EVAL. Business Workplace inbox auto-forwarding is used to forward all incoming mails to a particular inbox, e.g. the inbox of a generic user dedicated to processing the incoming mails. Then the background program periodically processes all new mail in that inbox. Successfully processed mails are deleted.

Additional points you should bear in mind are:

▶ The e-mail address of the incoming e-mail decision must be checked against the user IDs of the possible agents to make sure that the decision was truly made by one of the group of agents assigned to this step. This step is extremely important because the e-mail could be forwarded to anyone but it is your duty to ensure that only valid agents can affect the work item.

▶ Mails will be returned by the e-mail daemons when an e-mail address is no longer valid (particularly external users). These returns must be processed automatically so that the an administrator can take corrective action, not just for the workflow but also in terms of the user data. You could ignore the mails and wait for a deadline to expire, but this would slow the process down.

▶ The users may reply to the mails instead of making the decision by clicking on the URL. These replies are usually not decisions, so they must be dealt with by somebody else, possibly automatically via a polite auto-response that recommends consulting a relevant FAQ on the web.

A.2.5 Customizing Considerations

Mail sending will take place in the background and is therefore executed by the WF-BATCH user, unless you specify another user (e.g. as an import parameter for the office API or method that sends the mail). This user must have a valid e-mail address (i.e. a sender address) and the necessary authorization. Whenever the system sends mails there is a very good chance that users will reply to WF-BATCH directly. Try to reduce the number of replies by including a notice to this effect in all the e-mails that are sent. Giving WF-BATCH an e-mail address along the lines of DoNotReply@mycompany.com will also help cut down the replies, but most effective of all is to mention an alternative feedback channel, such as a web site or a help desk number.

WF-BATCH will also receive auto-response mails when a recipient is on vacation or the mail demon cannot locate an e-mail address. The most important rule to observe here is *not* to reply to such mails automatically. Although it is tempting to send an auto-reply yourself, saying "Please do not send me any mails" this can start an avalanche of mails between both systems as they auto-respond to each other. Only auto-respond if you have implemented a counter that limits the number of responses (easily accomplished with a workflow).

The best way of dealing with replies of this sort is to configure an administrator as a mail substitute for WF-BATCH who can periodically go in and check the incoming mails. The administrator can delete mails and correct erroneous e-mail addresses in the system.

Whenever WF-BATCH sends a mail, it creates a copy in its outbox (unless the "no outbox copy" flag is set in the function call). The easiest way of deleting these mails is by configuring a periodic batch job to do this for you.

Here is a summary of the steps that need to be performed before the workflow can transmit e-mails.

1. Configure SMTP Gateway (or Microsoft Exchange Connector for SAP or the Lotus MTA, which is part of the Lotus Connector for SAP R/3 from IBM).
2. Configure e-mail address for WF-BATCH using transaction SU01.
3. Make sure that WF-BATCH has sufficient authorization to send mails (if you have not changed the authorizations given to WF-BATCH it will have the relevant authorization since WF-BATCH is assigned the authorization profile SAP_ALL as a default).
4. The WF-BATCH user's default login language should be set to the desired e-mail language.

A.3   Showing the Decision Maker in a Follow-On Step

Showing the decision maker in a follow-on step is very handy for e-mail notifications and rejections. It lets you suggest that the user contact the decision maker if they need more information about why the decision was made, especially if the decision maker has neglected to include an explanation in an attachment.

In the decision step, you capture the actual agent (technical ID _WI_ACTUAL_AGENT) in the binding from task to workflow. Place the value in a workflow container element, e.g. ZActualAgent, of ABAP Dictionary type WFSYST-AGENT.

However, if you want to use the agent's attributes as well (e.g. title, telephone number or full name) then you will need an object reference to the agent. The simplest way of doing this is to capture a reference to the decision work item itself in the workflow container. The work item object has an attribute ExecutedBy-User, which is based on the object type USR01. This is exactly what you need and this does not cost any extra storage space or performance, because you are only capturing a reference.

To implement this, create a workflow container element (E.g. DecisionStep) based on the object type WORKINGWI. All dialog work items are of this type. In the workflow step that you need to capture, create an exporting binding from the _Workitem element to the newly created workflow container element.

> **Tip** Show the lines of the exporting binding definition first in order to make the `_Workitem` element visible.

You can then pass `DecisionStep.ExecutedByUser` to follow-on steps. For instance, you might want to display the decision maker's name in a subsequent e-mail. So in your send mail task you would:

▶ Include a task container element referring to object type `USR01` to hold the user object instance, e.g. `ZdecisionMaker`

▶ Bind `DecisionStep.ExecutedByUser` to `ZDecisionMaker` in the matching workflow step.

▶ Refer to attributes of `ZDecisionMaker` in your work item text, .e.g. "Unfortunately, your request has been rejected by `&ZDecisionMaker.Name&`. Please contact `&ZDecisionMaker.Name&` at `&ZDecisionMaker.Telephone&` if you require further details ..."

An additional bonus of capturing in this way is that there are other useful attributes of `DecisionStep` *that you can also use, such as* `DecisionStep.ActualEndDate`—*the day the decision was made.*

A.4   URLs in the Work Item Display

URLs can be added to the work item description or as attachments.

URLs in the description are most appropriate when using a Web-sympathetic inbox that recognizes HTML tags or when sending an e-mail. However, you should remember that the long description is limited. Therefore, if your URL is longer than allowed you may need to add it as an attachment. For most tasks, the maximum instruction line length is 70, but for send mail (`SelfItem.SendTaskDescription`) steps, you can use the `LineWidth` parameter to increase the length to 132.

To add a URL to the work item long description, you need to edit it in line editor mode instead of using the pc-mode SAPscript editor. You can change editor mode once you are in the editor. The line editor is less easy to use but gives you more control over the line feeds and allows you to enter raw strings such as HTML code. Add the HTML code as raw strings using the format control / * which is usually reserved for comments.

Make sure you add both the URL and the HTML tags around it to turn it into a hyperlink. For instance,

```
<a href=http://www.ourcompany.com> Our Company </a> or
<img src="http://www.abc.com/mylogo.jpg">
```

You can insert container elements into the URL just like any other text if you wish, remembering that the line length restricts the generated URL.

> **Tip** By delimiting the URL with "<" and ">" your URL will be clickable in many mail clients even if the URL is split over several lines.

Refer to SAP Note 375669 for a full treatment of URLs in work items.

A.5 Creating your Own User Decision Template

Sometimes it is useful to create your own user decision task, especially when you need to restrict the agent assignment for the decision (since the standard user decision task is a general task), or change the text instructions presented during execution.

The standard user decision task is TS00008267. Before you create your own user decision task, make sure you familiarize yourself with the standard task.

To create your own user decision task, create a new task based on object DECI-SION and method PROCESS, or just copy TS00008267 as a starting point. The easiest way to do this is to create a standard user decision step, then use the *Copy from Template* button on the *Control* tab page of the workflow step definition.

Enter your own texts and agent assignment for your new task. You can also add new container elements if you wish, especially if you want to add dynamic values to your instructions. Make sure you check any bindings.

> **Tip** If you do not want your user decision to appear in a pop-up screen, remove the standard work item display, overriding settings from the *WI Display* tab page in the step definition.

A.6 Using Secondary, Before, and After Methods

A.6.1 Secondary Methods

If you want to help an agent to make a decision by bringing extra assistance to them, i.e. more than just text instructions, you can use secondary methods. For instance, if an agent has been asked to approve or reject the vacation request of a subordinate, it might be helpful to see a report showing who else in their team is going to be on leave at the same time. You could do this by defining a secondary method "*Display team vacation schedule*" against the "*Approve vacation request*" workflow step.

When the agent executes the work item, a second session window is opened and the secondary method is executed there. For example, the agent might see the vacation request and the approve/reject options in the first session window and the team vacation schedule in the second session window. While making the decision, the agent can switch between the two session windows, checking the vacation request details and comparing them with the team vacation schedule before making a final decision and completing the work item. When the work item is completed, the system automatically closes the secondary method session. If the agent cancels the work item execution, and later re-executes it, the secondary method will be restarted each time the work item is executed.

The secondary method session runs asynchronously to the work item execution session, i.e. it is not aware of what is happening in the work item execution session.

Note that because a second session window must be opened, this technique depends heavily on how the work items are delivered to an agent. If the work item is presented using SAP GUI for Windows, then the second session window can be created. However, other work item delivery mechanisms, such as the Web inbox or external inboxes as in Microsoft Outlook or Lotus Notes, may not have the facility to open a second session window, in which case the secondary method is ignored.

As secondary methods are not part of the main workflow and not included in the workflow log, they are primarily designed for display methods, e.g. for showing extra data or statistics or a report.

To use secondary methods, in the *Methods* tab of your *activity* or *user decision* workflow step, you specify in the *Secondary methods* section your container element holding the relevant object instance and the method to be executed. Only automated binding is possible, i.e. the method container of the step's main task-based method is passed to the secondary method. Of course, only import parameters can be used for the secondary method, since the secondary method session runs asynchronously and therefore never returns results to the workflow. You can specify multiple secondary methods if you wish. An alternative is to append the report in the form of a business object to the work item (an attachment) so that the users can launch it from the work item when they need it.

A.6.2 Before and After Methods

Before and after methods[1] are similar to secondary methods in that:

▶ They are specified in the *Methods* tab of the workflow step.

▶ They require you to specify a container element holding the object instance, and the method to be executed.

▶ You can only use automated binding, i.e. the method container of the step's task-based method is passed to the before and after methods.

▶ You can specify multiple *before* and *after* methods if you wish.

▶ They are executed every time the work item is executed. In particular the after method is *always* executed after the synchronous part of the work item execution is complete, regardless of whether the work item is waiting on a terminating event or has ended in error.

▶ They have no effect on the execution of the work item itself.

However, *before* and *after* methods are called modally, i.e. as if they were extra steps in the same session as the work item. This means they can be used to manipulate the method container if you wish, to influence the main task-based method, or subsequent steps in the workflow.

Whereas *secondary* methods are best for displaying additional information to the agent, *before* and *after* methods are best for background tasks you want to call each time the work item is executed. You might wish to use *before* and *after* methods for such activities as:

▶ Collecting additional statistics on the workflow into your own database tables for later analysis.[2]

▶ Converting values returned by the work item in an *after* method.

▶ Notifying someone that the work item has been started in a *before* method, e.g. in the vacation request scenario, to let an employee know that the approving agent has at least seen their vacation request form.

▶ Notifying someone of the work item result in an *after* method. Of course this could also be done as part of the main workflow; however, it may be expedient to use an *after* method to avoid complicating the main workflow.

▶ Starting and stopping the ArchiveLink viewer.

---

1 Available from Release 6.10
2 From Release 6.20 use user exits in the workflow definition instead to write the data.

Note that the object instance being used in a *before* or *after* method must exist before the work item is executed, e.g. you cannot use a *before* method to create an object instance.

A.7 Looping Through a Multiline List

If you have a list of values in the workflow container, i.e. as a multiline element, you may want to perform a series of steps on the individual items of the list. One option is to use table driven dynamic parallel processing as described in chapter 7, *Creating a Workflow*. Table driven processing creates parallel-processed work items, one work item per row, for the same task or subworkflow. However, if you need to split the list into individual rows and loop over them one after another when the processing of one row is dependent on the processing of a prior row, you may need to take a different approach.

One example of how to split a list into individual rows is provided using the object type SYSTEM methods DescribeAgents and LoopAtAgents, which allow you to take a list of agents and separate out each individual agent for processing. This works as follows:

1. Use an *activity* step to call a task based on method SYSTEM.DescribeAgents. Pass the list of agents to the method. The number of agents in the list is returned. Store the number of agents in a workflow container element, e.g. NumOfAgents.

2. Use a loop step (*loop until* or *loop while*) to keep looping while NumOfAgents has a value greater than zero.

3. Within the loop, use another *activity* step to call a task based on method SYSTEM.LoopAtAgents. Pass it the list and the NumOfAgents value. The method will return the nth value of the list where n = NumOfAgents.

4. You can then do whatever processing you need to do on the agent returned, e.g. get their e-mail address and send them an e-mail.

5. As the final step within the loop, decrement the NumOfAgents value by one.

This process reads a list from highest value to lowest. The implementation of the DescribeAgents and LoopAtAgents methods is simple enough to reproduce in your own methods so that you can easily deal with any list of any data type, whether ABAP Dictionary or object reference.

A.8 Creating Object References Dynamically

Object references are very useful throughout workflow because you can use them to access all sorts of data, methods and events. For instance, because business object types can contain attributes pointing to other business object types, you can refer to attributes of object-referencing attributes of business objects, e.g. `SalesOrder.Customer.Name`, in container bindings and expressions such as in work item texts, the logical expressions in loop steps, or in start conditions.

For those situations where you can find the key data defining an object instance, but do not actually have access to the object instance in your workflow, object `SYSTEM` method `GenericInstantiate` can be used to create a new object reference dynamically. All you need to provide is the object key and the object type of the instance you want to access.

This is particularly useful when using utility objects such as the deadline object in appendix A.9. Or you might want to create an object instance based on attributes from two or more different object instances you are using in your workflow. Usually you will need to calculate the key itself in a prior step (e.g. by using a container operation), or use an alternative binding (mentioned in chapter 7, *Creating a Workflow*) to pass it to `SYSTEM.GenericInstantiate`.

A.9 Deadlines Based on the Factory Calendar

Deadlines are based on a reference date/time plus an absolute offset period. That is, deadline date/time is calculated simply by adding the offset period to the reference date/time. Weekends and holidays are not taken into account.

If you want to ensure that your deadline is escalated on a working day, you need to use factory calendars, which hold the relevant weekends and holidays. Factory calendars can be maintained using transaction `SCAL`.

To calculate the deadline date/time based on factory calendars you will need to:

▶ Create a deadline object that calculates the next working date/time based on the current, i.e. work item creation, date/time
▶ Set up a workflow container element based on your deadline object
▶ Instantiate the deadline object in your workflow prior to the step with the deadline
▶ Use the deadline object as the reference date / time in your deadline.

A.9.1   Creating the Deadline Object

The deadline business object described below is essentially a utility to calculate a date and time based on a factory calendar and the current system date and time. At runtime, when the deadline object is referenced from the workflow step, the current system date and time would be equivalent to the work item creation date and time.

The deadline object has no super-type.

The key is:

▶ **Offset**
A numerical offset relating to work item creation time.

▶ **Unit**
The time unit for the offset.

▶ **Calid**
Factory calendar ID, which must be active in the system.

The attributes are:

▶ **Date**
The calculated factory calendar date, based on data type SY-DATUM. This is a virtual attribute that calls function module END_TIME_DETERMINE to calculate the date.

▶ **Time**
The calculated factory calendar time, based on data type SY-UZEIT. This is a virtual attribute that calls function module END_TIME_DETERMINE to calculate the time.

Note that there is no buffering of the date and time attributes, so that even though you may instantiate the deadline object early in your workflow, when it is used to calculate a deadline it will always use the current system date and time, i.e. the work item creation time, as its starting point. If you need to pass in a specific date/time you could make the starting date/time method parameters or part of the object key.

```
PROGRAM ZDEADLINE.
*---------------------------------------------------------------
-
*---------------------------------------------------------------
-
```

```
INCLUDE <OBJECT>.
BEGIN_DATA OBJECT. " Do not change.. DATA is generated
* only private members may be inserted into structure private
DATA:
" begin of private,
"   to declare private attributes remove comments and
"   insert private attributes here ...
" end of private,
   BEGIN OF KEY,
        OFFSET LIKE SY-MSGNO,
        UNIT LIKE SWD_SDYNP-LATE_END_U,
        CALID LIKE SCAL-FCALID,
     END OF KEY,
        DATE LIKE SY-DATUM,
        TIME LIKE SY-UZEIT.
END_DATA OBJECT. " Do not change.. DATA is generated
*-----------------------------------------------------------------
--

GET_PROPERTY DATE CHANGING CONTAINER.
  DATA: DEADLINE_DATE LIKE SY-DATUM,
        DEADLINE_TIME LIKE SY-UZEIT.
* Calculate deadline end date and end time using SY-DATUM /
* SY-UZEIT as work item creation date and time
* Use object-key-values as defaults for offset, unit and calid
   PERFORM CALCULATE_DEADLINE
        USING SY-DATUM SY-UZEIT
             OBJECT-KEY-OFFSET OBJECT-KEY-UNIT OBJECT-KEY-CALID
             DEADLINE_DATE DEADLINE_TIME.
* Put the calculated date into the container, skip the time
   SWC_SET_ELEMENT CONTAINER 'Date' DEADLINE_DATE .
END_PROPERTY.
*-----------------------------------------------------------------
--

GET_PROPERTY TIME CHANGING CONTAINER.
  DATA: DEADLINE_DATE LIKE SY-DATUM,
        DEADLINE_TIME LIKE SY-UZEIT.
* Calculate deadline end date and end time  just like above
   PERFORM CALCULATE_DEADLINE
        USING SY-DATUM SY-UZEIT
             OBJECT-KEY-OFFSET OBJECT-KEY-UNIT OBJECT-KEY-CALID
             DEADLINE_DATE DEADLINE_TIME.
```

```
* Put the calculated time into the container, skip the date
  SWC_SET_ELEMENT CONTAINER 'Time' DEADLINE_TIME.
END_PROPERTY.
*---------------------------------------------------------------
--
FORM CALCULATE_DEADLINE USING VALUE(I_DATE) LIKE SY-DATUM
                              VALUE(I_TIME) LIKE SY-UZEIT
                              VALUE(I_OFFSET) VALUE(I_UNIT)
                              VALUE(I_CALID)
                              E_DATE LIKE SY-DATUM
                              E_TIME LIKE SY-UZEIT.
  DATA: OFFSET(10) TYPE N, UNIT(3), CALID LIKE SCAL-FCALID.

* Calculate deadline date/time based on factory calendar
  CALL FUNCTION 'END_TIME_DETERMINE'
     EXPORTING
          DURATION               = I_OFFSET
          UNIT                   = I_UNIT
          FACTORY_CALENDAR       = I_CALID
     IMPORTING
          END_DATE               = E_DATE
          END_TIME               = E_TIME
     CHANGING
          START_DATE             = I_DATE
          START_TIME             = I_TIME
       EXCEPTIONS
            OTHERS               = 1.

  IF SY-SUBRC <> 0.

*     If there are any problems, provide a default date and
time,
*     e.g. by calling END_TIME_DETERMINE without parameter
*     FACTORY_CALENDAR.

  CALL FUNCTION 'END_TIME_DETERMINE'
     EXPORTING
          DURATION               = I_OFFSET
          UNIT                   = I_UNIT
     IMPORTING
```

```
                END_DATE                 = E_DATE
                END_TIME                 = E_TIME
          CHANGING
                START_DATE               = I_DATE
                START_TIME               = I_TIME
            EXCEPTIONS
                OTHERS                   = 1.


      ENDIF.
  ENDFORM.
```

Listing A.1 Using Factory Calendar for Deadlines

A.9.2 Using the Deadline Object in Your Workflow

To use the deadline object in your workflow, create a workflow container element, e.g. ZFactoryDeadline referencing object type ZDEADLINE.

In the workflow step to be monitored, turn on the relevant deadline (requested start, latest start, requested end, or latest end) and set the reference date/time to the expression:

```
Date = ZFactoryDeadline.DATE
Time = ZFactoryDeadline.TIME
```

You can also set the offset if you wish.

The deadline object must be instantiated before it is used at runtime. There are a number of ways to do this including:

▶ Using the initial values option of the workflow container to set a default offset, unit, and factory calendar ID for ZFactoryDeadline.

▶ In a prior workflow step, use a task based on object SYSTEM method GENERICINSTANTIATE to instantiate ZFactoryDeadline using the appropriate offset, unit and factory calendar ID.

The result will be a deadline date/time created based on a factory calendar. Note that the reference date/time gives the date/time based on the factory calendar, but any offset will simply be added to the reference date/time as normal.

A.10 Making the Most of Modeled Deadlines

A.10.1 Taking Alternative Action

One of the most useful workflow techniques is a modeled deadline. This makes it possible to take an alternative action when a deadline is exceeded. If you have not used this technique before, using the *Model deadline monitoring* wizard will help. The basic process is:

▶ On the appropriate deadline tab of the step to be monitored, you enter the deadline reference date/time, offset period, and your *deadline exceeded* outcome.

▶ On the step to be monitored, activate the *processing obsolete* outcome.

The step to be monitored will now have two additional outcomes as well as its usual outcomes, *deadline exceeded* and *processing obsolete*.

Under the *deadline exceeded* outcome you can then add a number of steps, e.g. you might want to insert a step to notify someone the deadline has been exceeded. The last step under the *deadline exceeded* outcome should be a *process control* step. You use the process control step to make the monitored work item obsolete, thus triggering the *processing obsolete* outcome. You can now add your alternative actions after the processing obsolete outcome.

Why have separate outcomes for *deadline exceeded* versus *processing obsolete*? Consider the following scenarios as a couple of examples that make this separation very useful:

▶ You want to notify several different groups of people, or the same people of when a deadline is exceeded rather than take alternative action and you want this to repeat until the work is done. Using the deadline outcome on its own will let you do this without upsetting the normal operation and outcome of the monitored step.

▶ You want to take the same alternative actions if the deadline was exceeded or if the original agent rejects the work item. Having the alternative actions in the one place, under the processing obsolete outcome, enables you to trigger it from either the *deadline exceeded* outcome or the *processing rejected* outcome.

A.10.2 Modeled Deadlines for (Repeated) Notifications

You do not have to use the modeled deadline pattern as-is. It is quite useful to modify it so as to notify people via e-mail when a deadline is exceeded. For instance, you could add a send mail step after your *deadline exceeded* outcome.

You might even want to send more than one notification, for instance, to notify someone that a work item is late every day until it is completed. To do this, create a *loop until* step after your deadline exceeded outcome checking a container element flag to see whether the main step has completed. You will need to make sure that after the main work item has been completed you fill this flag via a container operation step. In the loop, you would send your mail; a requested start deadline can be used to ensure it is not sent until the next day. You could use a *process control* step to clear up any remaining waiting send mail work items once the main work item is complete.

B   Checklists

These checklists should be used as guidelines. Not every question will be relevant in every case, and you may want to add your own questions relevant to your company. However they should give you an idea of the sorts of questions to ask throughout the lifecycle of workflow practices.

The checklists for workflow projects are taken from the SAP service portal for the WebFlow Engine (*http://service.sap.com/webflow*). These may be updated from time to time.

B.1   Gathering Requirements

You may find that not all questions will be able to be answered in full at this stage, particularly with regard to data and step requirements. However, as much information as possible should be gathered to form a starting point for the workflow design, and to identify what answers are outstanding.

Process Name

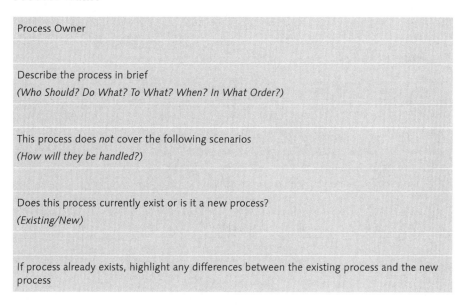

Process Owner
Describe the process in brief *(Who Should? Do What? To What? When? In What Order?)*
This process does *not* cover the following scenarios *(How will they be handled?)*
Does this process currently exist or is it a new process? *(Existing/New)*
If process already exists, highlight any differences between the existing process and the new process

Business Drivers for the Process

Expected benefits and success criteria

(Benefits may be tangible or intangible; success criteria should be quantitative so that they can be measured)

How will the success criteria be measured?

(New reports required? Statistics to be gathered? Who is responsible for gathering/measuring success criteria?)

The Process in Theory

What documentation currently exists describing this process?

(E.g. Business Procedure manual references)

List all activities that will be automated by this process

List all activities within this process that require the participation of an agent

The Process in Practice

What common problems occur with the existing process?

What problems are expected to occur with the new process?

Any suggestions for improving the process generally

Any suggestions for improving the information given to agents

What is the minimum/average/maximum time taken to complete the existing process?

Agent Determination

What criteria will be used to determine agents?

Who will maintain the data used to determine agents?

Are all agents internal employees?
(If not, specify)

Do all agents currently have user IDs in the system?
(If not, specify proportion of employees who currently have user IDs. Specify whether it is planned to give user IDs to employees who do not currently have user IDs, and if not, why not.)

What proportion of agents are already experienced workflow agents?

Work Item Delivery Requirements

To what types of inboxes will the work items be delivered?
(E.g. Business Workplace, Web inbox, Workplace inbox, Microsoft Outlook, Lotus Notes)

What proportion of all agents currently uses these types of inboxes?

What proportion of all agents requires e-mail notifications of new work items?

What supplementary inbox features are necessary to make the process work (e.g. attachments, work item forwarding)?

Will it be acceptable to use several different inboxes according to the type of agent involved?

Are offline processing capabilities required?

Data Requirements

List all data required to start the process
(E.g. initiator of the process, key business entities on which the process is based)

List all data required for texts/instructions

List all data required to execute activities within this process, per activity

List all data required to determine agents

List all data required to control the process
(E.g. retry counts, iteration counts)

Escalation Requirements

Will any deadlines be required? On what activities of the process?

Specify the deadline type (latest start, requested end, or latest end) and period for all activities requiring deadlines

Who is responsible for escalating delayed processes?

How will escalators be contacted? Via e-mail or work item?

Administration Requirements

What volume and frequency of workflows is expected?
(I.e. how often will this process be started?)

What is the pattern of work frequency?
(I.e. are there any significant peaks and troughs of activity)

How long will a single instance of the process take to complete?
(Expected minimum/average/maximum)

What are the critical points of the process?

Who is responsible for maintaining security and access rights for agents?

Communication/Education Requirements

Who is responsible for communicating the process to agents and affected parties throughout design, implementation, and go-live?

How will changes in the process be communicated?
(E.g. via newsletter, e-mail, web-based help desk)

Who is responsible for developing training material for agents?

Who is responsible for delivering training to agents?

How will agents be trained?
(E.g. classroom, one-on-one, remote sessions)

When will agents be trained?

Sign-Offs

Process Owner

Workflow Developer

Workflow Administrator

B.2   Return on Investment (ROI)

This list is a guide to the sort of questions and calculations that help to determine the return on investment. The actual calculation depends largely on the individual process, its impact on company revenue, and the extent of process improvement.

The list is not exhaustive and makes some assumptions, e.g. that total processing time of all objects will remain the same. Savings are assumed to be collected per year, but of course any appropriate time period could be used.

Process Name

Process Owner

Describe the current process
(Who Should? Do What? To What? When? In What Order?)

Describe the planned process
(Who Should? Do What? To What? When? In What Order?)

Revenue Gains due to Reduction in Cycle Time

Current average elapsed time to process one object in the current process

Number of objects currently processed per year

Total Current Processing Time
*(= number of objects * current average elapsed time per object)*

Expected average elapsed time to process one object (to-be process)

Expected number of objects processed per year
(= Total Current Processing Time / expected average elapsed time per object)

Note: This assumes that the overall processing time will remain the same. Also that the potential number of objects that can be processed per year is limited only by the speed of the process. Therefore this figure may need to be adjusted if these assumptions do not hold true for the process in question.

Average value per object to be processed

(i.e. average revenue gain from successfully processing one object)

Revenue Gains due to Reduction in Cycle Time per year

(= average value per object * (expected number of objects processed per year—current number of objects processed per year))

Labor Cost Savings

Average cost of labor of personnel currently involved in processing one object

(e.g. $ per hour)

Current average number of personnel involved in processing one object (as-is process)

Expected average number of personnel involved in processing one object (to-be process)

Current average time spent per person in processing one object (as-is process)

Expected average time spent per person in processing one object (to-be process)

Labor savings per object

(= (expected average time per person * expected average number of personnel)—(current average time per person * current average number of personnel))

Labor Cost Savings per year

(= total number of objects per year * labor savings per object * average cost of labor)

Savings due to Reductions in Process Failure

Total savings in legal costs per year due to expected reductions in process failure

Total savings reimbursement costs per year due to expected reductions in process failure

Other cost savings due to expected reductions in process failure

Savings due to Reductions in Process Failure per year
(= *total legal cost savings + total reimbursement cost savings + other cost savings*)

Revenue Gains from Process Improvement

Total expected revenue per year from utilization of discounts

Total expected revenue per year from achieving bonuses

Other revenue gains

Revenue Gains per year
(= *revenue from discounts + revenue from bonuses + other revenue gains*)

Intangible Benefits

Reduced training and support

Reliable audit control

Increased goodwill

Improved job satisfaction

Labor freed for other activities

Improved knowledge via statistics

Scalable
(ability to cope with volume growth)

Total estimated value of intangible benefits
(= sum of all intangible benefits)

Cost of Workflow Implementation

Cost of gathering requirements (once-only)
(Includes labor cost of personnel gathering requirements and labor cost of personnel from whom requirements are gathered)

Cost of workflow design (once-only)
(Includes labor cost of designer, labor costs of process owner assisting design, and cost of quality assurance review)

Cost of workflow development (once-only)
(Includes labor cost of developer, system costs for development, and cost of quality assurance review)

Cost of testing (once-only)
(Includes labor cost of developer, system costs for testing, and labor cost of testers)

Cost of support per year (on-going)
(Includes workflow administration costs, help desk costs and cost of maintaining support web site)

Training costs per year (on-going)
(Consider number of personnel to be trained, average training time, labor cost of personnel to be trained, labor cost of trainers)

Total cost of workflow implementation
(= sum of all costs of workflow implementation)

ROI Calculation

Savings
(= Gains due to Reduction in Cycle Time + Labor Cost Savings + Revenue Gains + Gains due to Reduction in Failure + estimated value of intangible benefits)

ROI
*(= Savings * 100 / Total cost of workflow implementation)*

B.3   Quality Assurance Design Review

For the quality assurance design review, the original requirements-gathering document and design documentation should be available.

Process Name

Process Owner

Workflow Designer

Workflow Name

Process Impact

Describe the workflow in detail.
(A text description and a flowchart should be used)

Does the workflow design match the business process requirements as specified by the process owner? If not, what is different and why?

Describe how the workflow will achieve the expected benefits and success criteria.
(Be specific, e.g. automation of posting step is expected to save 10 minutes per process instance)

Describe what metrics will be used to measure the success criteria.
(Include references to what reports/statistics will be used, and references to design specifications of any new reports/programs created to support the gathering of statistics and measurement of criteria)

Workflow Design

Is the workflow design well structured?
(Specify how the workflow will be broken into subworkflows if necessary)

Is exception handling consistent throughout the workflow? If not, why not?

Is retry handling of failed automated (background) tasks consistent throughout the workflow? If not, why not?

Is deadline handling consistent throughout the workflow? If not, why not?

How does the workflow design ensure good performance?
(E.g. Justify choice of transactions, BAPIs, function modules, CATTs, BDCs to be used in underlying methods, justify choice of background versus dialog tasks, specify any start conditions or check function modules used to prevent unwanted workflow instances from being created)

Does the workflow design make maximum use of existing workflow components such as object types, tasks, subworkflows?
(Where existing components have not been used, justify why new components were needed.)

Does the workflow design cope with other system activities occurring while the workflow is in progress? If not, why not.
(E.g. In an approvals process, change/deletion of the object to be approved should be detected and handled by the workflow.)

Does the workflow design allow for restart in the event of error? If not, why not.
(Indicate how the workflow will be restarted or corrected in the event of possible errors.)

Organizational Impact on Agents

List all dialog steps, i.e. all steps requiring agent participation.

Per dialog step, estimate the number and frequency of work items.

Per dialog step, estimate the average and maximum number of work items per agent.

(E.g. 100 work items/day split between 20 agents = Average 5 work items/day)

Per dialog step, estimate the average time required to complete a work item.

Per dialog step, calculate the total time to be spent per agent per day executing work items .

How does the workflow design help to ensure maximum speed of work item execution?

(Describe critical information to be provided in the work item instructions, describe any other features used, e.g. secondary methods)

Organizational Impact on Data Maintenance

Describe how agents will be determined for each dialog step.

(Include any rules that will be used, including references to the design of any new rules to be created)

What data will be used to determine agents?

Estimate the volume of data to be maintained for correct agent determination.

(Indicate whether the data already exists or will be created for the workflow.)

If existing data used for agent determination needs to be cleansed before use, specify who will cleanse the data and estimate the time required.

For any new data to be maintained, specify who will maintain the data and time required to do so.

(Eg. 2 hours prior to go-live, 10 minutes per day after go-live)

Who will be responsible for determining the correct agent in the event of agent determination failure?

(This should be a business contact not a technical person.)

Apart from agent determination data, is there any other new or existing data that will require maintenance (additional to current maintenance)? If so, specify who is responsible for maintaining this data and estimate the additional maintenance burden.

Communication and Support Impact

Who is responsible for communicating the workflow design and any changes to agents and other affected personnel?

How will the workflow design and changes be communicated?

(E.g. Newsletter, website, meeting)

Who is responsible for handling support issues from agents and affected personnel?

(E.g. Help desk)

How does the workflow design help to minimize support issues and resolution time?

(E.g. self-help included in work items such as "You have received this work item because...", plans for instructions to be written or vetted by experienced agents.)

Estimate the criticality of error resolution, i.e. at what time will unresolved errors in an instance workflow cause significant pain to the organisation, and what steps are most critical.

(E.g. All errors up to and including the posting step must be resolved within 3 days otherwise a financial/legal/goodwill loss will result due to...)

Training Impact

What proportion of agents will require basic workflow training?

(E.g. training in how to access, execute, complete work items, optimum inbox usage.)

Estimate time required per agent for basic workflow training.

Estimate time required per agent for workflow training for this specific workflow.

Estimate time required to train support personnel in resolving issues with the new workflow.

Who is responsible for preparing and delivering training?

Will any other personnel require training as a result of this workflow?

(E.g. Escalators, personnel sent automatic e-mail notifications from the workflow)

System Impact

Estimate the number of new workflow instances that will be created per day.

Estimate the number of new work items created per day.

Estimate the number of new events, triggering and terminating, that will be created per day.
(Include events that will be raised but never used due to check function modules or start conditions.)

Estimate the number of deadlines that will be created per day.
(I.e. the number of deadlines to be checked, regardless of whether the deadline is exceeded or not)

Estimate any peaks and troughs in the creation of workflow, work item, event, or deadline instances.
(E.g. 60% of all events raised between 08:00 and 09:30)

Describe any hardware or network changes that will be required to support this workflow.
(E.g. Setting up network connection between SAP system and inbox used for work item delivery)

Describe any new background jobs to be scheduled or changed to support this workflow.
(E.g. If this is the first workflow to use deadlines, the deadline background job SWWDHEX will need to be scheduled.)

Security Impact

Estimate number of new user Ids to be created for agents.

Estimate number of agents who will require changes to their security profile.

Describe what security changes will need to be made.
(Include possible agent assignment, i.e. consider whether assignments will be to job/position/profile generator role, and whether non-Basis security will be involved, such as HR structural authorizations)

Who is responsible for creating/changing user profiles?

Sign-Offs

Process Owner
Workflow Designer
Workflow Developer
Workflow Administrator
System Administrator
Security Administrator
Support Representative
Education Representative

B.4   Verification Tests

Note that most test tools are available via the Workflow Diagnosis transaction (SWUD).

Components of Object Types

Test Purpose	Testing Tool
Attribute	
Attribute value is correct for all object instances	Test option in Business Object Builder (SWO1)
If attribute value does not exist, an empty value is returned not an error	
Method	
Execution works correctly	Test option in Business Object Builder (SWO1)

Test Purpose	Testing Tool
Asynchronous methods only: Execution triggers terminating event only when method has been successfully executed	Test option in Business Object Builder (SW01) and Event trace (SWELS/SWEL)
Input Parameters can be entered and affect the method as expected	Test option in Business Object Builder (SW01)
Output Parameters and Results return expected values	
Exceptions are raised as expected including: Object does not exist Bad input parameters Improper end of execution (especially important for synchronous methods) Error returned by underlying code such as CATTs and "Call transaction using"	

Single-Step Task

Test Purpose	Testing Tool
Dialog Task	
Work item and long texts appear correctly	Test task (transaction SWUS), workflow log and SAPOffice work item display
Possible agents are correct	
Execution works correctly	Test task (transaction SWUS) and workflow log Check effect on application via relevant application transactions
Successful execution completes the work item (Includes testing terminating events)	Test task (transaction SWUS) and workflow log
Cancelled execution does *not* complete the work item	Test task (transaction SWUS), workflow log and SAPGUI work item display
Background task	
Execution works correctly *in background*	Test task (transaction SWUS) and workflow log Check affect on application via relevant application transactions
Successful execution completes the work item (Includes testing terminating events)	Test task (transaction SWUS) and workflow log Check terminating event linkage via SAPGUI work item display, event instance linkage log (SWEINST), and workflow log

Test Purpose	Testing Tool
Unsuccessful execution does *not* complete the work item	Workflow log
Recovery or restart of unsuccessful execution is possible	Workflow log and administration reports that include restart options (e.g. transaction SWI1)

Rule

Test Purpose	Testing Tool
Rule container allows entry of expected criteria combinations	Agent-determination-rule test option (transaction PFAC)
Responsibility rules—results are as expected, including use of responsibilities with different priorities	
Function module rules—rule container read successfully	Agent-determination-rule test option (transaction PFAC) and function module test option (transaction SE37)
Function module rules—agent determination is correct	
Function module rules—no agent found returned correctly	

Workflow

Test Purpose	Testing Tool
Triggering event starts the workflow	Event trace (SWELS/SWEL) Determine instances for task
All necessary details passed from triggering event to workflow	Workflow log
All steps tested	
Workflow completes correctly	
All underlying tasks tested (new and existing)	Test task (transaction SWUS)
All data passed from workflow to tasks/rules correctly	Workflow log Container monitor
All agent assignment works correctly	Workflow log Work item—check all agents for each step (selected/possible/excluded)

Event

Test Purpose	Testing Tool
Application raises event correctly	Event trace (SWELS/SWEL)
Start conditions/check function modules exclude unwanted workflows	Event trace (SWELS/SWEL) Generate event (SWUE)—for debugging
Triggered event starts the correct workflows	Event trace (SWELS/SWEL)

B.5 Quality Assurance Implementation Review

For the quality assurance implementation review, the original requirements-gathering document, design documentation, and development documentation should be available, as well as system access to view the workflow itself.

Process Name

Process Owner
Workflow Designer
Workflow Developer
Workflow ID *(if there are subworkflows this should be the main workflow ID, or else complete one document per workflow and for each subworkflow)*

Per Object Type

Question	☑
Is object type new or existing?	
Which standard SAP business object has been used as a parent? If no standard SAP business object has been used as a parent, why not?	
Has the standard SAP business object type been delegated to the new business object type? If not, why not?	
Have naming conventions for business object, attributes, methods, events been correctly applied?	

Question	☑
Have attributes, methods, and events been assigned correctly to the business object according to good object-oriented design and maximum reusability? *(Look for close relationships between attributes/methods/events and the object to which they belong, look for use of attributes based on object references to allow maximum reuse of other objects.)*	
Have attributes and methods been coded for optimum performance? *(Consider use of buffering within the object, consider choice of background tasks versus virtual attributes, consider techniques used in underlying code, e.g. BAPIs should be used rather than BDCs where possible.)*	
Have attributes been coded to ensure that when no value exists an empty value is returned, not an error?	
Do method parameters have meaningful names and appropriate data dictionary or object type references?	
Have methods been coded to ensure that possible errors in the underlying code are adequately reported via exceptions?	
Have all exceptions been appropriate marked as temporary, application or system to ensure appropriate action is taken in the event of an error? *(Affects whether the work item sits in the inbox awaiting manual retry or is reported to a workflow administrator)*	
Is the choice of synchronous versus asynchronous appropriate for each method? *(As a rule of thumb, display methods should be synchronous; change methods should be asynchronous. Justify any non-standard choices)*	
Is the choice of background versus dialog method appropriate for each method? *(Check that the agent is adding value via the dialog method; otherwise the method should be automated, i.e. background)*	
Have appropriate object interface relationships been used? *(Generic programming should be encouraged. In particular interface IFFIND should always be implemented, so that maximum use can be made of standard workflow reports.)*	
Is the object type adequately documented on-line? *(Check for use of documentation areas, and good comments in attribute/method code.)*	

Per Task

Question	☑
Have naming conventions been correctly applied?	
Does the task have appropriate and effective work item texts and instructions? *(Most salient details should be towards the start/top of any texts so that experienced agents can make decisions quickly; texts/instructions should be viewed and signed off by an experienced agent familiar with the activity to be executed via this task. Ensure that even background tasks have good work item texts to assist error resolution.)*	
Have background processing/confirm end of processing options been set appropriately?	

Question	☑
Have appropriate terminating events been defined for asynchronous tasks?	
Have appropriate possible agents been assigned to the task? In particular, any use of the general-task attribute must be justified. *(Look for appropriate use of assignments to profile generator roles, jobs, or positions)*	
Has the task been adequately documented on-line?	

Per Rule

Question	☑
Have naming conventions been correctly applied?	
Is the type of rule appropriate? *(E.g. Responsibility rule used in preference to function module rule where possible)*	
Is the rule container correctly defined? *(Look for appropriate use of data dictionary and object type references, and meaningful names assigned to container elements.)*	
Have realistic combinations of criteria been tested against the rule?	
Have "no valid agent" scenarios been tested?	
Has the "terminate if rule resolution has no result" flag been set appropriately?	
For responsibility rules: Has the effect of priority settings on agent choice been tested?	
For function module rules: Has the function module been coded for best possible performance?	
Has the rule been adequately documented on-line, including instructions for related data maintenance?	

Per Event

Question	☑
How will the event be raised by the application? *(Include what data maintenance if any will be needed to configure the raising of the event and event linkage in the production environment.)*	
Will any check function modules or start conditions be used to limit the number of workflow instances created? If not, why not?	
For each start condition: Is the logical expression well-formulated and does it match the business requirements?	

Question	☑
For each check function module: Has the check function module been coded for best possible performance?	
For each check function module: Is the code appropriate for the business requirements?	

Per Workflow

Question	☑
Have naming conventions been correctly applied?	
Is the workflow well structured? *(Look for appropriate use of subworkflows and lack of redundancy)*	
Is exception handling consistent throughout the workflow? If not, why not?	
Is retry handling consistent throughout the workflow? If not, why not?	
Is deadline handing consistent throughout the workflow? If not, why not?	
Do workflow container elements have meaningful names?	
Is the binding correct between Triggering event and workflow? Tasks and workflow? Rules and workflow? *(Check whether any hard-coded constants are justified; check that there are no unnecessary bindings, since these cost unnecessary processing time.)*	
Do all dialog tasks have appropriate agent assignments? *(Check possible, responsible, excluded, deadline and notification agents as necessary. Responsible agents should be assigned to rules or expressions. Possible agents should be assigned to profile generator roles, jobs or positions.)*	
Have all modelled deadlines have been structured correctly? *(Use the modelled deadline wizard as a guide.)*	
Have all steps that send e-mails been implemented as send mail steps (for clarity)? *(I.e. Rather than use a normal activity step)*	
For any loop/until steps: Check the loop expression cannot result in an infinite loop, i.e. that it will end.	
Does the workflow permit restart in the event of error from any point where error is likely to occur? If not, why not. *(Check especially that if background tasks fail the workflow can be restarted. Details of the restart process should be in the troubleshooting guide provided to the support/workflow administrator.)*	

Question	☑
Does the workflow cope with other system activities occurring while the workflow is in progress? If not, why not?	
Do all steps and outcomes have meaningful descriptions?	

Metrics

How will the success criteria for the workflow be measured?
(Detail any new reports/programs to be used to gather and/or evaluate workflow statistics.)

General

Question	☑
Have all components of the workflow and the workflow as a whole been tested adequately? *(Preferably testing should involve one or more agents who then sign off the testing.)*	
Has the work item delivery method been tested? *(Particularly necessary if work items are to be delivered to an external inbox.)*	
Has a troubleshooting guide been created and signed off by Support Representative and Workflow Administrator?	
Has appropriate documentation and examples been given to the Education Representative for training preparation and delivery?	
Has appropriate offline documentation been created for future workflow designers/developers? *(Must be sufficient documentation to allow workflow designers/developers to understand what has been developed and why.)*	

Sign-Offs

Process Owner
Workflow Developer
Workflow Administrator

B.6 Going Live

This checklist includes final checks to be made before go-live.

Process Name

Process Owner
Workflow Designer
Workflow Developer
Workflow ID *(if there are subworkflows this should be the main workflow ID, or else complete one document per workflow and for each subworkflow.)*

Workflow Readiness

Question	☑
Have all components of the workflow including the workflow itself been transported to the production environment? *(Ensure all business object types, object type delegation settings, event triggering, event linkage, start conditions, check function modules, rules, tasks, subworkflows, etc. have been transported and checked. Make sure all object types have been generated and all function modules are active.)*	
Has the correct version of the workflow been activated?	
Have appropriate possible agents been assigned to all tasks?	

Data Readiness

Question	☑
Has all agent determination data been entered or cleansed?	
Has any other data critical to the workflow been entered or cleansed? *(E.g. Configuration changes to the application, master data changes)*	

Agent Readiness

Question	☑
Have all agents been trained in basic workflow and inbox use?	
Have all agents been trained for their activities in this specific workflow?	
Have all agents been assigned appropriate user Ids?	
Have all agents been assigned appropriate security access?	
Have all agents been informed of the go-live date?	
Have any last minute changes, support contact numbers and/or web sites been communicated to agents? *(E.g. As a day 1 "survival pack" newsletter or e-mail)*	

System Readiness

Question	☑
Has the workflow environment been activated? (This should only need to be done if this is the first workflow to be used in the production environment)	
Have all hardware and network connections been changed as necessary?	
Have all new/changed background jobs been included in the job schedule?	

Support Readiness

Question	☑
Has the troubleshooting guide been given to Support Representative/Workflow Administrator?	

Sign-Offs

Process Owner	
Workflow Developer	
Workflow Administrator	
System Administrator	

Security Administrator	
Support Representative	
Education Representative	

B.7 Housekeeping

This checklist includes checks to be made periodically in the production environment.

Workflow System Health Check

The health check takes approximately 10 minutes to perform.

Perform the health check approximately once a week depending on how critical your processes are. You may wish to perform it more often, e.g. once a day, the first week after going live in your production environment with your first workflow.

In the steps that use date ranges as input parameters make sure that the range is equivalent to the frequency of the checks, e.g. daily, weekly or monthly.

Question	☑
Check there are no workflows or work items in error.	
Use transaction SWI2_DIAG. *Enter an appropriate date range. Expected result: No work items found.*	
Check that the workflow system customization is valid.	
Use transaction SWU3. *In the workflow runtime environment, all items should have a green tick. If the RFC destination shows a red cross, use the Test RFC option to check that it is working correctly (red cross should change to green tick).*	
Check there are no hanging event linkages or background tasks on the transaction RFC queue.	
Use transaction SM58. *Enter the workflow system user (*WF-BATCH*) and an appropriate date range. Expected result: No entries found.*	
Check that the event log is switched off.	
(Active event logs are a drain on system performance). Use transaction SWELS.	
Check that the technical trace for outgoing mails and work items is off.	
(Active traces are a drain on system performance). Use transaction SCOT *and menu option Goto → Trace. The trace should be off for all communication types.*	

Question

Check scheduled background jobs are running successfully.

Use transaction SM37. Search for the job name (as indicated in the Scheduled Background jobs to be monitored section below). Check that the jobs exist, that they have finished successfully. Compare how often the jobs actually run against their expected schedule.

Scheduled Background Jobs to be Monitored

Question ☑

SWWERRE—This job initiates re-execution of failed background tasks (up to a maximum number of retries), and reports errors to the workflow administrator.

SWWDHEX—This job evaluates work items with deadlines for outstanding deadlines and initiates the deadline response (as implemented in the workflow). This job should *only* be regularly scheduled if "periodic" monitoring has been chosen in transaction SWWA. Note that deadlines are evaluated only when the job is run, therefore:

Total time to raise deadline = baseline date/time for deadline + deadline period + time until next SWWDHEX job runs.

Archiving Requirements

Question ☑

Per workflow, how long do the workflow logs need to be accessible?

(This decision affects how often archiving should be performed and whether additional reports need to be written to keep a summary of the workflow logs.)

C   Step-by-Step Troubleshooting Guide

This is a practical guide to troubleshooting some of the thornier problems that you may run into in the development environment. It does not make interesting reading, but it may nevertheless be useful to you when you develop your own workflows.

This guide may be updated to take into account more recent discoveries. If so, they will be available from the publisher's Web site: *www.sap-press.com*.

When investigating a problem your first point of attack is the diagnosis transaction (SWUD). Start by selecting the most appropriage item from the list-menu.

C.1   A Workflow That Does Not Start

The source of a workflow's triggering problems is straightforward to locate when you select the second item from the new list-menu: *Problem: Task does not start* from the diagnosis transaction (SWUD). The first check is to see whether the workflow really did not start, or whether it was started but did not create a work item in the correct inbox.

Did it Really Fail to Start?

Choose the first item in the new list-menu (*Determine instances for task*) to determine whether or not the list of instances is empty.

The new list shows you all the workflow work items created on that day for the particular workflow definition that you are investigating. If you want to view the work items created on another day, change the date in the preceding screen. If you want to search over a date range, then call up a work item list report (such as transaction SWI1) directly.

An empty list shows clearly that your workflow really did not start—you should proceed with the next test (section: Is the Triggering Event Set Up Correctly?). However, if a workflow work item was created, then you can examine the log of the workflow to see if the first work item was created and to whom it was assigned. This being the case, you can skip this section and move to the section: Investigating a Workflow that Stops in Mid-Track

Is the Triggering Event Set Up Correctly?

So your workflow really did *not* start. You are now a significant step closer to finding the solution. If the flow is started by an event then you will need to follow the list of checks relating to events. If this is *not* the case, jump to the next section: What is Preventing the Workflow from Starting?

You will verify in the following tests:

- ▶ Whether the event was raised correctly:
  - ▶ Check whether the event was raised
  - ▶ Check whether there is a `COMMIT WORK` statement in the code following the event creation (this only needs to be checked if you are investigating a home made event-creation).
  - ▶ Check whether the event is not released until after the application object has been committed to the database.
- ▶ Whether the event to workflow linkage occurred as expected:
  - ▶ Check whether the event linkage is correct
  - ▶ Check whether any start conditions or check function modules used returned the correct result
  - ▶ Check whether the mandatory data required by the workflow is being passed by the event
- ▶ If the event is okay but the first work item has failed to appear:
  - ▶ Check whether an agent has been assigned to the first step in the workflow

The event checks are relatively straightforward. These are presented to you in the menu. The only thing that you need to do is choose from the list the event that should trigger the workflow (if more than one event is possible).

Now perform the checks one after another.

Check the RFC Queue to See if the Event Raising Has Aborted Midway

Check the RFC queue to verify that it is empty. This is a simple check that usually returns a positive result allowing you to move swiftly to the next test. When you perform this check, make sure that the "started by" user ID is that of the person who called the transaction that should have raised this event (usually your own). If there is an entry, take a look at the time stamp and estimate whether or not it came from your test. An entry in this queue implies that the failure is either due to an incorrectly customized system (but you did check this earlier didn't you?), an incorrect binding between the event and the workflow or mandatory data missing in the event container.

Check the event trace to see if the event really was raised and that the start condition or check function module (if any) did not return an exception. Remember that, technically, start conditions are also implemented as a check function module, so if your start conditions have failed this will also show up as a check function module exception. If the event is not found, make sure that the event trace is switched on and repeating the test if necessary.

If the event still does not appear in the log, it has not been raised. The most likely cause is:

▶ Incorrect application customizing or lack of a call to the ABAP statement COM-MIT WORK after the call to function module SWE_CREATE_EVENT (custom transaction).

▶ The SWE_CREATE_EVENT call is not being reached by the transaction (verify this with the ABAP debugger). If the event occurs twice the application customizing is incorrect. This will happen if you have configured the event to be raised upon a status change, but the application is raising the event directly, too.

The error *object does not exist* (message OL826) shows that the event is failing because the object does not yet exist in the database. This is most likely to happen when an object is created for the first time and the CREATED event is triggered by incorrect program code. In other words, the event is triggered before the object has been committed to the database because it is still in the update task queue at the time the event is raised.

Note that in an incorrectly programmed custom transaction an event can be raised when the user has cancelled the transaction; i.e. the status-change that the event is reporting did not actually happen. This is most likely to happen if the event is raised without due regard to the logical unit of work in the transaction; for example, if it was raised in the dialog task instead of the update task.

Refer back to chapter 13, *Custom Programs,* to find out how to raise such events correctly.

Check the Consistency of the Workflow Definition

This consistency check is worth performing next because it is so simple to perform but sometimes identifies the root problem very quickly. If the results of the test show that your workflow definition is correct, then you can jump straight to the next test.

The test will make sure that your workflow definition is correct, that agents have been assigned to the tasks in the workflow and that the event bindings are defined properly. In early releases, if no agent has been assigned to the dialog task used in the first step in the workflow, the event will fail to trigger the workflow. Similarly, a workflow definition that contains errors will also fail to start.

Simulate the Event

Simulate the event to check the event linkage, using the menu in the diagnosis program. This will show you all the workflows that are linked to the event and reason codes explaining why any of the workflows cannot be triggered. The reasons for failure will vary from release to release (the workflow system has become more fault tolerant) but you will see at a glance if everything is okay. More often than not, if you reach this test you may find that the event linkage has been automatically disabled by the workflow system.

When event queues are *not* used (Prior to Release 4.6C), if a fatal error prevented a workflow from triggering, the event linkage is disabled by the system to prevent the RFC queue from choking. This means that once you have enabled the event linkage you should always raise the event again and make sure that the workflow starts correctly. If the event linkage is deactivated again by the system, then you should look deeper for the cause of the problem. This is most likely to be a missing obligatory element in the event container or an inactive workflow definition.

To avoid event linkages being disabled, activate event queues as described in chapter 10, *Business Interfaces*. Event queues are also particularly useful when a lot of events fail before you can fix the error, since they collect all failed events and give you an easy way to restart them en masse.

If none of the above tests finds anything, the next step is to start the workflow directly and follow the checks described in the next section.

What is Preventing the Workflow from Starting?

By now you have established that the event customizing is correct (or that no triggering events are involved).

Now start the workflow directly from the test environment of the diagnosis transaction or from the Workflow Builder.

This has the advantage that any error messages that occur while the workflow is starting are displayed directly on the screen. If the workflow starts correctly and does not display any error messages on the screen, then the most likely source of the problem is that the parameters passed to the workflow in the test scenario are different from those passed from the triggering transaction. There are two ways of investigating the parameters that are passed by an event. You can either use the workflow trace, as described in chapter 14, *Advanced Diagnostics*, or you can use the function module SWE_EVENT_MAIL.

If you want to be notified of an event being raised, regardless of whether a workflow is started, then function module SWE_EVENT_MAIL can be used to send a mail whenever the event occurs. Simply create an event linkage (transaction SWE-TYPV) for your event, listing your user ID as the receiver type and SWE_EVENT_MAIL as the receiver function module.

When the event is raised, an SAP Office mail is sent to you in your inbox. This mail includes a list of the event's container elements. Check that these elements include all the mandatory elements required by the workflow. Check , too, that the elements have the correct format as expected by the workflow. For example check that the leading zeros match and that the key of the object is complete. You may find it useful to consult the section: Business Object Does Not Exis, if you find that the key is correct but the workflow cannot find the object.

C.2   A Workflow that Stops in Mid-Track

Troubleshooting a workflow to find out why it has stopped is the trickiest part of workflow diagnostics, due in part to the fact that it can be difficult to reproduce the problem. For this reason it is well worth investing effort in making a workflow robust from the outset rather than trying to track the errors down later.

Most problems are caused by hastily built background methods. Bear in mind that a background method that does not trap exceptions will terminate with an error message displayed on a virtual screen with no one there to view it. If the exception is not trapped, all clues will simply evaporate into space and not even Sherlock Holmes can solve the mystery. However, if the exception is trapped via an exception defined in the method definition, this will be logged in the workflow log when the exception occurs and even Sherlock's ineffectual friend Watson will see at a glance what the trouble is.

> **Caution** Be particularly careful when building background methods based on BDC (batch input) communication and CATTs to use the relevant options (e.g. MESSAGES parameter in the CALL TRANSACTION USING statement) to trap any errors.

When you select the *Problem: Workflow is hanging* suggestion in the diagnosis transaction, the first suggestion that you are presented with is the option to see the list of workflows running (*Determine instances for task*) so that you can inspect the workflow's technical log. Make sure you have selected the technical view. The error messages are marked clearly with red traffic lights to help you pick them out. Choosing the red light will bring up the error message. Usually the long text of the error message describes exactly what has gone wrong. Choosing the very first red light in a workflow will bring up an analysis of the relevant errors. For simple problems this is a great help, but for more complex problems you need to take the analysis with a pinch of salt, since it may have been oversimplified. As a rule of thumb, check the suggested analysis first, but as soon as you suspect that this is not the solution, do not dwell on it any longer; follow your own nose instead.

If the work item has stopped with an error, the parent workflow work item goes into the ERROR status, too, and a new message (WL394) is logged against the parent workflow's work item. This message simply tells you which step caused the fatal error. Having located this step (usually the last step executed) you should put all your attention into investigating the error logged against this delinquent work item.

There are four types of error messages that you will find

▶ Workflow system errors (Message ID WL)

▶ Errors that occur in business objects when expression evaluation fails, such as during a binding. (Message ID OL)

▶ Errors that occur during agent determination (Message ID 5W)

▶ Exceptions from the business object methods called within the tasks (Message IDs other than the above message IDs[1] usually come from the application your method is calling).

It is sometimes a little tricky distinguishing knock-on errors from those that clearly point to the root of the problem. The best method is to view the technical display of the work item itself. You can view the actual error message that caused the work item to abort by pressing ![i] displayed to the right of the work item's status. In normal circumstances (no error) the button will not be displayed at all or will display a temporary error message such as "cancelled by user". However, an erroneous work item will show the exception generated within the method, such as "invoice locked", "master record does not exist" or "no authorization to perform this task". It is now child's play to solve the problem.

Of course, if no exception has been defined in the method, no message is logged and you will have to continue the search by trying to reproduce the problem. It is often simpler to change the method to capture exceptions and then rerun the failed scenario than try to guess what went wrong.

C.3   The Most Likely Causes (and How to Avoid Them)

Background Work Items Aborting in the Middle

Background work items that abort in the middle (without an exception) will not return a result to the workflow system so they will remain in the status STARTED.

---

1   The exceptions to this rule are the method exceptions WZ, which occur in the demo scenario FORMABSENC. This is only relevant when you are setting up this particular demo.

There is a background job, SWWERRE, which periodically searches for such work items and switches them to ERROR status with the appropriate WL message in the error log. Since the error message will not tell you much, the best course of action here is to test the method directly and try to reproduce the error.

A common cause of background method failure is incorrect or insufficient data passed to the method. You can use the workflow trace to determine exactly which parameters are being passed to the method.

Another common cause of background method failure is a method that unexpectedly requires dialog input to continue. This is most likely to arise when the background method is based on transactions executed via BDC (batch input, including CALL TRANSACTION USING) or CATT procedures, particularly after an upgrade. It can also occur when the preferences (e.g. for date and decimal format) of WF-BATCH are different from that of the user used to create and test the BDC routine. Usually you will need to correct the method's code to make it more robust.

Methods can be tested using transaction SW01, the Business Object Builder. This allows you to vary the parameters being passed to the method. One thing that you cannot test with this is whether the workflow agent or workflow batch user (WF-BATCH) has enough authorization to execute the method. This can only be checked before going live using real agents, or test agents having strict production security. If you have HR implemented in your SAP component, watch out for HR structural authorizations to workflow here, since these are often forgotten.

The diagnosis transaction also checks for short dumps under the WF-BATCH user caused by errant background methods. If it finds any, you will usually have to correct the method's program code to correct the problem.

Business Object Does Not Exist

When the workflow tries to execute a method or evaluate an obligatory expression based on an object that does not exist you will see an OL826 message in the log. The most probable cause is that either

▶ The binding is incorrect in the workflow definition or

▶ The object does not yet exist in the database.

The latter is the case when the workflow has been hastily modeled and a race between the update task and the workflow system sporadically causes this effect (shown in Figure C.1). The read operation (marked with the number 2 in diagram) occurs before the write operation (marked with the number 1).

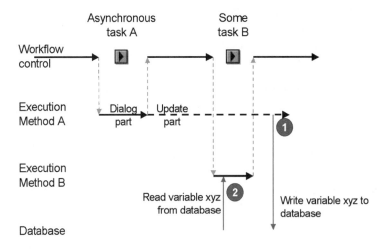

Figure C.1 Diagram Showing Update Task Race

This problem is most likely to appear following a release change. The workflow system performance has improved in every new release, making the chances of the workflow system winning the race higher with each new Release.

The answer to the problem is to ensure that the workflow is in fact modeled correctly. Any one of the following three suggestions can be followed, but they are listed in order of preference. Note that all of these approaches imply some additional performance cost, either in event creation, in background job execution, or in additional method execution, so it is up to you to ensure you use best practice options, such as event queues, to minimize system impact. Remember that the cost of business process failure is always higher than any performance cost.[2]

Method	Advantage	Disadvantage
1. Make the update task an asynchronous task so that it is completed by an event coming from the update task which confirms that the data has been successfully committed to the database. E.g. `object CREATED` or `status CHANGED`	Workflow continues as soon as the data is ready. This solution always works.	Tricky for beginners to set up (but worth learning)[2]. You have to establish a suitable event creation mechanism if there is no standard event raised by the application.

Table C.1 Dealing with a race between the update task and theWebFlow Engine

---

2   Read the sections on this in chapter 8, *Business Objects*, Chapter 10, *Business Interfaces*, and chapter 13, *Custom Programs*, for how to set up asynchronous tasks and terminating events.

Method	Advantage	Disadvantage
2. *Complete execution* condition in the workflow step. The workflow step is completed only after the condition *object exists* is true.	Simple to set up. The solution always works.	*Complete execution* conditions are not available before Release 6.20. The periodic evaluation of conditions means that the workflow will take several minutes before it continues with the next step. *Create work item* conditions for the next workflow step can be used instead. These have the advantage that they are available in Release 6.10 onwards.
3. Set a requested start deadline in the next step so that the workflow always waits ,say five minutes, before the next step is started.	Simple to set up.	This is not a watertight solution. If the update task takes longer than five minutes or fails then the next step will fail.

Table C.1 Dealing with a race between the update task and theWebFlow Engine (cont.)

Inconsistent Definition

The workflow runtime system determines the path to follow on the fly. This is an essential ingredient of the workflow system, allowing it to support ad hoc workflow processing and versioning. If the system arrives at a point where it cannot determine which is the next step or where it expects to call a task that no longer exists, the workflow has no choice but to put the workflow work item into status ERROR with the error ID W8.

If this happens, first verify that the version on the workflow work item really is the latest active version. You can find the version by running the workflow list report (SWI1) with the *Additional Data* flag set so that the version of each workflow work item is displayed in a separate column, or you can examine the attributes of the workflow work item in the workflow container via the technical log. If the workflow is following the current version then the most likely source of the problem is a corrupted or incompletely generated workflow runtime definition. This is occasionally caused by transport problems.

You can regenerate the workflow runtime version from the Workflow Builder in display mode or activate it again. The next time the workflow runs it will follow the correct path.

Workflow Step Must be Confirmed Manually

Occasionally in the production environment, new users may report that the work item does not disappear even when they have executed it. Check that the workflow step does not require manual confirmation. If it does, make sure that the agent is confirming confirmation after executing it.

Condition Set Up Incorrectly

If the workflow contains complex conditions, which appear to yield incorrect results and the simulation of the condition in the condition editor fails to find the source of the problem, use the workflow trace to capture the results (and the analysis) of the conditions as the workflow executes.

C.4   Binding Problems with the Workflow Trace

The symptoms of binding problems are not easy to spot straight away. Usually you are faced with another problem, such as the work item refusing to execute or the wrong agents receiving the work item. However, in such cases you will often be confronted with the fact that data is not being passed through the workflow correctly. Either the data is being lost along the way, or the wrong data is being passed to the next step.

The cure is simply to correct the workflow definition so that the correct data is passed to the relevant step, but how do you locate the part of the workflow that is wrongly defined?

There are two approaches. Either inspect the workflow definition checking every binding definition that has been made, or monitor each binding as it passes through the workflow instance. Even though the Workflow Builder offers a very useful cross-reference for container elements in the workflow definition (from Release 4.5B), you will often find it simpler to monitor the data as it is passed through the workflow at run time. This is because the bindings often use expressions, such as the attributes of an object (or the attributes of attributes), so it is not simply a question of which container element is used where. The Workflow trace described at the beginning of this chapter is the tool used to monitor the bindings.

Bear in mind that there is usually no binding between a task and a method (and vice versa) because this particular binding defaults to copying the task container straight to the method container (and vice versa). So you should concentrate on the *workflow · task*, and *task · workflow bindings* when you are having problems with the execution of a workflow. If you are having problems with agent determination then you will need to start with the *workflow · rule bindings* and may need to extend your investigation to the other types of bindings once you have determined that the workflow container is incorrect at the time of the rule binding.

Text bindings (for the task descriptions), which account for many of the bindings in a workflow, can be ignored.

C.5 Why Duplicate or Multiple Workflows are Triggered

If the workflow is being started twice, or more than one workflow is being started by the same event, the application configuration is probably incorrect. Bear in mind that some applications (e.g. Engineering Change) trigger the workflow directly from customizing tables and not from events. So if you have configured the workflow to be triggered by an event, too, the workflow will be triggered once by your event and once again by the application directly! Check the online documentation of the application to determine how the workflow should be triggered.

To begin with, with, look at the list of workflows started (transaction SWI1). By examining the list of workflows started and checking the *Task ID,* column you will be able to see if the problem results from one workflow definition that is being triggered twice or two separate workflows.

Use the *Problem: Task does not start* suggestion of the diagnosis transaction to examine the event trace (are two events being triggered?) and to check the event simulation to determine whether or not two workflows are being configured to trigger from the same event.

Possible causes:

▶ **Two workflows are triggered by the same event**
Solution: Disable one of the event linkages.

▶ **Start conditions are used to determine which workflow should be triggered by a particular event, but the start conditions overlap**
Solution: Correct the start conditions.

▶ **One workflow is triggered by a subtype event, and the other workflow is triggered by the supertype event**
Solution: Use delegation so that just one event is raised, or disable one of the event linkages, or use start conditions (or a check function module) to decide which workflow should be started.

▶ **Workflow is triggered directly by a customizing table and also by an event**
Solution: Check the online documentation for this workflow and if necessary disable the event linkage.

C.6 Why an Agent Does Not Receive a Work Item

In a production system the cause of this problem is likely to differ from that of a development system, but the administrator must be trained for all eventualities.

While investigating why the user has not received the work item in his inbox, bear in mind the prerequisites for receiving a work item.

1. The user has been assigned to the task as a possible agent (or it is a general task).

2. The workflow step's agent determination technique (expression, rule resolution, etc.) has found this user, assuming an agent determination technique is defined.

3. The default agent determination rule on the task level has found this user, assuming a default resolution is defined. The default agent determination rule will only be called if no step agent determination rule has been defined or if the step agent determination rule fails to find a user.

4. The agent is not on the list of excluded agents.

5. The work item has not been reserved by anybody else and has not been forwarded to anybody else.

6. The organizational management buffers are up-to-date with respect to this user; otherwise the agent will be displayed as an actual agent but will not see the work item in his inbox.

7. The user has sufficient security authorization to view and execute work items. Especially be careful of HR structural authorizations since they are often forgotten.

Check That the Agent Is Assigned to the Work Item

In the workflow log view the list of actual agents and make sure that the user's name is included in this list. To be doubly sure switch to the user ID view (it has been known for several users to exist in the system with the same name but different user IDs).

If the agent is displayed but the user does not see the work item in his inbox, then this user's buffered information is not up-to-date. In a production system the user can refresh the buffer from the Business Workplace via the *workflow settings* menu, or the workflow administrator can refresh it for him by using transaction SWU_OBUF. If the work item does not appear, he may need to log off and log on again, depending on the release of the SAP component.

In a development system you can refresh the buffer for all users from the diagnosis transaction (*Problem: Task does not start*). Try to avoid this in the production system because it makes the inbox slower the first time a user calls it (subsequent calls are not affected).

Check That the Agent Is Assigned to the Task

In the technical workflow log, view the list of possible agents and check that the agent's name is included in the list. You may need to expand the list to show the user view, rather than the view of organizational management objects. If the agent is not a possible agent, check that the task is a general task. If this is not the case, then the problem is that the agent has not been assigned to the task. The administrator will need to correct this.

Check That the Agent Has Not Been Excluded from This Work Item

This is not very likely but it is very quick and easy to check. Look at the list of excluded agents for this work item (from the workflow log) and verify that this agent is not one of those excluded.

Check That the Agent Determination Rule Has Selected an Agent

Agent determination rule resolution is easy to check by calling the test facility in the agent determination rule definition tool. In a development system you may want to use the workflow trace to make sure that the rule container is being filled with the correct data.

C.7 Why the Wrong Agent Receives the Work Item

When a user receives a work item that he should not have received, the tests that you need to perform are the same as when an agent fails to receive a work item (described above).

However, there is one important distinction. Because the agent has actually received something in the inbox, you can give him access to information about how to solve the problem himself, or how to accelerate the procedure for getting it solved. This is important because the faster the problems are solved, the faster the workflow executes.

In other words, if the work item contains information on how the agent may have been chosen (e.g. "You have received this work item because you have been identified as the manager of cost center 9999"), and the contact details for getting this corrected ("If you are not the manager of cost centre 9999, please contact the help desk on extension 1111") in the long text of the work item, the agent can see at a glance if something has gone wrong. Further, a proactive environment for the user encourages him to understand the process rather than just react to it.

This would improve when the work item contains a URL to an Intranet site containing a FAQ list, which might even allow them to solve the problem himself. For example:

▶ Buffers need refreshing: Can be solved by the agent himself.

▶ Organizational Management not up to date: Must be solved by the administrator.

▶ Security settings not up to date. Must be solved by the administrator.

C.8   Why the Work Item Follows the Wrong Route

This could be caused by an incorrect expression in a branch or the wrong workflow version being used, or the container element data evaluated in the branch being wrong.

Solution: Correct the workflow definition.

D   Administrator's First Aid Guide

This guide offers suggestions for repairing rare problems that may occur in the production system. Use the troubleshooting guide in appendix C to locate the cause.

This guide may be updated to take into account more recent discoveries. If so, they will be available from the publisher's Web site: *www.sap-press.com*.

D.1   Resolving Work Item Errors

Good workflow design and thorough testing of the workflow in a development environment can prevent most work item errors.

These errors come in two broad categories:

▶ **Work items in Error status**
These work items are easy to find, and the messages in the work item display and workflow log are helpful when diagnosing the problem.

▶ **Work items that don't behave as expected**
These can very difficult to track down, especially if the problem is not discovered until after the work item is completed. You cannot reactivate a completed work item, so you may need to fix the problem manually. If many work items have been affected, it may be worthwhile creating a program specifically to fix the problem. However, this is the worst case. If the work item is still active (e.g. in READY or STARTED status) you can usually resolve the problem readily.

Watch out for work items that take an unusually long time to complete, since this can indicate an error situation. For instance, the delay may be caused by terminating events or escalation procedures (deadlines) that have failed, a background process that has started but not completed correctly, or it could be that no agent has been assigned to the work item. Of course, it could also be that the assigned agent has simply been slow to act.

Common problems with work items include:

▶ **Work item in Error status with the message Object does not exist**
This could be the result of binding problems (i.e. object was not passed correctly), sequencing problems (i.e. the object did not exist when the work item was first created/executed), or inadequate process design (e.g. the workflow did not take into account the fact that the object may occasionaly be deleted manually)

▶ **Work item in Error status with the message Mail could not be sent**
This is usually due to missing configuration information. It could be that the office settings do not allow for mails to be sent to the given mail type (e.g. HR objects). Or, if you are sending mails externally via a mail server, there could be a problem in the configuration between the SAP Web Application Server and the mail server. This can be a considerable nuisance, since if the workflow runs frequently a lot of workflows will be stopping with this error. If most e-mails are working and just a particular instance of a workflow is not working, the problem may be simply a binding error.

▶ **Work item in Error status with an application message, i.e. the underlying object method has failed**
This type of error occurs when the object method executes the underlying applications and routines. There are many possible causes for this such as: changes in configuration, changes in the data used, underlying transactions executed in an unexpected way, changes in user-exits or BAdIs. Usually the problem is not the workflow itself, but you still need to co-ordinate problem resolution and restart the workflow once the error has been fixed.

▶ **A dialog work item that never completes because a terminating event did not occur**
This may be due to an agent who has not completed the work correctly, i.e. since the work has not been done, the terminating event is not raised; or it may be an event linkage problem.

▶ **Background work items that start but never complete**
If the background work item is waiting on a terminating event, this could be an event linkage problem.

The background work item may have failed because of a severe error in the underlying method. It is worthwhile checking for matching ABAP short dumps to see if this is the case. Fix the problem and re-execute.

If the background work item is trying to execute a dialog step, execute the failed routine from the transactional RFC monitor and process the dialog step.

Most other problems can be resolved by using the option to re-execute the background item. However if that fails, another option is to do the work manually, then manually complete the background work item.

▶ *Problem:* Work item deadline has not been escalated even though the deadline has expired.
Repair:

▶ This may simply be a timing issue. Remember that deadlines are not escalated immediately when the deadline time is exceeded but only when the next deadline job runs. This means the timing of the deadline job is dependent on whether the deadline job is scheduled on a case-specific or periodic basis and the efficiency of the background queue.

▶ If the deadline-monitoring job (background job SWWDHEX) has already been scheduled and released but is being held up the background queue, you may need to discuss this with the system administrators. For instance, you may need to increase the job priority, or more background queues may need to be added to cope with the background job load.

▶ If you find that there are too many deadline-monitoring jobs (background job SWWDHEX) in the background queue and they are blocking each other, you may need to reassess the scheduling of this job. In particular, if the job is being scheduled on a case-specific basis you may need to switch to periodic monitoring. Since every deadline job assesses all exceeded deadlines on all work items being monitored, you can cancel the unnecessary deadline jobs to allow the currently active job to complete.

▶ If the deadline job has not been scheduled at all, it is usually sufficient to restart the deadline-monitoring job (background job SWWDHEX) using workflow customizing (transaction SWU3).

▶ *Problem:* Work item has completed successfully even though an error occurred, i.e. the object method did not report the error. These cases can be extremely difficult to diagnose, in part because it can be some time before anyone realizes that an apparently successful workflow process has failed to achieve the business result. If the data used is temporary and is deleted at the end of the workflow this can be a real problem.

Repair:

▶ If the workflow is still in progress, you may be able to manually correct the data, then change the containers of any failed work items and restart the failed workflows.

▶ If the workflow has finished, you may be able to manually correct the data. If it was some time before the problem was detected, you may need a developer to write a program to fix the data en masse.

Preventing Work Item Problems from Reoccurring

Once you are confident the immediate problem is solved, you need to ensure that it does not reappear. This may mean:

▶ Initiating changes to the workflow design (e.g. to cope with the object being manually deleted while the workflow is still running) to fix binding errors, or to better handle common application errors.

▶ Improving quality assurance checklists to catch more problems. For example, check that every workflow design considers the impact of non-workflow activity on the workflow.

▶ Making sure that all workflows using temporary objects or deleting objects as part of the workflow include enough information in work item texts or container elements to give you a starting point for fixing problems after the workflow has completed. It can even be worthwhile putting redundant container elements in the workflow to hold this extra information.

▶ Re-examining the deadline job to see if it should have a higher job priority, or be switched from case-specific to periodic monitoring.

Support Tools for Work Item Problems

Here are some more reports and functions that you may find useful in dealing with work item errors:

Diagnosis of Workflows with Errors

Administration · Workflow Runtime · Diagnosis of Workflows with Errors (transaction `SWI2_DIAG`)

This function displays all workflows with errors and groups them according to error cause (agent, deadlines, binding, or other). This report helps you to assess whether particular types of errors are reoccurring across many workflows, or whether the problem is specific to just a particular work item. You can also fix and restart the workflow from this report.

> **Tip** The system determines highest-level work items with errors, i.e. if a work item is in error status, the work item shown will belong to the highest workflow in error hierarchically above it.

Workflow Restart After Error

Administration · Workflow Runtime · Workflow Restart After Error (transaction `SWPR`)

This report can be used to display a list of workflows with errors for a particular selection period, and then restart them. The benefit of this report is that it allows you to perform a mass restart of workflows.

Deadline Monitoring for Work Items

Administration · Workflow Runtime · Work Item Deadline Monitoring (transaction `SWI2_DEAD`).

Tasks with deadlines also have deadline monitoring based on a background job. You can change the period duration of the background job, schedule it, display it, or execute it manually.

Work Item Rule Monitoring

Administration · Workflow Runtime · Work Item Rule Monitoring.

If conditions are defined for the work item start or work item end for steps in the workflow, these conditions must be regularly checked. This task is performed by a report that is controlled by a background job. You can schedule or display the background job. You can also start the report manually using *Execute Work Item Rule Monitoring*.

D.2 Resolving Workflow Instance Errors

Usually errors in workflows are simply due to errors in work items. To resolve these you usually fix the work items, then restart the workflow (see appendix D.1 for more details).

Make sure you distinguish workflow instance errors from work item errors. When a work item is in ERROR status, the system also puts the workflow instance into ERROR status, but the cause of the error is at the work item level. You know you have a workflow instance error when only the workflow instance is in error and the underlying work items are okay.

There are a few problems that are specific to the workflow itself. These include:

▶ Wrong version is active

▶ No workflow definition is active

▶ Binding errors

▶ Workflow appears to be successful but the work has not been done

  See appendix D.1 for more details about "unreported work item errors".

The majority of workflow instance errors are preventable if new and changed workflows are adequately designed and thoroughly tested prior to being moved to a production environment.

Fixing Workflow Instances in Error

Diagnosing why a workflow instance has failed is a topic in itself. Use the troubleshooting guide in appendix C to locate the cause. Knowing the cause will help you solve the problem.

▶ *Cause:* Wrong version of workflow is active.

Repair:

▶ Verify that the production environment contains the correct version of the workflow definition. It may be that the workflow was not transported correctly or at all, or only part of the workflow was transported.

▶ If necessary, manually activate the correct workflow definition.

In either case, all current workflows will be using the old version. You will need to decide with the business process owner whether that is okay, or whether you should stop those workflows and trigger new versions of the workflows, e.g. via *Generate Event* (transaction SWUE). Obviously this depends on what the difference is between the versions and how far the workflow has progressed. If the workflow is still in the initial stages, it is usually easier to stop and re-trigger it, but if agents have already taken several actions it may not be practical to stop the existing workflow.

▶ *Cause:* Workflow has failed due to binding errors.

Repair: Since the workflow instance has its own (type F) work item, you can change the workflow container via the work item technical display. Then restart the workflow.

Preventing Workflow Instance Problems from Reoccurring

Once you are confident the immediate problem is solved, you need to ensure that this does not happen again. This may mean:

▶ Ensuring transport logs are checked carefully after transporting workflows, and that after transport the version, activation of the workflow definition, event linkage activation and start conditions are checked.

▶ Improving quality assurance checklists, e.g. to make sure the workflow has been thoroughly tested.

Support Tools for Workflow Instance Errors

In addition to the support tools listed in appendix D.1, the following transaction will also be useful.

Continue Workflow After System Crash

Administration · Workflow Runtime · Continue Workflow After System Crash (transaction SWPC)

You can use this report to select and continue workflows that have had the status STARTED for longer than a day. This means that workflows that have come to a halt after system errors can be continued.

D.3 Finding Workflows That Appear to Have Disappeared

This is a common complaint soon after a workflow goes live, but it becomes less and less frequent as the users become familiar with the WebFlow Engine. There has never been a case of a workflow physically disappearing on its own.

Cause

The complaint arises when a user expects to receive a work item but does not. In nearly all cases this is simply because the agent has not been assigned to the task.

From the user's point of view, if one agent processes his work item so that it disappears from his inbox, but the next work item does not appear in the next user's inbox, he will claim that the "workflow has disappeared".

Repair

As an administrator, once the problem is reported to you, you can sort this out easily by checking the workflow log and work item display, but it is more efficient to have a description of what users should do (e.g. how to report the problem, how to find out where the workflow went) in the Intranet support site. Bear in mind that the agents are not familiar with workflow technology, so your FAQ section should include a section along the lines "What to do if the workflow disappears!"

Useful pointers for self-help are descriptions of how to locate the workflow (e.g. the outbox of the first agent or generic object services for the object) and how to establish who has received the work item by checking the workflow log.

D.4 Resolving Event Linkage Errors

Event linkage problems prevent workflows from being started and/or work items from being completed (assuming the work item is waiting on a terminating event). Be careful not to confuse event linkage errors with workflow instance errors where the workflow has started but has hung, since these problems have very different solutions. The majority of event linkage errors are preventable if new and changed event linkages are thoroughly tested prior to being moved to a production environment. In production environments the most common problems are:

- The application that is supposed to raise the event has failed to do so because the workflow environment configuration or the application configuration is missing or incorrect.
- The event-linkage has not been activated. Do not forget that events need to be 'switched on'
- The event object doesn't satisfy the start conditions (if used), or the start condition is incorrect.
- The object instance doesn't satisfy the check function modules (if used).
- The event linkage binding contains errors.

You can counteract most of these problems by raising the event again manually, for example by using the *Generate Event* transaction (SWUE). However, you need to be careful that you raise the event with all of the necessary data, including a designated workflow initiator.

Another related problem may be delays in event-processing. This can result from impaired system performance, or could be deliberate if the events have been placed in an event queue. Event queues are an advanced technique used to spread the workload of raising events over time. Check with the developer if you suspect an event queue has been used. Note that via the event linkage configuration (transaction SWE2) and the event queue configuration (transaction SWEQADM) you can also opt to send failed events to an event queue, rather than have the system deactivate the event linkage (refer to chapter 10, *Business Interfaces*). You can then redeliver the event (with all the original data used during event creation) via the event queue.

> **Tip** Don't forget that if you have set up workflow error monitoring, event linkages that fail due to binding problems and/or are automatically deactivated by the system will be reported to you (as the workflow administrator) via your inbox. You should make sure that you check your inbox regularly.

Once the immediate problem has been solved, don't forget to make sure the problem doesn't happen again.

Fixing Workflows That Didn't Start

- *Cause:* Event was not raised at all.

    Repair:

    - If nothing is found on the event log or in the transactional RFC monitor, check that workflow customizing has been done for the current client and the workflow logical destination is working. If necessary, complete the workflow customizing, or change the workflow logical destination, then use *Generate Event* to raise the event manually.

▶ If the configuration for raising the event is not correct, complete the configuration. Then use *Generate Event* to raise the event manually.

When you use *Generate Event* (transaction SWUE) to raise the event manually, be careful to fill in all necessary data. Take care when doing this, since the person raising the event will then be the event initiator. This variable may be referred to later in the workflow (e.g. to determine agents). If necessary, you may need to ask the real initiator to log on and generate the event using their user ID.

▶ *Cause:* Event linkage was deactivated.

Repair:

▶ The linkage can be reactivated using the *Simulate Event* function (transaction SWU0). However, if the event has a start condition, the linkage should be reactivated from the *Start Condition* function (transaction SWB_COND).

▶ Then, if you can, raise the event again using the application.

▶ If this is not possible, use *Generate Event* (transaction SWUE) to raise the event again manually, be careful to fill in all necessary data. Take care when doing this, since the person raising the event will then be made the event initiator, which may be used later in the workflow e.g. for determing agents. If necessary, you may need to ask the real initiator to log on and raise the event using their user ID.

▶ *Cause:* A start condition disqualified the event linkage.

Repair:

▶ If the logical expression is incorrect, use the *Start Condition* function (transaction SWB_COND) to correct it.

▶ Then, if you can, raise the event again using the application.

▶ If this is not possible, use *Generate Event* (transaction SWUE) to raise the event again manually, being careful to fill in all necessary data. Take care when doing this, since the person raising the event will then be made the event initiator, which may be used later in the workflow, e.g. to determine agents. If necessary, you may need to ask the real initiator to log on and raise the event using their user ID.

▶ *Cause:* A check function module disqualified the event linkage.

Repair: Check and if necessary correct the underlying event data. Then use *Generate Event* (transaction SWUE) to raise the event again manually, being careful to fill in all necessary data. Take care when doing this, since the person raising the event will then be made the event initiator, which may be used later in the workflow, e.g. to determine agents. If necessary, you may need to ask the real initiator to log on and raise the event using their user ID.

▶ *Cause:* The event linkage failed due to binding errors.

Repair:

▷ If the event binding is incorrect and it is a triggering event for a workflow, don't use *Generate Event* to trigger a missing workflow. Instead use *Test Workflow* (transaction SWUS) to manually start the workflow, being careful to fill in all necessary data, including workflow initiator.

▷ If the event binding is incorrect and it is a terminating event, you may be able to use the work item display to fill the container with the correct return values, and manually complete the work item. However, this particular problem is rare for terminating events.

Preventing Error Linkage Problems from Reoccurring

Once you are confident the immediate problem is solved, you need to ensure that this does not happen again. This may require you to ensure that:

▶ Binding problems, or failed check function modules, are fixed by the workflow developers, and improve quality assurance checklists for new and changed workflows.

▶ Any failures in the transactional RFC monitor are resolved in the system. These may be due to configuration changes in the application or changes to the event linkage configuration.

▶ All event-raising configuration has been done prior to the workflow being started.

▶ Transport logs are checked carefully for workflows, and that after transport the version, activation of the workflow definition version, event linkage activation and start conditions are correct.

Support Tools for Event Linkage Problems

Workflow RFC Monitor

Administration · Workflow Runtime · Workflow RFC monitor (transaction SWU2)

You can use this function to display the log file of the transactional RFC. The log entries are displayed with the target system (logical destination) WORKFLOW_ LOCAL_<client>. Use this report to follow up errors that have occurred in connection with the feedback from work items to the workflow runtime system after their execution.

D.5 Resolving Internet-Specific Errors

If agents are executing workflows via the web, then problems with the web environment (such as web server or ITS (Internet Transaction Server)) may be blamed on the workflow. Problems may also occur if a user has an inappropriate web browser version, i.e. an old version of a web browser or an unsupported web browser, so always first check that the user has the correct web browser and version (including service pack) level.

Possible problems include:

▶ Agent cannot access the work item/workflow because the web server or ITS server is down or has a severe error. You will need to contact your system/web administrators to have this fixed. Sometimes the errors are timing problems (e.g. session terminated or connection lost) and once the problem is fixed, the agent simply needs to logon again to complete the work item.

▶ Agents cannot execute the work item because it has been locked by a prior ITS session that is still active in the background. Resolve this by unlocking the work item (e.g. via transaction SM12).

▶ Agent cannot execute work item because of a "template missing" error. This is usually not due to a template being missing, but is more likely the result of a short dump or bad hyperlink. Check first whether a short dump has been created, and contact the web/workflow developers to have the problem fixed. If the work item has gone into ERROR status (it may simply remain in STARTED status), restart the workflow once the error has been corrected.

▶ Agents cannot execute work items because ITS service/templates are incorrect. For instance, they don't trigger completion of the work item, or they have HTML or JavaScript errors that are preventing execution. You will need to contact workflow/web developers to have these errors corrected and correct templates republished to the ITS.

E   Workflow Macros

Whenever workflow programming is involved, workflow macros are required to define and access object references, attributes, methods, and containers. There are a few macros specific to object type programming, but most macros are available for all workflow programs whether object type programs, agent determination rules, check function modules, receiver type function modules, or custom programs for monitoring and reporting on workflows.

E.1   Macros Specific to Object Type Programs

All the macros needed for general workflow programming are defined in the include program `<OBJECT>` (note the <> brackets are part of the name). This is automatically included in the object type program using the statement:

▶ `INCLUDE <OBJECT>.`
The following macros are specific to the object type program.

▶ `BEGIN_DATA Object.`
Start of the object declaration.

▶ `END_DATA.`
End of the object declaration.

▶ `GET_PROPERTY <Attribute> CHANGING CONTAINER.`
Start of a virtual attribute implementation.

▶ `GET_TABLE_PROPERTY <Tablename>.`
Start of a database attribute implementation.

▶ `END_PROPERTY.`
End of an attribute implementation.

▶ `BEGIN_METHOD <Method> CHANGING CONTANER.`
Start of a method implementation.

▶ `END_METHOD.`
End of a method implementation.

▶ `SWC_SET_OBJECTKEY <ObjectKey>.`
Sets the object key of the current object. Usually only instance-independent methods use this to return a reference to an object instance of the current object.

Macros for Method Exceptions

▶ `EXIT_OBJECT_NOT_FOUND`
Tells workflow that an object does not exist.

- ► EXIT_CANCELLED
  Tells workflow that the user cancelled execution of a method.

- ► EXIT_RETURN ⟨Exception⟩ ⟨MessageVariable1⟩ ⟨MessageVariable2⟩
  ⟨MessageVariable3⟩ ⟨MessageVariable4⟩.
  Tells workflow that an error has occurred.

- ► EXIT_NOT_IMPLEMENTED
  Tells workflow that a method is not implemented.

- ► EXIT_PARAMETER_NOT_FOUND
  Tells workflow that a mandatory parameter of a method is missing.

E.2   Macros for General Workflow Programming

All the macros needed for general workflow programming are defined in the include program ⟨CNTN01⟩ (note the <> brackets are part of the name). Apart from the object type program, which already includes this program as part of the include program ⟨OBJECT⟩, you must add the include program to your own workflow program using the statement:

INCLUDE ⟨CNTN01⟩.

Macros to Process a Container as a Whole

- ► SWC_CONTAINER ⟨Container⟩.
  Declares a container.

- ► SWC_CREATE_CONTAINER ⟨Container⟩.
  Initializes a container. The makros SWC_RELEASE_CONTAINER and SWC_CLEAR_CONTAINER have the same functions.

Runtime Versus Persistent Containers

A runtime container only exists within the environment of the current program, for example the object container. A persistent container can be passed to another program. For example, if you want to change the event container within a check function module or receiver type function module, or you want to pass the container to a function module such as a WAPI (refer to chapter 13, *Custom Programs*) or SWE_EVENT_CREATE.

- ► SWC_CONTAINER_TO_PERSISTENT ⟨Container⟩.
  Makes a runtime container persistent.

- ► SWC_CONTAINER_TO_RUNTIME ⟨Container⟩.
  Makes a persistent container runtime.

Macros to Process Elements from the Container

▶ SWC_GET_ELEMENT <Container> <ContainerElement> <Variable>.
Read single value element from the container into a variable.

▶ SWC_SET_ELEMENT <Container> <ContainerElement> <Variable>.
Write single value element from a variable to the container.

▶ SWC_SET_TABLE <Container> <ContainerElement> <InternalTable>.
Read multiline element from the container into an internal table.

▶ SWC_GET_TABLE <Container> <ContainerElement> <InternalTable>.
Write multiline element from an internal table to the container.

▶ SWC_COPY_ELEMENT <SourceContainer> <SourceContainerElement> <TargetContainer> <TargetContainerElement>.
Copies a container element from a source container to a target container.

▶ SWC_DELETE_ELEMENT <Container> <ContainerElement>.
Deletes a container element.

Macros for processing object references

▶ SWC_CREATE_OBJECT <Object> <ObjectType> <ObjectKey>.
Create an object reference from an object type and object key.

▶ SWC_REFRESH_OBJECT <Object>.
Invalidates the object reference buffer so that all attributes will be recalculated when they are next called.

▶ SWC_GET_OBJECT_KEY <Object> <ObjectKey>.
Returns the object key of an object reference. Used in generic object programming.

▶ SWC_GET_OBJECT_TYPE <Object> <ObjectType>.
Returns the object type of an object reference. Used in a generic object programming.

▶ SWC_OBJECT_FROM_PERSISTENT <Variable> <Object>.
Convert a persistent object reference to a runtime reference.

Macros for Retrieving Object Attributes

▶ SWC_GET_PROPERTY <Object> <Attribute> <Variable>.
Retrieve a single value attribute of an object into a variable.

SWC_GET_TABLE_PROPERTY <Object> <Attribute> <InternalVariable>.
Retrieve a multiline attribute of an object into an internal table.

Macros for Calling Object Methods

▶ SWC_CALL_METHOD `<Object>` `<Method>` `<Container>`.
Calls the method of an object. All parameters are passed to/from the method as contents of the container.

F   SAP Workflow Training

F.1   BC600 Workflow Introduction

In addition to an introduction to the fundamental terms, concept, and architecture of the WebFlow Engine, participants learn about how workflow can be used during this two-day course. They also learn how they can get an overview of the business processes predefined by SAP (and the relevant documentation) and how they can adapt and activate these SAP workflows in a particular scope.

Additional parts of this course cover the use of the Business Workplace as an end user interface for editing work items, the use of simple possibilities of runtime control and the use of the organization management for agent determination.

BC600 is designed for workflow project leaders and team leaders.

F.2   BC601 Build and Use Workflows

In this five-day course, participants learn about the definition tools of the WebFlow Engine and how to implement their own workflows from the ground up. In addition, they can customize a SAP system to use the WebFlow Engine, trigger workflows using events or start transactions, and determine agents dynamically at runtime. The modeled deadline monitoring, the use of wizards, and the implementation of workflows in Internet scenarios are further topics.

The participants learn about the necessary test tools and monitoring tools and how to use these when developing their own workflows.

BC601 is designed for workflow project members and administrators.

F.3   BC610 Workflow Programming

In this three-day course, participants are shown how to perform customer-specific extensions of workflows that cannot be modeled with the definition tools, using Workflow Interface programming.

This covers: Objects, events, methods, attributes, and rules (for agent determination).

Participants also learn about the creation, functions, and administration of the runtime system.

BC610 is designed for workflow developers and consultants.

F.4 BIT603 Web Scenarios and the WebFlow Engine

In this two-day course, participants learn how to use workflows in Internet scenarios and intranet scenarios and how they call external Web services or Web forms. They learn how to build workflows that use the Wf-XML interface and therefore can communicate with workflows in other systems. Use of the Wf-XML interface enables communication between both SAP systems and also SAP systems and non-SAP systems.

This course is aimed at workflow modelers, workflow developers, and consultants.

F.5 TAWF10 Workflow Academy

This two-week course teaches the participants how to carry out WebFlow Engine projects. It prepares participants for certification and concludes with the certification exam. In addition to the fundamentals such as concept, architecture, and implementation areas of the WebFlow Engine, participants learn about the use of tools for the development of their own workflows, for reporting, and for runtime monitoring. Working with the organization management and the definition of rules for agent determination is also covered, as is the use of integration technologies. In addition, the course deals with the relevant special features of workflow roles (user, developer, system integrator, administrator, project manager) and project implementation with ASAP.

The target group of this certification course is technical consultants with SAP experience, administrators, and project members from partners who want to undertake large workflow projects.

F.6 Further Information

You can find more detailed information about these courses as well as the dates and locations by visiting *www.sap.com/education/*.

The service marketplace for WebFlow is *http://service.sap.com/webflow*.

G Glossary

Activity   Step type in a workflow definition for executing a task at runtime. The task can be a single-step task or a workflow. At runtime, an activity is represented by a work item of one of the following types:

▶ Dialog work item (type W)

▶ Background work item (type B)

▶ Workflow work item (type F)

Advance with immediate dialog   Execution property of the workflow system. A work item for which this indicator is set is executed immediately, if the actual agent of the preceding dialog work item is also a recipient of this work item.
This user does not have to call their Business Workplace to execute the work item.

Agent   Umbrella term for a system user who participates actively in SAP Business Workflow and executes work items.
There are various types of agent:
Current agent

▶ Recipient

▶ Responsible agent

▶ Excluded agent

▶ Possible agent

Agent determination rule   Method of establishing a user at runtime. This user can be used as a responsible agent or a recipient of certain notifications.
A role can be defined in the following ways:

▶ Responsibilities

▶ Organizational data

▶ User-programmed function to be executed

Roles are assigned in the step definition.
Example:

▶ Rule: "Superior of <user>"

▶ Rule: "MRP controller for <material>"

▶ Rule: "Employee responsible for <customer> from <order total>"

Asynchronous method   Method that does not report back directly to the calling component (in this case the work item manager) after its execution. It does not return any *result*, any *parameters* or any *exceptions*. At least one terminating event *must* be defined for a single-step task described with an asynchronous object method. An asynchronous method must enter its results itself. Import parameters can be passed to it only.
At runtime, the relevant work item is only completed if one of the defined terminating events occurs.

Attachment   Additional information for a work item, which can be entered by the current agent of the work item. Attachments are displayed to the agents of the subsequent steps of a workflow in read-only form.
Attachments can be SAPscript editor texts or PC documents.

Attribute   Object type component: Property or characteristic of an object.
The attributes of an object are defined and implemented as part of the object type definition in the Business Object Repository. The object type Material can, for example, have the attributes Material type, Division and Purchase order.
Attributes can be used to formulate conditions in the workflow definition. At runtime, the attribute values are read or calculated, and can also be used to control the workflow.

Background work item   Work item representing a single-step task whose execution does not require any dialog and can therefore be controlled by the system.
Work items of type B are not displayed in the Business Workplace, but can be found using the selection report for work items of all types.

Binding   Assignment of values to a container element at runtime.
The assignment rules to be observed are first defined in the binding definition.

Binding definition   Specification of assignment rules describing the assignment of data to a container element (initial value assignment) or the exchange of data between two container elements.

Block   Elementary structure element of a workflow definition.
A block always contains a consistent arrangement of steps and operators. A block has one beginning and one end.
The consistency and robustness of a workflow definition is ensured by the fact that a block is always created when a new step is created or an undefined step changed. Similarly, when individual steps are deleted, cut or inserted, the entire block in which the step is located is affected.

Business Add-In (BadI)   The location in a program defined by the developer at which software recipient layers such as industries, partners and customers can insert additional code without modifying the original object.
You can create Business Add-Ins at every level of a multi-level system infrastructure such as SAP, country version, IS solution, partner and customer. You can also create and deliver implementations in all software layers.
Enhancements with Business Add-Ins allows you to distinguish between enhancements that can have no more than one implementation and those that can be actively used by any number of customers at the same time. You can also define Business Add-Ins that depend on a filter value. Enhancements to the program code are implemented with ABAP Objects.

Business Application Programming Interface (BAPI)   A standardized programming interface that facilitates external access to business processes and data in the SAP System.
You define Business Application Programming Interfaces (BAPIs) in the Business Object Repository (BOR) as methods of SAP business objects or SAP interface types.
BAPIs offer an object-oriented view of business components in the SAP System. They

are implemented and stored as RFC-enabled function modules in the Function Builder of the ABAP Workbench.

Business Object Builder   Tool for creating and processing business object types.
You can use the Business Object Builder for direct access to the definition of an object type. You can also check or generate the business object type, as well as get a where-used list.
You can also create subtypes for an existing business object type.

Business Object Repository   Directory of all object types in a hierarchy format. The object types are each assigned to a development class (and hence indirectly to an application component as well).

Business Workplace   A user's integrated work area for:
▶ Processing work items
▶ Receiving and sending messages
▶ Managing documents and work processes
▶ Distributing and processing information for the whole enterprise or within a particular group.

Condition   Step type in a workflow definition to execute one of two defined paths in the definition ("two-way fork").
The Workflow system decides on the path on the basis of the defined conditions and information contained in the Workflow container as values.
You define conditions using the conditions editor, which allows you to define complex and multilevel conditions.

Container   Basic common data structure of the various definition and execution components of the WebFlow Engine. Containers have container elements for holding the following:
▶ Values (constants)
▶ Structures
▶ Object references
▶ Complex types (XML)

The container elements can be used to control the execution of work items and workflows. The container elements are addressed using an identifying name, and may consist of several lines.

Container definition   General information about the structure of the data to be stored in a container.
A container definition specifies the elements included in a container and the properties of those elements (ID, name, data type).
A container is always defined when working with one of the definition tools (object type definition, role definition, task definition, workflow definition).

Container element   Entry in a container. It is defined by specifying the following:
▶ ID
▶ Name
▶ Data type reference

Current agent   User who actually processes (or has processed) a work item.
The current agent of a work item is therefore one of the recipients of a work item.

Deadline monitoring   Functions in the workflow runtime system, which monitor start and end deadlines for the processing of selected work items.
In deadline monitoring the deadline notification agents are notified with a "missed deadline work items".
The monitoring of the requested start ensures that the work item appears in a Business Workplace at a defined point in time, and not before.
If a latest end, a latest start or a requested end is missed, there are two possible reactions:
▶ Missed deadline notification
Recipients of a missed deadline message are notified with a missed deadline work item in their Business Workplaces.
▶ Modeled deadline monitoring
The reaction is modeled in the workflow definition.

Delegation type   Object type whose definition is considered at runtime instead of the definition of another object type, although this other object type is specified in all definition components (for example task and workflow definition, linkage tables). In all definition tools you can still refer to the original object type, but the system uses the definition of the delegation type for every access.
The delegation type must always be a subtype of the object type it is to replace. The delegation type can have different or additional methods, attributes and events.
A delegation type is always defined for an object type on a system-wide and cross-client basis.

Development system   The SAP transaction where development and Customizing work is performed.
From here, the system data can be transferred to the quality assurance system.

Dialog work item   Type W work item that represents a single-step task at runtime, which requires dialog with the user. Dialog work items are usually displayed in the Business Workplace.
When a dialog work item is executed, the object method underlying the single-step task is called. Dialog work item execution can be deadline-monitored.

Evaluation path   An evaluation path describes a relationship chain that exists in a hierarchical structure between particular objects.
For example, the evaluation path ORGEH describes the relationship chain Organizational unit > Position > Person. Evaluation paths are used for the selection of objects in evaluations.
After you have specified an evaluation path, the system evaluates the structure along this evaluation path and only takes into account the objects found via the specified evaluation path.

Event   Status change of an object, which is 'published' throughout the system. Examples: "invoice entered", "purchase order released".

The list of possible events is defined with the relevant object type in the Business Object Builder. This list can be extended according to customer requirements using the delegation concept. You have to ensure that the events added are actually created. Each event carries information from its creation context in its event container. This information is available to the receiver of the event and can be used for event-driven control and communication mechanisms. An event may start, terminate or continue tasks and workflows.

Event container   Container that contains the event parameters of an event. The event must be defined as an object type component in the Business Object Repository (BOR).
Event containers can have bindings with workflow containers or task containers.

Exception   Object type component: Error which may occur during method execution and indicates whether a method was successful.
Exception categories:

▶ Application and system error

▶ Temporary error

Temporary errors can occur when system resources are not available. So it might make sense to call the method up again later.
You can account for application or system errors in Workflow by defining steps to be carried out when an exception occurs.

Excluded agent   User who is excluded from processing a work item.
Excluded agents can be established at runtime so that information from the workflow execution environment (agents of previous steps for example) or from the context of the processed application objects can be taken into account.

Expression   Umbrella term for constant, variable and system field.
In the context of an expression the following terms have the following meanings:

▶ Constant

  Fixed value or fixed object reference

▶ Variable

  ▶ Container element or
  ▶ Attribute referenced indirectly via a container element

▶ System field

  Field from table SYST

Expressions are used, for example, to describe the source or destination of data to be transferred in a binding definition.

Extensible Markup Language XML   XML is a developed subset of the Standard Generalized Markup Language (SGML) for applications in the World Wide Web. XML documents consist of entities which include either analyzed (parsed) or not analyzed (unparsed) data. An analyzed entity includes text, which is a sequence of characters. There are the following types of characters:

▶ Character data

▶ Markup (start tags, end tags, tags for empty elements, entity references, character references, comments, limitations for CDTA sections, document type declarations, and processing instructions)

General task   Indicator for a task or a workflow. Tasks with this indicator can be executed or started by any user.
The following apply to a work item of this type:

▶ Recipients are all users, providing no restriction has been imposed by defining responsible agents.

▶ It can be forwarded to any user by its recipient.

It can be executed by any employee who finds it using work item selection or the workflow log.

Inheritance   Relationship between object types allowing common attributes and methods to be passed on automatically from supertypes to subtypes.
With inheritance the subtype usually has the same key fields as its supertype but greater functionality.

Logical Unit of Work (LUW)   Inseparable sequence of database operations that must be executed either in its entirety by a database commit, or not at all.

From the point of view of a database system, Logical Units of Work play an important role in ensuring data integrity.

Method   Object type component: Operation that can be executed on an object. The methods of an object type are specified and implemented in the Business Object Builder.

Methods usually refer to existing ABAP functions, such as function modules, transactions and dialog modules as well as services over the Internet. They are called using a standard interface, which is determined basically by the method ID and the method parameters. The actual implementation of a method is not externally apparent.

You can specify the following for each method:

▶ Import parameters (for synchronous and asynchronous methods)

▶ A result (only synchronous methods)

▶ Export parameters (only synchronous methods)

▶ Exceptions (only synchronous methods)

Object   Any type of related information, which can be accessed uniquely under an identifying key. Most of this information is generally stored in an ABAP Dictionary table.

Objects are created at runtime and are the specific instances of a previously defined object type, which have been assigned values.

Object reference   Reference to the data of an object in the Business Object Repository. Object data is made available at runtime in an internal table. The object reference contains a reference to this internal table.

Object type   Description of data (objects) in the system created at definition time in the Business Object Builder. Examples:

▶ Documents (invoices, purchase requisitions, job applications, and so on)

▶ Master data (customer, material, vendor, and so on)

▶ Transaction data (order, quotation, and so on)

Object types are described and implemented by specifying the following components:

▶ Basic data

▶ Key fields

▶ Attributes

▶ Methods with parameters, result and exceptions

▶ Events with parameters

▶ Implementation program

The Business Object Repository provides a full directory of all object types.

The object type must be defined before its data (objects) can be used in the system.

Organizational Management object   Certain Organizational Management objects are important for the integration of Web-Flow and PD Organizational Management. The objects are identified using a 2-character identifier for their object type and an 8-digit number or 12-character name.

The follow object types are used for the organizational plan and for the specification of agents and responsibilities:

▶ Organizational unit (O)

▶ Job (C), position (S)

▶ User (US), employee (P)

▶ Work center (A)

▶ Agent determination rule (AC)

The Organizational Management objects also have an abbreviation (which is not necessarily unique) and a descriptive name.

Possible agent   User who is organizationally authorized to start a task and execute the associated work item.

The possible agents are not usually expressed with a full list of all user names, but with organizational units, positions and jobs. The possible agents of a task are specified in the task definition.

Without possible agents a task cannot be executed or started in dialog.

Production system   The live SAP System used for normal operations and where the organization's data is recorded.
This can also be described as a delivery system.

Recipient   User who may actually process a work item and hence sees it in their Business Workplace.
When a single-step task is used in a workflow definition, a user is only included among the recipients of a work item, if they are a possible agent of the single-step task and a responsible agent of the activity.

Responsible agent   User assigned locally to a step in the workflow definition.
The system establishes the recipients of a work item from the intersection of responsible and possible agents.

SAP workflow   Executable workflows supplied by SAP.
You can:
▶ Use them as models for defining your own workflow templates
▶ Configure them making your own agent and deadline entries

Step   Elementary module of a workflow definition.
The individual steps are arranged and processed sequentially. Only steps in forks can be executed simultaneously.
Steps within a workflow definition can only be changed or inserted according to certain rules, taking into account block orientation.

Subtype   Copy of an object type, which has inherited all the attributes, events and methods. The subtype can be modified and extended.
Subtypes are used to edit or extend object types supplied by SAP.

Subworkflows   Workflow template or workflow task used in an activity in a workflow definition.
At runtime the workflow referenced in the activity is executed when the step is executed.

Supertype   Object type from which another object type (subtype) has inherited all object type components. Changes to the object type components of the supertype only affect the object type components of the subtype if the components have not been redefined for the subtype.

Synchronous method   Method that assumes process control for the duration of its execution and reports back to the calling component (in this case the work item manager) after its execution.
Terminating events can be defined for a single-step task described with a synchronous object method. At runtime, the relevant work item is completed either when the method has been processed or when one of the events occurs.
A synchronous method can return the following data to the workflow:
▶ Return parameters
▶ **One** result
▶ Exceptions

Task   Goal-oriented business activity description.
The following tasks exist in the workflow context:
▶ Single-step task
   Activity in which an object method is executed on a specific object.
▶ Multistep task (workflow)
   Activity whose description includes reference to a workflow definition.

Task container   Container of a task for storing data from the task environment. The task container contains the control information in the form of constants and object references:
▶ Information on execution of the object method (object reference to the object to be processed, current agent of work item, and so on)
▶ Information available after processing the method
The task container already contains some defined workflow system variables.

You can define other container elements in the task container, which are of interest, for example, for variable replacement in connection with the notifications.

Task group   Collection of tasks, workflows and other task groups, which are used in a common context.

You can set up hierarchies of task groups by inserting task groups into other task groups. Task groups can be cross-application. They can include tasks from within one application component as well as tasks from different application components.

Terminating event   Event whose occurrence terminates a single-step task.

If the indicator *confirm end of processing* is set for the single-step task, the end of processing must be confirmed by a recipient even after the event has occurred.

The event is entered as a terminating event of the single-step task. A single-step task can have several terminating events.

Tasks that refer to an asynchronous method must have at least one terminating event. Tasks that refer to a synchronous method can have terminating events.

Tasks with terminating events can be terminated as follows:

▶ By the event occurring

▶ By an agent executing the work item and (possibly) setting it to 'Done' (only for single-step tasks that use synchronous object type methods)

Transport   The transfer of SAP System components from one system to another. The components to be transported are specified in the object list of a transport request.Each transport consists of an export process and an import process:

▶ The export process reads objects from the source system and stores them in a data file at operating system level.

▶ The import process reads objects from the data file and writes them to the database of the target system.

The SAP System maintains a transport log of all actions during export and import.

Triggering event   Event whose occurrence starts a task or a workflow.

The event must be entered as a triggering event for the task to be started, and the event linkage must be activated. A task or workflow can have several triggering events.

Information from the event creation context can be passed in the binding from the event container to the task or workflow container.

The event must be defined as an object type component in the *Business Object Builder*.

Wizard   Dialog-driven user guide for the definition of workflows in standard situations.

There are wizards that create sequences of steps within a workflow definition. These can be found in the Workflow Builder. Wizards that create a new workflow definition are located in the Workflow Wizard Explorer. You can, however, also use these wizards in existing workflow definitions. In this case, a new workflow definition is not created.

Work item   Runtime representation of a task or a step in the workflow definition. There are various types of work item.

Work item container   Runtime representation of the task container of a single-step task.

Work item type   There are various types of work item.

The work item type determines the internal processing. The type also determines which statuses and status transitions are allowed. Certain work items are displayed to a user in their Business Workplace, depending on the type. Other work items are only used and processed internally within the system. Work items of the following types are displayed in the Business Workplace:

▶ Dialog work item (type W)

  Runtime representation of single-step tasks requiring user dialog.

▶ Missed deadline work item (type D)
Work item for notification upon missed deadline.

▶ Work queue work item (type A)
Runtime representation of a work queue.

There are other work item types that can only be seen using the selection report for displaying work items.

Workflow   A workflow consists of a sequence of steps, which are processed either by people or automatically by the system.
The chronological and logical sequence of the steps, linked to the evaluation of conditions, is monitored by the WebFlow Engine and can be controlled flexibly with event-related response mechanisms.

Workflow Application Programming Interface (WAPI)   Workflow API.

Workflow Builder   Modeling tool for creating a workflow definition.
You can create and process workflow definitions in the Workflow Builder. The workflow definitions created can be tested and activated. You can include existing tasks and subworkflows into the workflow definition using the integrated Workflow Explorer. The workflow container cannot be processed directly.

Workflow container   The workflow container contains workflow-specific system variables and other container elements to be defined explicitly.
The container elements for which the import or export indicator is set form the data interface of the workflow. This interface applies to all versions of the workflow definition.
Container elements for which no import or export indicators are set are local container elements in the workflow definition. They are subject to versioning and are only valid in the versions of the workflow definition in which they were defined. They can be used as indicators or internal counters amongst other things.

Workflow definition   Technical description of a workflow.
A workflow definition is made up of individual steps and events with one step and one or more events making up one unit. These units can be arranged in sequence or in parallel.

Workflow definition version   Management information about a workflow definition.
Several versions of a workflow definition can be managed simultaneously.
One version of a workflow definition is marked as active. All workflows started refer to the version of the workflow definition, which was active when they were started.
It is possible to make an older version the active version again.

Workflow log   Log for a workflow, which contains all the workflow steps whose processing has been at least started so far.
You can double-click in a workflow log to display work items (and change them if you have the appropriate authorization).
Any errors during a workflow are displayed in the workflow log and can be analyzed with the help of the error messages displayed.
You can go to the following, amongst other things, from the workflow log:

▶ Attachments
▶ Ad hoc objects
▶ Processed work items
▶ Subworkflows
▶ Agents involved

Worklist   List of all work items that are assigned to a specific user at a particular time. This user is one of the recipients of each work item.
The worklist is located in the workflow inbox in the Business Workplace.

Workload   Workload of individual employees, positions, jobs, or organizational units.

Authors

Alan Rickayzen

Alan Rickayzen is the WebFlow Product Manager. He has been with SAP since 1992 and in data processing since 1988. In 1995 he joined the SAP Business Workflow group performing development work as well as consulting for various major US customers. During this time he amassed a good technical knowledge of the product before moving in 1998 to workflow product management. He is the principal liaison for the SAP workflow user groups through which he has a good insight into the project factors and WebFlow features that make a customer implementation a success. He writes regularly for SAP Insider and other journals. Alan Rickayzen graduated from Kings College, London with a BSc in physics.

Jocelyn Dart

Jocelyn Dart is a Senior Product Consultant specializing in Enterprise Buyer Professional (EBP) and Workflow. She has been involved with SAP products since 1990, and has been in data processing far longer than she wants to admit. In 1994, she joined SAP Australia as a help desk support consultant. Later she became an SAP instructor giving courses in ABAP, Internet Transaction Server, Workflow and EBP. Explaining and demonstrating workflow to students, and generally tinkering around, has given her a unique appreciation of the breadth and depth of the WebFlow Engine. She is currently in Professional Services, performing development work at and advising various major Australian and New Zealand customers. She is acknowledged as a regional expert in both Workflow and EBP development, and is frequently called upon to assist international consultants with EBP and Workflow issues. Jocelyn Dart has a B.App.Sc.(Computing Science) from the University of Technology, Sydney.

Dr. Carsten Brennecke

Dr. Carsten Brennecke has been involved in Workflow Management since 1995. In 1998 he joined SAP AG to work in workflow development. Carsten Brennecke is responsible for workflow documentation and he is directly involved in the planning and development of the WebFlow Engine. In addition, he takes an active role in the development WebFlow training and on occasion delivers training courses himself.

Markus Schneider

Markus Schneider has an MA in linguistics from Aachen Technical University. During this course he developed a new training and documentation concept for a local IT company. Markus Schneider joined SAP AG in 1998 to develop documentation and training material for SAP workflow. He is now in the WebFlow Engine development team and has a deep understanding of the underlying architecture.

Index